Learning

RED HAT

LINUX

Learning

RED HAT
LINUX

BILL McCARTY

O'REILLY®

Beijing · Cambridge · Farnham · Köln · Paris · Sebastopol · Taipei · Tokyo

Learning Red Hat Linux
by Bill McCarty

Published by O'Reilly & Associates, Inc., 101 Morris Street, Sebastopol, CA 95472.

Editor: Mark Stone

Production Editor: David Futato

Printing History:

September 1999:	First Edition.

ISBN: 1-56592-627-7

TABLE OF CONTENTS

PREFACE

Lately it seems that two topics crop up in conversation after conversation: the stock market and Linux. As for the stock market, I'm something of a pessimist. When friends and even perfect strangers continually recount their recent financial successes, I conclude that a stock market correction is overdue. (I've shifted my investments to bonds.)

As for Linux, I'm considerably more—perhaps wildly—optimistic. When my realtor tells me about the TV feature on Linux she saw on CNN, I see it as a harbinger of Linux Spring. Like her, my cable TV repairman, and my colleague in the next office, you've probably heard about Linux from a magazine, radio or TV program, or a friend. You're wondering what Linux is about and whether you should give it a try. If so, particularly if you currently use Microsoft Windows, this book was written for you.

Not long ago, Linux was the plaything of the technical elite. Today, however, Linux is much easier to use. Every day brings a new tool or feature designed for ease of use. If you work with Microsoft Windows and have dabbled a bit in MS-DOS, or are curious about what happens inside Windows, you can install and configure Linux. Thousands of people from all walks of life—even journalists, who are notorious for their technical ineptitude—have already done so.

This book will make your Linux journey easier, by giving you the big picture, providing you with step-by-step procedures, and getting you started doing useful or fun activities, such as word processing or games. This book focuses on the needs of the new Linux user and on desktop Linux applications. You'll learn about networks and servers, but the details of those topics are left for more advanced books.

This book includes a CD-ROM that contains Red Hat Linux, so you have in your hand all you need to get started using Linux. Much of the material in this book applies to Linux generally and not merely to Red Hat Linux; so, even if you prefer to use another Linux distribution, you'll probably find this book useful.

Organization of This Book

Chapter 1, *Why Run Linux?*, is designed to introduce you to Linux and help you determine whether Linux is appropriate for you.

Chapter 2, *Preparing to Install Linux*, helps you understand what's involved in installing Linux and guides you through a procedure to gather information needed to successfully install Linux.

Chapter 3, *Installing Linux*, takes you step-by-step through the installation of Linux.

Chapter 4, *Issuing Linux Commands*, describes the basics of how to use the Linux command-line interface, which resembles MS-DOS but is much more powerful and sophisticated.

Chapter 5, *Installing and Configuring the X Window System*, shows you how to install and configure X. Generally, the Red Hat Linux installation program will successfully install and configure X. However, if your video hardware is unusual, you may need to refer to the procedures in this chapter.

Chapter 6, *Using the X Window System*, shows you how to use X, the graphical user interface included with Red Hat Linux. If you've used Microsoft Windows, you'll find X familiar and easy to use.

Chapter 7, *Configuring and Administering Linux*, shows you how to configure your Linux system. Administering a multi-user operating system such as Linux is somewhat more complicated than administering a single-user operating system, but Linux includes tools that simplify the work.

Chapter 8, *Using Linux Applications and Clients*, describes several of the most popular applications available for Linux, including desktop suites and word processors.

Chapter 9, *Playing Linux Games*, describes several of the most popular games available for Linux. The chapter also shows you how to run your favorite Microsoft Windows games under Linux.

Chapter 10, *Setting Up a Linux-Based LAN*, shows you how to connect your Linux system to other systems on your local area network.

Chapter 11, *Getting Connected to the Internet*, shows you how to connect via your Internet Service Provider (ISP) to the Internet. Once connected, you can use your Linux system to surf the Web and access other familiar Internet services.

Chapter 12, *Setting Up a Linux-Based WAN*, shows you how to set up servers that users around the world can access via the Internet. For example, you'll learn how to install and configure Apache, the world's most popular web server.

Chapter 13, *Conquering the BASH Shell*, digs deeper into the BASH shell, the Linux command-line interface first introduced in Chapter 4. Here you'll see firsthand just how powerful and easy to use Linux can be.

Appendix A, *Linux Directory Tree*, describes the structure of the principal Red Hat Linux directories.

Appendix B, *Principal Linux Files*, describes the principal Red Hat Linux configuration files.

Appendix C, *The Red Hat Package Manager*, describes the utilities provided by Red Hat Linux for working with packages. These utilities let you install applications, uninstall applications, and query a database that describes installed applications. This appendix also includes commands for installing the applications described in this book.

Appendix D, *Managing the Boot Process*, explains how PCs boot and describes how to configure your system to conveniently boot Linux.

Appendix E, *Linux Command Quick Reference*, briefly describes the most useful Linux commands. It also presents Linux equivalents for common MS-DOS commands.

The glossary defines terms used in the book. Use it to spare yourself the effort of searching the index to discover the page on which a term is defined.

Conventions Used in This Book

The following typographical conventions are used in this book:

Boldface
> indicates a keyboard command, such as **Enter**.

`Constant width`
> indicates command-line computer output, code examples, and keyboard accelerators (See "Keyboard Accelerators" later in this section).

`Constant width italic`
> indicates variables in examples.

`Constant width bold`
> indicates user input in examples.

Italic
> introduces new terms and indicates URLs or user-defined files and directories, commands, command options, file extensions, filenames, directory or folder names, and pathnames.

Path Notation

I use a shorthand notation to indicate paths. Instead of writing "Click on the Start menu, then click on Find, then Files or Folders," I write: Start → Find → Files or Folders. I distinguish menus, dialog boxes, buttons, or other GUI elements only when the context would otherwise be unclear. Simply look for the GUI element whose label matches an element of the path.

Keyboard Accelerators

In a keyboard accelerator (such as **Ctrl-Alt-Del**), a dash indicates that the keys should be held down simultaneously, whereas a space means that the keys should be pressed sequentially. For example, **Ctrl-Esc** indicates that the **Ctrl** and **Esc** keys should be held down simultaneously; whereas **Ctrl Esc** means that the **Ctrl** and **Esc** keys should be pressed sequentially.

Where a keyboard accelerator contains an uppercase letter, you should not type the **Shift** key unless it's given explicitly. For example, **Ctrl-C** indicates that you should press the **Ctrl** and C keys; **Ctrl-Shift-C** indicates that you should press the **Ctrl**, **Shift**, and C keys.

We'd Like to Hear from You

I tested and verified the information in this book to the best of my ability, but you may find that features have changed or that I've made a mistake. Please let O'Reilly know about any errors you find, by writing:

O'Reilly & Associates, Inc.
101 Morris Street
Sebastopol, CA 95472
800-998-9938 (U.S. and Canada)
707-829-0515 (International and local)
707-829-0104 (fax)

To ask technical questions or to comment on this book, please send email to *bookquestions@oreilly.com*.

Acknowledgments

I owe my editor, Mark Stone, a huge debt (non-monetary, I hope) for his help in carrying this book through to completion. From the initial outline to the last editorial query, Mark's suggestions and assistance were indispensable. Thanks, Mark.

Katie Gardner helped me understand O'Reilly's authorship process, steered me clear of obstacles, and fixed many dumb mistakes without chiding me about them. Thanks, Katie.

Thanks also to Margot Maley of Waterside Productions, Inc., who brought this authorship opportunity to my attention.

Several reviewers, some working for O'Reilly & Associates and some working elsewhere, commented on the manuscript and suggested helpful corrections and improvements. I greatly appreciate their assistance and readily confess that any errors in the manuscript were added by me after their reviews, and so are entirely my responsibility.

My family—Jennifer, Patrick, and Sara—provided compassion and assistance during this latest authorship experience. Their efforts are worthy of special note, because we sold two houses and purchased a new one during the preparation of this book. They generously undertook more than their share of work on our turn of the (21st) century home, so that I could focus on writing. Thanks, guys.

I also acknowledge the love, concern, and support of my savior, Jesus Christ. His perfect love is entirely undeserved.

## CHAPTER ONE

WHY RUN LINUX?

This chapter introduces you to the upstart operating system Linux. It helps you determine whether Linux is right for you, by surveying the features and performance that Linux offers. It demonstrates that choosing Linux is a practical—even wise—decision for many computer users. The chapter also helps you feel at home with Linux and other Linux users, by introducing you to the history and culture of Linux. Finally, it points you to some popular gathering places on the Internet where you can correspond with other Linux users, get up-to-the-minute Linux news and information, and obtain free technical support.

Linux at Home and at Work

Perhaps you learned about Linux from a trusted friend, whose enthusiasm and ready answers convinced you to learn more about Linux, or perhaps an article or anecdote that mentioned Linux simply sparked your curiosity. In any case, you may find it interesting to learn what other computer users, ranging from PC hobbyist to guru, have accomplished by using Linux:

- Tired of slow telephone modem transfer rates, a PC owner leases a cable modem that provides high-speed transfers. He installs the new modem in a Linux system that routes packets to and from the computers of other family members. Now the entire family can simultaneously surf the Web at warp speed.

- Struggling to complete a dissertation, a graduate student determines that most of his problems stem from bugs and inadequate features of his word processing program. Dumping Microsoft Windows and Microsoft Word, he loads Linux onto his computer and uses free text processing software he downloads from the Web. In contrast to the frequent system hangs and lost work he experienced with Windows, his new system runs for over 100 days before needing to be shutdown for installation of new hardware.

- Considered among the world's best, the experienced graphics artists at Digital Domain have generated visual effects for such films as *Apollo 13, Dante's Peak, The Fifth Element, Interview with the Vampire,* and *True Lies.* But when director James Cameron selected Digital Domain to conjure visual effects for *Titanic,* the artists faced a task of unprecedented size and complexity. Concerned to obtain enormous computing power at the lowest cost, they purchased 160 DEC Alpha computers. Most DEC Alpha users run Microsoft Windows NT or Digital Unix as an operating system. However, Digital Domain chose to run Linux on 105 of their new computers. If you've seen *Titanic* and Digital Domain's breathtaking effects, you know what a good decision this was.

- Needing a supercomputer, but having a budget sufficient for only a minicomputer, scientists at the Los Alamos National Laboratory created Avalon, a system of 70 networked computers that run Linux. Instead of millions of dollars, the scientists spent only about $152,000—none of it on software, because Linux is free. Their Avalon system performs more than 10 billion floating-point operations per second, roughly on par with the Silicon Graphics Origin2000 system, which costs $1.8 million. Linux-based Avalon ranks as the 315th fastest computer in the world.

Linux began as a hacker's playground, but has become progressively easier to use and consequently more popular: today, perhaps as many as 7.5 million computers run Linux. Many Linux users are not hackers, but relatively ordinary computer users. Linux has become an operating system of formidable appeal and potential:

- In 1996, computing trade magazine *Infoworld* named Linux "Best Computer Desktop Operating System." A year later, they named the Linux community "Best Tech Support Organization."

- The cover of the August 10, 1998, issue of the influential business magazine *Forbes* featured super-programmer Linus Torvalds, author of the Linux kernel. The article pointed out that Intel, IBM, Netscape, Oracle, and other computing industry giants have taken a keen commercial interest in Linux and other open-source software.

- Market research firm International Data Corporation reported that in 1998, Linux held 17.2% of the server operating system market, up 212% from 1997. In contrast, Microsoft's flagship operating system, Windows NT, held a 36% market share—barely twice as great.

- Lawyers defending Microsoft against the U.S. government's antitrust charges argued that Linux poses a real threat to Microsoft's domination of the desktop operating systems market.

What is Linux?

Linux is an operating system, a software program that controls your computer. Most vendors load an operating system onto the hard drive of a PC before delivering the PC, so, unless the hard drive of your PC has failed, you may not understand the function of an operating system.

An operating system solves several problems arising from hardware variation. As you're aware, no two PC models (or models of other computers, for that matter) have identical hardware. For example, some PCs have an IDE hard drive, whereas others have a SCSI hard drive. Some PCs have one hard drive, others have two or more. Most PCs have a CD-ROM drive, but some do not. Some PCs have an Intel Pentium CPU, whereas others have an AMD K-6, and so on. Suppose that, in a world without operating systems, you're programming a new PC application, perhaps a new multimedia word processor. Your application must cope with all the possible variations of PC hardware. As a result, it becomes bulky and complex. Users don't like it because it consumes too much hard drive space, takes a long time to load, and—because of its size and complexity—has more bugs than it should.

Operating systems solve this problem by providing a single standard way for applications to access hardware devices. When an operating system exists, applications can be more compact, because they share the commonly used code for accessing the hardware. Applications can also be more reliable because this code is written only once, and by expert programmers, rather than by application programmers.

As you'll soon learn, operating systems do many other things as well; for example, they generally provide a filesystem so that you can store and retrieve data, and a user interface so that you can control the operation of your computer. However, if you think of a computer's operating system as its subconscious mind, you won't be far off the mark. It's the computer's conscious mind—applications such as word processors and spreadsheets—that do useful work. But, without the subconscious—the operating system—the computer would cease breathing and applications would not function.

PC Operating Systems

Now that you know what an operating system is, you may be wondering what operating system your PC uses. Chances are, your PC operating system was provided by Microsoft. Table 1-1 shows the sales of several popular desktop operating systems during 1997 and projected sales for 2001.* Bear in mind that, because Linux is a free operating system, Linux sales are a mere fraction of Linux installations. Moreover, unlike most commercial operating systems, Linux is not sold

---

* Source: International Data Corporation.

Pronouncing Linux

Internet newsgroup participants have long debated the proper pronunciation of *Linux*. Because the name Linux was conferred by Linux kernel author Linus Torvalds, his pronunciation of the word should reign as standard as I see it. However, Linus is Finnish and his pronunciation of Linux is difficult for English speakers to approximate. Consequently, many variations in pronunciation have arisen. The most popular pronunciation sounds as though the word were spelled *Linnucks*, with the stress on the first syllable.

If your computer has a sound card, you can hear how Linus Torvalds pronounces Linux: *http://www.ssc.com/lj/linuxsay.html.*

---

under terms of a per-seat license; a company is free to purchase a single Linux CD-ROM diskette and install Linux on as many computer systems as they like.

Table 1-1. Sales of Popular Desktop Operating Systems

Operating System	1997[a]	2001 (est.)[b]
Windows 95/98	69.4%	65.0%
Windows NT Workstation	9.2	26.2
DOS with Windows 3.x	7.7	0.3
MacOS	4.6	1.9
Linux	2.4	4.2
DOS without Windows	2.3	0.3
Unix	1.0	0.5
OS/2 Warp	0.8	1.2
Other	2.7	0.5

[a] U.S. sales of desktop operating systems as percent of market.
[b] Includes IBM, Digital Research (DR), and Microsoft versions of DOS.

As the table shows, your desktop computer is probably running Microsoft Windows 95 or Windows 98, which together accounted for over 69% of 1997 sales. The sales of Linux were miniscule in comparison: a mere 2.4%. As explained, these figures don't do full justice to the ubiquity of Linux. Nevertheless, notice that sales of Linux are expected to almost double, whereas those of Windows 95/98 are expected to slightly contract.

Later in this chapter you'll learn how Linux is distributed, but recall that Linux was termed a *free* operating system. If you have a high-speed Internet connection, you can download, install, and use Linux without paying anyone for anything (except perhaps your Internet Service Provider, who may impose a connection fee). It's anyone's guess how many people have downloaded Linux, but estimates indicate that between 7 and 10 million computers run Linux.

Moreover, many Linux users run Linux not as a desktop computer but as a server, which is powered up and online 24 hours per day, connected (at least occasionally) to the Internet, and ready to provide services to requesting clients. For example, many Linux users run web servers, hosting web sites browsed by users worldwide. But, the number of desktop Linux users—those who power on their computer to use it and power it off when they're done—is rising.

Desktop use of Linux is the focus of this book. However, if you're unfamiliar with Linux and Unix, this book is right for you even if you plan to establish a Linux server. This book will take you through the basics of setting up and using Linux. After you've mastered what this book offers, you should consult *Running Linux, Third Edition*, Matt Welsh, Matthias Kalle Dalheimer and Lar Kaufman (O'Reilly, 1999), a more advanced book that focuses on setting up and using Linux servers.

How Linux is Different

Linux is distinguished from many popular operating systems in three important ways.

- Linux is a cross-platform operating system that runs on many computer models. Only Unix, an ancestor of Linux, rivals Linux in this respect. In comparison, Windows 95 and Windows 98 run only on CPUs having the Intel architecture. Windows NT runs only on CPUs having the Intel architecture or the DEC Alpha.

- Linux is free, in two senses. First, you may pay nothing to obtain and use Linux. On the other hand, you may choose to purchase Linux from a vendor who bundles Linux with special documentation or applications, or who provides technical support. However, even in this case, the cost of Linux is likely to be a fraction of what you'd pay for another operating system. So, Linux is free or nearly free in an economic sense.

    Second, and more important, Linux and many Linux applications are distributed in source form. This makes it possible for you and others to modify or improve them. You're not free to do this with most operating systems, which are distributed in binary form. For example, you can't make changes to Microsoft Windows or Microsoft Word—only Microsoft can do that. Because of this freedom, Linux is being constantly improved and updated, far outpacing the rate of progress of any other operating system. For example, Linux will likely be the first operating system to support Intel's forthcoming Merced 64-bit CPU.

- Linux has attractive features and performance. Free access to Linux source code lets programmers around the world implement new features, and tweak Linux to improve its performance and reliability. The best of these features and tweaks are incorporated in the standard Linux kernel or made available as kernel patches or applications. Not even Microsoft can mobilize and support a software development team as large and dedicated as the volunteer Linux software development team, which numbers in the hundreds of thousands, including programmers, code reviewers, and testers.

The origins of Linux

Linux traces its ancestry back to a mainframe operating system known as Multics (Multiplexed Information and Computing Service). Begun in 1965, Multics was one of the first multi-user computer systems and remains in use today. Bell Telephone Labs participated in the development of Multics, along with the Massachusetts Institute of Technology and General Electric.

Two Bell Labs software engineers, Ken Thompson and Dennis Richie, worked on Multics until Bell Labs withdrew from the project in 1969. One of their favorite pastimes during the project had been playing a multi-user game called Space Travel. Now, without access to a Multics computer, they found themselves unable to indulge their fantasies of flying around the galaxy. Resolved to remedy this, they decided to port the Space Travel game to run on an otherwise unused PDP-7 computer. Eventually, they implemented a rudimentary operating system they named *Unics*, as a pun on *Multics*. Somehow, the spelling of the name became *Unix*.

Their operating system was novel in several respects, most notably portability. Most previous operating systems had been written for a specific target computer. Just as a tailor-made suit fits only its owner, such an operating system could not be easily adapted to run on an unfamiliar computer. In order to create a portable operating system, Ritchie and Thompson first created a programming language, called *C*. Like assembly language, C let a programmer access low-level hardware facilities not available to programmers writing in a high-level language such as FORTRAN or COBOL. But, like FORTRAN and COBOL, a C program was not bound to a particular computer. Just as a ready-made suit can be lengthened or shortened here and there to fit a purchaser, writing Unix in C made it possible to easily adapt Unix to run on computers other than the PDP-7.

As word of their work spread and interest grew, Ritchie and Thompson made copies of Unix freely available to programmers around the world. These programmers revised and improved Unix, sending word of their changes back to Ritchie and Thompson, who incorporated the best such changes in their version of Unix. Eventually, several Unix variants arose. Prominent among these was BSD (Berkeley Systems Division) Unix, written at the University of California, Berkeley, in

1978. Bill Joy, one of the principals of the BSD project, later became a founder of Sun Microsystems, which sold another Unix variant (SunOS) to power its workstations. In 1984, AT&T, the parent company of Bell Labs, began selling its own version of Unix, known as System V.

Free software

What Ritchie and Thompson had begun in a distinctly non-commercial fashion ended up spawning several legal squabbles. When AT&T grasped the commercial potential of Unix, it claimed Unix as its intellectual property and began charging a hefty license fee to those who wanted to use its Unix. Soon, others who had implemented Unix-like operating systems were distributing licenses only for a fee. Understandably, those who had contributed improvements to Unix considered it unfair for AT&T and others to appropriate the fruits of their labors. This concern for profit was unlike the democratic, share-and-share-alike spirit of the early days of Unix.

Some, including MIT scientist Richard Stallman, yearned for the return of those happier times and the mutual cooperation of programmers that then existed. So, in 1983, Stallman launched the GNU (GNU's not Unix) project, which aimed at creating a free Unix-like operating system. Like early Unix, the GNU operating system was to be distributed in source form so that programmers could read, modify, and redistribute it without restriction. Stallman's work at MIT had taught him that, by using the Internet as a means of communication, programmers the world over could improve and adapt software at incredible speed, far outpacing the fastest rate possible using traditional software development models, in which few programmers actually see one another's source code.

As a means of organizing work on the GNU project, Stallman and others created the Free Software Foundation (FSF), a non-profit corporation that seeks to promote free software and eliminate restrictions on the copying, redistribution, understanding, and modification of software. Among other activities, the FSF accepts tax-deductible charitable contributions and distributes copies of software and documentation for a small fee, using this revenue to fund its operations and support the GNU project.

If you find it peculiar that the FSF charges a fee—even a small fee—for "free" software, you should understand that the FSF intends the word *free* to refer primarily to freedom, not price. The FSF believes in three fundamental software freedoms:

- You can copy GNU software and give it away to anyone you choose.

- If you're a programmer, you can modify GNU software any way you like, because you have access to the source code.

- You can distribute improved versions of GNU software. However, you cannot charge anyone a fee for using your improved version (although you can charge a fee for providing a user with a physical copy of your software).

Copyleft

Commercial software vendors protect their proprietary rights to software by copyrighting the software. In contrast, the FSF protects software freedom by *copylefting* its software. If the FSF placed its software in the public domain, others would be free to transform it into a proprietary product, denying users the freedom intended by the original author of the software. For example, a company might distribute the software in binary rather than source form and require payment of a license fee for the privilege of making additional copies.

To copyleft software, the FSF uses the same legal instrument used by proprietary software vendors—the copyright—but the FSF adds special terms that guarantee freedom to users of the software. These terms, referred to as the *GNU Public License*, give everyone the right to use, modify, and redistribute the software (or any software derived from it), but only if the distribution terms are unchanged. Thus someone who attempts to transform FSF software into a proprietary product has no right to use, modify, or distribute the product. As the FSF puts it, "Proprietary software developers use copyright to take away the users' freedom; we use copyright to guarantee their freedom. That's why we reverse the name, changing *copyright* into *copyleft*."

The Linux kernel

By the early 1990s, the FSF had obtained or written all the major components of the GNU operating system except for one: the kernel. About that time, Linus Torvalds, a Finnish computer science student, began work on a kernel for a Unix-like system. Linus had been working with Minix, a Unix-like operating system written by Andrew Tannenbaum primarily for pedagogical use. Linus was disappointed by the performance of the Minix kernel and believed that he could do better. He shared his preliminary work with others on Internet newsgroups. Soon, programmers around the world were working together to extend and improve his kernel, which he called Linux (for *Linus's Minix*). As Table 1-2 shows, Linux grew rapidly. Within three years of its October 5, 1991 initial release, Linux was released as production software; version 1.0 was released in March of 1994. However, as early as 1992, Linux had been integrated with other GNU software to produce a fully functional operating system, which took as its name the name of its kernel.

Table 1-2. The History of Linux

Year	Version	Users	Kernel size (Bytes)	Milestone(s)
1991	0.01	100	63,362	Linus Torvalds writes Linux kernel
1992	0.99	1000	431,591	GNU software integrated with Linux kernel, producing a fully functional operating system
1993	0.99	20,000	937,917	High rate of code contributions prompts Linus to delegate code review responsibility
1994	1.0	100,000	1,016,601	First production release
1995	1.2	500,000	1,850,182	Linux adapted to non-Intel processors
1996	2.0	1,500,000	4,718,270	Linux supports multiple processors, IP masquerading, and Java
1999	2.2	7,500,000	10,600,000[a]	Linux growth rate exceeds that of Microsoft Windows NT

[a] estimated

However, work on Linux did not cease. Since the initial production release, the pace of development has accelerated as Linux has been adapted to include support for non-Intel processors and even multiple processors, sophisticated TCP/IP networking facilities such as IP masquerading, and more. Versions of Linux are now available for such computer models as the Apple PowerPC, the DEC Alpha, the Motorola 68k, the Sun SPARC, the Mips, and many others. Moreover, Linux does not implement an obscure Unix variant: it generally complies with the POSIX (Portable Operating System Interface) standard that forms the basis of the X/Open specifications of The Open Group.

The X Window System

Another important component of Linux is its graphical user interface, the X Window System. Unix was originally a mouseless, text-based system that used noisy teletype machines rather than modern CRT monitors. The Unix command interface is very sophisticated and, even today, some power users prefer it to a point-and-click graphical environment, using their CRT monitor as though it were a noiseless teletype. Consequently, some remain unaware that Unix long ago outgrew its text-based childhood, and now provides users a choice of graphical or command interfaces.

The X Window System (or simply X) was developed as part of the Massachusetts Institute of Technology's (MIT) Project Athena, which it began in 1984. By 1988, MIT released X to the public. MIT has since turned development of X over to the X Consortium, which released version 6 in September 1995.

X is a unique graphical user interface in two major respects. First, X integrates with a computer network, letting users access local and remote applications. For example, X lets you open a window that represents an application running on a remote server: the remote server does the heavy-duty computing; all your computer need do is pass the server your input and display the server's output.

Second, X lets you configure its look and feel to an amazing degree. To do so, you run a special application—called a *window manager*—on top of X. A variety of window managers is available, including some that closely mimic the look and feel of Microsoft Windows.

Linux distributions

Because Linux can be freely redistributed, you can obtain it in a variety of ways. Various individuals and organizations package Linux, often combining it with free or proprietary applications. Such a package that includes all the software you need to install and run Linux is called a *Linux distribution*. Table 1-3 shows some of the most popular Linux distributions.

Table 1-3. Popular Linux Distributions and Their Web Home Pages

Distribution	Home Page
Caldera OpenLinux	*http://www.caldera.com/*
Debian Linux	*http://www.debian.org/*
Slackware Linux	*http://www.cdrom.com/titles/os/slackwar.htm/*
Red Hat Linux	*http://www.redhat.com/*
SuSE. Linux	*http://www.suse.com/*

Caldera, Red Hat, Slackware, and SuSE are packaged by commercial companies, which seek to profit by selling Linux-related products and services. However, because Linux is distributed under the GNU GPL, you can download these distributions from the respective companies' web sites or make additional copies of a Linux distribution you purchase from them. (Note, however, that you cannot necessarily make additional copies of proprietary software that these companies may distribute with their Linux distribution.) Debian Linux is the product of volunteer effort conducted under the auspices of Software In The Public Interest, Inc., a nonprofit corporation. This book is bundled with a copy of Linux, which you can install and run on your PC.

Linux Features and Performance

The origins of Linux and the availability of its source code set it apart from other operating systems. But most users choose an operating system based on features and performance—and Linux delivers these in spades. Table 1-4 compares certain features and performance characteristics of a specific Linux distribution—Red Hat Linux 5.1—with those of Microsoft Windows NT 4.0 and Sun Microsystems Solaris 2.6.* Each of these three operating systems can be run on an Intel-architecture PC.

Table 1-4. Linux Features and Performance Comparison

Characteristic	Red Hat Linux	Windows NT	Solaris
Range of compatible hardware	Very wide	Modest	Narrow
Minimal hardware	386 PC	486 PC	Pentium
Representative cost of hardware	$200	$1300	$1600
Average downtime	Very low	As low as 30 min./week	Very low
Performance	High	Comparable to Linux	Half of Linux to same as Linux
Multi-processing capabilities	Excellent	Modest	Excellent
IP Security (IPSec)	Yes	Planned	1999
IPv6	Available	Privately demonstrated	Beta
Overall user satisfaction, per *Datapro*	Highest	Lowest	Medium
Source code readily available	Yes	No	No
Installed base	Millions	Millions	Hundreds of thousands

As you can see, Linux fares well in this comparison. It runs on a wider range of hardware platforms and runs adequately on less costly and powerful systems. Moreover, the typical downtime of a Linux system is less than that of a Windows NT system and its performance surpasses that of a Solaris system. Its multi-processing capabilities exceed those of Windows NT and its support of advanced TCP/IP networking facilities is superior to that of Windows NT and Solaris. As a group, Linux users are more satisfied than Windows NT users and Solaris users. Linux source code is readily available. And, the Linux installed base dwarfs that of Solaris and approaches that of Windows NT.

---

* Source: Adapted from *SunWorld*, August 1998.

But this impressive inventory of selling points doesn't end the matter. Let's consider some other technical characteristics of Linux that distinguish it from the pack. Foremost in the minds of many is the low cost of Linux. Comparable server operating systems can cost more than $100,000. The low cost of Linux makes it practical for use even as a desktop operating system. In that mode, it truly eclipses the competition.

Many desktop systems are occasionally, even regularly, employed as servers. Because Linux was designed for use as a server operating system, its features and performance readily outshine those of desktop operating systems used as makeshift servers. For example, Microsoft's software license for Windows NT Workstation restricts the number of simultaneous client connections to 10; if your Windows NT Workstation computer accepts more than 10 client connections, it is operating in breach of license. However, Linux imposes no such restriction: your Linux desktop is free to accept as many client connections as you think it can handle.

Again, because it was designed as a server, Linux provides more reliable data storage than competing desktop operating systems. Most Linux users store their disk data using the EXT2 filesystem, which is superior in performance and reliability to filesystems (partition types) provided by Microsoft operating systems, including FAT, FAT32, and NTFS. Of course, Microsoft claims that its NTFS filesystem is so reliable that you'll probably never need to use special software tools to recover lost data—truth is, Microsoft provides no such tools. Despite Microsoft's ambitious claims, users report that NTFS reliability is not perfect. Here's a case in point:

> When my Windows NT Workstation computer crashed a little over a year ago, I discovered that its NTFS file system was damaged. I searched the Microsoft web site for recovery instructions and tools and found nothing that helped. So, I went to my local software store and purchased a third party disk recovery tool for Windows NT. When I opened the box, I was angered to discover that it supported recovery of FAT and FAT32 data, but not NTFS data.

> Eventually, I recovered 95 percent of my data by using a free Linux utility that was able to open the damaged NTFS partition and copy its files. If I'd been without Linux, I'd be without my data.

Like other server operating systems, Linux provides advanced disk management (RAID), which makes it possible to automatically duplicate stored data on several hard drives. This greatly improves the reliability of data storage; if one hard drive fails, the data can be read from another. Competing desktop operating systems such as Microsoft Windows 95/98 do not support this capability (though several third parties sell drivers that let you add this capability to your desktop operating system).

If you're an old computer dog who remembers the days of MS-DOS, you may have a fondness for what's now called the MS-DOS Prompt window. However, if you've worked exclusively within the Microsoft Windows point-and-click environment, you may not fully understand what the MS-DOS Prompt window is about. The MS-DOS Prompt window provides what's called a *command-line interface.* By typing commands, chosen from a list of commands the operating system understands, you can direct the computer to perform a variety of tasks.

For most users, the command interface is not as convenient as the point-and-click interface offered by Microsoft Windows. That's because you must know the commands the operating system understands, and must type them correctly, if you expect the operating system to do your bidding.

However, the MS-DOS Prompt window lets you accomplish tasks that would be cumbersome and time-consuming if performed by pointing and clicking. Linux comes with a similar command interface, known as the *shell.* But, the word "similar" fails to do justice to the Linux shell's capabilities, because the MS-DOS command line provides a fraction of the capabilities provided by the Linux shell.

In particular, the MS-DOS command line lacks many ease-of-use features found in the Linux shell. You may have used the MS-DOS command line and, finding it distastefully cumbersome, forever rejected it in favor of pointing and clicking. If so, you'll be pleasantly surprised to see how easy it is to use the Linux shell. You'll certainly be pleased—perhaps amazed—by the enormous power it offers. You'll learn more about the Linux shell in Chapter 4, *Issuing Linux Commands.*

If you're a programmer, you'll also admire the ease with which it's possible to develop portable, Unix-compliant software by using Linux. Linux comes with a complete suite of software development tools, including an assembler, C compiler, C++ compiler, `make` application, and source code librarian. All of these are freely distributable programs made available under the terms of the GNU GPL.

Reasons to Choose or Not Choose Linux

Here are several reasons for running Linux. The more of these that are true of you, the likelier you are to be happy in running Linux:

You want a stable and reliable computing platform.
No other popular operating system is more stable and reliable than Linux. If you're tired of crashes and hangs and the lost time and data they entail, you're a candidate for Linux.

You want a high performance computing platform.
Linux can coax blazingly fast performance out of hardware below the minimum required to load and run other popular operating systems. And, with ample memory and a fast CPU, Linux goes toe-to-toe with anything Microsoft or other vendors offer. If speed is your thing, Linux is your hot rod.

You need a low-cost or free operating system.

If you're someone on a budget, such as a student, or if you need to set up many systems, the low cost of Linux will let you reserve your hard-earned capital for hardware or other resources. Linux is the best operating system value on the planet.

You're a heavy network or Internet user.

If you use networks, especially the Internet, Linux's advanced support for TCP/IP may light up your life. Linux makes it easy to construct firewalls that protect your system against hackers or routers that let several computers share a single network connection.

You want to learn Unix or TCP/IP networking.

The best way—perhaps the only way—to learn more about Unix or TCP/IP networking (or computers generally) is through hands-on experience. Whether you're interested in such experience owing to personal curiosity or career ambition (system administrators are often handsomely paid), Linux affords you the opportunity to gain such experience at low cost, without leaving the comfort of your home.

You seek an alternative to Microsoft's vision of computing's future.

If you're tired of marching to the relentless drumbeat of the Redmond juggernaut, Linux offers a viable way to cut the umbilical cord and set about creating a new computing destiny for yourself and others.

You want to enjoy enhanced peer esteem.

If you're a technical worker, such as a programmer or engineer, you may acquire enhanced status among your peers by being an early adopter of Linux. (Of course, in many peer groups, it's already too late to become an early adopter of Linux; but at least you won't become a late adopter). You can even obtain decals and bumper stickers to advertise your good taste in operating systems (see the Linux Mall at *http://www.all-linux.com/index.html*).

You want to have fun.

Hopefully, you've discovered that one of the best reasons for doing anything is that it's fun. Many Linux users report that they've never had so much fun with a computer. There's no better reason for running Linux than that.

To be both blunt and honest, some folks shouldn't run Linux. If you're one or more of the following are true of you, you should run Linux only if you have a good friend who's knowledgeable about Linux, available by phone at odd hours, and works cheap:

You're scared of computers.

If you're scared of computers, you should spend more time working with Microsoft Windows 95 or Windows 98 before venturing into the Linux world. Linux may indeed be right for you, but it's not right just yet.

You don't like to learn.

Setting up and running Linux will require you to learn new concepts and skills. None of these are especially difficult, but if you don't like to learn, setting up and running Linux will stress you out. Instead, you should stick with the familiar.

You're married to certain Windows applications.

You can run some Windows applications under Linux's WINE emulation (over 100 applications at the time of writing, Microsoft's Minesweeper and FreeCell among them). However, this isn't true of every Windows application. Before putting your toe in the Linux waters, you should obtain up-to-date information on the status of WINE emulation of your favorite Windows applications (see *http://www.winehq.com/*).

Rather than convert your desktop system to run Linux, you may prefer to install Linux on a second system or convert your existing Windows system into a dual-boot system that can run Windows or Linux. That way, you have your choice of running your favorite Windows applications or Linux.

Linux Resources on the Internet

This section points you to up-to-the-minute information about Linux available though web pages and Internet newsgroups. You may find this information helpful in completing your installation of Linux and you'll certainly find it helpful in using your Linux system.

Web Pages

Table 1-5 lists the URLs of some popular Linux web pages. Check these out to get the latest information about Linux. Perhaps the most useful is the home page of the Linux Documentation Project. There, you can find almost anything you want to know about Linux. The Linux Documentation Project web site includes a search engine that makes it easy to find what you need.

Table 1-5. Recommended Linux Web Pages

Web page	URL
Eric S. Raymond's Linux Reading List HOWTO	*http://metalab.unc.edu/LDP/HOWTO/Reading-List-HOWTO.html*
Gary Singleton's Gary's Place: Linux News Tips and Links	*http://gary.singleton.net/*
Joshua Go's Linux Guide	*http://jgo.local.net/LinuxGuide/*
Linux Documentation Project	*http://metalab.unc.edu/linux/*
Linux Journal Web Page	*http://www.linuxjournal.com/*

Table 1-5. Recommended Linux Web Pages (continued)

Web page	URL
Linux Journal's Linux Gazette	*http://www.linuxgazette.com/*
Linux Resources	*http://www.linuxresources.com/*
Linux Web Ring	*http://nll.interl.net/lwr/*
Linux Weekly News	*http://lwn.net/*
O'Reilly & Associates Linux Center	*http://linux.oreilly.com/*
Red Hat Linux Users FAQ	*http://www.best.com/%7Eaturner/RedHat-FAQ/*
Renaissoft's Linux Resources	*http://www.renaissoft.com/linux.html*
Robert Kiesling's Linux Frequently Asked Questions with Answers (FAQ)	*http://metalab.unc.edu/LDP/FAQ/Linux-FAQ.html*
Slashdot	*http://slashdot.org/*
Victoria, British Columbia Linux Users Group	*http://vlug.org/vlug/*

The Linux Webring offers another convenient way to explore a variety of Linux-related web sites. Participating web sites present links to one another; by following these links you can circumnavigate the entire ring or you can use the Webring's home page to seek exactly the sort of page you're interested in.

Linux Journal is a popular magazine among Linux users. You can subscribe to the hard copy edition or peruse any of several web sites supported by *Linux Journal*.

A FAQ (Frequently Asked Questions) list summarizes questions and answers commonly appearing on an Internet newsgroup or other venue. FAQs are among the most valuable sources of information about any topic because they answer a high percentage of potential questions. You should consult FAQs early and often.

The motto of the Slashdot web site is "News for nerds. Stuff that matters." You'll find a great deal of interesting news and information there, concerning not only Linux but the open source community and computing generally.

Newsgroups

Internet newsgroups are a popular gathering place for Linux users. There, they give and receive help in setting up and using Linux systems and share pointers to the latest Linux software. Table 1-6 lists some popular Linux-related newsgroups. If your Internet Service Provider supports access to newsgroups, you can view them using Microsoft Internet Explorer, Netscape Communicator, or a special newsgroup client application.

Table 1-6. Popular Linux-related Internet Newsgroups

Newsgroup	Topic
comp.os.linux.advocacy	Arguing the benefits of Linux in comparison to other operating systems
comp.os.linux.alpha	Linux on DEC Alpha computers
comp.os.linux.announce	Announcements important to the Linux community (Also visit the archive site)
comp.os.linux.answers	FAQs, HOWTOs, READMEs, etc.
comp.os.linux.development.apps	Writing Linux applications and porting applications to Linux
comp.os.linux.development.system	Linux kernels, device drivers, and modules
comp.os.linux.hardware	Hardware compatibility with the Linux operating system
comp.os.linux.misc	Topics not covered by other groups
comp.os.linux.networking	Networking and communication.
comp.os.linux.powerpc	Linux systems running on the PowerPC
comp.os.linux.setup	Linux installation and system administration
comp.os.linux.x	X servers, clients, libs, and fonts

## CHAPTER TWO

PREPARING TO INSTALL LINUX

This chapter presents information you need to know and tasks you need to perform before installing Linux. It helps you make certain that your IBM-compatible PC meets the minimum hardware requirements for Linux. It shows you how to document your system configuration so that you can respond to questions presented by the Linux install procedure. It also describes the three types of Red Hat Linux installations (for most new users of Linux, the workstation installation type is the most appropriate). Finally, it shows you how to prepare your hard disk for Linux.

Minimum Hardware Requirements

Linux supports a wide range of PC hardware; but not even Linux supports every known device and system. Your PC must meet certain minimum requirements in order to run Linux. The following sections present these minimum requirements; however, for the latest and most complete information, you should check Red Hat's web site at *http://www.redhat.com/hardware/*. Red Hat's web site will also help you determine whether Linux supports all the devices installed in your system.

Central Processing Unit (CPU)

Linux does not support the Intel 286 and earlier processors. However, it fully supports the Intel 80386, 80486, Pentium, Pentium Pro, Pentium II, and Pentium III processors. Nevertheless, some users feel that their 80386 Linux systems respond sluggishly, particularly when running X. So, if you want optimum performance, you should install Linux on a PC having an 80486 processor or better.

Linux also supports non-Intel processors such as the Cyrix 6x86 and the AMD K5 and K6. Most Linux users have systems that use Intel chips; if your system uses a non-Intel chip, you may find it somewhat more difficult to resolve possible problems.

TIP	Red Hat reports that some AMD K6 systems freeze during the Linux install. Some users have solved this problem by updating their system BIOS or replacing their system motherboards. The author's Linux system uses an AMD K6 and has presented no special problems.

Motherboard

Linux supports the standard ISA, EISA, PCI, and VESA (VLB) system buses used on most IBM-compatible PCs. Linux recently gained support for IBM's MCA bus, used in IBM's PS/2 series of computers. However, at the time of this writing, Red Hat has not announced support for the MCA bus. If you have an IBM PS/2, you may be unable to install Red Hat Linux (check the Red Hat web site for the latest available information on support for the MCA bus).

Your motherboard should include at least 16 MB of RAM for optimum Linux performance. Some users have managed to coax Linux into working on systems with as little as 4 MB of RAM. However, if your system has less than 16 MB of RAM, you probably won't be pleased with its performance. If you plan to run X, you may wish to install more than 16 MB of RAM—perhaps 64 MB. Although X operates well with 16 MB of RAM, you can open more windows and switch between them more quickly if you have additional memory.

A handful of motherboards present special problems when installing Linux. Generally, the problem stems from a bad BIOS, for which a fix is often available. Check the Red Hat web site for details.

Drives

An anonymous wag once quipped that one can never be too thin, too rich, or have too much hard disk space. Fortunately, Linux is not too hungry for disk space. To install and use Linux, you should have at least 250 MB of free hard disk space. (The absolute minimum is about 101 MB, but installing Linux on a system with so little disk space will compel you to omit many useful applications and will leave you with little room to work.)

More realistically, if you plan to use your Linux system as a workstation, you should have at least 600 MB of free disk space; if you plan to user your Linux system as a server, you should have at least 1.6 GB (1,600 MB) of free disk space.

For convenient installation using the CD-ROM included with this book, your system should include an IDE or SCSI CD-ROM drive. It's also possible to install Linux from a PCMCIA CD-ROM drive, an FTP site, an NFS server, an SMB shared volume, or a hard drive. Consult the Red Hat web site for details.

Your system should also include a 3.5-inch floppy drive. You'll use the floppy drive to boot your system from a special Linux diskette you create.

Collecting Information About Your System

In order to be able to complete the installation procedure smoothly, you should collect certain information about your system before beginning the installation. Often the installation utility will be able to determine your system configuration automatically but when it fails to do so, you must be prepared to supply the needed information. Otherwise, you'll be forced to terminate the installation procedure, obtain the information, and restart the installation.

Information You Need

Table 2-1 specifies the configuration information you need. To obtain this information, you can consult your system documentation and the documentation for any devices installed by you. If your documentation is missing or incomplete, you may need to contact your hardware vendor or manufacturer. Alternatively, you may be able to find the needed information on the manufacturer's web site; use a search engine such as Yahoo! or AltaVista to discover the URL of the web site.

Table 2-1. Configuration Information Needed to Install Linux

Device	Information needed
Hard Drive(s)	The number, size, and type of each hard drive.
	Which hard drive is first, second, and so on
	Which adapter type (IDE or SCSI) is used by each drive.
	For each IDE drive, whether or not the BIOS is set for LBA mode
RAM memory	The amount of installed RAM
CD-ROM Drive(s)	Which adapter type (IDE, SCSI, or other) is used by each drive
	For each drive using a non-IDE, non-SCSI adapter, the make and model of the drive
SCSI Adapter (if any)	The make and model of the card
Network Adapter (if any)	The make and model of the card
Mouse	The type (serial, PS/2, or bus)
	The protocol (Microsoft, Logitech, MouseMan, etc.)
	The number of buttons
	For a serial mouse, the serial port to which it's connected

Table 2-1. Configuration Information Needed to Install Linux (continued)

Device	Information needed
Video Adapter	The make and model of the card
	The amount of video RAM

To obtain the needed information, you may need to examine your system's BIOS settings or open your system's case and examine the installed hardware. Consult your system documentation to learn how to do so.

Collecting Configuration Information by Using Windows

If you run Microsoft Windows 95 or Windows 98, you can obtain much of the needed information by using the Windows System Properties dialog box, which you can launch by using the Control Panel:

1. Click on the Start menu. A popup menu appears.

2. Select Settings on the popup menu and click on Control Panel in the sub-menu. The Control Panel appears.

3. Double click on System. The System Properties dialog box appears. If necessary, click on the General tab, so that the dialog box resembles Figure 2-1.

    The General tab of the System Properties dialog box shows the type of your system's processor and the amount of installed RAM.

4. Click on the Device Manager tab. The appearance of the dialog box changes to resemble Figure 2-2.

    You can double click on an icon (or single click on the plus key adjacent to an icon) to obtain additional information. For example, by double clicking on the Disk Drives icon you can determine whether a disk drive uses an IDE or SCSI interface.

    If you have a printer, you can use the Print button to print information about your system's devices.

From the Device Manager tab, you can learn the following information:

* The number and type (IDE or SCSI) of your system's hard drives.

* The make and model of CD-ROM drives.

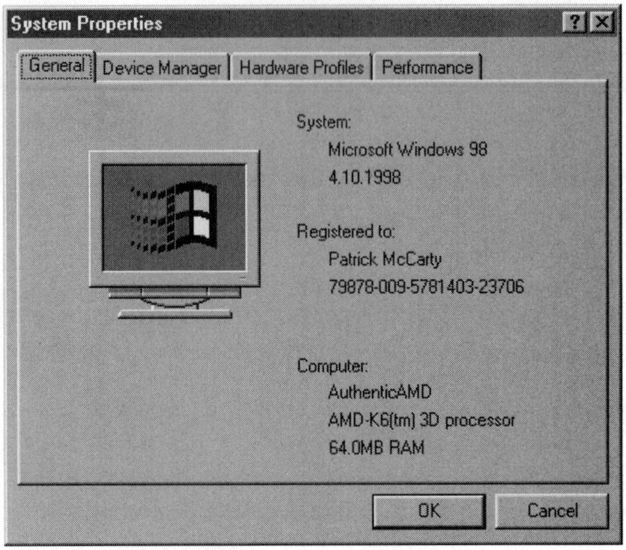

Figure 2-1. The General tab of the System Properties dialog box

---

| *TIP* | Some installed CD-ROM drives do not appear in the Device Manager tab of the System Properties dialog box. Often the *CONFIG.SYS* file will contain clues that help you learn more about such drives. |

- The type of mouse installed.

- The make and model of the video adapter.

- The make and model of multimedia adapters, such as sound cards, if any.

- The make and model of network adapters, if any.

- The make and model of SCSI adapters, if any.

Installation Types

Red Hat Linux defines three installation types: Workstation, Server, and Custom.

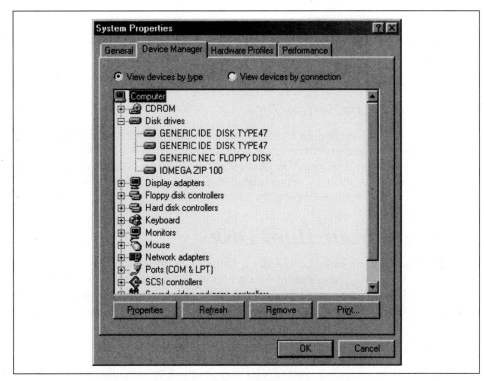

Figure 2-2. The Device Manager tab of the System Properties dialog box

The Workstation Installation Type

If you're new to Linux, the workstation installation type is probably the most appropriate for you, especially if you currently run Microsoft Windows. In that case, the workstation installation procedure will automatically configure your system to dual boot—whenever you start your system, a Linux utility known as LILO will give you the choice of starting Microsoft Windows or Linux. Both operating systems can reside on a single system. A workstation installation requires about 600 MB of free disk space.

The Server Installation Type

The server installation type automatically removes *all* existing data from your hard disk. You should use it when you want your system to run only Linux. A server installation requires about 1.6 GB of free disk space.

WARNING   The server installation type *destroys all data* on your hard drive. Do
not perform a server installation if you want to preserve any data on
your system.

The Custom Installation Type

The custom installation type gives you complete control over the installation process. You specify whether to configure your system for dual boot, what software packages to install, and so on. The custom install is covered in detail in the next chapter, but a workstation or server install can offer a quick way to get started unless you need to preserve data on the target machine.

Preparing Your Hard Disk

To prepare your hard disk for installing Linux, you must allocate the space in which Linux will reside. You'll learn how to do so in this section. First, you'll learn how hard disks are organized, then you'll learn how to view the structure of a hard disk. Finally, you'll learn how to alter the structure of a hard disk.

How Hard Disks are Organized

Let's start by reviewing facts you've probably learned by working with Microsoft Windows. Most operating systems, including Microsoft Windows 95 and Windows 98, manage hard disk drives by dividing their storage space into units known as *partitions*. So that you can access a partition, Windows 95 and Windows 98 associate a drive letter (such as C: or D:) with it. Before you can store data on a partition, you must *format* it. Formatting a partition organizes the associated space into what is called a *filesystem*, which provides space for storing the names and attributes of files as well as the data they contain. Microsoft Windows supports several types of filesystems, such as FAT and FAT32, a newer filesystem type that provides more efficient storage, launches programs faster, and supports very large hard disk drives.

Partitions comprise the *logical structure* of a disk drive, the way humans and most computer programs understand the structure. However, disk drives have an underlying *physical structure* that more closely resembles the actual structure of the hardware. Figure 2-3 shows the logical and physical structure of a disk drive.

Mechanically, a hard disk is constructed of platters that resemble the phonograph records found in a old-fashioned juke box. Each platter is associated with a read/write *head* that works much like the read/write head on a VCR, encoding data as a series of electromagnetic pulses. As the platter spins, the heads record data in concentric rings known as *tracks*, which are numbered beginning with zero. A hard disk may have hundreds or thousands of tracks.

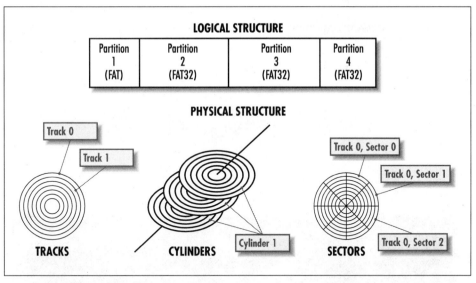

Figure 2-3. The structure of a hard disk

All the tracks with the same radius are known as a *cylinder*. Like tracks, cylinders are numbered beginning with zero. The number of platters and cylinders of a drive determine the drive's *geometry*. Most PCs require you to specify the geometry of a drive in the BIOS setup.

Most operating systems prefer to read or write only part of a track, rather than an entire track. Consequently, tracks are divided into a series of *sectors*, each of which holds a fixed number of bytes, usually 512.

To correctly access a sector, a program needs to know the geometry of the drive. Because it's sometimes inconvenient to specify the geometry of a drive, some PC BIOS programs let you specify *logical block addressing* (LBA). LBA sequentially numbers sectors, letting programs read or write a specified sector without the burden of specifying a cylinder or head number.

Viewing Partition Information

The first step in preparing your hard disk is viewing its partition information. Once you know how your hard disk is organized, you'll be able to determine how to reorganize it to accommodate Linux. To view the partitions that exist on your hard disk drives, you can use the `fdisk` utility:

1.   Click on the Start menu. The Start popup menu appears.

2. Select Programs. The Programs submenu appears.

3. From the Programs submenu, click on MS-DOS Prompt. An MS-DOS Prompt window appears.

4. Type *fdisk* and press **Enter**. The *fdisk* menu appears, as shown in Figure 2-4.

TIP The *fdisk* menu may not appear immediately. Instead, Windows may ask if you want to enable large disk support. If this occurs, type N and press **Enter**. You don't need to enable large disk support to view partition information.

Figure 2-4. The fdisk Options screen

5. Type 5 and press **Enter**. This takes you to a screen, resembling the one shown in Figure 2-5, that lets you specify the current fixed disk drive. This screen displays partition information in a more readable format than the screen you obtain by using menu item 4, "Display Partition Information."

    The screen shows each hard disk drive and its size, numbering the drives beginning with 1. If a drive contains free space not allocated to a partition, the screen shows the amount of free space available. The screen also shows how much of the drive's space has been allocated to partitions, as a percentage of the total drive space.

Under the information describing a drive, the screen shows the size of each partition that resides on the drive. The screen also shows the associated drive letter, if any.

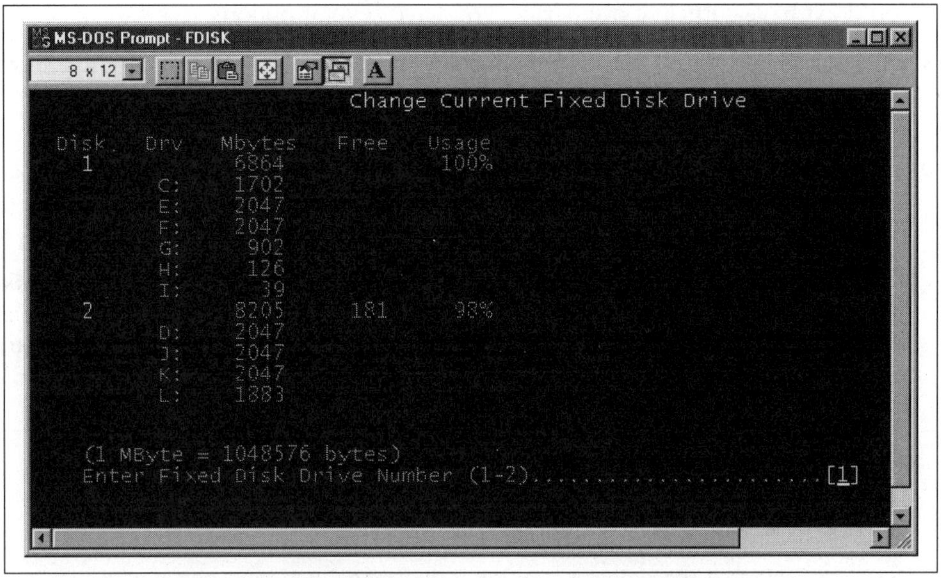

Figure 2-5. The fdisk Change Current Fixed Disk Drive screen

6. When you're done viewing partition information, press **Esc** twice to exit *fdisk* and return to an MS-DOS prompt. You can then close the MS-DOS Prompt window by clicking on the close icon in the upper right corner of the window or by typing `exit` and pressing **Enter**.

Obtaining Sufficient Disk Space

You cannot install Linux to a partition already in use. By viewing the partitions on your hard drive, you can determine which of the following two cases best describes your system:

*   You have available free (unpartitioned) disk space large enough to accommodate Linux (600 MB to 1.6 GB, depending on the type of installation you want).

    In this case, make a note of the drive that holds the free disk space. You can then begin the installation process described in Chapter 3, *Installing Linux.* However, see the following tip on PC BIOS limitations.

- You don't have enough free (unpartitioned) disk space to accommodate Linux.

  The procedures given in this section will help you obtain the necessary free space.

If you don't have sufficient disk space, you have several options:

- If your system has room for an additional disk drive, you can install a new drive and use it to hold Linux. The section titled "Installing a new disk drive" offers some considerations and tips on installing a new drive.

- If you have one or more unneeded partitions, you can delete them and use the space you gain to hold Linux. The section titled "Identifying an unused partition" shows you how to identify an unused partition.

- If you have one or more partitions that are larger than needed, you can shrink them and use the space you gain to hold Linux. The section titled "Shrinking a partition" shows you how to determine whether a partition is larger than needed and how to free the excess space.

TIP   The BIOS of most PCs cannot access more than two hard drives and cannot access data on or beyond cylinder 1023 of a hard drive. In order to boot Linux, the installation program must create a 16 MB (or larger) boot partition in an area accessible by BIOS. If your available free space does not satisfy these criteria, you must obtain additional free space as described in the following sections.

If you're unsure whether your free space satisfies these criteria, simply begin the installation; the installation program will notify you if it is unable to proceed. In that case, you can return to this chapter and obtain additional free space.

Installing a new disk drive

Often, the easiest way to install Linux is to install a new disk drive. If your system has only a single hard disk drive, you can probably install a second drive and place Linux on the new drive. Before purchasing a drive, you should make sure that the system provides room to mount the new drive and that you have the proper data and power cables. You'll also need to plan how to move data from your existing hard drive to the new hard drive. Consult your system vendor for assistance, if necessary.

If your system already has two disk drives, you probably can't simply add a third disk drive: the BIOS of most PCs lets you boot the system from only the first or second hard drive. In such a case, you can probably replace one of your existing drives with a larger drive adequate to support your existing needs and Linux.

Identifying an unused partition

You can use the drive letter information provided by *fdisk* to examine the contents of a partition in the Windows Explorer. If you can find a partition that holds no useful data but that is large enough to accommodate the type of Linux installation you want, you can delete the partition and use the free space to hold Linux.

The easiest way to delete a partition is to use the Red Hat install utility. Make note of the partition you wish to delete and then simply begin the installation process described in the next chapter.

Shrinking a partition

Even if all of your partitions contain useful data, one or more partitions may be larger than required. In that case, you can reduce the size of each such partition and reorganize the drive to include contiguous unused space that you can use to hold Linux.

You can use the Windows Explorer to determine the amount of free disk space in a partition. Simply right click on the drive icon and click on Properties in the popup menu. The Properties dialog box that appears shows the amount of used and free disk space associated with the drive.

If you are able to find one or more partitions that have sufficient free space for a Linux installation, you can use a special utility to split the used and unused portions of a partition into separate partitions. The Linux CD-ROM includes the GPL *fips* utility, which can split FAT and FAT32 partitions. For information on using *fips*, see the next section.

WARNING   If you make a mistake while attempting to shrink a partition or if the software malfunctions, you may lose all data in one or more partitions. You should not attempt to shrink a partition until you've completely backed up your system and made sure that your backup is usable.

Many Linux users find PowerQuest's PartitionMagic utility helpful. Unlike *fips*, PartitionMagic is commercial software; however, it supports partition types and operations not supported by *fips*. For example, PartitionMagic can split NTFS, HPFS, and Linux `ext2` partitions.

Using the fips utility

The *fips* utility lets you split a FAT partition into two partitions, one containing the data of the original partition and the other containing no data. Version 2 of the *fips* utility lets you split a FAT or FAT32 partition. Once you've run *fips*, you can use the *fdisk* program to delete the new empty partition, creating free space for installing Linux.

TIP   The *fips* utility will not split a partition unless there is at least about 10 MB of free space at the end of the drive. Moreover, *fips* requires a free entry in the disk's partition table; it will not work if your drive already contains four partitions.

This section describes the procedure for using *fips*. It assumes that you're running Microsoft Windows 9x. If you're running another operating system, consult the *fips* documentation for special instructions.

WARNING   In the words of its author, *fips* is "somewhat experimental." Neither the author of this book nor the publisher can accept responsibility or liability for damage resulting from your use or misuse of *fips*. You should not attempt to use *fips* until you've completely backed up your system and made sure that your backup is usable.

Also, your Microsoft operating system may assign different letters to drives after you use *fips* to split a partition. For example, your D: drive may become E:. The *fips* utility ensures that the C: drive remains C: so that you will generally be able to boot your system; however, you may not be able to properly access programs or files that reside on drives other than C:.

Before running *fips*, you should check the condition of your hard drive by running *chkdsk*, ScanDisk, Norton Disk Doctor, or a similar program. To launch the Scan-Disk program, click Start → Programs → Accessories → System Tools → ScanDisk. If your program reports errors, you should not attempt to split the partition until you resolve them.

Next, you must defragment your hard drive. Defragmenting a drive moves all its data to the beginning of the drive, leaving all the free space at the end. You can defragment your drive by using the Microsoft *defrag* utility. Simply click Start → Programs → Accessories → System Tools → Disk Defragmenter. However, you can use another defragmentation program if you prefer; the Norton Speedisk program, PCTool's Compress program, and various shareware programs are suitable.

TIP | The Microsoft *defrag* program doesn't always defragment a drive as thoroughly as possible. It sometimes erroneously regards some disk blocks as bad or immovable, and thus can fail to clear space that another program would successfully reclaim. If you find the results of using *defrag* disappointing, you should consider using a different program.

Next, you should disable virtual memory. Launch the Control Panel by clicking Start → Settings → Control Panel. Then, double click on the System icon. The System Properties dialog box appears. Select the Performance tab and click on "Virtual Memory . . . " The Virtual Memory dialog box appears. Make a note of the current setting. Then, click on "Let me specify my own virtual memory settings" and then click on "Disable virtual memory." Click on OK to dismiss the Virtual Memory dialog box. Finally, click on OK to dismiss the System Properties dialog box.

Next, create a boot floppy, by using the Add/Remove Programs control panel applet. Double click on the Add/Remove Programs icon in the Control Panel. The Add/Remove Program Properties dialog box appears. Click on the Startup Disk tab and then click the Create Disk button. A progress bar appears on the Add/Remove Program Properties dialog box. When prompted by the program, insert your Windows 9x CD-ROM. After reading from the CD-ROM, the program will prompt you to insert a formatted floppy disk into your system's floppy drive. Label a floppy disk "FIPS" and insert it into the drive. As the boot disk is being written, the progress bar informs you of the task's status. After a few minutes, the progress bar will disappear, informing you that the boot disk has been created. Click on OK to dismiss the Add/Remove Program Properties dialog box.

Do not remove the diskette from the drive. Instead, copy the following files from the CD-ROM onto the floppy disk:

\dosutils\fips20\restorrb.exe
\dosutils\fips20\fips.exe
\dosutils\fips20\errors.txt

If you use IMAGE or MIRROR or if your *config.sys* or *autoexec.bat* file invokes programs that write to your hard disk, use the Windows Explorer to temporarily rename *config.sys* to *config.fip* and *autoexec.bat* to *autoexec.fip*. If you're unsure what programs your *config.sys* and *autoexec.bat* files invoke, play it safe by renaming both files.

Now, boot your system by using the floppy diskette you created. When the MS-DOS command prompt appears, type *fips* and press **Enter** to launch the *fips* utility. If you have more than one hard disk drive, *fips* asks which disk it should access. Respond by identifying the appropriate disk drive.

Next, *fips* gives you the opportunity to create a backup file on your A: drive. You should allow *fips* to create the file. Then, if something goes wrong in using *fips*, you can boot from your floppy diskette and run the *restorrb* program to return your hard drive to its original state.

The *fips* utility then displays the partitions found on your hard disk. You need pay attention to only the first and last columns of the display, which indicate the number and size of each partition.

The *fips* utility performs some analysis of your hard drive. Then, if your hard drive contains more than one partition, *fips* asks you which partition you wish to split. Type the number of the partition and press **Enter**.

After performing some further analysis, *fips* asks you to enter the number of the cylinder on which the new partition should begin. Use the left cursor key to decrease the number and the right cursor key to increase it. As you increase or decrease the cylinder number, *fips* displays the size of the two partitions it will create. After setting the proper cylinder number, press **Enter**.

TIP

You may find that the maximum size of the empty partition is much smaller than you expected. If so, this is probably due to the presence of a hidden file that your defragmentation program was unable to move.

To identify such files, open an MS-DOS Prompt window, type the command `dir /a:h /s` and press **Enter**. Ignore any files with names similar to *ibmbio.com* or *ibmdos.com*. Try to determine what program created any remaining hidden files. If you can identify the program, you may be able to create a larger empty partition by uninstalling the program, splitting the partition, and reinstalling the program.

The *fips* utility displays the new partition information. You can type Y to save your changes and exit, or type C to make additional changes.

After exiting *fips*, you should *immediately* boot Windows 9x and run ScanDisk to verify that the partitions created by *fips* are valid. *Do not write anything to the disk before rebooting*; otherwise, you may destroy information on your hard drive.

Next, you should re-enable virtual memory. To do so, launch the Control Panel by clicking Start → Settings → Control Panel. Then, double click on the System icon. The System Properties dialog box appears. Select the Performance tab and click on

Virtual Memory. Return the settings to the values you earlier noted, then click on OK to dismiss the Virtual Memory dialog box. Then, click on OK to dismiss the System Properties dialog box.

If you renamed your *config.sys* and *autoexec.bat* files, restore the original names by using Windows Explorer.

Finally, reboot your system so that the changes to your system's virtual memory settings become active. Now you're ready to install Linux to the new empty partition.

CHAPTER THREE

INSTALLING LINUX

In this chapter, you'll learn how to install Linux by following a simple, step-by-step procedure. Most users will be able to complete the installation procedure without difficulty; however, the chapter includes a section that describes how you can obtain help if you encounter installation problems. Once you successfully complete the installation procedure, you'll have your own working Linux system.

Installing the Operating System and Applications

To install Linux, you follow a simple, step-by-step procedure that has three main phases:

- Installing the operating system and applications

- Configuring devices and services

- Completing the installation

This section describes the procedure for installing the operating system and applications. The following sections describe the remaining phases.

WARNING   Although the Linux installation procedure is generally troublefree, errors or malfunctions that occur during the installation of an operating system can result in loss of data. You should not begin the installation procedure until you have backed up all data on your system and determined that your backup is error-free.

34

The Installation Program User Interface

Like other modern Linux distributions, Red Hat Linux includes a screen-based install program that simplifies the installation and initial configuration of Linux. However, the install program works somewhat differently than a typical Microsoft Windows application. For instance, it does not support use of a mouse or other pointing device; all input is via the keyboard. So that you can make effective use of the install program, the next three sections describe the user-interface controls used by the install program, present the special keystrokes recognized by the install program, and explain the use of Linux's virtual consoles.

User-interface controls

Figure 3-1 shows a typical screen displayed by the install program. This screen includes the following elements:

A main window

The install program runs in a full screen window. The upper right corner of the window displays the name of the current installation step. In Figure 3-1, the current step is "Setup filesystems." You cannot minimize or change the size of the install program's main window.

Dialog boxes

Like Microsoft Windows, the install program uses dialog boxes to obtain user input. The install program consists of a series of dialog boxes that accept information needed to install and configure your Linux system. In Figure 3-1, two dialog boxes are visible: one titled "Current Disk Partitions," and another titled "Edit New Partition." You dismiss a dialog by using its Ok or Cancel button. You cannot minimize or move an install program dialog box.

The cursor

Like Windows programs, the installation program has a cursor on screen. Unlike Windows, the cursor movement and cursor actions are keyboard, rather than mouse controlled. The location of the cursor is called the input focus. At any time, exactly one control has the input focus, which lets it respond to keyboard input. The install program displays a rectangular cursor that identifies the field having the input focus. In Figure 3-1, the "Mount Point" field has the input focus.

Text boxes

Text boxes let you type text that is sent to the install program when you dismiss the dialog box by using the Ok button. In Figure 3-1, the field labeled "Mount Point" is a text box.

Checkboxes

Checkboxes let you specify that an option is enabled or disabled. An asterisk (*) indicates an enabled option; an empty checkbox indicates a disabled option. When a checkbox has the input focus, you can press the space bar to

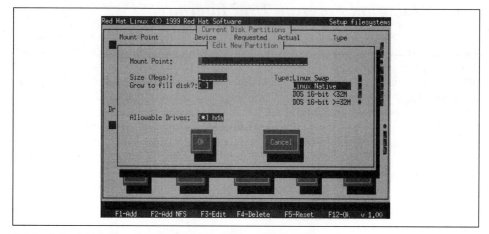

Figure 3-1. A typical screen displayed by the install program

toggle the checkbox between its enabled and disabled states. In Figure 3-1, the fields labeled "Grow to fill disk" and "Allowable drives" are checkboxes.

A scrollable list

Scrollable lists contain other controls, such as checkboxes, or labeled text. Scrollable lists have an associated scrollbar that lets you page through a list of items that may be too long to display all at once. At any time, one line in the scrollable list is active, as indicated by a # character to the right of the line. When a scrollable list has the input focus, the Up and Down arrow keys let you choose a different active item.

If the active item is a checkbox and the scrollable list has the input focus, you can use the space bar to toggle the state of the checkbox. Labeled text controls work like text boxes with predefined contents; when they appear within a scrollable list they let you quickly choose an option from a group of options. If the active item is labeled text, you can press **Enter** to select it. The contents of all selected entries with a scrollable list are sent to the install program when you dismiss the dialog box.

Buttons

When you press a button, the install program performs a corresponding action. For example, pressing the Ok button of a dialog box tells the install program to accept the dialog box inputs and proceed to the next dialog. Similarly, pressing the Cancel button of a dialog box tells the install program to ignore the dialog box inputs. Many dialog boxes include a helpful Back button that lets you return to the previous dialog box. When a button has the input focus, you can press it by pressing **Enter** or **Space**.

Common keystrokes

Several keystrokes let you direct the operation of the install program. For example, you can use the **Tab** key to move the input focus from one control to the next. Table 3-1 summarizes the keystrokes that the install program recognizes. You may want to keep this table handy as you work with the install program.

Table 3-1. Keystrokes Recognized by the Install Program

Keystroke	Meaning
Enter	Button: send a button press to the install program
	Scrollable list: toggle the selection state of the active item
Tab	Move the input focus to the next field
Alt-Tab	Move the input focus to the previous field
Down	Move the cursor down
Up	Move the cursor up
Left	Move the cursor left
Right	Move the cursor right
Space	Button: send a button press to the install program
	Checkbox: toggle the state of the checkbox
F12	Accept the inputs of the current dialog box and move to the next dialog box

---

WARNING You should press keys only when an installation program dialog box is active. Pressing keys at other times can send keystrokes to programs invoked by the install program, which may interpret your input in an unpredictable fashion.

Using virtual consoles

A console is a combination of a keyboard and a display device, such as a video monitor. A console provides a basic user interface adequate to communicate with a computer: you can type characters on the keyboard and view text on the display device.

Although a home computer system seldom has more than one console, Linux systems provide several virtual consoles. By pressing a special combination of keys, you can control which console your system's keyboard and monitor are connected to. Table 3-2 describes the virtual consoles used by the install program. The main installation dialog appears in virtual console #1. If you like, you can use the indicated keystroke to view a different virtual console. The contents of virtual consoles #2–5 can be useful in troubleshooting; however, you will not usually need to switch from one virtual console to another. Nevertheless, you may find it interesting to view the contents of the virtual consoles.

Table 3-2. Virtual Consoles Used by the Install Program

Console	Keystroke	Contents
1	Alt-F1	The installation dialog
2	Alt-F2	A shell prompt that lets you enter commands to be processed by Linux
3	Alt-F3	The installation log, containing messages from the install program
4	Alt-F4	The system log, containing messages from the Linux kernel and other system programs
5	Alt-F5	Other messages

Starting the Installation

To begin installing Linux, you must boot your system from a floppy diskette containing the boot kernel. Creating the boot disk requires some special measures; you can't simply copy files onto a disk and then boot it.

To create the boot disk, perform the following steps:

1. Insert the Linux CD-ROM diskette in your CD-ROM drive.

2. Start an MS-DOS Prompt window by clicking on Start → Programs → MS-DOS Prompt.

3. In the MS-DOS window, change to the drive letter that corresponds to your CD-ROM drive, for example, *m:* (see Figure 3-2).

4. In the MS-DOS window, type the command `dosutils\rawrite` and press **Enter**.

5. When prompted, specify the file name of the disk image source as *images\boot.img* and press **Enter**.

6. When prompted, specify the drive letter of your floppy drive, for example, *a:* .

7. As instructed by the program, place a formatted floppy diskette in your floppy drive and press **Enter**.

It takes perhaps a minute or so for the `rawrite` utility to create the floppy diskette. Wait for the utility to complete and then restart your system using the floppy diskette. When you see the `boot:` prompt, press **Enter** to begin the installation process.

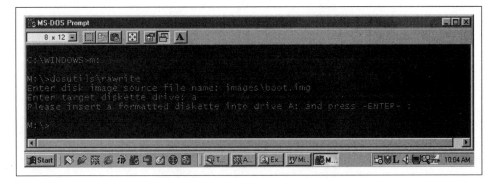

Figure 3-2. Using rawrite to make a boot diskette

TIP   The **boot:** prompt lets you enter various kernel options. Most sys-
      tems can be started without using any kernel options. However, if
      you cannot successfully boot your system from a CD-ROM or floppy
      diskette, you should suspect that a kernel option is needed. Seek
      help as described in the section titled "Getting Help," near the end
      of this chapter.

If your CD-ROM drive is attached to a SCSI controller on your system's PCMCIA
bus, you'll need to make a second floppy diskette, called the *supplemental
diskette*. Repeat the procedure for making the boot diskette, substituting *images\
supp.img* as the name of the disk image source in step #5.

Choosing a language

Once the install program starts, it first displays the Choose a Language dialog box,
shown in Figure 3-3, which asks what language should be used during the installation process. Use the UP and DOWN keys to move to the language you prefer and
press **Enter** to select it. The Keyboard Type dialog box appears.

Selecting a keyboard type

The Keyboard Type dialog box, shown in Figure 3-4, lets you specify the type of
keyboard attached to your system. Use the UP and DOWN keys to choose "us" to
specify a U.S.–style keyboard, or choose one of the other entries to specify a keyboard that provides special characters used by your preferred language. Press
Enter to dismiss the dialog box. If the install program determines that your computer supports PCMCIA devices, the PCMCIA Support dialog box appears next;
otherwise the Installation Method dialog box appears.

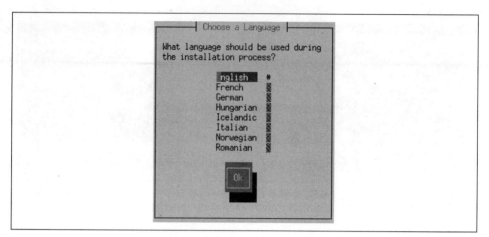

Figure 3-3. The Choose a Language dialog box

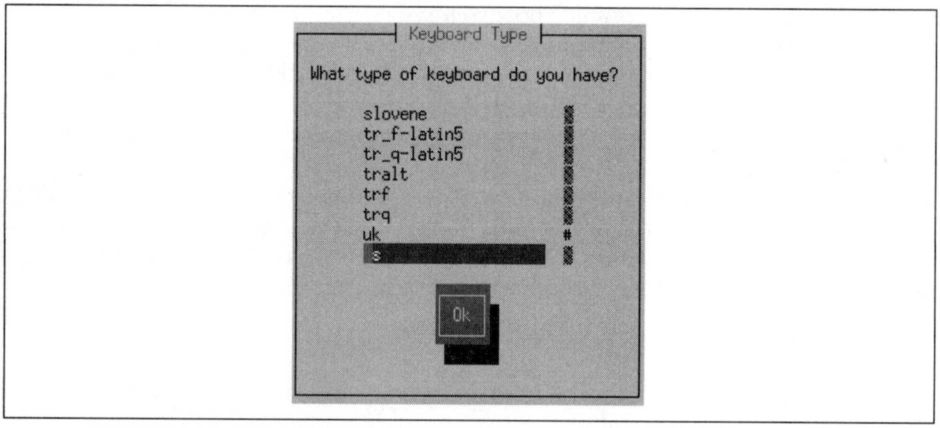

Figure 3-4. The Keyboard Type dialog box

Selecting PCMCIA support

The PCMCIA Support dialog box asks whether you require PCMCIA support during the installation process. If your CD-ROM drive is attached to a SCSI controller on your system's PCMCIA bus, you must enable PCMCIA support by selecting Yes; otherwise you should select No. If you select Yes, the install program will prompt you to insert the supplemental diskette you created earlier. When the install program has finished configuring PCMCIA support, the Installation Method dialog box appears.

TIP   You need not select this option merely because your computer has a
         PCMCIA slot. You need to select the option only if Linux must recog-
         nize your PCMCIA card in order to find the CD-ROM drive. Normal
         PCMCIA setup will occur later in the installation process.

Selecting Installation Options

In the next phase of system installation, you select an installation method, specify
whether this is a fresh install or an upgrade, and select the class of installation you
desire (workstation, server, or custom).

Selecting the installation method

When the Installation Method dialog box (shown in Figure 3-5) appears, select the
"Local CDROM" entry and press **Enter**. The install program prompts you to insert
the Linux CD-ROM diskette; make sure the diskette is in the CD-ROM drive and
then press **Enter**. The install program attempts to detect your CD-ROM drive. If it
encounters difficulty, it may prompt you to specify whether your CD-ROM drive
uses a SCSI interface (type SCSI) or a non-IDE, non-SCSI interface (type Other).
Once the install program has successfully detected your CD-ROM drive, the Installation Path dialog box appears.

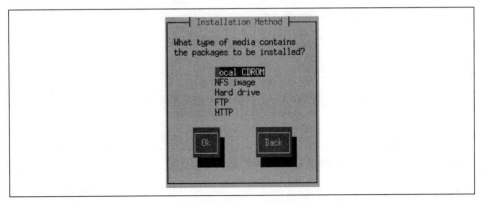

Figure 3-5. The Installation Method dialog box

TIP	If the install program fails to detected your IDE CD-ROM drive, you can restart the installation process and type the following option in response to the **boot:** prompt:

```
linux hdX=cdrom
```

where *X* indicates the drive configuration, as follows:

a Drive attached to first IDE controller and configured as master

b Drive attached to first IDE controller and configured as slave

c Drive attached to second IDE controller and configured as master

d Drive attached to second IDE controller and configured as slave

Upgrading or installing

The Installation Path dialog box, shown in Figure 3-6, lets you specify whether you're installing a new Linux system or upgrading a system that already contains Red Hat Linux 2.0 or later. Unless you've previously installed Red Hat Linux, you should select Install and press **Enter**. The Installation Class dialog box appears.

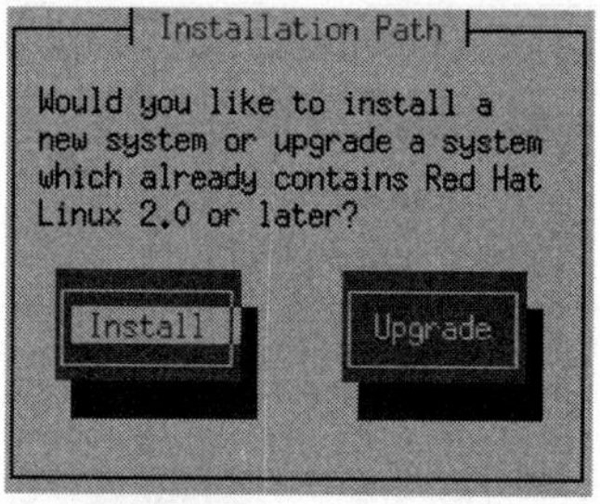

Figure 3-6. The Installation Path dialog box

Selecting the installation class

The Installation Class dialog box, shown in Figure 3-7, lets you choose to create a Workstation or Server system, or perform a Custom installation. You should choose Custom, because doing so gives you control over important installation options. This is particularly important if your system's hard drive already contains an installed operating system that you wish not to disturb.

The install program next asks if your system includes one or more SCSI adapters, as shown in Figure 3-8. If so, select Yes and press **Enter**. The install program will

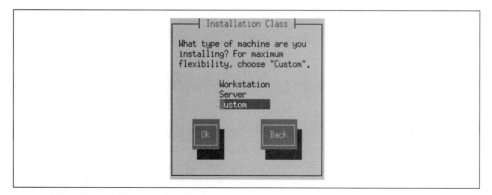

Figure 3-7. The Installation Class dialog box

ask what driver it should try, as shown in Figure 3-9. Highlight the driver that corresponds to your adapter, select Ok, and press **Enter.**

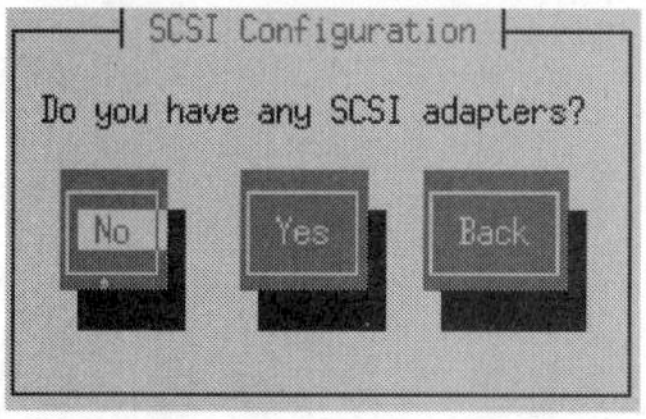

Figure 3-8. The SCSI Configuration dialog box

Creating Partitions

In the next phase of the installation procedure, you use the Disk Druid program to establish partitions on your hard disk drive. First, the Disk Setup dialog box (shown in Figure 3-10) appears. Most users should select Disk Druid and press **Enter;** however, if you have extensive Linux experience, you may prefer to use the Linux `fdisk` utility to establish partitions.

Using Disk Druid

Figure 3-11 shows the Disk Druid display screen, which is titled "Current Disk Partitions." The top part of the display contains a scrollable list that describes each existing partition. The middle part of the display contains a scrollable list that describes each disk drive. The bottom part of the display contains buttons that control the operation of Disk Druid. You use Disk Druid to add, edit, and delete Linux partitions.

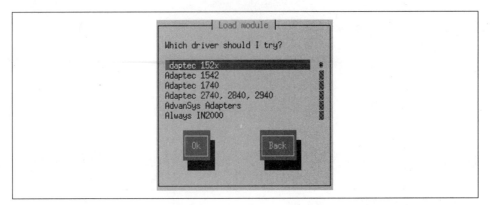

Figure 3-9. The Load Module dialog box

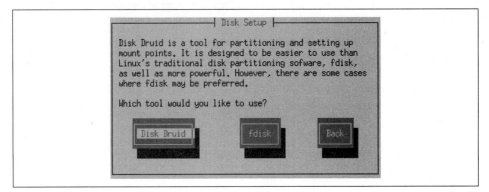

Figure 3-10. The Disk Setup dialog box

Adding a partition

As a minimum, you must establish two partitions. One, a Linux native partition, will hold the Linux operating system. The other, a Linux swap partition, will provide a work area used by Linux to efficiently manage your system's RAM memory.

To add a partition, select the Add button and press **Enter** (or simply press the F1 key). The Edit New Partition dialog box appears. To add the required Linux native partition, enter the following values:

Mount point
> Type a forward slash (/).

Size
> Specify the size in megabytes of the Linux native partition, which should be at least 600 MB.

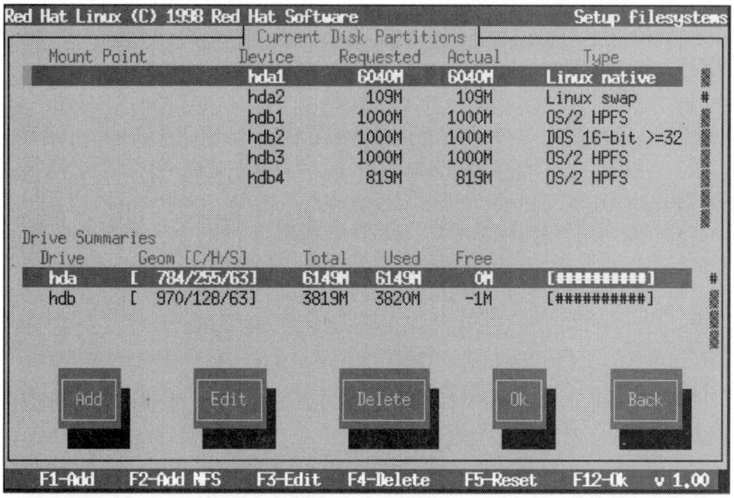

Figure 3-11. The Current Disk Partitions dialog box

Grow to fill to disk?

If you specify that a partition is growable by checking the "Grow to fill to disk?" box, the size you specify is treated as a minimum size. Disk Druid will distribute any remaining free disk space among the growable partitions. If you want your disk drive to contain some free space for later use, do not specify any growable partitions.

Type

Select Linux native.

Allowable drives

Choose one or more hard disk drives on which to place the partition. If you select more than one hard disk drive, Disk Druid will choose a drive from among those you specify; Disk Druid will never create a partition that spans multiple disk drives.

Select the Ok button and press **Enter** to accept the input values; or, if you don't want to create the partition, select the Cancel button and press **Enter**. The Current Disk Partitions dialog box returns to the front of the display.

TIP   If you enter an inappropriate value, Disk Druid may be unable to create the partition. In such a case, it displays a dialog box that explains the reason why the partition could not be created. Study the dialog box to determine what you did wrong and try again.

To add the required Linux Swap partition, select the Add button and press **Enter** to launch the Edit New Partition dialog box. Enter the following values:

Mount point
> Leave this field blank.

Size
> If your system has 16 MB of RAM or more, specify the amount of RAM in your system; but do not specify more than 127 MB. If your system has less than 16 MB of RAM, specify 16 MB

Grow to fill to disk?
> If this box is checked, uncheck it.

Type
> Select Linux Swap.

Allowable drives
> Choose one or more hard disk drives on which to place the partition. If you select more than one hard disk drive, Disk Druid will choose a drive from among those you specify; Disk Druid will never create a partition that spans multiple disk drives.

Select the Ok button and press **Enter** to accept the input values; or, if you don't want to create the partition, select the Cancel button and press **Enter**. The Current Disk Partitions dialog box returns to the front of the display.

Editing a partition

If you wish to change one or more values associated with a partition, highlight the partition you wish to change, select the Edit button and press **Enter** (or simply press the F3 key). Disk Druid launches the Edit Partition dialog box, shown in Figure 3-12. You can use this dialog box to change the mount point of a previously existing partition or other options of a partition you've just created. You cannot use this dialog box to change the size, grow option, or type of a previously existing partition; instead you must delete such a partition and recreate it.

Deleting a partition

If you wish to delete a partition, highlight it, select the Delete button, and press **Enter** (or simply press the F4 key). Disk Druid presents the Delete Partition dialog box, shown in Figure 3-13, which asks you to confirm the operation. Select Yes and press **Enter** to delete the partition or select No and press **Enter** to leave the partition intact.

WARNING   Deleting a partition destroys all the data it contains. Exercise great care to delete only unneeded partitions.

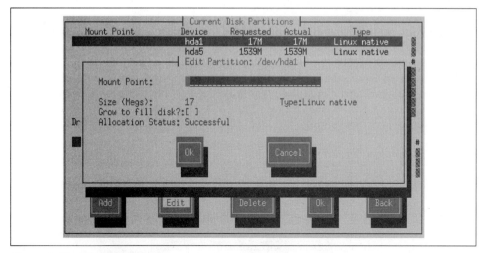

Figure 3-12. Editing a partition

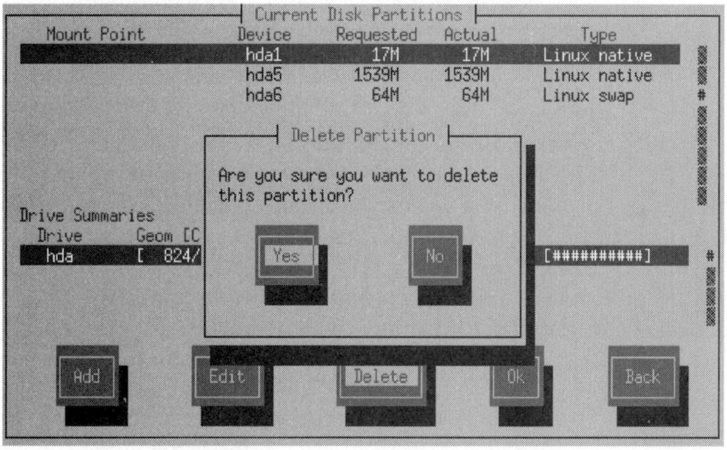

Figure 3-13. Deleting a partition

Starting over

If you determine that you've made mistakes and want to abandon the changes you've specified, simply press the F5 key. Disk Druid resets all partitions to their original state.

Saving your changes

To save your changes and proceed with the installation, select the Ok button and press **Enter** (or simply press the F12 key). Disk Druid completes its processing and the install program looks for active swap partitions. After it finds them, it presents the Active Swap Space dialog box, shown in Figure 3-14, which lets you initialize the swap partitions and check them for bad blocks. Check the swap partition you wish to use, check the "Check for bad blocks during format" option, select Ok and press **Enter**.

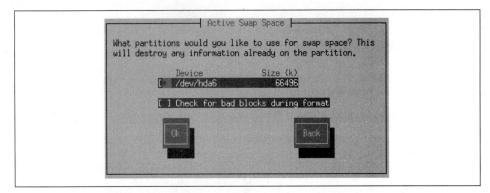

Figure 3-14. The Active Swap Space dialog box

Next, the install program presents the Partitions To Format dialog box, shown in Figure 3-15. This dialog box lets you choose which Linux native partitions to format. If this is the first time you've installed Linux on this system, you can safely format all Linux native partitions. Check each partition and check the "Check for bad blocks during format" option. If you've installed Linux on this system previously, you must be more discreet: Format only those partitions that contain no important data. To authorize formatting (which the install program will perform later), select Ok and press **Enter**. The Components to Install dialog box appears.

WARNING   Formatting a partition destroys all data in the partition. Be sure you
              format only partitions that contain no data you need.

The install program now formats any partitions you earlier specified for formatting. It may require several minutes to complete this step. When formatting is done, the Install Status dialog box appears and the install program begins installing packages.

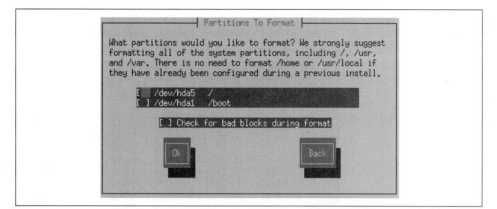

Figure 3-15. The Partitions To Format dialog box

Selecting and Installing Packages

To install an application under Linux, you install a *package*, which contains all the files needed by the application. If you like, you can specify the individual packages you want to install; however, the large number of available packages makes it tedious to specify them one at a time. Instead, you can specify *components* you want to install. A component is simply a group of related packages.

Selecting components

The Components to Install dialog box, shown in Figure 3-16, lets you choose which components you want to install. Simply select each desired component and press **Space** to mark the associated checkbox. The install program has pre-selected several components for you. If you don't know what components to select, don't worry; you can install additional components after setting up your Linux system. If, on the other hand, you want to be able to select individual packages as well as components, check the Select Individual Packages checkbox by selecting it and pressing **Space**. When you're satisfied with your choices, select the Ok button and press **Enter**.

Selecting packages

If you checked the Select Individual Packages check box, the Select Group dialog box appears, as shown in Figure 3-17. This dialog box works like a table of contents, letting you call up a dialog box that lets you select from a group of individual packages. To use the dialog box, select a group and press **Enter**. Or, if you prefer, you can highlight a group, select the Edit button and press **Enter**.

The Select Packages dialog box, shown in Figure 3-18, appears. To use the Select Packages dialog box, select the package or packages you wish to install, by

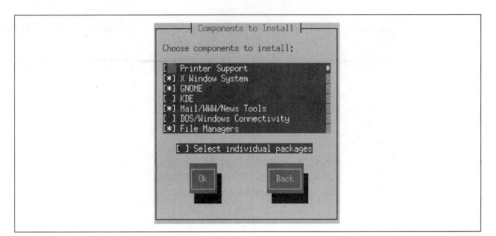

Figure 3-16. The Components to Install dialog box

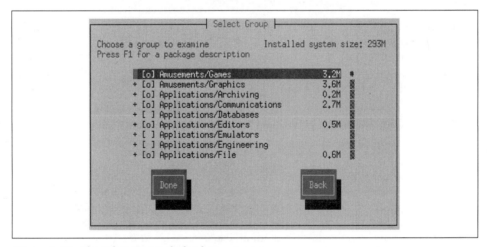

Figure 3-17. The Select Group dialog box

moving the cursor to the associated checkbox and pressing **Space**. You can view a description of the currently highlighted package by pressing F1.

When you've selected all the desired packages within a group, select the Ok button and press **Enter**. Or, if you want the install program to ignore the selections you've just made, you can select the Cancel button and press **Enter**. In either case, the Select Group dialog box returns to the front of the screen.

When you've selected all the desired packages, you can exit the Select Group dialog box by selecting the Done button and pressing **Enter**. Some packages work independently of others; but many packages depend on other packages, which

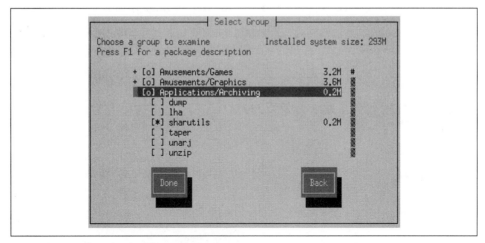

Figure 3-18. The Select Packages dialog box

provide files or services they need. After you've selected the packages you desire, the install program checks whether any additional packages are needed. If it finds that additional packages are needed, it presents a list of unresolved dependencies. You can, and should, select an option that causes the install program to automatically install the missing packages.

When the install program is ready to begin installing packages, it presents the Install Log dialog box, shown in Figure 3-19. This dialog box informs you of the location of a list of installed packages, which will be helpful to you in maintaining your system. Note the location of the log file and then select Ok and press **Enter**.

Figure 3-19. The Install Log dialog box

The install program now formats any partitions you earlier specified for formatting. It may require several minutes to complete this step. When formatting is done, the

Install Status dialog box appears and the install program begins installing packages. This dialog box displays the name of each package as it is installed, and presents a progress bar that shows the relative progress of the installation process. When all the packages have been installed, you're ready to configure devices and services.

Configuring Devices and Services

To help you configure devices and services, the install program presents a series of dialog boxes that let you configure:

- A mouse

- The X Window System

- Networking

- The system clock

- Services

- Printers

TIP   If you're unable to configure one or more devices or services during installation, you'll be able to configure them later.

Configuring a Mouse

Next, the install program probes your system to locate a mouse. If the install program successfully finds and identifies your mouse, it presents one or two simple dialog boxes like those shown in Figure 3-20 and Figure 3-21. These ask you to confirm the install program's findings and possibly select from several options. Simply make the appropriate choices and continue to the next step.

If the install program cannot find and identify your mouse, it presents a Configure Mouse dialog box, which lists supported mouse types. If you can find your mouse or an exact equivalent, highlight the appropriate choice; otherwise, highlight one of the "Generic" entries, whichever best resembles the type of interface and number of buttons of your mouse. If you followed the procedure given in Chapter 2, *Preparing to Install Linux*, you know whether your mouse uses a serial interface or PS/2 interface. If not, the shape of the connector is a somewhat reliable guide: A round connector indicates a PS/2 interface whereas a rounded rectangular connector indicates a serial mouse.

If your mouse has a serial interface, the install program presents a Mouse Port dialog box that asks you to identify the COM port to which your mouse is attached.

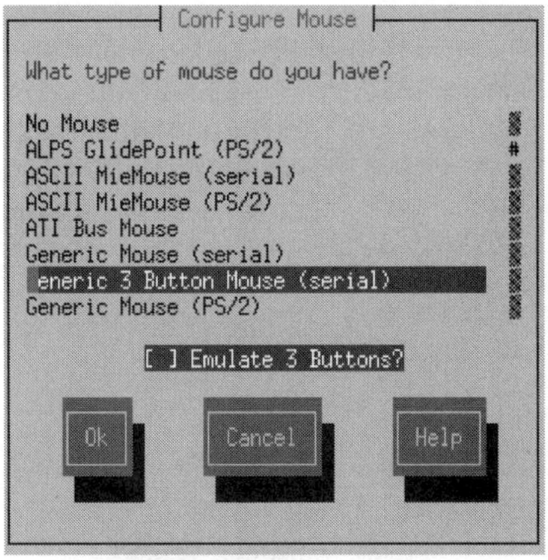

Figure 3-20. The Configure Mouse dialog box

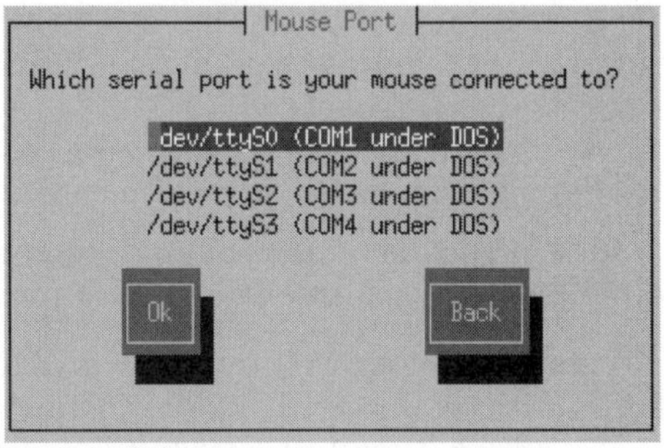

Figure 3-21. The Mouse Port dialog box

Again, if you followed the procedure given in Chapter 2, you know which port this is. Otherwise, you can try to identify the port by tracing the mouse cable and referring to your system documentation.

TIP   If you fail to correctly configure your mouse, you can re-configure it
                 after installation is complete by using the *mouseconfig* command.

Configuring Networking

After configuring your mouse, the installation program presents the Network Configuration dialog box, shown in Figure 3-22. If your computer is attached to a Local Area Network (LAN), you can use the network configuration dialog to configure networking. Select Yes and press **Enter** to configure networking; if your computer is not attached to a LAN, select No and press **Enter**.

Figure 3-22. The Network Configuration dialog box

If your computer is part of a LAN, your networking needs will fall into one of two categories:

*   You're making a dialup connection to the Internet; or

*   You're on a LAN with a permanent connection to other machines on the LAN and connection to the Internet via a gateway.

This isn't so different from Windows. Windows has a place under the Control Panel where you identify and configure what kind of hardware you have (modem and/or ethernet adapter), and what kind of protocol that hardware uses to communicate (such as TCP/IP). Windows has a separate utility, "Dial-up Networking," for making actual modem connections.

In Linux, you'll do much the same. First you need to establish what kind of network connections you'll be making (Ethernet and/or modem), and provide some basic information about the type of network you're connecting to. Later, after you've set up your Linux system, you'll use a separate program to actually make a dialup modem connection.

First, the install program probes for a network adapter card. If it cannot locate a card, it presents a dialog box that lets you specify the type of network adapter card present in your system. A second dialog box lets you specify whether to autoprobe for the adapter. You should generally allow the installation program to do so. Because probes sometimes fail, the dialog box gives you the option of specifying the I/O port address and IRQ associated with your card. Don't bother to specify these unless the installation program has previously failed to successfully probe your card.

Next, the installation program presents a set of network configuration dialog boxes, beginning with the Boot Protocol dialog box, shown in Figure 3-23. The Boot Protocol dialog box lets you specify how your computer's network address (IP address) is determined. You have three choices:

Static IP address
Lets you type in your computer's network address.

BOOTP
Tells your computer that it will determine its network address whenever you start it, by querying a BOOTP server.

DHCP
Tells your computer that it will determine its network address whenever you start it, by querying a DHCP server.

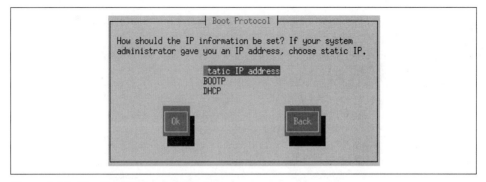

Figure 3-23. The Boot Protocol dialog box

If you choose BOOTP or DHCP, the install program skips the remaining steps of the network configuration dialog, because the computer can automatically determine the required information by querying the BOOTP or DHCP server.

TIP   If you choose BOOTP or DHCP, your LAN must provide an active BOOTP or DHCP server; otherwise networking will not operate properly.

If you chose Static IP Address, the install program presents the Configure TCP/IP dialog box, shown in Figure 3-24. Consult your LAN administrator to determine the proper values for these fields.

IP address
The network address of your system (for example, 192.168.1.2).

Netmask
> A bitmask that specifies the portion of your system's network address that uniquely identifies the network (for example, 255.255.255.0). The install program guesses this value; you can change it if it's incorrect.

Default gateway
> The network address of the router your system uses to send packets beyond its local network (for example, 192.168.1.1). The install program guesses this value; you can change it if it's incorrect.

Primary nameserver
> The network address of the system that provides hostname lookup services to your system (for example, 192.168.1.1). The install program guesses this value; you can change it if it's incorrect.

When you've filled in all the fields, select Ok and press **Enter**.

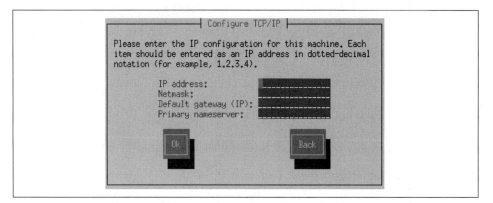

Figure 3-24. The Configure TCP/IP dialog box

The install program next presents the Configure Network dialog box, shown in Figure 3-25. Supply values for the following fields:

Domain name
> The domain name of your system (for example, `redhat.com`).

Host name
> The hostname of your system, including the domain name (for example, `newbie.redhat.com`)

Secondary nameserver
> The network address of the system used to look up hostnames if the primary name server is unavailable (optional).

Tertiary nameserver

The network address of the system used to look up hostnames if the primary and secondary name servers are unavailable (optional).

When you've entered the appropriate data, select the Ok button and press **Enter**.

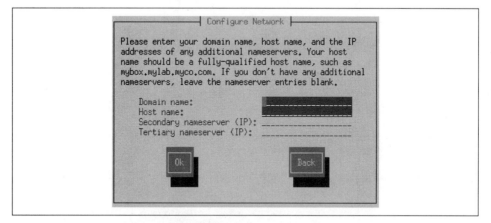

Figure 3-25. The Configure Network dialog box

Configuring the System Clock

When you bypass or complete the network configuration dialog, the install program presents the Configure Timezones dialog box, shown in Figure 3-26. Select the timezone you want your system to use and press **Enter**.

TIP   You can change the timezone setting after completing the installation, by using the *timeconfig* command.

Configuring Services

Next, the install program presents the Services dialog box, shown in Figure 3-27. This dialog box lets you choose the services that will be started when you boot your system. Several services are pre-selected. Highlight a service and press **Space** to toggle its selection state. If you're uncertain which services to select, you can accept the default selections. Pressing F1 provides a brief description of the currently highlighted service. When you've selected the services you want, select the Ok button and press **Enter**.

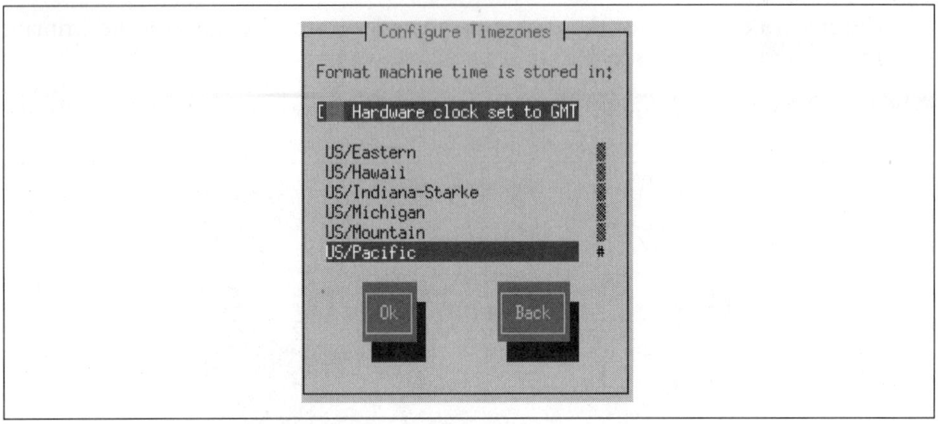

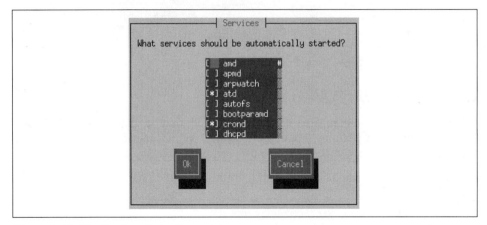

Figure 3-26. The Configure Timezones dialog box

Figure 3-27. The Services dialog box

Configuring a Printer

Next, the install program presents the Configure Printer dialog box, shown in Figure 3-28. If you have a locally attached printer or LAN access to a remote printer, you can use the printer configuration dialog to configure one or more printers. Select Ok and press **Enter** to configure a printer; or, select No and press **Enter** to skip printer configuration.

If you selected Yes, the install program presents the Select Printer Connection dialog box, shown in Figure 3-29. Three types of printers are supported:

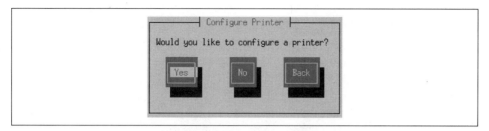

Figure 3-28. The Configure Printer dialog box

- Local printers attached to the parallel port(s) of your system.

- Remote printers accessed via the LAN. These can be:

  - Remote printers provided by a UNIX or Linux lpd daemon.

  - Remote printers provided by a LAN Manager or SMB server.

Highlight the proper printer type, select the Ok button and press **Enter**.

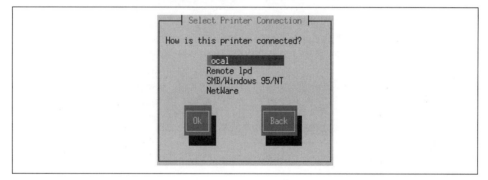

Figure 3-29. The Select Printer Connection dialog box

Next, the install program presents the Standard Printer Options dialog box, shown in Figure 3-30. You can simply accept the default information. Select the Ok button and press **Enter**.

Configuring a local printer

If you specified a local printer, the install program presents the Local Printer Device dialog box, shown in Figure 3-31. This dialog box lets you choose the parallel port to which your printer is attached. If your printer is attached to LPT1:, specify */dev/lp0*; if it is attached to LPT2:, specify */dev/lp1*; and so on. To help you correctly specify the device, the install program attempts to detect and display the available parallel ports. When you've specified the correct device, select the Ok button and press **Enter**.

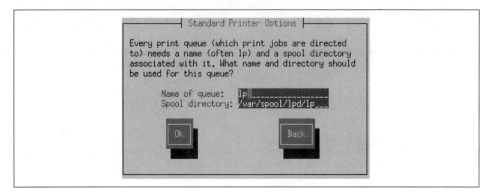

Figure 3-30. The Standard Printer Options dialog box

```
┌──────────┤ Local Printer Device ├──────────┐
│                                             │
│ What device is your printer connected to   │
│ (note that /dev/lp0 is equivalent to LPT1:)?│
│                                             │
│        Printer Device: /dev/lp0 _____      │
│                                             │
│   Auto-detected ports:                      │
│                                             │
│     /dev/lp0: Detected                      │
│     /dev/lp1: Not Detected                  │
│     /dev/lp2: Not Detected                  │
│                                             │
│         ┌──────┐        ┌──────┐            │
│         │  Ok  │        │ Back │            │
│         └──────┘        └──────┘            │
│                                             │
└─────────────────────────────────────────────┘
```

Figure 3-31. The Local Printer Device dialog box

Configuring a remote printer

If you specified a remote printer provided by an lpd daemon, the install program presents the Remote lpd Printer Options dialog box. There, you specify the remote hostname and queue that correspond to the remote printer. Consult your LAN administrator to determine the proper values.

If you specified a remote printer provided by a LAN Manager or SMB server, the install program presents the LAN Manager Printer Options dialog box. There, you specify:

LAN Manager Host
    The LAN Manager hostname of the server.

LAN Manager IP
> The network address of the server.

Share name
> The name by which the printer is known to the network.

Username
> A valid username permitting access to the printer.

Password
> The password corresponding to the username.

Consult your LAN administrator to determine the proper values.

TIP	The LAN Manager hostname is not always the same as the TCP/IP hostname.

Completing printer setup

Whether you specified a local or remote printer, the install program next presents the Configure Printer dialog box, shown in Figure 3-32. Highlight the printer most similar to the printer you wish to access. Then, select the Ok button and press **Enter**.

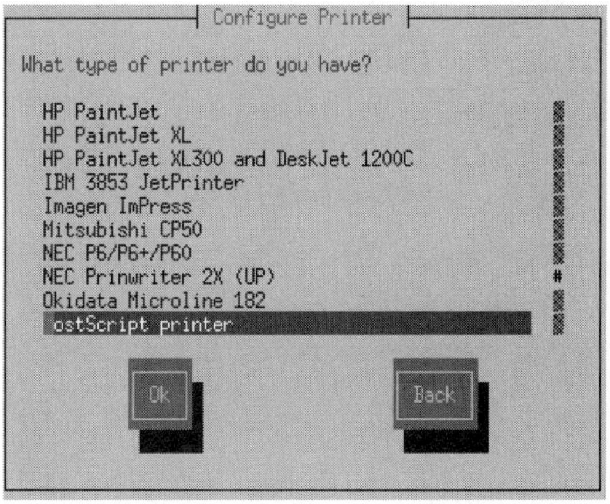

Figure 3-32. The Configure Printer dialog box

Next, the install program presents a dialog box similar to the PostScript printer dialog box shown in Figure 3-33. The title and contents of the dialog box vary according to the type of printer you specified in the preceding step. Use this dialog box to specify the characteristics of your printer. If your printer does not automatically perform a carriage return at the end of each line, check the Fix Stair-Stepping of Text checkbox. When you're done, select the Ok button and press **Enter**.

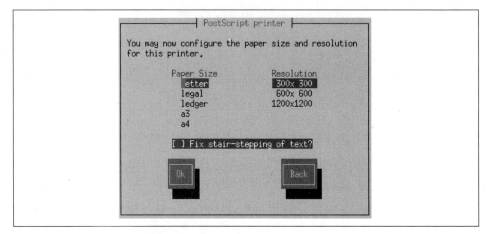

Figure 3-33. The Postscript printer dialog box

The install program presents the Verify Printer Configuration dialog box, shown in Figure 3-34. This dialog box lets you verify all the options pertaining to your printer. If an option is wrong, you can use the Back button to return to the appropriate dialog and change the option. Otherwise, select the Ok button and press **Enter**.

Completing the Installation

Once you've skipped or completed the printer configuration dialog, you're ready to complete the installation of Linux. This involves:

- Setting a password for the system administrator

- Configuring your system to boot

Setting root's Password

The user who administers a Linux system is known as *root*. To protect your system against mischief and misadventure, you should protect the root user's login with a password. To help you do so, the install program presents the Root Password dialog box, shown in Figure 3-35. Simply choose a password and type it in each text field. Then, select the Ok button and press **Enter**. You'll need to use this password when you log in after booting Linux for the first time.

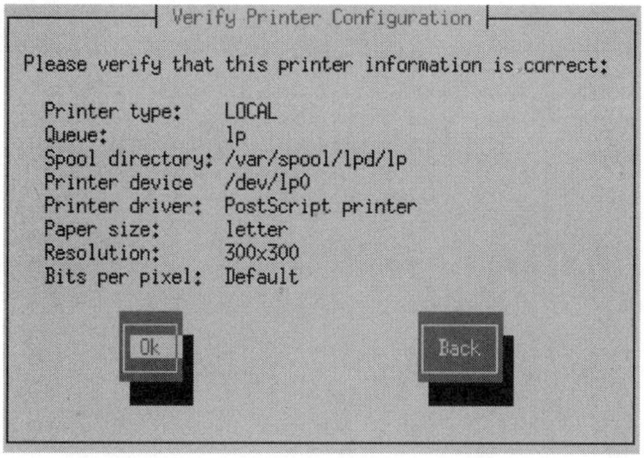

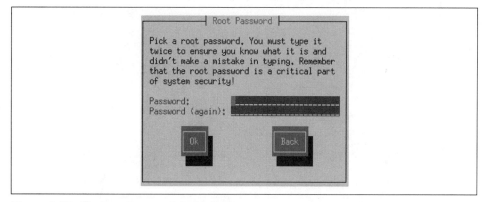

Figure 3-34. The Verify Printer Configuration dialog box

Figure 3-35. The Root Password dialog box

Next, the installation program shows the Authentication Configuration dialog box, shown in Figure 3-36. Disable the NIS option and enable both the Use Shadow Passwords and MD5 Passwords options. Select Ok and press **Enter**.

Creating a Boot Diskette

The install program next gives you the opportunity to create a boot diskette, by presenting the Bootdisk dialog box shown in Figure 3-37. You should take the opportunity, because a boot diskette will let you boot your Linux system even if the bootloader fails to install properly and even if the system boot information is damaged. To create a boot diskette, select Yes and press **Enter**. The install program will prompt you to insert a blank diskette in your system's diskette drive. Insert the diskette, select the Ok button, and press **Enter**. It may take several minutes for the install program to create the boot diskette.

Figure 3-36. The Authentication Configuration dialog box

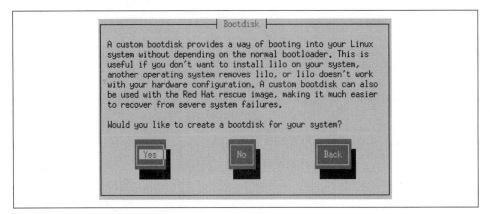

Figure 3-37. The Bootdisk dialog box

Installing the LILO Bootloader

Once the install program has created a boot diskette, it presents the Lilo Installation dialog box, shown in Figure 3-38. This dialog box lets you specify the location where LILO will be installed. LILO is a special program used to start Linux—or another operating system—when you boot your system.

Generally, Linux users install LILO on the Master Boot Record (MBR). However, doing so poses some risk. If your system currently boots using System Commander, the OS/2 Boot Manager, or the Microsoft Windows NT loader, installing LILO on the MBR will prevent you from booting any operating system other than Linux until you specially configure LILO. Moreover, some anti-virus applications detect changes to the MBR and roll them back. The bottom line is that, for many users, LILO can present some headaches.

Figure 3-38. The first Lilo Installation dialog box

You can easily avoid LILO either of two ways. First, you can boot Linux by using the boot diskette prepared earlier. Linux won't boot as quickly as it might, but you won't face the prospect of disabling your other operating systems. If booting from a floppy diskette seems antediluvian, you can use LOADLIN, an MS-DOS program that can start Linux. Appendix D, *Managing the Boot Process* explains how to use LOADLIN to boot Linux.

In view of the potential problems it poses, you're advised to skip installation of LILO. However, if you prefer to install it and you're using special boot software, then specify that LILO should be installed on the first sector of the boot partition rather than the MBR. Then, you can configure your special boot software to start LILO, which will boot Linux.

When you've made the proper selection, Ok or Skip, press **Enter**.

Configuring LILO options

If you specified that LILO should be installed, the install program presents the Lilo Installation dialog box, shown in Figure 3-39. This dialog box lets you specify kernel options; LILO will pass any options you specify to the kernel at boot time. Generally, no kernel options are needed. However, if you discover that a kernel option is required (for example, to access a CD-ROM drive with a proprietary interface), you can specify it here.

If your computer accesses the boot drive using linear byte addressing (LBA), set the Use Linear Mode option by selecting it and pressing **Space**.

When you've specified the proper options, select the Ok button and press **Enter**.

Booting other operating systems

Next, the install program presents the Bootable Partitions dialog box, shown in Figure 3-40. This dialog box lets you select the operating systems that LILO will let you boot. When LILO loads, it displays a `boot:` prompt. By pressing the **Tab** key, you can obtain a list of bootable operating systems. Typing the name of an

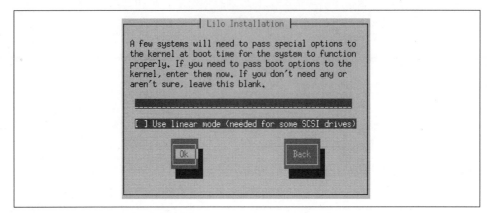

Figure 3-39. The second Lilo Installation dialog box

operating system and pressing **Enter** boots the specified operating system. Alternatively, you can press **Enter**, which causes LILO to boot the default operating system. To specify the default operating system, highlight the corresponding partition in the Bootable Partitions dialog box and press F2. The install program pre-selects Linux as the default operating system.

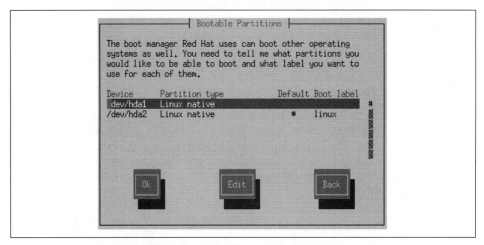

Figure 3-40. The Bootable Partitions dialog box

If you have an MS-DOS or Microsoft Windows partition, the install program will automatically select the corresponding device as bootable. If you want to be able to boot other operating systems, highlight the corresponding device, select the Edit button, and press **Enter**. The install program presents a dialog box that lets you assign a boot name to the selected device. LILO displays this boot name when you press the **Tab** key in response to its `boot:` prompt.

When you've specified all the bootable partitions, select the Ok button and press **Enter**.

Configuring X

If you specified that X should be installed (package XFree86), the install program launches the *Xconfigurator* utility, which helps you configure X. The utility first attempts to identify your video card, as shown in Figure 3-41; if it fails to do so, it presents a list of video cards from which you can choose. Simply highlight the appropriate card and press **Enter**.

TIP   If your video card is not listed, you may be able to use the "Unlisted Card" entry; however, you'll need to know the video chipset employed by your card.

Figure 3-41. The PCI Probe dialog box

The utility next attempts to identify your video monitor, as shown in Figure 3-42. Again, it presents a list of supported devices. Simply highlight the appropriate monitor and press **Enter**.

WARNING   An apparently similar monitor model may have capabilities in excess of those of your monitor. Failing to select the appropriate monitor, or selecting an inappropriate custom setup, may result in permanent damage to your monitor. If your monitor displays a scrambled image, turn it off promptly and recheck your configuration.

If you can't find your monitor listed, you can highlight Custom and press **Enter**. This causes the install program to provide a series of dialog boxes that ask you about your monitor's characteristics. As the dialog box shown in Figure 3-43 explains, you'll need to know the vertical sync rate (also known as the *vertical*

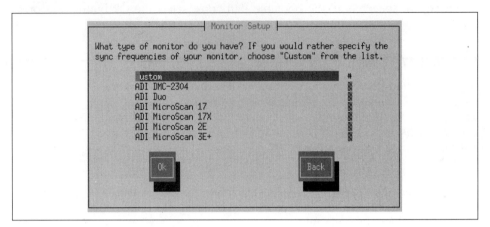

Figure 3-42. The Monitor Setup dialog box

refresh rate) and the horizontal sync rate of your monitor, which you can generally obtain from the owner's manual or from the manufacturers' web site. If you can't find this information there, try the file */usr/X11R6/lib/X11/doc/Monitors*. If you fail to find the information there, you can try some conservative values that are unlikely to damage all but the oldest of monitors. For example, try setting the horizontal sync to Standard VGA, as shown in Figure 3-44, and the vertical sync rate to 50-70, as shown in Figure 3-45.

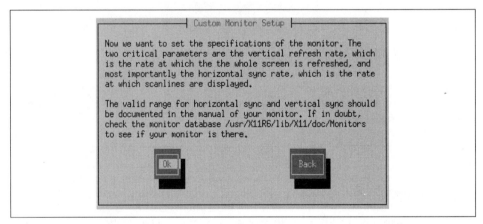

Figure 3-43. The Custom Monitor Setup dialog box

Next, the utility asks you to specify the amount of video memory installed on your video card. Specifying a value that is too large will probably prevent X from starting. If you followed the procedure given in Chapter 2, you may have learned the amount of video memory installed on your card; otherwise consult your video

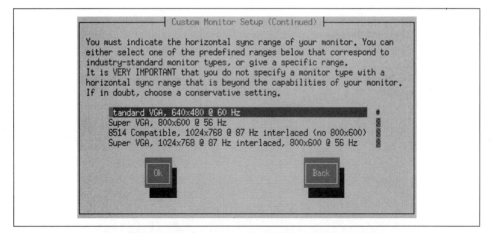

Figure 3-44. The Custom Monitor Setup (Continued) dialog box

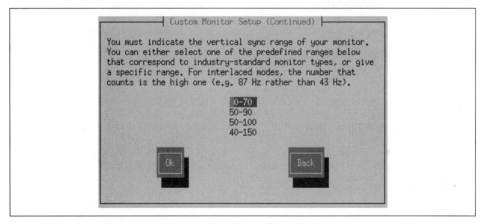

Figure 3-45. The Custom Monitor Setup (Continued) dialog box

card's documentation to determine the proper value. If you can't locate the information, select a conservatively low value; choosing a value that's too low will prevent you from using high-resolution video modes but won't damage your monitor.

If the utility suspects that your video card may have a video clockchip, it presents a list of clockchips. Choose the "No Clockchip" setting, because X can generally detect the proper clockchip automatically.

Finally, the utility announces that probing is finished, as shown in Figure 3-46, and proposes a default video mode in which X will operate. A video mode is associated with a video resolution, which has exactly the same meaning under X and

Windows, namely the number of horizontal and vertical dots (pixels) that comprise the display area. For example, 800×600 means that the display has 800 horizontal dots and 600 vertical dots.

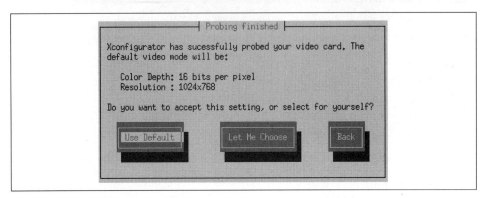

Figure 3-46. The Probing finished dialog box

A video mode also specifies a color depth, which refers to the number of colors that can be displayed:

- A color depth of 8 bits (per pixel) yields 256 colors, a mode Microsoft Windows video drivers often refer to as 256-Color.

- A color depth of 16 bits (per pixel) yields 65,536 colors, a mode Microsoft Windows video drivers often refer to as Thousands of Colors or High Color.

- A color depth of 24 bits (per pixel) yields about 16 million colors, a mode Microsoft Windows video drivers often refer to as Millions of Colors or True Color.

If you want to enable video modes other than the one proposed by the utility, you can select the Let Me Choose option, which launches the dialog box shown in Figure 3-47. Simply select each mode you want to use and press **Space**. Then select Ok and press **Enter**.

The install program now asks to start X in order to test your configuration, as shown in Figure 3-48. Select Ok and press **Enter**.

When X starts, you'll see a small dialog box that asks you whether you can read its message. Click on Yes to dismiss the dialog box. You'll need to do so within 10 seconds, or `Xconfigurator` will assume that X failed. This time limit is intended to avoid damage to your video hardware if the configuration is incorrect; however, some hardware can suffer damage even during such a brief interval.

A dialog box pops up, asking whether you'd like to automatically start X the next time you boot your system. Answer Yes nor No, according to your preference. If

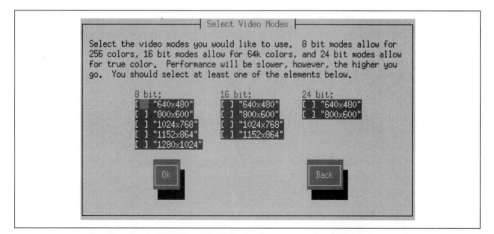

Figure 3-47. The Select Video Modes dialog box

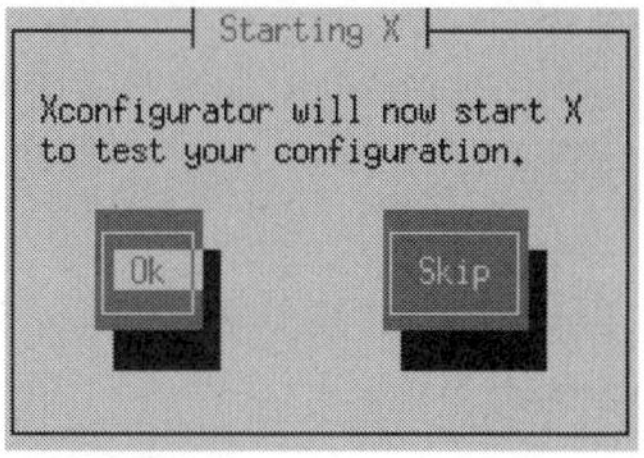

Figure 3-48. The Starting X dialog box

you don't specify that X should start automatically, you can start X at any time, by using commands described in Chapter 7, *Configuring and Administering Linux.*

The install program then presents its final dialog box, shown in Figure 3-49, which explains that Linux has been successfully installed. If you configured LILO, follow the instruction to remove any floppy diskette from your system's floppy drive; otherwise, ignore that instruction and insert your boot diskette in your system's floppy drive. press **Enter** to boot your system. If your system successfully boots Linux, you're ready to move on to Chapter 4, *Issuing Linux Commands*, which shows you how to begin using your new Linux system. If your system fails to boot, consult the next section, which tells you how to get help.

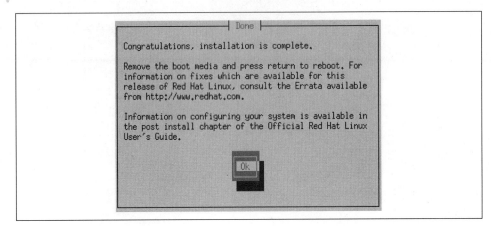

Figure 3-49. The Done dialog box

Getting Help

If your system fails to boot, or if you're unable to complete the Linux installation process, don't despair. The help you need is probably close by, in one of these sources:

- Linux FAQs (Frequently Asked Questions)

- Linux HOWTOs

- The Red Hat mailing list

- Usenet newsgroups

The following sections describe these sources and explain how to access and use them. You should generally consult them in the order specified.

FAQs

Linux FAQs present commonly asked questions and answers. The Red Hat Linux Installation Support FAQ is available online at *http://www.redhat.com/support/docs/rhl/RedHat-FAQ/RedHat-FAQ.html*. Also useful is the Red Hat Linux 5.2 Errata, found online at *http://www.redhat.com/support/docs/rhl/rh52-errata-general.html*.

You can find additional FAQs on the CD-ROM diskette, in the */Doc/Faq* directory. You can also find these FAQs online at *http://metalab.unc.edu/linux/intro.html*. The main Linux FAQ is known simply as the Linux FAQ. You can find it on-line at *http://metalab.unc.edu/linux/FAQ/Linux-FAQ.html*.

The FAQs on the CD-ROM diskette are available in several formats. If your system has an installed web browser, you'll probably find the HTML-formatted files convenient; they're located in the *HTML/* subdirectory. Alternatively, you can use Microsoft Windows WordPad, or another text editor of your choice, to access the plain test documents located in the *TXT/* subdirectory.

HOWTOs

Linux HOWTOs address specific topics of interest to Linux users. They're found on the CD-ROM diskette in the */Doc/Howto* directory. You can also find them online at *http://metalab.unc.edu/linux/intro.html*. At this point in your Linux experience, you'll probably find the Installation-HOWTO useful. Use it to find workarounds for your installation and configuration problems.

The HOWTOs are generally available in plain text format. You can use Microsoft Windows WordPad, or another text editor of your choice, to access them.

The Red Hat Mailing List

Several Internet mailing lists address Red Hat Linux. You can find a list of these at *http://archive.redhat.com/*. Perhaps the most pertinent is the RedHat-Install-List, archived at *http://archive.redhat.com/redhat-install-list/*. You can access the archives to read recently posted messages. Read the periodic posting to learn how to subscribe to the mailing list. By subscribing to the mailing list, you can post queries to which other subscribers may respond. You can also read the queries of other subscribers and respond to them.

Usenet Newsgroups

Several Internet newsgroups also address Red Hat Linux. You can find a list of these at *http://metalab.unc.edu/linux/intro.html*. If your Internet Service Provider (ISP) provides access to these newsgroups—as most do—you can read and post messages read by other Linux users around the world. If necessary, consult your ISP for information on accessing these newsgroups.

Don't post blindly to these newsgroups or you may draw angry responses; instead, you should first attempt to find answers to your questions in the Linux FAQs and HOWTOs. Generally, the Linux community is quite willing to help even those who ask what some consider dumb questions; as a courtesy to all, however, it's best if you do some work on your own before seeking the help of others.

CHAPTER FOUR

ISSUING LINUX COMMANDS

This chapter shows you how to begin using your Linux system. It shows you how to boot your system, log in, issue commands, log out, and shut down your system. It also explains how to use the *man* command, which provides help on using other commands. The chapter describes how Linux organizes data as filesystems, directories, and files and how you can work with removable media, such as diskettes. It describes how to query the status of your system. And, finally, it explains how to use *pico*, a simple text editor.

The System Use Cycle

This section introduces you to the cycle of Linux system use. If you're a user of Microsoft Windows, you're accustomed to a pattern of system use that forms a cycle:

- Boot the system

- Identify yourself to the system

- Use the system

- Shutdown the system

The cycle of Linux system use is similar, even though you perform the tasks somewhat differently.

Booting the System

Most Linux users boot their system from its hard drive. Of course, if you made a boot diskette during system installation, you can use it to boot your system.

First, you must prepare your system for booting. If your system is running, you must shut it down by following the proper procedure for shutting down the operating system that's active. For example, if you're running Microsoft Windows, click Start → Shut Down and select the Shut Down option in the Shut Down dialog box. Press OK to begin the system shutdown. After a few seconds, Windows displays a screen telling you that it's safe to turn off power to your system. Turn off the power or, if your system automatically powers down, wait a few seconds until the system powers itself down.

Next, you must set your system to boot from the desired device. To boot your system from its hard drive, remove any floppy diskette from your system's floppy drive. To boot your system from a floppy diskette, insert your Linux boot diskette into your system's floppy drive.

Now, you're ready to boot your system. Switch your system on (or press your system's reset button, if your system is powered on) and watch as it performs its self test. Shortly thereafter, you should see a `boot:` prompt on the system's monitor. If you like, you can list the available boot configurations stored on the boot device by pressing **Tab**. To boot the system, type the name of the desired configuration and press **Enter**, or simply press **Enter** to boot using the default configuration.

Once it loads, Linux begins probing your system and its devices, printing status information on your system's monitor. This status information is helpful if your system fails to boot properly, because it discloses the point in the boot process where the problem occurred.

When Linux has completed its boot process, your system's monitor will display a login prompt similar to this:

```
Red Hat Linux release 6.0 (Hedwig)
Kernel 2.2.5 on an i586
login:
```

Logging In

Before you can use the system, you must identify yourself by logging in. The install program created a special user named `root`; by identifying yourself as the `root` user, you can gain access to the system. Normally, you use the `root` userid only when performing system administration tasks, because the `root` user has special capabilities that other users lack. However, because `root` is currently the only userid that has access to your system, you must log in as `root`. Later, you'll add one or more userids.

To log on, type `root` and press **Enter**. The system prompts you for the password associated with the `root` userid. Type the password you established during the installation process and press **Enter**. To prevent anyone nearby from learning your password, Linux does not display it as you type. If you suspect you've typed it incorrectly, simply press **Enter** and start over; or press **Backspace** once (or more) for each character you've entered and then re-enter it. If you type the userid or password incorrectly, Linux displays the message "login incorrect" and prompts you to try again.

TIP   Like other members of the Unix family, the Linux operating system is case sensitive. Be sure to type the userid `root` just as it appears, using all lowercase characters. Similarly, you must type the password in exactly the same way you entered it in the Root Password dialog box during system installation.

When you've successfully logged in, you'll see a command prompt that looks something like this:

```
[root@desktop /root]#
```

This prompt tells you that the Linux **bash** shell is ready to accept your commands.

Issuing Commands

The component of Linux that interprets and executes commands is called the *shell.* Linux supports a variety of different shells, but the most popular is the **bash** shell. This chapter presents the basics of using the **bash** shell; you'll learn more about the shell in Chapter 13, *Conquering the BASH Shell.*

The Linux **bash** shell presents the user with a command-line interface (CLI). CLIs are familiar to Windows users who have worked in the MS-DOS window, and indeed the Microsoft Windows MS-DOS Prompt window is a kind of command-line shell for Windows. The Linux **bash** shell works much like the MS-DOS Prompt window. You type text commands and the system responds by displaying text replies. As your first Linux command, type *w* and press **Enter**. Your screen should look something like this:

```
[root@desktop /root]# w
11:12am  up 6 min,  1 user,  load average: 0.00, 0.08, 0.05
USER     TTY     FROM            LOGIN@   IDLE   JCPU   PCPU  WHAT
root     tty1                    11:13am  0.00s  0.20s  0.11s -bash
```

The *w* command tells Linux to display the system status and a list of all system users. In the example, the output of the command tells you that it's now 11:12 a.m., that the system has been up for 6 minutes, and that only one user—**root**— is currently logged in. Notice that the command output is very terse, packing much information into a few lines. Such output is typical of Linux commands. At first, you may find Linux output cryptic and difficult to read, but over time you'll grow to appreciate the efficiency with which Linux communicates information.

Linux provides many commands besides the *w* command; so many that you may despair of learning and recalling them. Actually, the number of commands you'll use regularly is fairly small. Soon, these will become second nature to you.

Now try a second command, the *date* command:

```
[root@desktop /root]# date
Tue Feb 23 11:15:20 PST 1999
```

The *date* command displays the current date and time.

TIP   If you find working with MS-DOS distasteful or intimidating, you may not immediately enjoy working with the Linux command line. However, give yourself some time to adjust. The Linux command line has several features that make it easier to use, and more powerful, than MS-DOS. If, after working with the Linux command line for several days, you don't find yourself at home, don't despair. Linux provides a graphical user interface in addition to its command-line interface. You'll learn about the graphical user interface in Chapter 6, *Using the X Window System.*

Correcting Commands

Sometimes you may type a command incorrectly, causing Linux to display an error message. For example, suppose you typed dat instead of *date*:

```
[root@desktop /root]# dat
bash: dat: command not found
```

In such a case, carefully check the spelling of the command and try again. If you notice an error before pressing **Enter**, you can use the **Backspace** key to return to the point of the error and then type the correct characters.

Just as a web browser keeps track of recently visited sites, Linux's BASH shell keeps track of recently issued commands. This list is called the history list, and you can scroll back through it using the Up arrow key, or back down using the Down arrow key, just as you would with the Back and Forward buttons on a web browser. In fact, the history list provides several powerful ways to remember and reuse frequently issued commands, as we'll see in Chapter 13.

The Up and Down arrow keys let you scroll through a list of commands recently issued. This feature is handy when you want to repeat a command. Simply use the Up arrow key to find the command and press **Enter** to re-execute it. You can also use this feature when you want to issue a command similar to one you recently issued. Use the Up arrow key to find the original command. Then, use the Left and Right arrow keys to position the cursor and make whatever changes to the command you like. Finally, press **Enter** to execute the command.

Using Virtual Consoles

In Microsoft Windows, you can have several MS-DOS Prompt windows simultaneously active. Although the bash shell doesn't have a graphical user interface, you can nevertheless work with several instances of the shell, by using Linux virtual consoles. Linux provides six virtual consoles; you can use special keystrokes to switch between them. The keystroke **Alt-F**n, where n is the number of a virtual console (1–6), causes Linux to display virtual console n. For example, you can display virtual console 2 by typing **Alt-F2**. You can view only a single console at a time, but you can switch rapidly between consoles by using the appropriate keystroke.

Virtual consoles are handy when you've started a time-consuming task and want to be able to perform an unrelated task while the original task is working. You'll also find them useful after you've established several userids on your system, because you can log on as one userid on one virtual console while you're logged on as another userid on a different console.

Virtual consoles have a screen saver feature like that found on Microsoft Windows. If a virtual console is inactive for an extended period, Linux blanks the monitor screen. To restore the screen without disturbing its contents, simply press the **Shift** key.

Logging Out

When you're done using a virtual console, you should log out by typing the command *exit* and pressing **Enter**. When you log out, the system frees memory and other resources that were allocated when you logged in, making those resources available to other users.

When the system logs you out, it immediately displays a login prompt. If you change your mind and want to access the system, you can login simply by supplying your userid and password.

Shutting Down the System

You shouldn't turn off power to a computer while it's running Linux; instead, you should shut down the operating system and then turn off power. To shut down a Linux system, you use the *shutdown* command, which resides in a directory named */sbin*:

```
[root@desktop /root]# /sbin/shutdown -h now
```

Don't type the prompt, which automatically appears on the command line. Only the `root` user can issue the *shutdown* command. If you want to restart a Linux system, you can use an alternative form of the *shutdown* command:

```
[root@desktop /root]# /sbin/shutdown -r now
```

Or, even more conveniently, you can use the familiar MS-DOS "three-finger salute": **Ctrl-Alt-Del**, which simply issues a *shutdown* command on your behalf.

When you shut down a system, Linux automatically logs off all users, terminates all running programs, and closes all open files. Before shutting down a system, you should check each virtual console to determine if an important operation is in progress. If so, you should delay shutting the system down until the operation completes.

Working with the Linux Command Prompt

To make Linux commands easy to use, they share a simple, common structure. This section describes their common structure and explains how you can obtain helpful information on the commands available to you.

Command Structure

Linux commands share the common form:

```
command option(s) argument(s)
```

The `command` identifies the command you want Linux to execute. The name of a Linux command almost always consists of lowercase letters and digits. Remember that, unlike Microsoft Windows, Linux is case sensitive; be sure to type each character of a command in the proper case.

Most commands let you specify options or arguments. However, in any given case, you may not need to do so. For example, typing the *w* command without options and arguments causes Linux to display a list of current users.

Options modify the way that a command works. Most options consist of a single letter, prefixed by a dash. Often, you can specify more than one option; when you do so, you separate each option with a space or tab. For example, the *–h* option of the *w* command causes the output of the command to omit the header lines that give the time and the names of the fields. Typing:

```
[root@desktop /root]# w -h
```

prints a list of users without the header lines.

Arguments specify filenames or other targets that direct the action of the command. For example, the *w* command lets you specify a userid as an argument, which causes the command to list only logins that pertain to the specified userid. Typing:

```
[root@desktop /root]# w root
```

prints a list of current logins by the `root` user. Some commands let you specify a series of arguments; you must separate each argument with a space or tab.

Getting Help

Because Linux provides so many commands and because Linux commands provide so many possible options, you can't expect to recall all of them. To help you, Linux provides the *man* command and the *apropos* command, which let you access a help database that describes each command and its options.

Using man

Each Linux command is described by a special file called a *manual page*. The manual pages are stored in a group of subdirectories comprising a help database. To access this database, you use the *man* command, which resembles the MS-DOS *help* command. For example, to get help on using the *w* command, type:

```
[root@desktop /root]# man w
```

Figure 4-1 shows the resulting output, which the command displays one page at a time. Notice the colon prompt, which appears at the bottom left of the screen. To page forward, press the **Space** key; to page backward, press the **b** key. To exit the *man* program, press the **q** key.

The manual pages are organized according to a common format. At the beginning of a manual page, you'll find the name of the page and the section of the manual page database from which the page comes, shown in parentheses. For example, the figure shows the manual page named *w*, which comes from section 1 of the manual page database. Table 4-1 describes the sections of the manual page database; most sections are primarily of interest to programmers. As a user and administrator, you'll be interested primarily in sections 1 and 8.

Table 4-1. Manual Page Sections

Section	Description
1	Executable programs and shell commands
2	System calls (provided by the kernel)
3	Library calls (provided by system libraries)
4	Special files (for example, device files)

Table 4-1. Manual Page Sections (continued)

Section	Description
5	File formats and conventions
6	Games
7	Macro packages and conventions
8	System administration commands
9	Non-standard kernel routines

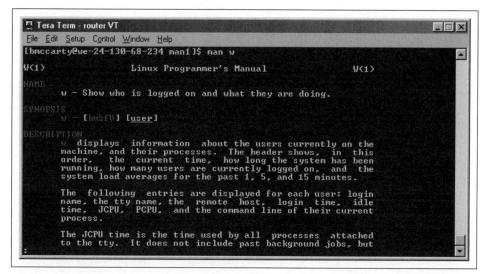

Figure 4-1. A typical man page

Next in the output comes the name and brief description of the command. Then comes a synopsis of the command, which shows the options and arguments that you can specify. Brackets enclose parts of a command that you can choose to include or omit. Next comes a detailed description of the operation of the command, followed by a description of its options.

As you're learning your way around Linux, you may find it convenient to reserve a virtual console for running the *man* command. That way, you can enter commands in a separate virtual console, switching between consoles to refresh your recollection of the options and arguments of commands as you type them.

Using apropos

The *man* command searches the manual pages and displays detailed information about a specified command. The *apropos* command also searches the manual pages; however, it displays summary information about manual pages that contain a specified keyword. (The search is limited to the short description that appears at the beginning of each manual page). For example, typing the command:

```
[root@desktop /root]# apropos files
```

displays a list of manual pages that contain the word *files*, as shown in Figure 4-2.

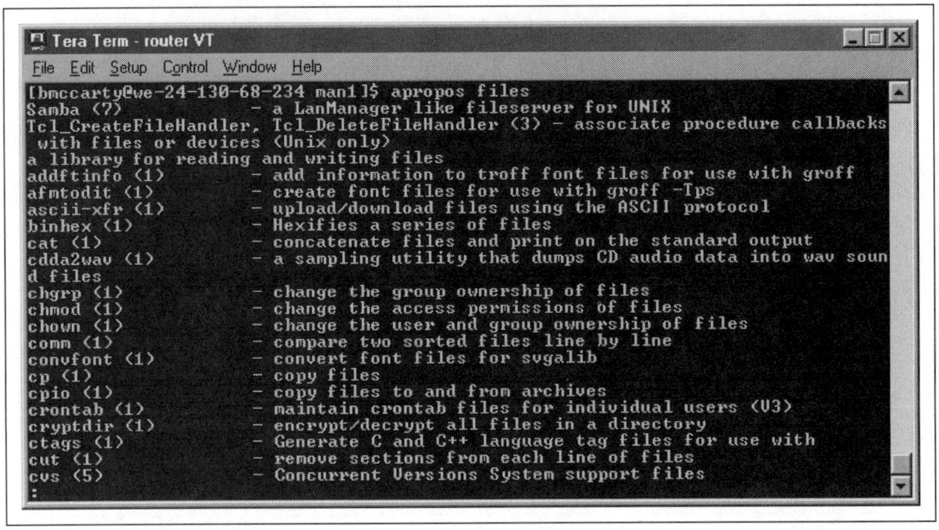

Figure 4-2. Output of the apropos command

The *apropos* command is useful when you don't recall the name of a Linux command. By typing a related keyword, you can obtain a list of commands and search the list for the command you need.

How Linux Organizes Data

In order to make the most effective use of your Linux system, you must understand how Linux organizes data. If you're familiar with Microsoft Windows or another operating system, you'll find it easy to learn how Linux organizes data, because most operating systems organize data in rather similar ways. This section explains how Linux organizes data. It also introduces you to several important Linux commands that work with directories and files.

Devices

Linux receives data from, sends data to, and stores data on *devices*. A device usually corresponds to a hardware unit, such as a keyboard or serial port. However, a device may have no hardware counterpart: the kernel creates several *pseudo-devices* that you can access as devices but that have no physical existence. Moreover, a single hardware unit may correspond to several devices—for example, Linux defines each partition of a disk drive as a distinct device. Table 4-2 describes some typical Linux devices; not every system provides all these devices and some systems provide devices not shown in the table.

Table 4-2. Typical Linux Devices

Device	Description
atibm	Bus mouse
audio	Sound card
cdrom	CD-ROM drive
console	Current virtual console
fd$n$	Floppy drive (n designates the drive; for example, fd0 is the first floppy drive)
ftape	Streaming tape drive not supporting rewind
hdxn	Non-SCSI hard drive (x designates the drive and n designates the partition; for example, hda1 is the first partition of the first non-SCSI hard drive)
inportbm	Bus mouse
lp$n$	Parallel port (n designates the device number; for example, lp0 is the first parallel port)
modem	Modem
mouse	Mouse
nftape	Streaming tape drive supporting rewind
nrft$n$	Streaming tape drive supporting rewind (n designates the device number; for example, nrft0 is the first streaming tape drive)
nst$n$	Streaming SCSI tape drive not supporting rewind (n designates the device number; for example, nst0 is the first streaming SCSI tape drive)
null	Pseudodevice that accepts unlimited output
printer	Printer
psaux	Auxiliary pointing device, such as a trackball, or the knob on IBM's Thinkpad
rft$n$	Streaming tape drive not supporting rewind (n designates the device number; for example, rft0 is the first streaming tape drive)
scd$n$	SCSI device (n designates the device number; for example, scd0 is the first SCSI device)

Table 4-2. Typical Linux Devices (continued)

Device	Description
sdxn	SCSI hard drive (x designates the drive and n designates the partition; for example, sda1 is the first partition of the firs SCSI hard drive)
srn	SCSI CD-ROM (n designates the drive; for example, sr0 is the first SCSI CD-ROM)
stn	Streaming SCSI tape drive supporting rewind (n designates the device number; for example, st0 is the first streaming SCSI tape drive)
ttyn	Virtual console (n designates the particular virtual console; for example, tty0 is the first virtual console)
ttySn	Modem (n designates the port; for example, ttyS0 is an incoming modem connection on the first serial port)
zero	Pseudodevice that supplies an inexhaustible stream of zero-bytes

Filesystems

Whether you're using Microsoft Windows or Linux, you must format a partition before you can store data on it. When you format a partition, Linux writes special data, called a *filesystem*, on the partition. The filesystem organizes the available space and provides a directory that lets you assign a name to each *file*, which is a set of stored data. You can also group files into *directories*, which function much like the folders you create using the Microsoft Windows Explorer: directories store information about the files they contain.

Every CD-ROM and floppy diskette must also have a filesystem. The filesystem of a CD-ROM is written when the disk is created; the filesystem of a floppy diskette is rewritten each time you format it.

Microsoft Windows 95 lets you choose to format a partition as a FAT or FAT32. Linux supports a wider variety of filesystem types; Table 4-3 summarizes the most common ones. The most important filesystem types are ext2; which is used for Linux native partitions, msdos, which is used for FAT partitions (and floppy diskettes) of the sort created by MS-DOS and Microsoft Windows; and iso9660, which is used for CD-ROMs. Linux also provides the vfat filesystem, which is used for FAT32 partitions of the sort created by Microsoft Windows 9x. Linux also supports reading of Windows NT NTFS filesystems; however, the support for writing such partitions is not yet stable.

Table 4-3. Common Filesystem Types

Filesystem	Description
coherent	A filesystem compatible with that used by Coherent Unix
ext	The predecessor of the `ext2` filesystem; supported for compatibility
ext2	The standard Linux filesystem
hpfs	A filesystem compatible with that used by IBM's OS/2
iso9660	The standard filesystem used on CD-ROMs
minix	An old Linux filesystem, still occasionally used on floppy diskettes
msdos	A filesystem compatible with Microsoft's FAT filesystem, used by MS-DOS and Windows
nfs	A filesystem compatible with Sun's Network File System
ntfs	A filesystem compatible with that used by Microsoft Windows NT's NTFS filesystem
sysv	A filesystem compatible with that used by AT&T's System V Unix
vfat	A filesystem compatible with Microsoft's FAT32 filesystem, used by Windows 9x
xenix	A filesystem compatible with that used by Xenix

Directories

If you've used MS-DOS, you're familiar with the concepts of file and directory, and with various MS-DOS commands that work with files and directories. Under Linux, files and directories work much as they do under MS-DOS.

Home and working directories

When you login to Linux, you're placed in a special directory known as your *home directory*. Generally, each user has a distinct home directory, where the user creates personal files. This makes it simple for the user to find files previously created, because they're kept separate from the files of other users.

The *working directory*—or *current working directory*, as it's sometimes called—is the directory you're currently working in. When you login to Linux, your home directory is your working directory. By using the *cd* command (which you'll meet in a moment) you can change your working directory.

The directory tree

The directories of a Linux system are organized as a hierarchy. Unlike MS-DOS, which provides a separate hierarchy for each partition, Linux provides a single hierarchy that includes every partition. The topmost directory of the directory tree is the *root directory*, which is written using a forward slash (/), not the backward slash (\) used by MS-DOS to designate a root directory.

Figure 4-3 shows a hypothetical Linux directory tree. The root directory contains six subdirectories: *bin, dev, etc, home, tmp,* and *usr.* The *home* directory has two subdirectories; each is the home directory of a user and has the same name as the user who owns it. The user named *bill* has created two subdirectories in his home directory: *books* and *school.* The user named *patrick* has created a single subdirectory in his home directory: *school.*

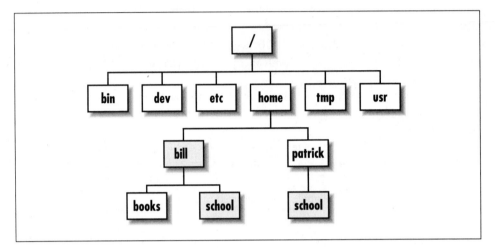

Figure 4-3. A hypothetical Linux directory tree

Each directory (other than the root directory) is contained in a directory known as its parent directory. For example, the parent directory of the *bill* directory is *home.*

Absolute and relative pathnames

Notice in the figure that two directories named *school* exist: One is a subdirectory of *bill* and the other is a subdirectory of *patrick.* To avoid confusion that could result when several directories have the same name, directories are specified using *pathnames.* Two kinds of pathnames exist: *absolute* and *relative.* The absolute pathname of a directory traces the location of the directory beginning at the root directory; you form the pathname as a list of directories, separated by forward slashes (/). For example, the absolute pathname of the unique directory named *bill* is */home/bill.* The absolute pathname of the *school* subdirectory of the *bill* directory is */home/bill/school.* The absolute pathname of the identically named *school* subdirectory of the *patrick* directory is */home/patrick/school.*

When a subdirectory is many levels below the root directory, its absolute pathname may be long and cumbersome. In such a case, it may be more convenient to use a relative path name, which uses the current directory, rather than the root directory, as its starting point. For example, suppose that the *bill* directory is the current working directory; you can refer to its *books* subdirectory by the relative pathname *books*. Notice that a relative pathname can never begin with a forward slash, whereas an absolute pathname must begin with a forward slash. As a second example, suppose that the *home* directory is the current working directory. The relative pathname of the *school* subdirectory of the *bill* directory would be *bill/school*; the relative pathname of the identically named subdirectory of the *patrick* directory would be *patrick/school*.

Linux provides two special directory names. Using a single dot (.) as a directory name is equivalent to specifying the working directory. Using two dots (..) within a pathname takes you up one level in the current path, to the parent directory. For example, if the working directory is */home/bill*, .. refers to the */home* directory. Similarly, the path *../patrick/school* refers to the directory */home/patrick/school*.

Commands That Work with Directories

Now that you understand the fundamentals of how Linux organizes data, you're ready to learn some commands that work with directories. Rather than simply read this section, you should login to your Linux system and try the commands for yourself. Only by doing so will you begin to develop skill in working with shell commands.

Displaying the working directory

To display the current working directory, issue the *pwd* command. The *pwd* command requires no options or arguments.

```
[root@desktop /root]# pwd
/root
```

The *pwd* command displays the absolute pathname of the working directory.

Changing the working directory

To change the working directory, issue the *cd* command, specifying the pathname of the new working directory as an argument. You can use an absolute or relative pathname. For example, to change the working directory to the */bin* directory, type:

```
[root@desktop /root]# cd /bin
[root@desktop /bin]#
```

Notice how the prompt changes to indicate that */bin* is now the working directory.

You can quickly return to your home directory by issuing the *cd* command without an argument:

```
[root@desktop /bin]# cd
[root@desktop /root]#
```

Again, notice how the prompt changes to indicate the new working directory.

If you attempt to change the working directory to a directory that doesn't exist, Linux displays an error message:

```
[root@desktop /root]# cd nowhere
bash: nowhere: No such file or directory
```

Displaying directory contents

To display the contents of a directory, you use the *ls* command. The *ls* command provides many useful options that let you tailor its operation and output to your liking.

The simplest form of the *ls* command takes no options or arguments. It simply lists the contents of the working directory, including files and subdirectories (your own output will differ, reflecting the files present in your working directory):

```
[root@desktop /root]# ls
GNUstep                 firewall              sniff
Xrootenv.0              linux                 ssh-1.2.26
audio.cddb              mail                  ssh-1.2.26.tar.gz
audio.wav               mirror                support
axhome                  mirror-2.8.tar.gz     temp
conf                    nlxb3181.tar          test
corel                   openn                 test.doc
drivec.img              scan                  tulip.c
dynip_2.00.tar.gz       screen-3.7.6-0.i386.rpm  win95
[root@desktop /root]#
```

Here, the output is presented in lexical (dictionary) order, as three columns of data. Notice that filenames beginning with uppercase letters appear before those beginning with lowercase letters.

A more sophisticated form of the *ls* command that includes the *−l* option displays descriptive information along with the filenames, as shown in Figure 4-4.

The first line of the output shows the amount of disk space used by the working directory and its subdirectories, measured in 1K blocks. Each remaining line describes a single file or directory. The columns are:

Type
> The type of file: a directory (d), or an ordinary file (−). If your system supports color, Linux displays output lines that pertain to directories in blue and lines that pertain to files in white.

```
[root@desktop /root] # ls — l
total 558414
d rwxr-xr-x    5  root    root         1024 Dec 23 13:48 GNUstep
- rw-r--r--    1  root    root          331 Feb 11 10:19 Xrootenv.0
- rw-rw-r--    1  root    root          490 Jan  6 15:07 audio.cddb
- rw-r--r--    1  root    root     45254876 Jan  6 15:08 audio.wav
d rwxr-xr-x    2  root    root         1024 Feb 20 16:41 axhome
- rw-r--r--    1  root    root          900 Jan 18 20:15 conf
d rwxr-xr-x    2  root    root         1024 Dec 25 10:03 corel
- rw-r--r--    1  root    root          915 Jan 18 20:57 firewall
d rwxrwxr-x    2  root    root         1024 Jan  6 15:42 linux
d rwx------    2  root    root         1024 Jan  4 02:19 mail
d rwxr-xr-x    3  root    root         1024 Jan  4 01:49 mirror
- rwxr--r--    1  root    root           29 Dec 27 15:07 openn
d rwxr-xr-x    3  root    root         1024 Dec 26 13:24 scan
d rwxrwxr-x    3  root    root         1024 Jan  4 02:34 sniff
```

type	access modes	# of links	owner	group	size (bytes)	modification date and time	name

Figure 4-4. Output of the ls command

Access modes
> The access mode, which determines what users can access the file or directory.

Links
> The number of files or directories linked to this one.

Group
> The group that owns the file or directory.

Size
> The size of the file or directory, in bytes.

Modification date
> The date and time when the file or directory was last modified.

Name
> The name of the file or directory.

You'll learn more about access modes, links, and groups in subsequent sections of this chapter.

If a directory contains many files, the listing will fill more than one screen. To view the output one screen at a time, use the command:

```
ls -1 | more
```

This command employs the pipe redirector (|, explained in Chapter 13), sending output of the *ls* subcommand to the *more* subcommand, which presents the output one screen at a time. You can control the operation of the *more* command by using the following keys:

- **Space** moves you one page forward

- *b* moves you one page back

- *q* exits the program and returns you to the command prompt

If you want to list a directory other than the working directory, you can type the name of the directory as an argument of the *ls* command. Linux displays the contents of the directory, but does not change the working directory. Similarly, you can display information about a file by typing its name as an argument of the *ls* command. Moreover, the *ls* command accepts indefinitely many arguments, so you can type a series of directories and filenames as arguments, separating each with one or more spaces or tabs.

When the name of a directory or file begins with a dot (.), the output of the *ls* command does not normally include the directory or file, which is said to be *hidden*. To cause the output of the *ls* command to include hidden directories and files, use the *−a* option. For example, to list all the files and subdirectories in the current directory—including hidden ones—type:

```
[root@desktop /root]# ls -a -l
```

If you prefer, you can combine the *−a* and *−l* options, typing the command like this:

```
[root@desktop /root]# ls -al
```

A user's home directory generally includes several hidden files containing configuration information for various programs. For example, the *.profile* file contains configuration information for the Linux shell.

The *ls* command provides a host of additional useful options; see its manual page for details.

Creating a directory

You can create directories by using the *mkdir* command. Just type the name of the new directory as an argument of the command. Linux creates the directory as a subdirectory of the working directory. For example, this command creates a subdirectory named *office*:

```
[root@desktop /root]# mkdir office
```

If you don't want to create the new directory as a subdirectory of the working directory, type an absolute or relative pathname as the argument. For example, to create a directory named */root/documents*, type:

```
[root@desktop /root]# mkdir /root/documents
```

The name of a directory or file must follow certain rules. For example, it must not contain a slash (/) character. Directory and file names usually include letters (either uppercase or lowercase), digits, dots, and underscores (_). You can use other characters, such as spaces, but such names present problems, because the shell gives them special meaning. If you simply must use a name containing special characters, enclose the name within single quotes ('). The quotes don't become part of the name that is stored on the disk. This technique is useful when accessing files on a Microsoft Windows filesystem; otherwise you'll have trouble working with files in directories such as *My Documents*, which have names containing spaces.

Most MS-DOS filenames contain a dot, but most Linux filenames do not. In MS-DOS, the dot separates the main part of the filename from a part known as the extension, which denotes the type of the file. For example, the MS-DOS file *memo.txt* would contain text. Most Linux programs determine the type of a file automatically, so Linux filenames don't require an extension.

Removing a directory

To remove a directory, use the *rmdir* command. For example, to remove *unwanted*, a subdirectory of the working directory, type:

```
[root@desktop /root]# rmdir unwanted
```

If the directory you want to delete is not a subdirectory of the working directory, remove it by typing an absolute or relative pathname.

You cannot remove a directory that contains files or subdirectories; you must first delete the files in the directory and then remove the directory itself.

Working with Files

Directories contain files and other directories. You use files to store data. This section introduces you to several useful commands for working with files.

Displaying the contents of a file

Linux files, like Microsoft Windows files, can contain text or binary information. The contents of a binary file are meaningful only to skilled programmers, but you can easily view the contents of a text file. Simply type the *cat* command, specifying the name of the text file as an argument. For example:

```
[root@desktop /root]# cat /etc/passwd
```

displays the contents of the */etc/passwd* file, which lists the valid system logons.

If a file is too large to be displayed on a single screen, the first part of the file will whiz past you and you'll see only the last few lines of the file. To avoid this, you can use the *more* command:

```
[root@desktop /root]# more /etc/passwd
```

This command displays the contents of a file in the same way the *man* command displays a manual page. You can use **Space** and the **b** key to page forward and backward through the file and the **q** key to exit the command.

Removing a file

To remove a file, type the *rm* command, specifying the name of the file as an argument. For example:

```
[root@desktop /root]# rm badfile
```

removes the file named *badfile* contained in the working directory. If a file is located elsewhere, you can remove it by specifying an absolute or relative pathname.

WARNING   Once you remove a Linux file, its contents are lost forever. Be careful to avoid removing a file that contains needed information.

The *−i* option causes the *rm* command to prompt you to verify your decision to remove a file. If you don't trust your typing skills, you may find this option helpful. Linux automatically supplies the *−i* option even if you don't type it.

Copying a file

To copy a file, use the *cp* command, specifying the name (or path) of the file you want to copy and the name (or path) to which you want to copy it. For example:

```
[root@desktop /root]# cp /etc/passwd sample
```

copies the */etc/passwd* file to a file named *sample* in the working directory.

If the destination file already exists, Linux overwrites it. You must therefoı careful to avoid overwriting a file that contains needed data. Before copying ¿ use the *ls* command to ensure that no file will be overwritten; alternatively, use the −*i* option of the *cp* command, which prompts you to verify the overwriting of an existing file. Linux automatically supplies the −*i* option even if you don't type it.

Renaming or moving a file

To rename a file, use the *mv* command, specifying the name (or path) of the file and the new name (or path). For example:

```
[root@desktop /root]# mv old new
```

renames the file named *old* as *new*. If the destination file already exists, Linux overwrites it, so you must be careful. Before moving a file, use the *ls* command to ensure that no file will be overwritten; or, use the −*i* option of the *mv* command, which prompts you to verify the overwriting of an existing file. Linux automatically supplies the −*i* option even if you don't type it.

The *mv* command can rename a directory, but cannot move a directory from one device to another. To move a directory to a new device, first copy the directory and its contents and then remove the original.

Finding a file

If you know the name of a file, but do not know what directory contains it, you can use the *find* command to locate the file. For example:

```
[root@desktop /root]# find . -name 'missing' -print
```

attempts to find a file named *missing*, located in (or beneath) the current working directory (.). If the command finds the file, it displays its absolute pathname.

If you know only part of the file name, you can surround the part you know with asterisks (*):

```
[root@desktop /root]# find / -name '*iss*' -print
```

This command will find any file whose name includes the characters *iss*, searching every subdirectory of the root directory (that is, the entire system).

Printing a file

If your system includes a printer, you can print a file by using the *lpr* command. For example:

```
[root@desktop /root]# lpr /etc/passwd
```

sends the file */etc/passwd* to the printer.

If a file is lengthy, it may require some time to print. You can send other files to the printer while a file is printing. The *lpq* command lets you see what files are queued to be printed:

```
[root@desktop /root]# lpq
lp is ready and printing
Rank    Owner     Job  Files                              Total Size
active root        155  /etc/passwd                        1030 bytes
```

Each waiting or active file has an assigned print job number. You can use the *lprm* to cancel printing of a file, by specifying the print job number. For example:

```
[root@desktop /root]# lprm 155
```

cancels printing of job number 155. However, only the user who requested that a file be printed (or the root user) can cancel printing of the file.

Working with compressed files

To save disk space and expedite downloads, you can compress a data file. By convention, compressed files are named ending in *.gz*; however, Linux doesn't require or enforce this convention.

To expand a compressed file, use the *gunzip* command. For example, suppose the file *bigfile.gz* has been compressed. Typing the command:

```
[root@desktop /root]# gunzip bigfile.gz
```

extracts the file *bigfile* and removes the file *bigfile.gz*.

To compress a file, use the *gzip* command. For example, to compress the file *bigfile*, type the command:

```
[root@desktop /root]# gzip bigfile
```

The command creates the file *bigfile.gz* and removes the file *bigfile*.

Sometimes it's convenient to store several files (or the contents of several subdirectories) in a single file. This is useful, for example, in creating a backup or archive copy of files. The Linux *tar* command creates a single file that contains data from several files. Unlike the *gzip* command, the *tar* command doesn't disturb the original files. To create a *tar file*, as a file created by the *tar* command is called, a command like this:

```
tar -cvf tarfile files-or-directories
```

Substitute `tarfile` with the name of the tar file you want to create and `files-or-directories` with a list of files and directories, separating the list elements by one or more spaces or tabs. You can use absolute or relative pathnames to specify the files or directories. By convention, the name of a tar file ends with *.tar*, but Linux does not require or enforce this convention.

For example, to create a tar file named *backup.tar* that contains all the files in all subdirectories of the directory */home/bill*, type:

```
tar -cvf backup.tar /home/bill
```

The command creates the file *backup.tar* in the current working directory.

You can list the contents of a tar file by using a command that follows this pattern:

```
tar -tvf tarfile | more
```

The | more causes the output to be sent to the *more* command, so that you can page through multiple pages. If the tar file holds only a few files, you can omit the | more.

To extract the contents of a tar file, use a command that follows this pattern:

```
tar -xvf tarfile
```

This command expands the files and directories contained within the tar file as files and subdirectories of the working directory. If a file or subdirectory already exists, it is silently overwritten.

The *tar* command provides a host of useful options; see its manual page for details.

It's common to compress a tar file. You can easily accomplish this by specifying the options *–czvf* instead of *–cvf*. Compressed tar files are conventionally named ending with *.tgz*. To expand a compressed tar file, specify the options *–xzvf* instead of *–xvf*.

The *tar* command doesn't use the common ZIP method of compression common in the Microsoft Windows world. However, Linux can easily work with, or even create, ZIP files. To create a ZIP file that holds compressed files or directories, issue a command like this one:

```
zip -r zipfile files_to_zip
```

where `zipfile` names the ZIP file that will be created and `files_to_zip` specifies the files and directories to be included in the ZIP file.

To expand an existing ZIP file, issue a command like this one:

```
unzip zipfile
```

Working with links

Microsoft Windows 9x supports shortcuts, which let you refer to a file or directory (folder) by several names. Shortcuts also let you include a file in several directories or a subdirectory within multiple parent directories. In Linux, you accomplish these results by using the *ln* command, which links multiple names to a single file or directory. These names are called *symbolic links*, *soft links*, or simply *links*.

To link a new name to an existing file or directory, type a command that follows this pattern:

```
ln -s old new
```

For example, suppose that the current working directory contains the file *william*. To be able to refer to this same file by the alternative name *bill*, type the command:

```
[root@desktop /root]# ln -s william bill
```

The *ls* command shows the result:

```
[root@desktop /root]# ls -l
lrwxrwxrwx   1 root      root            7 Feb 27 13:58 bill->william
-rw-r--r--   1 root      root         1030 Feb 27 13:26 william
```

The new file (*bill*) has type 1, which indicates it's a link, rather than a file or directory. Moreover, the *ls* command helpfully shows the name of the file to which the link refers (*william*).

If you omit the *–s* option, Linux creates what's called a *hard link*. A hard link must be stored on the same filesystem as the file to which it refers, a restriction that does not apply to symbolic links. The link count displayed by the *ls* command reflects only hard links; symbolic links are ignored.

Working with file permissions

Unlike Windows 98, but like other varieties of Unix and Windows NT, Linux is a multi-user operating system. Therefore, it includes mechanisms that protect data from unauthorized access. The primary protection mechanism restricts access to directories and files, based on the identity of the user who requests access and on *access modes* assigned to each directory and file.

Each directory and file has an associated user, called the *owner*, who created the directory or file. Each user belongs to one or more sets of users known as *groups*. Each directory and file has an associated group, which is assigned when the directory or file is created.

Access permissions determine what operations a user can perform on a directory or file. Table 4-4 lists the possible permissions and explains the meaning of each. Notice that permissions work differently for directories than for files. For example, permission *r* denotes the ability to list the contents of a directory or read the contents of a file. A directory or file can have more than one permission. Only the listed permissions are granted; any other operations are prohibited. For example, a user who had file permission *rw* could read or write the file, but could not execute it.

Table 4-4. Access Permissions

Permission	Meaning for directory	Meaning for file
r	List the directory	Read contents
w	Create or remove files	Write contents
x	Access files and subdirectories	Execute

The access modes of a directory of file consist of three permissions:

owner
> Applies to the owner of the file

group
> Applies to users who are members of the group assigned to the file

other
> Applies to other users

The *ls* command lists the file access modes in the second column of its long output format, as shown in Figure 4-5. The column contains nine characters: the first three specify the access allowed the owner of the directory or file, the second three specify the access allowed users in the same group as the directory or file, and the final three specify the access allowed to other users (see Figure 4-6).

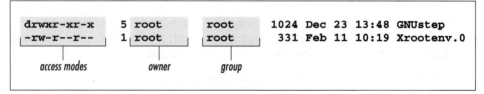

Figure 4-5. Access modes as shown by the ls command

You set the access modes of a directory or file by using the *chmod* command, which has the following pattern:

```
chmod nnn directory-or-file
```

The argument *nnn* is a three-digit number, which gives the access mode for the owner, group, and other users. Table 4-5 shows each possible digit and the equivalent access permission. For example, the argument 751 is equivalent to **rwxr-x--x**, which gives the owner every possible permission, gives the group read and execute permission, and gives other users execute permission.

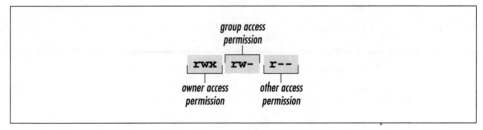

Figure 4-6. Access modes specify three permissions

Table 4-5. Numerical Access Mode Values

Value	Meaning
0	---
1	--x
2	-w-
3	-wx
4	r--
5	r-x
6	rw-
7	rwx

If you're the owner of a file or directory (or if you're the root user), you can change its ownership by using the *chown* command. For example, the following command assigns *newuser* as the owner of the file *hotpotato*:

```
[root@desktop /root]# chown newuser hotpotato
```

The owner of a file or directory (and the root user) can also change the group of a file. For example, the following command assigns *newgroup* as the new group of the file *hotpotato*:

```
[root@desktop /root]# chgrp newgroup hotpotato
```

The group you assign to a file or directory must have been previously established by the root user. The valid groups appear in the file */etc/group*, which only the root user can alter.

The root user can assign each user to one or more groups. When you log on to the system, you are assigned to one of these groups—your *login group*—by default. To change to another of your assigned groups, you can use the *newgrp* command. For example, to change to the group named *secondgroup*, use the following command:

```
[root@desktop /root]# newgrp secondgroup
```

If you attempt to change to a group that does not exist, or to which you have not been assigned, your command will fail. When you create a file or directory, it is automatically assigned your current group as its owning group.

Running programs

In Linux, as in MS-DOS and Microsoft Windows, programs are stored in files. Often, you can launch a program by simply typing its filename. However, this assumes that the file is stored in one of a series of directories known as the *path*. A directory included in this series is said to be *on the path*. If you've worked with MS-DOS, you're familiar with the MS-DOS path, which works much like the Linux path. You'll learn more about working with the Linux path in Chapter 13.

If the file you want to launch is not stored in a directory on the path, you can simply type the absolute pathname of the file. Linux will then launch the program even though it's not on the path. If the file you want to launch is stored in the working directory, type ./ followed by the name of the program file. Again, Linux will launch the program even though it's not on the path.

For example, suppose the program *bigdeal* is stored in the directory */home/bob*, which is the current directory and which happens to be on the path. You could launch the program any of these ways:

```
bigdeal
./bigdeal
/home/bob/bigdeal
```

The first command assumes that the program is on the path. The second assumes that the program resides in the current working directory. The third makes no assumptions about the location of the file.

Working with Devices

This section presents commands that work with devices. You'll learn how to mount and unmount devices and how to format a floppy diskette.

Mounting and Unmounting Drives

You cannot access a hard drive partition, CD-ROM, or floppy diskette until the related device or partition is *mounted*. Mounting a device checks the status of the device and readies it for access. Linux can be configured to automatically mount a device or partition when it boots; but you must manually mount other devices and partitions.

TIP   If a device uses removable media, the media may not be present when the system boots. If the system is configured to automatically mount such a device and the media is not present, an error occurs. Therefore, devices that use removable media are not generally configured for automatic mounting.

Before you can remove media from a device, you must unmount it. The system also unmounts devices when it shuts down. Mounting and unmounting devices is a privileged operation; generally, only the root user can manually mount and unmount devices.

To mount a device or partition, you use the *mount* command, which has the following pattern:

```
mount options device directory
```

The *mount* command provides many options. However, you can generally use the *mount* command without any options; consult the manual page to learn about the available options.

TIP   The reason you can use the *mount* command without options is that the file */etc/fstab* describes your system's devices and the type of filesystem each is likely to contain. If you add a new device to your system, you may need to revise the contents of */etc/fstab* or specify appropriate options when you mount the device.

You must specify the device that you want to mount and a directory, known as the *mount point*. To make it convenient to access various devices, Linux treats a mounted device as a directory; mounting the device associates it with the named directory. For example, a common operation is mounting a CD-ROM. You can accomplish this with the command:

```
[root@desktop /root]# mount /dev/cdrom /mnt/cdrom
```

The file */dev/cdrom* is a link that points to the actual device file associated with your system's CD-ROM drive. The directory */mnt/cdrom* is a directory created by the install program; this directory is conventionally used as the mounting point for CD-ROMs. After the command has completed, you can access files and directories on the CD-ROM just as you would access ordinary files and directories on the path */mnt/cdrom*. For example, to list the top-level files and directories of the CD-ROM simply type:

```
[root@desktop /root]# ls /mnt/cdrom
```

To mount a floppy diskette in your *a:* drive, type:

```
[root@desktop /root]# mount /dev/fd0 /mnt/floppy
```

To unmount a device, specify its mount point as an argument of the *umount* command. For example, to unmount a CD-ROM diskette, type:

```
[root@desktop /root]# umount /mnt/cdrom
```

Only the root user can unmount a device. Moreover, a device can be unmounted only if it's not in use. If, for example, the working directory of a user is a directory of the device, the device cannot be unmounted.

TIP   If you can't unmount a device, check each virtual console to see if one of them has a session that's using the device as its working directory. If so, either exit the session or change to a working directory that isn't associated with the device.

Formatting Floppy Diskettes

Before you can write data on a floppy diskette, you must format it. The Linux command to format a floppy is *fdformat*. Simply follow the command with an argument that specifies the floppy drive and the capacity of the diskette; the available arguments are listed in Table 4-6. For example, to format a 1.44 MB floppy in your system's a: drive, type:

```
[root@desktop /root]# fdformat /dev/fd0H1440
```

Once you've formatted the floppy, you can mount it and then read and write it. Be sure you unmount the floppy diskette before you remove it. Unmounting the floppy diskette ensures that all pending data has been written to it; otherwise, the floppy diskette may be unusable due to corrupt data.

Useful Linux Programs

This section presents several programs you may find helpful in working with your Linux system. You'll learn several commands that report system status and you'll learn how to use *pico*, a simple text editor.

Table 4-6. Floppy Drive Designators

Designation	Meaning
/dev/fd0	3.5-inch diskette in *a:* (1.44 MB)
/dev/fd0d360	5.25-inch diskette in *a:* (360 kB)
/dev/fd0D720	3.5-inch diskette in *a:* (720 kB)
/dev/fd0h1200	5.25-inch diskette in *a:* (1.2 MB)
/dev/fd0H1440	3.5-inch diskette in *a:* (1.44 MB)
/dev/fd0H2880	3.5-inch diskette in *a:* (2.88 MB)
/dev/fd1	3.5-inch diskette in *b:* (1.44 MB)
/dev/fd1d360	5.25-inch diskette in *b:* (360 kB)
/dev/fd1D720	3.5-inch diskette in *b:* (720 kB)
/dev/fd1h1200	5.25-inch diskette in *b:* (1.2 MB)
/dev/fd1H1440	3.5-inch diskette in *b:* (1.44 MB)
/dev/fd1H2880	3.5-inch diskette in *b:* (2.88 MB)

Viewing System Information

Linux provides a number of commands that report system status. The most commonly used commands are shown in Table 4-7. These commands can help you troubleshoot system problems and identify resource bottlenecks. Although each command can be used without options or arguments, each supports options and arguments that let you customize operation and output; consult the appropriate manual page for details.

Table 4-7. Useful System Commands

Command	Function
df	Shows the amount of free disk space (in 1K blocks) on each mounted filesystem.
du	Shows the amount of disk space (in 1K blocks) used by the working directory and its subdirectories.
free	Shows memory usage statistics, including total free memory, memory used, physical memory, swap memory, shared memory, and buffers used by the kernel.
ps	Shows the active processes (instances of running programs) associated with this login session. Use the −*a* option to list all processes.
top	Shows a continually updated display of active processes, and the resources they are using. Type the q key to exit.
uptime	Shows the current time, the amount of time logged in, the number of users logged in, and system load averages.

Table 4-7. Useful System Commands (continued)

Command	Function
users	Shows each login session.
w	Shows a summary of system usage, currently logged-in users, and active processes.
who	Shows the names of users currently logged in, the terminal each is using, the time each has been logged in, and the name of the host from which each logged in (if any).

Using the pico Editor

The *pico* editor is a simple text editor that you can think of as the Linux equivalent of the Microsoft Windows *Notepad* accessory. To start *pico*, simply type *pico* at the shell prompt; or, if you want to edit a particular file, type *pico* followed by the name of the file (or the file's path, if the file is not in the working directory). For example, to edit the file *mydata*, type:

```
[root@desktop /root]# pico mydata
```

TIP   If *pico* fails to start, you probably did not install the *pine* package, which contains it. You can install that package by following the instructions given in Appendix C, *The Red Hat Package Manager*.

Figure 4-7 shows *pico*'s standard display. At the top of the display is a status line, which shows the version of the program and the name of the file being edited (or "New Buffer," if the file is new). If the file has been modified, the upper right corner of the display contains the word *Modified*. The bottom two lines of the display list the available editing commands. Most of the commands require you to type a control character, so that commands can be distinguished from characters you want to add to the buffer. Typing an ordinary character inserts it at the current cursor position. You can use the cursor keys to move around the display; you can use the delete or backspace key to erase unwanted characters. Some commands use the third line from the bottom to report status and obtain additional input.

Table 4-8 summarizes *pico*'s commands. Notice that the command **Ctrl-G** accesses *pico*'s help system. You can access several of the commands by using function keys; for example, pressing **F1** has the same result as typing **Ctrl-G**.

Figure 4-7. The pico editor

Table 4-8. Summary of pico Commands

Command	Description
Ctrl-^	Mark the cursor position as beginning of selected text.
Ctrl-A	Move to the beginning of the current line.
Ctrl-B	Move backward one character.
Ctrl-C (F11)	Report the current cursor position.
Ctrl-D	Delete the character at the cursor position.
Ctrl-E	Move to the end of the current line.
Ctrl-F	Move forward one character.
Ctrl-G (F1)	Display help.
Ctrl-I	Insert a tab at the current cursor position.
Ctrl-J (F4)	Format the current paragraph.
Ctrl-K (F9)	Cut selected text.
Ctrl-L	Refresh the display.
Ctrl-N	Move to the next line.
Ctrl-O (F3)	Save the current buffer to a file.
Ctrl-P	Move to the previous line.
Ctrl-R (F5)	Insert an external file at the current cursor position.
Ctrl-T (F12)	Invoke the spelling checker.
Ctrl-U (F10)	Paste text at the current cursor position.
Ctrl-V (F8)	Move forward one page of text.
Ctrl-W (F6)	Search for text, neglecting case.
Ctrl-X (F2)	Exit *pico*, saving the edit buffer.
Ctrl-Y (F7)	Move backward one page of text.

## CHAPTER FIVE

INSTALLING AND CONFIGURING THE X WINDOW SYSTEM

This chapter helps you install, configure, and use the X Window System (often known simply as X). If your graphics card is of a common variety and you correctly specified its characteristics during the Linux installation procedure, the install program may have successfully installed and configured X. Otherwise, you'll need to install and configure X by using the more sophisticated procedures given in this chapter. Once X is up and running, you can choose how to start X. This chapter explains your options and also gives some tips on optimizing the performance of X.

What is X?

X is the standard graphical user interface for Linux. Like other graphical user interfaces such as Microsoft Windows and Mac OS, X lets you interact with programs by using a mouse (or other pointing device) to point and click, providing a simple means of communicating with your computer.

Originally implemented as a collaborative effort of Digital Equipment Corporation and Massachusetts Institute of Technology, X was first released in 1987. Subsequently, the X Consortium, Inc. became responsible for the continued development and publication of X.

Despite its age, X is a remarkable and very modern software system: a cross-platform, network-oriented, graphical user interface. It runs on a wide variety of platforms, including essentially every variety of Unix. X Clients are available for use, for example, under Windows 3.x, 9x, and NT. The sophisticated networking capabilities of X let you run a program on one computer while viewing the graphical output on another computer, connected to the first via a network. With the advent of the Internet, which interconnected a sizable fraction of the computers on the planet, X achieved a new height of importance and power.

Most Linux users run XFree86, a freely available software system compatible with X. XFree86 was developed by the XFree86 software team, which began work in 1992. In 1994, The XFree86 Project assumed responsibility for ongoing research and development of XFree86.

Installing X

Getting a proper X Window System up and running used to be a real challenge on Linux, almost a rite of passage. Today, device drivers are available for a much wider array of hardware, and configuration tools to assist in the setup process have greatly improved. While still tricky at times—especially with unusual hardware—X setup and configuration is no longer the daunting process it once was, and should be relatively easy.

You'll go through two stages before you have X successfully running. The first stage involves installing the needed programs that enable X to run. These can be grouped into several categories:

- Basic XFree86 program
- X servers
- Window Managers
- Applications
- Fonts

This stage is very straightforward and may well have been done as part of the basic installation process, if you selected the relevant X packages during that step.

In the second stage you configure X to run properly on your system. This is a matter of identifying an X server compatible with your graphics card, and tuning the server for your graphics card. If you have a common card and all the documentation for it, this second stage will be relatively simple. Missing information makes the process harder, but not impossible.

As shown in Appendix C, *The Red Hat Package Manager*, X consists of many RPM packages. Consequently, the easiest way to install X is to install the X Window System component during the installation procedure. If you omitted the X Window System component, you should consider redoing the installation procedure, as this may be the simplest way to install X. However, if you prefer, you can use the information in Appendix C to install X without redoing the installation.

Once you've installed the necessary packages, you're ready to configure X. The first step is to establish a symbolic link to the X server you want to use. RPM installed your X server in the directory */usr/X11R6/bin*. So, if you installed the SVGA server, the full path name of the server is */usr/X11R6/bin/XF86_SVGA*. The symbolic link */etc/X11/X* must point to this file. You can accomplish this by logging in as root and issuing the command:

```
ln -sf /usr/X11R6/bin/XF86_SVGA /etc/X11/X
```

If you installed a server other than *XF86_SVGA*, substitute the name of your server in the above command. To determine the name of your server, consult Table C-3 if you installed a basic server or Table C-2 if you installed an accelerated server.

If you're unsure what servers you installed, use this command:

```
ls /usr/X11R6/bin/XF*
```

Among the files listed will be the installed servers.

WARNING   You should exercise due care while configuring X to run on your system. If you incorrectly or incompletely configure X, your system can be permanently damaged. In particular, if you configure your monitor for a refresh rate that exceeds its capacity, you can damage the monitor. Older fixed-frequency monitors are particularly susceptible to such damage. The author and publisher have taken pains to make this chapter clear and accurate, but their efforts don't ensure that the procedure presented in this chapter will work correctly with your hardware. Consequently, the author and publisher cannot be held responsible for damages resulting from a faulty installation or configuration of X.

If you have a card or monitor of unknown manufacture or model, and feel that you must guess, at least start with a narrow range of middle values, and gradually expand that range to see if you can find a value that works. Don't let a monitor that displays an unstable or garbled image run any longer than the time it takes you to cut power to the monitor.

Configuration Using Xconfigurator

A configuration file named *XF86Config* controls the operation of X. Linux places this file in the */etc/X11* directory. You can edit this file by using *pico* or another text editor; but it's much easier to use *Xconfigurator*, which asks a few questions about your system and then builds the file for you.

To launch *Xconfigurator*, log in as root and type the command:

```
Xconfigurator
```

Xconfigurator displays its opening screen, shown in Figure 5-1. The configuration process that ensues is very similar to the one performed by the install program; but, as you'll see, there are a few differences, mostly minor. Select the Ok button and press **Enter** to continue.

WARNING   *Xconfigurator* overwrites the contents of the *XF86Config* file. If you already have a working X setup, you should create a backup copy of *XF86Config* before running *Xconfigurator.*

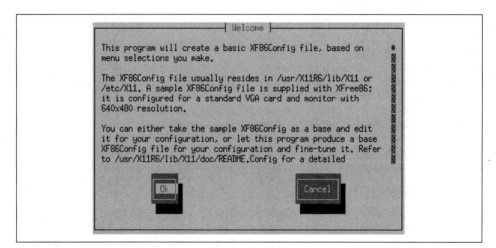

Figure 5-1. The Xconfigurator Welcome dialog box

As shown in Figure 5-2, *Xconfigurator* probes your system to determine the characteristics of your video card. If the probe fails, you should suspect that you installed an X server that's not compatible with your video card; install the proper server and try running *Xconfigurator* again. If the probe succeeded, you can select the Ok button and press **Enter**.

Xconfigurator may present a dialog box that asks you to specify your video card. If so, consult Figure 5-2 and select the video card that most nearly resembles the video card installed in your system.

Xconfigurator may also ask you to specify the amount of memory installed on your video card by presenting a dialog box like that shown in Figure 5-3. If so, specify the proper amount of memory, select the Ok button, and press **Enter**.

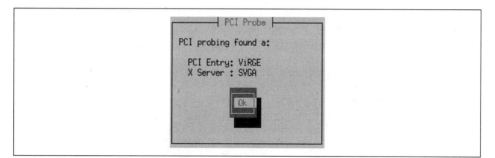

Figure 5-2. The PCI Probe dialog box

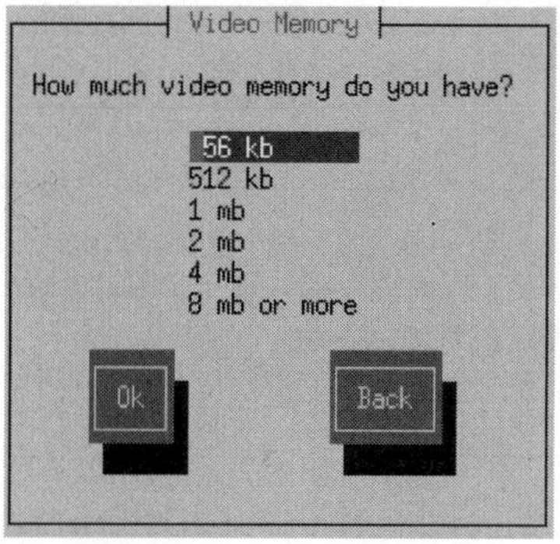

Figure 5-3. The Video Memory dialog box

Next, *Xconfigurator* presents a dialog box, shown in Figure 5-4, that asks you to specify your system's monitor. If you can't find your monitor listed, select Custom; *Xconfigurator* will then let you specify your monitor's characteristics.

If you specified Custom, the dialog box shown in Figure 5-5 appears. As the dialog box explains, the two parameters needed to configure up your monitor are its vertical refresh rate and horizontal sync rate. You can find these values by:

- Consulting your monitor's documentation.

- Consulting the file */usr/X11R6/lib/X11/doc/Monitors*, which may list your monitor. Use *pico* or another text editor to view the file.

- Viewing the monitor manufacturer's web support page.

- Posting a question to the newsgroup *comp.os.linux.setup*.

- Contacting the monitor manufacturer's technical support group and requesting the information.

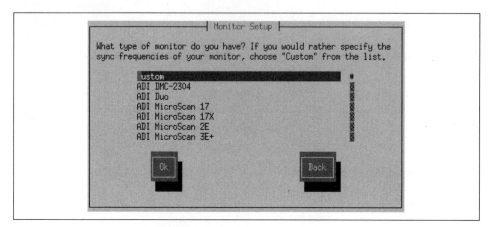

Figure 5-4. The Monitor Setup dialog box

WARNING   Often, otherwise similar monitor models have different horizontal sync rates. It is crucial that you accurately determine the horizontal sync rate of your monitor. If you configure X to use an inappropriate horizontal sync rate, you can permanently damage your monitor.

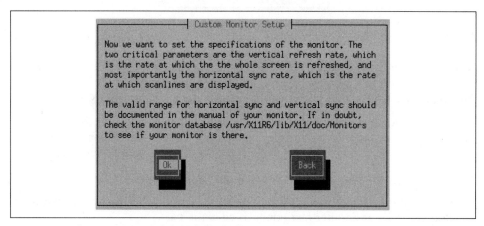

Figure 5-5. The Custom Monitor Setup dialog box

When you select the Ok button and press **Enter**, *Xconfigurator* presents a dialog box that lets you specify the horizontal sync rate of your monitor, as shown in Figure 5-6. Choose the appropriate sync rate, select the Ok button and press **Enter**.

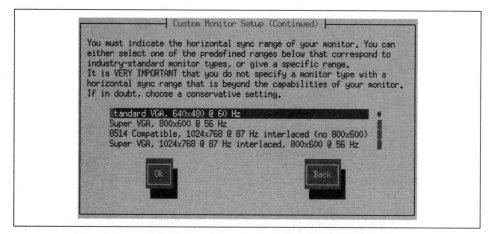

Figure 5-6. The Custom Monitor Setup (Continued) dialog box specifying horizontal sync

Xconfigurator next presents a dialog box, shown in Figure 5-7, that lets you choose your monitor's vertical refresh (sync) rate. As the dialog box explains, interlaced modes provide a sync rate that is approximately double the specified rate; if your documentation specifies two rates for an interlaced mode, specify the higher of the two rates. After choosing the proper rate, select the Ok button and press **Enter**.

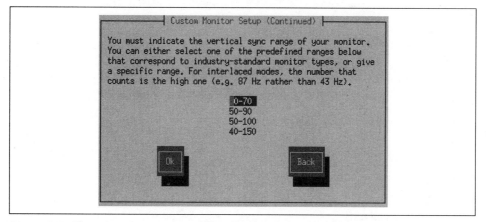

Figure 5-7. The Custom Monitor Setup (Continued) dialog box specifying vertical refresh

After you've specified your monitor or its sync rates, *Xconfigurator* probes your system to discover additional video characteristics. It displays the dialog box shown in Figure 5-8 before beginning. Select the Ok button and press **Enter** to begin the probe. Your screen may flicker or blink a bit while *Xconfigurator* probes your system.

Figure 5-8. The Probing to begin dialog box

When *Xconfigurator* has probed your system, it displays the dialog box shown in Figure 5-9. The dialog box displays the default video mode in which X will oper-ate. If you prefer more or less color depth or resolution, you can use the Let Me Choose button to specify your choice. Table 5-1 shows the relationship between color depth and the number of displayed colors.

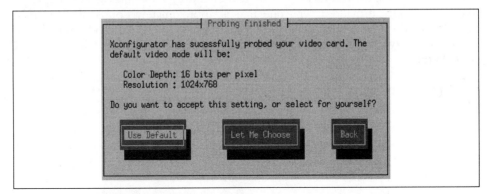

Figure 5-9. The Probing finished dialog box

Table 5-1. Color Depth and Number of Colors

Color depth	Number of colors
8	256
16	Thousands
24	Millions

Xconfigurator now asks permission to start X in order to test your configuration, as shown in Figure 5-10. Normally, you should allow it to do so, by selecting the Ok button and pressing **Enter**.

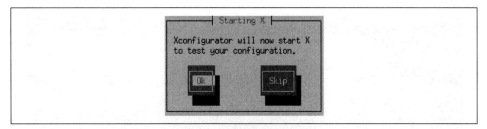

Figure 5-10. Xconfigurator's Starting X dialog box

When X starts, you'll see a small dialog box that asks you to whether you can read its message. Click on Yes to dismiss the dialog box. You'll need to do so within 10 seconds, or *Xconfigurator* will assume that X failed. This time limit is intended to avoid damage to your video hardware if the configuration is incorrect; however, some hardware can suffer damage even during such a brief interval.

A dialog box pops up, asking whether you'd like to automatically start X the next time you boot your system. Answer Yes nor No, according to your preference. *Xconfigurator* then presents its final dialog box, which explains that X has been successfully installed. Select the Ok button and press **Enter** to exit *Xconfigurator*.

Configuration Using xf86config

Xconfigurator is not always able to successfully probe a system. The *xf86config* utility, though somewhat less convenient to use, is more often successful. If *Xconfigurator* failed to properly configure your system to use X, you can follow the instructions in this section to configure your system by using *xf86config*. If you successfully configured your system you can skip to the next section, which shows you how to launch X.

To launch *xf86config*, log in as `root` and type the command:

```
xf86config
```

Figure 5-11 shows the beginning of the *xf86config* dialog. As you can see, unlike *Xconfigurator*, *xf86config* is a text-mode program; it does not support use of the mouse and it presents its questions teletype-style, using black-and-white text.

TIP   In working with *xf86config*, you may find that your **Backspace** key
             doesn't work as expected. If so, use **Ctrl-Backspace** instead.

When you press **Enter**, *xf86config* asks you to confirm that the PATH is correctly set, as shown in Figure 5-12. The install program should have properly configured the PATH. Press **Enter** to continue.

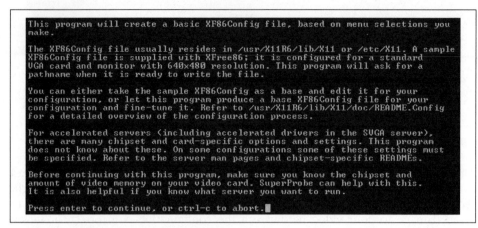

Figure 5-11. The beginning of the xf86config dialog

Figure 5-12. Confirming the PATH

Next, *xf86config* asks you to specify the type of mouse attached to your system, as shown in Figure 5-13. Type the number associated with your choice, and press **Enter**. For non-mouse pointing devices found on many laptops, you should most likely select PS/2 Mouse.

If you selected the Logitech MouseMan mouse, you should enable its third button by responding *y* to the question asking whether ChordMiddle should be enabled, as shown in Figure 5-14.

If your mouse has only two buttons, you should enable emulation of a three-button mouse by responding *y* to the question asking about Emulate3Buttons, as shown in Figure 5-15. If you enable this option you can simultaneously press both the buttons of your mouse to emulate pressing the third button.

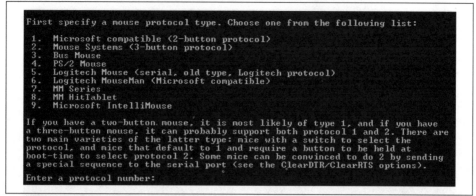

Figure 5-13. Specifying the mouse type

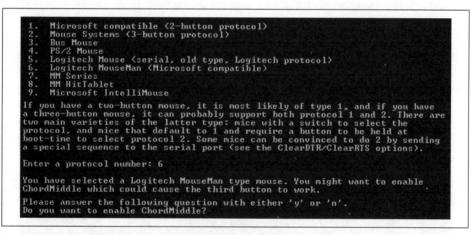

Figure 5-14. Specifying the ChordMiddle option

Next, you must specify the device file associated with the mouse, as shown in Figure 5-16. The install program should have associated your system's mouse with the device */dev/mouse*, which is the default choice. Simply press **Enter** to continue.

As described by the output shown in Figure 5-17, X provides special support for using extended keyboards. If you use a special keyboard layout to support national characters, you can type y to use *xkb*, which simplifies changing the keyboard map. After making your choice, press **Enter** to continue.

As shown in Figure 5-18, you can configure X to let you generate non-ASCII characters. If you want to use this capability, type y. After specifying your choice, press **Enter** to continue.

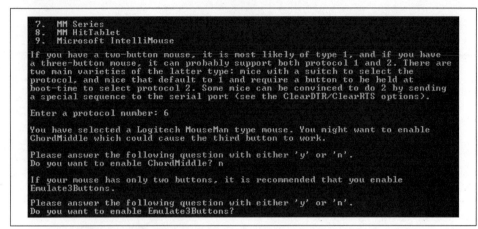

Figure 5-15. Specifying emulation of a three-button mouse

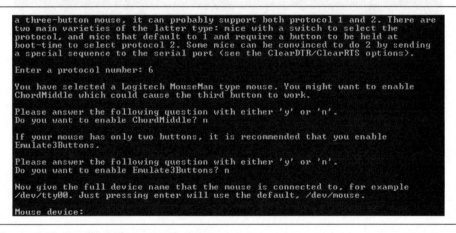

Figure 5-16. Specifying the mouse device

Next, as shown in Figure 5-19, you must specify the characteristics of your monitor. Consult the previous section for help in finding your monitor's characteristics. Press **Enter** to continue.

First, you must specify the horizontal sync rate of your monitor, as shown in Figure 5-20. Type the number associated with your choice and press **Enter**. To specify a range other than those listed, you can select choice 11; if you do so, you'll be prompted to enter the low and high values of the horizontal sync range.

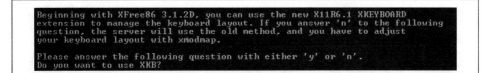

Figure 5-17. Specifying use of the keyboard extension

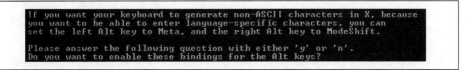

Figure 5-18. Specifying generation of non-ASCII characters

Figure 5-19. Preparing to specify monitor characteristics

WARNING   Often, otherwise similar monitor models have different horizontal sync rates. It is crucial that you accurately determine the horizontal sync rate of your monitor. If you configure X to use an inappropriate horizontal sync rate, you can permanently damage your monitor.

Next, as shown in Figure 5-21, you must specify the vertical sync (refresh) rate. Type the number associated with your choice and press **Enter**. To specify a range other than those listed, you can select choice 5; if you do so, you'll be prompted for the low and high values of the vertical sync range.

You must now specify identification and description strings for your monitor, as shown in Figure 5-22. You can enter any text you like. Press **Enter** after typing each string.

Next, you must specify your video card and its characteristics. The explanations provided by *xf86config*, shown in Figure 5-23, point out that you can choose to select your card from a database. However, even if you do so, you'll be given the opportunity to specify non-standard values. Unless you have a specific reason for doing so, you should not override the values in the database. Moreover, you

```
You must indicate the horizontal sync range of your monitor. You can either
select one of the predefined ranges below that correspond to industry-
standard monitor types, or give a specific range.

It is VERY IMPORTANT that you do not specify a monitor type with a horizontal
sync range that is beyond the capabilities of your monitor. If in doubt,
choose a conservative setting.

    hsync in kHz; monitor type with characteristic modes
 1  31.5; Standard VGA, 640x480 @ 60 Hz
 2  31.5 - 35.1; Super VGA, 800x600 @ 56 Hz
 3  31.5, 35.5; 8514 Compatible, 1024x768 @ 87 Hz interlaced (no 800x600)
 4  31.5, 35.15, 35.5; Super VGA, 1024x768 @ 87 Hz interlaced, 800x600 @ 56 Hz
 5  31.5 - 37.9; Extended Super VGA, 800x600 @ 60 Hz, 640x480 @ 72 Hz
 6  31.5 - 48.5; Non-Interlaced SVGA, 1024x768 @ 60 Hz, 800x600 @ 72 Hz
 7  31.5 - 57.0; High Frequency SVGA, 1024x768 @ 70 Hz
 8  31.5 - 64.3; Monitor that can do 1280x1024 @ 60 Hz
 9  31.5 - 79.0; Monitor that can do 1280x1024 @ 74 Hz
10  31.5 - 82.0; Monitor that can do 1280x1024 @ 76 Hz
11  Enter your own horizontal sync range

Enter your choice (1-11): 2
```

Figure 5-20. Specifying the horizontal sync rate

```
 3  31.5, 35.5; 8514 Compatible, 1024x768 @ 87 Hz interlaced (no 800x600)
 4  31.5, 35.15, 35.5; Super VGA, 1024x768 @ 87 Hz interlaced, 800x600 @ 56 Hz
 5  31.5 - 37.9; Extended Super VGA, 800x600 @ 60 Hz, 640x480 @ 72 Hz
 6  31.5 - 48.5; Non-Interlaced SVGA, 1024x768 @ 60 Hz, 800x600 @ 72 Hz
 7  31.5 - 57.0; High Frequency SVGA, 1024x768 @ 70 Hz
 8  31.5 - 64.3; Monitor that can do 1280x1024 @ 60 Hz
 9  31.5 - 79.0; Monitor that can do 1280x1024 @ 74 Hz
10  31.5 - 82.0; Monitor that can do 1280x1024 @ 76 Hz
11  Enter your own horizontal sync range

Enter your choice (1-11): 2

You must indicate the vertical sync range of your monitor. You can either
select one of the predefined ranges below that correspond to industry-
standard monitor types, or give a specific range. For interlaced modes,
the number that counts is the high one (e.g. 87 Hz rather than 43 Hz).

 1  50-70
 2  50-90
 3  50-100
 4  40-150
 5  Enter your own vertical sync range

Enter your choice: 1
```

Figure 5-21. Specifying the vertical sync rate

should be careful to choose only the database entry that exactly matches your card; cards having similar model names may have significantly different hardware characteristics.

Figure 5-24 shows the screen you use to choose your card. Simply type the number associated with your card and press **Enter**. If you suspect that your card appears on a subsequent page, press q to page forward through the database. If you accidentally page past your card, simply continue moving forward; when the program reaches the last entries of the database, it cycles back to the beginning.

After you choose your video card, *xf86config* reports your choice. As in Figure 5-25, *xf86config* may provide instructions, such as "Do NOT probe clocks." It's a

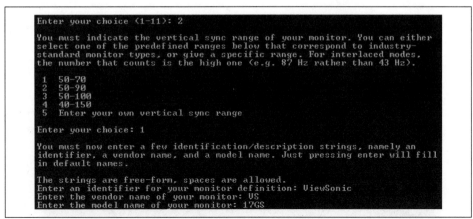

```
Enter your choice (1-11): 2

You must indicate the vertical sync range of your monitor. You can either
select one of the predefined ranges below that correspond to industry-
standard monitor types, or give a specific range. For interlaced modes,
the number that counts is the high one (e.g. 87 Hz rather than 43 Hz).

  1  50-70
  2  50-90
  3  50-100
  4  40-150
  5  Enter your own vertical sync range

Enter your choice: 1

You must now enter a few identification/description strings, namely an
identifier, a vendor name, and a model name. Just pressing enter will fill
in default names.

The strings are free-form, spaces are allowed.
Enter an identifier for your monitor definition: ViewSonic
Enter the vendor name of your monitor: VS
Enter the model name of your monitor: 17GS
```

Figure 5-22. Specifying the monitor identification and description strings

```
Now we must configure video card specific settings. At this point you can
choose to make a selection out of a database of video card definitions.
Because there can be variation in Ramdacs and clock generators even
between cards of the same model, it is not sensible to blindly copy
the settings (e.g. a Device section). For this reason, after you make a
selection, you will still be asked about the components of the card, with
the settings from the chosen database entry presented as a strong hint.

The database entries include information about the chipset, what server to
run, the Ramdac and ClockChip, and comments that will be included in the
Device section. However, a lot of definitions only hint about what server
to run (based on the chipset the card uses) and are untested.

If you can't find your card in the database, there's nothing to worry about.
You should only choose a database entry that is exactly the same model as
your card; choosing one that looks similar is just a bad idea (e.g. a
GemStone Snail 64 may be as different from a GemStone Snail 64+ in terms of
hardware as can be).

Do you want to look at the card database?
```

Figure 5-23. Preparing to examine the card database

good idea to write these down so that you remember to observe them even after
they've scrolled off the screen.

Next, you must specify the X server you want to use, as shown in Figure 5-26.
Consult Table C-2 to determine the appropriate server. Type the number associated
with the server and press **Enter** to continue. If you specify choice 4, you'll be
prompted to specify which accelerated server you want to use.

Next, as shown in Figure 5-27, *xf86config* asks whether it should set the required
symbolic link to your server. Respond by typing *y* and press **Enter**. Being able to
respond with *n* is helpful only if you've moved the X executables to a directory
other than the default directory.

Now, as shown in Figure 5-28, specify the amount of memory installed on your
video card by typing the appropriate number and pressing **Enter**.

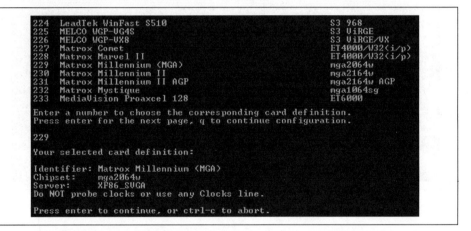

```
216  JAX 8241                          S3 801/805
217  Jaton Video-58P                   ET6000
218  Jaton Video-70P                   CL-GD5464
219  Jazz Multimedia G-Force 128       ET6000
220  LeadTek WinFast 3D S600           S3 ViRGE
221  LeadTek WinFast 3D S680           S3 ViRGE/GX2
222  LeadTek WinFast S200              ET4000/W32(i/p)
223  LeadTek WinFast S430              S3 968
224  LeadTek WinFast S510              S3 968
225  MELCO WGP-VG4S                    S3 ViRGE
226  MELCO WGP-VX8                     S3 ViRGE/VX
227  Matrox Comet                      ET4000/W32(i/p)
228  Matrox Marvel II                  ET4000/W32(i/p)
229  Matrox Millennium (MGA)           mga2064w
230  Matrox Millennium II              mga2164w
231  Matrox Millennium II AGP          mga2164w AGP
232  Matrox Mystique                   mga1064sg
233  MediaVision Proaxcel 128          ET6000

Enter a number to choose the corresponding card definition.
Press enter for the next page, q to continue configuration.

229
```

Figure 5-24. Examining the card database

```
224  LeadTek WinFast S510              S3 968
225  MELCO WGP-VG4S                    S3 ViRGE
226  MELCO WGP-VX8                     S3 ViRGE/VX
227  Matrox Comet                      ET4000/W32(i/p)
228  Matrox Marvel II                  ET4000/W32(i/p)
229  Matrox Millennium (MGA)           mga2064w
230  Matrox Millennium II              mga2164w
231  Matrox Millennium II AGP          mga2164w AGP
232  Matrox Mystique                   mga1064sg
233  MediaVision Proaxcel 128          ET6000
Enter a number to choose the corresponding card definition.
Press enter for the next page, q to continue configuration.

229

Your selected card definition:

Identifier: Matrox Millennium (MGA)
Chipset:    mga2064w
Server:     XF86_SVGA
Do NOT probe clocks or use any Clocks line.

Press enter to continue, or ctrl-c to abort.
```

Figure 5-25. The selected card definition

Just as you previously specified text strings that identify and describe your monitor, you should now specify strings that identify and describe your video card, as shown in Figure 5-29. Press **Enter** after typing each string.

If you selected an accelerated server, you can now enter the RAMDAC settings, as shown in Figure 5-30. Some SVGA servers also support RAMDACs. If you're not using an accelerated server, you can simply type *q* and press **Enter** to omit specification of a RAMDAC. Otherwise, type the number associated with the RAMDAC used by your card and press **Enter**. Determining the correct number may pose a bit of a puzzle. The descriptions given in the screen specify RAMDAC chips used on particular cards. If you can conveniently view your card, you can inspect it to see if it contains any of the listed chips. If it's not convenient to view your card,

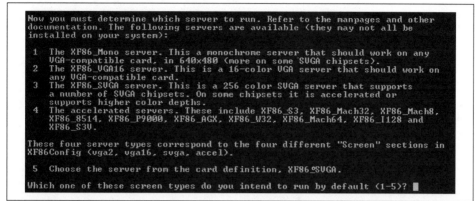

Figure 5-26. Specifying the server

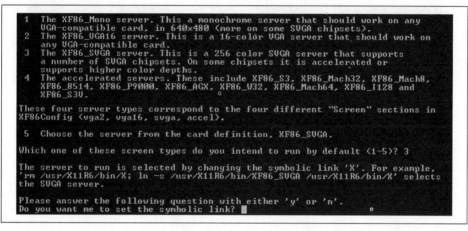

Figure 5-27. Setting the symbolic link

type q and press **Enter** to omit specification of a RAMDAC. X will autodetect most RAMDACs, so omitting the specification will not likely impair the performance of your video hardware.

Next, as shown in Figure 5-31, you can specify the programmable clock chip used by your video card. Most video cards lack such a chip; such cards require a `Clocks` line in the X configuration file. If your video card lacks a programmable clock chip, type q and press **Enter** to continue; otherwise type the number associated with your card's programmable clock chip and press **Enter**.

As shown in Figure 5-32, *xf86config* asks you to let it probe your system to determine proper clock timings. If you specified a programmable clock chip, you

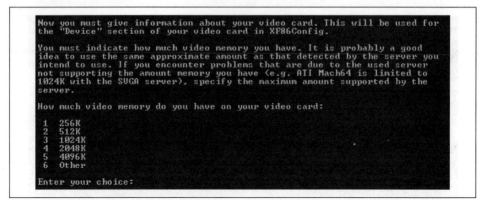

Figure 5-28. Specifying the amount of video memory

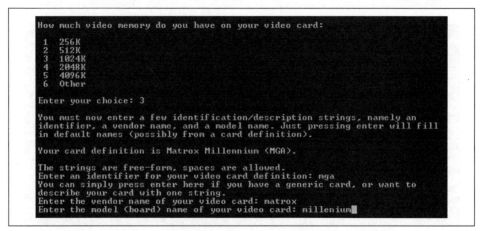

Figure 5-29. Specifying the video card identification and description strings

should omit the probe; type **n** and press **Enter** to continue. You should also omit the probe if you earlier noted that probing is not recommended for your card.

TIP   You can sometimes improve the accuracy of the clock timings by running the probe yourself after *xf86config* is done and adding an appropriate `Clocks` line to your X configuration. Consult the X documentation for information on how to do so.

Otherwise, you should let *xf86config* probe your system to determine appropriate clock settings: type **y** and press **Enter** to begin the probe.

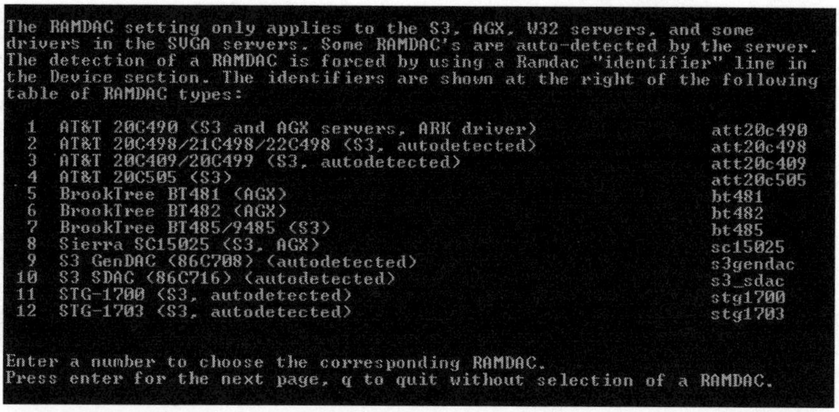

```
The RAMDAC setting only applies to the S3, AGX, W32 servers, and some
drivers in the SVGA servers. Some RAMDAC's are auto-detected by the server.
The detection of a RAMDAC is forced by using a Ramdac "identifier" line in
the Device section. The identifiers are shown at the right of the following
table of RAMDAC types:

  1  AT&T 20C490 (S3 and AGX servers, ARK driver)           att20c490
  2  AT&T 20C498/21C498/22C498 (S3, autodetected)           att20c498
  3  AT&T 20C409/20C499 (S3, autodetected)                  att20c409
  4  AT&T 20C505 (S3)                                        att20c505
  5  BrookTree BT481 (AGX)                                   bt481
  6  BrookTree BT482 (AGX)                                   bt482
  7  BrookTree BT485/9485 (S3)                               bt485
  8  Sierra SC15025 (S3, AGX)                                sc15025
  9  S3 GenDAC (86C708) (autodetected)                       s3gendac
 10  S3 SDAC (86C716) (autodetected)                         s3_sdac
 11  STG-1700 (S3, autodetected)                             stg1700
 12  STG-1703 (S3, autodetected)                             stg1703

Enter a number to choose the corresponding RAMDAC.
Press enter for the next page, q to quit without selection of a RAMDAC.
```

Figure 5-30. Specifying the RAMDAC settings

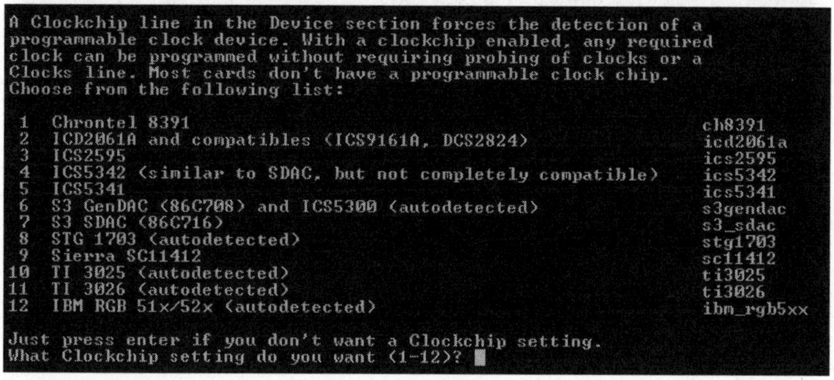

```
A Clockchip line in the Device section forces the detection of a
programmable clock device. With a clockchip enabled, any required
clock can be programmed without requiring probing of clocks or a
Clocks line. Most cards don't have a programmable clock chip.
Choose from the following list:

 1  Chrontel 8391                                          ch8391
 2  ICD2061A and compatibles (ICS9161A, DCS2824)           icd2061a
 3  ICS2595                                                ics2595
 4  ICS5342 (similar to SDAC, but not completely compatible)  ics5342
 5  ICS5341                                                ics5341
 6  S3 GenDAC (86C708) and ICS5300 (autodetected)          s3gendac
 7  S3 SDAC (86C716)                                       s3_sdac
 8  STG 1703 (autodetected)                                stg1703
 9  Sierra SC11412                                         sc11412
10  TI 3025 (autodetected)                                 ti3025
11  TI 3026 (autodetected)                                 ti3026
12  IBM RGB 51x/52x (autodetected)                         ibm_rgb5xx

Just press enter if you don't want a Clockchip setting.
What Clockchip setting do you want (1-12)?
```

Figure 5-31. Specifying the clock chip

WARNING If *xf86config* probes your system and the screen remains black for more than 30 seconds, immediately cancel the probe by turning off the monitor, pressing **Ctrl-C**, and restoring power to your monitor. If the probe fails, it can *permanently* damage your monitor.

Next, you can specify the color depths and resolutions in which X will operate, as shown in Figure 5-33. Generally, *xf86config*'s default choices are appropriate: you can type 5 and press **Enter** to continue. However, you can change the resolutions allowed when operating at a given color depth by typing the number associated with the color depth and specifying the desired resolution or resolutions.

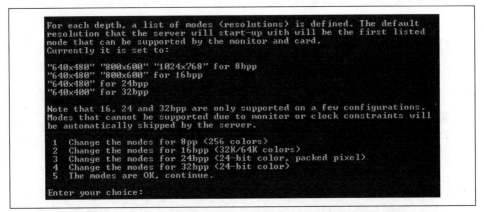

```
For most configurations, a Clocks line is useful since it prevents the slow
and nasty sounding clock probing at server start-up. Probed clocks are
displayed at server startup, along with other server and hardware
configuration info. You can save this information in a file by running
'X -probeonly 2>output_file'. Be warned that clock probing is inherently
imprecise; some clocks may be slightly too high (varies per run).

At this point I can run X -probeonly, and try to extract the clock information
from the output. It is recommended that you do this yourself and add a clocks
line (note that the list of clocks may be split over multiple Clocks lines) to
your Device section afterwards. Be aware that a clocks line is not
appropriate for drivers that have a fixed set of clocks and don't probe by
default (e.g. Cirrus). Also, for the P9000 server you must simply specify
clocks line that matches the modes you want to use. For the S3 server with
a programmable clock chip you need a 'ClockChip' line and no Clocks line.

You must be root to be able to run X -probeonly now.

The card definition says to NOT probe clocks.
Do you want me to run 'X -probeonly' now?
```

Figure 5-32. Beginning the automatic probe

```
For each depth, a list of modes (resolutions) is defined. The default
resolution that the server will start-up with will be the first listed
mode that can be supported by the monitor and card.
Currently it is set to:

"640x480" "800x600" "1024x768" for 8bpp
"640x480" "800x600" for 16bpp
"640x480" for 24bpp
"640x400" for 32bpp

Note that 16, 24 and 32bpp are only supported on a few configurations.
Modes that cannot be supported due to monitor or clock constraints will
be automatically skipped by the server.

1    Change the modes for 8bpp (256 colors)
2    Change the modes for 16bpp (32K/64K colors)
3    Change the modes for 24bpp (24-bit color, packed pixel)
4    Change the modes for 32bpp (24-bit color)
5    The modes are OK, continue.

Enter your choice:
```

Figure 5-33. Specifying the modes

Finally, as shown in Figure 5-34, *xf86config* is ready to write the configuration file it has prepared. Generally, you should let it write the file to */etc/X11/XF86Config*: simply type **y** and press **Enter**. However, if you prefer, you can type **n** and specify a different directory or filename.

```
I am going to write the XF86Config file now. Make sure you don't accidently
overwrite a previously configured one.

Shall I write it to /etc/X11/XF86Config?
```

Figure 5-34. Writing the configuration file

Once the file has been written, you're ready to start X.

Starting and Stopping X

Now that you've configured X by using *Xconfigurator* or *xf86config*, you're probably eager to see it work. To start X, type the command:

```
startx
```

Your system's screen should briefly go blank and then you should see X's graphical desktop. Chapter 6, *Using the X Window System,* will teach you how to use X effectively.

WARNING   If the screen is garbled or remains blank for more than about 30 seconds, your X configuration may be faulty. Immediately turn off your monitor or terminate X by pressing **Ctrl-Alt-Backspace**.

To exit X, click on an unused part of the desktop and a pop-up menu will appear. From the menu, select the Exit, Logout, or Quit menu item. X shuts down, returning you to the familiar text-based interface of the Linux shell prompt.

CHAPTER SIX

Using the X Window System

Using the X Window System means interacting with Linux on several different levels. X itself simply provides the graphics for displaying components of a graphical user interface: X draws the screen, draws objects on the screen, and tracks user input actions such as keyboard input and mouse operations. To organize all of this into familiar objects like windows, menus, and scrollbars, X relies on a separate program called a window manager. A window manager alone won't necessarily assure tight integration between applications running under X; that higher degree of integration comes from something called a desktop environment. While X itself is a single program, X under Linux supports several popular window managers, and two popular desktop environments.

To use X effectively, you'll learn the basic keyboard and mouse operations for communicating with X. If you're like most X users, you'll find it helpful to use a window manager and a desktop with X. You'll learn why window managers and desktops are useful and get help in choosing and setting up a window manager and a desktop.

Keyboard Operations

Using the keyboard with X closely resembles using the keyboard with Microsoft Windows. X sends your keyboard input to the active window, which is said to have the *input focus*. The active window is usually the window in which you most recently clicked the mouse; however, under some circumstances, it can be the window beneath the mouse cursor.

TIP   This chapter refers to your pointing device as a *mouse*. However, like Microsoft Windows, X supports a variety of pointing devices.

Microsoft Windows lets you choose to perform most operations by using the keyboard or mouse. In contrast, X was designed for use with mouse. If your mouse isn't functioning, you'll find it quite challenging or even impossible to use most X programs.

Similarly, X provides a few important functions that you can access only via the keyboard:

- Using virtual consoles

- Switching video modes

In addition, you can use the keyboard to terminate X.

Switching Video Modes

When you configured X, you specified the video modes in which X can operate. Recall that the current video mode determines the resolution and color depth of the image displayed by your monitor—for example 16 bits per pixel color depth and 1024×768 pixels screen resolution.

By pressing **Shift-Alt-+** (using the plus key on the numeric keypad), you command X to switch to the next video mode in sequence. X treats the video modes as a cycle: If X is operating in the last video mode, this key sequence causes X to return to the first video mode.

The similar key sequence **Shift-Alt- -** (using the minus key on the numeric keypad) causes X to switch to the previous video model. If you shift to a video mode that your monitor doesn't support—as demonstrated by a unsteady or garbled image—you can use this key sequence to return to a supported video mode, avoiding the inconvenience of terminating X.

Using Virtual Consoles with X

Even while X is running, you can access the Linux virtual consoles. To switch from graphical mode to a virtual console running in text mode, type **Ctrl-Alt-F***n*, where F*n* is a function key and *n* is the number of the desired virtual console. X uses virtual console 7, so only virtual consoles 1–6 are accessible while running X.

To switch from a virtual console back to X, type **Alt-F7**. Nothing is lost when you switch from X to a virtual console or back, so you can move freely between the graphical and text operating modes.

Terminating X

As you learned in the previous chapter, you can terminate X by typing **Ctrl-Alt-Backspace**. X immediately terminates each program running under X, closes each open window, and returns your system to text mode.

This key sequence terminates X abruptly; most window managers support gentler ways of terminating X. You'll learn about these later in this chapter.

While X is running, you cannot use the **Ctrl-Alt-Del** sequence to reboot your system. To reboot your system, you can terminate X and then use the **Ctrl-Alt-Del** sequence, or access a terminal window and enter the command:

```
shutdown -r now
```

The *shutdown* command terminates X and then reboots your system.

Terminal Windows

In Windows, you need not restart in DOS mode simply to have access to the DOS command line. Similarly, in X you need not switch to a virtual console simply to have access to the command line. X enables you to open a terminal window. A terminal window resembles the familiar Microsoft Windows MS-DOS Prompt window; like the Linux shell, it lets you type commands and view command output. Various window managers support different ways of accessing a terminal window.

Pop-Up Menus

The terminal window is just one example of a frequently used program under X that you'll want to access. Most window managers install with a default set of common programs that can be accessed by right-clicking with the mouse on the desktop. Most window managers, for example, let you right click on the desktop and select a terminal window program from the pop-up menu that appears. However, the pop-up menu displayed by a window manager may display program names rather than program functions. In this case, you may have some difficulty determining which entry on the pop-up menu corresponds to a terminal program. Many programs that provide terminal windows have names that include the sequences *xt* or *xterm*. Selecting such an entry will probably launch a terminal window. You'll learn more about window managers and how to use them later in this chapter.

Mouse Operations

Mouse operations under X are similar to mouse operations under Microsoft Windows, although you perform them differently. The most common mouse operations are:

- Copying and pasting text

- Using scrollbars

Copying and Pasting Text

To copy and paste text, you must first mark the text. To do so, you move the mouse cursor to the beginning of the text, press the left mouse button, and drag the mouse across the text to be marked. X automatically copies the marked text into a buffer; you don't need to press **Ctrl-C** or perform any other operation. If you find that you need to change the size of the marked text section, you can press the right mouse button and move the mouse to adjust the marked text.

TIP   Some window managers, including the Enlightenment window manager, display a pop-up menu when you click the right button, even when the mouse cursor is above text. When using such a window manager, you cannot use the right mouse button to adjust the size of the marked text section.

To paste the text, properly position the insertion point and press the middle mouse button. If your mouse has only two buttons, simultaneously press the left and right buttons to simulate pressing the middle mouse button. You may find that this operation requires a little practice before you get it right, but once you've mastered it you'll find it works almost as well as having a three-button mouse.

Using Scrollbars

Many X programs provide scrollbars that resemble those provided by Microsoft Windows programs. However, the operation of scrollbars under X differs significantly from that under Microsoft Windows.

To page forward using a X scrollbar, you click the left mouse button on the scrollbar. Clicking near the top of the scrollbar scrolls forward a short distance, as little as a single line. Clicking near the bottom of the scrollbar scrolls the window by a page.

To page backward, you click the right mouse button on the scrollbar. Again, clicking near the top of the scrollbar scrolls a short distance, as little as a single line. Clicking near the bottom of the scrollbar scrolls the window by a page.

TIP   Some X programs, redefine the operation of scrollbars to correspond to that provided by Microsoft Windows. If a scrollbar doesn't respond as you expect, try using the common Windows manipulations: left click below the scroll box to move forward, left click above the scroll box to move backward, or left drag the scroll box to a desired position.

Virtual Desktop

Under X, your desktop can be larger than the size of your monitor. For example, even if your monitor has a maximum resolution of 800 × 600, you might have a desktop of 1600 × 1200 or even 3200 × 2400. Such a desktop is known as a *virtual desktop*. Some desktop environments, including GNOME, provide a tool called a *pager*, which lets you move around the virtual desktop. The pager provides a thumbnail view of your virtual desktop; by clicking within the thumbnail, you center your actual desktop on the clicked location. Some window managers let you simply move the mouse to the edge of the desktop to scroll the virtual desktop.

Window Managers

Window managers create the borders, icons, and menus that provide a simple-to-use interface. Window managers also control the look and feel of X, letting you configure X to operate almost any way you desire. Some Linux users who are accustomed to the look and feel of Microsoft Windows 9x use the FVWM window manager to establish a user interface that resembles that of Windows 9x, both in appearance and operation. Other Linux users prefer to avoid anything resembling a Microsoft product. Table 6-1 describes the most popular Linux window managers. For detailed information about a variety of window managers, see the X11.Org web site at *http://www.x11.org/wm/*.

Table 6-1. Popular Window Managers

Window Manager	Description
AfterStep	Resembles the user interface of the NEXT computer (NEXTStep).
BlackBox	A small, simple, efficient window manager. Compatible with KWM.
Enlightenment	A highly configurable window manager.
FVWM	One of the most venerable and popular Linux window managers—small, efficient, and configurable. Can mimic the Microsoft Windows 9x user interface. Not compliant with GNOME desktop.
KWM	A window manager that sports an accompanying desktop, KDE. The combination of KWM and KDE provides a robust and efficient user interface. However, KWM includes some non-GPL code, inhibiting its adoption as the de facto standard Linux window manager. Not compliant with GNOME desktop.
SCWM	A window manager that has a powerful configuration language, based on the Scheme dialect of LISP.
Window Maker	Resembles the user interface of the NEXT computer (NEXTStep). Compatible with KWM.

At present, the two most important window managers appear to be FVWM and Enlightenment. The next two subsections describe these window managers in more detail.

FVWM

FVWM is perhaps the most popular Linux window manager. Several other window managers have borrowed from its code base, so many of its capabilities are found in other window managers. Although FVWM lacks the visual flashiness of more recent window managers, it is robust and highly configurable. However, FVWM is not fully compliant with the GNOME desktop; users who plan to use GNOME may prefer to choose a different window manager.

Enlightenment

Enlightenment is the window manager most often used with the GNOME desktop, which is described in the following section. Although Enlightenment is still under development, many Linux users find it stable enough for everyday use. Apart from being highly configurable, Enlightenment is written using CORBA (Common Object Request Broker Architecture). Programs written in any language can interact with Enlightenment via its CORBA interface. Red Hat is assisting in the development of Enlightenment, which may soon become the dominant Linux window manager.

Desktops

A desktop is a set of desktop tools and applications. The Microsoft Windows 9x desktop includes applications such as the Windows Explorer, accessories such as Notepad, games such as FreeCell and Minesweeper, and utilities such as the Control Panel and its applets. Although you can run X without a desktop, having a desktop helps you work more efficiently. The two most popular desktops used with X are KDE and GNOME.

KDE

KDE (the K Desktop Environment) is a freely available desktop that includes KWM, the K Window Manager, as an integral component. KDE provides a file manager, a help system, a configuration utility and a variety of accessories and applications, including:

- Games such as Kmines, Kpoker, and Ktetris

- Graphical applications such as Kfract, a fractal generator, and Kview, an image viewer

- Multimedia applications such as Kmix, a sound mixer, and Kmedia, a media player

- Network applications such as Kmail, a mail client, Knu, a network utility, and Krn, a news client

New KDE accessories and applications are available almost weekly. Work is underway on a complete open source office suite (KOffice) that runs under KDE. You can learn more about KDE and the status of KOffice by browsing the KDE web site at *http://www.kde.org/*.

Although KDE is freely redistributable, KDE uses the QT widget set to create user interface controls. This presents a problem, because QT is distributed under a license that many developers dislike. Therefore, the most popular desktop environment in the U.S. has been, and continues to be, GNOME rather than KDE.

GNOME

GNOME is a freely available desktop that can be used with any of several window managers, including Enlightenment. Unlike KDE, GNOME is open source software.

One of GNOME's most interesting features is session awareness. When you re-enter GNOME, it reconfigures your desktop to match the state at the time you exited, by launching each application that was open when you exited. GNOME even restores each application to its former state by, for example, moving to the page that was open when you exited.

GNOME provides desktop tools similar to those of KDE, including:

- Games such as FreeCell, Gnobots, Gnometris, and Gnome Mines

- The GNU Image Manipulation Program (GIMP)

- Network applications such as Mailman, which helps you track your mailing lists; Talk, which lets you exchanged typed messages with another user in real time; and Synchronize, which lets you synchronize files on multiple systems

- Multimedia applications such as Audio Mixer and CD Player

- General applications such as gEdit, a text editor, Netscape Navigator, a Linux version of the popular browser, and Gnumeric, a spreadsheet

- Utilities for configuring GNOME and your Linux system

GNOME developers, like KDE developers, release new applications regularly. Check the GNOME Web site at *http://www.gnome.org/* for the latest information.

Using GNOME and Enlightenment

In this section, you'll learn how to configure and use the GNOME desktop and the Enlightenment window manager. If you choose to use a different desktop or window manager, you should consult the documentation that accompanies each. However, you should read this section anyway, because the procedures for configuring various desktops and window managers are more similar than different: the way you perform each step may vary but the function of each step will not.

Launching GNOME and Enlightenment

Before starting GNOME, you must configure the X startup files. Move to the your home directory and enter the following command:

```
cp .Xclients .Xclients.SAVE
```

Be sure you include the dot before the file name. This command makes a copy of your *.Xclients* file so that you can restore it to its current state if something goes wrong. If you get an error informing you that the *.Xclients* file doesn't exist, simply ignore the error. Next, using *pico* or another text editor of your choice, edit your *.Xclients* file to contain only these lines:

```
#!/bin/bash
   gnome-session
##
```

If you want every user to be able to access GNOME, you could place a *.Xclients* file in each user's home directory. However, that would be tedious if your system had many users. Moreover, if you added a user, you'd need to create a *.Xclients* file before the new user could access GNOME.

Fortunately, Linux provides a better way. If no *.Xclients* file exists in a user's home directory, X executes the commands in */etc/X11/init/Xclients* when it starts. By placing the GNOME startup commands in that file, you can give every user access to GNOME without the need to create a *.Xclients* file in each user's home directory. As you'll learn in Chapter 13, *Conquering the BASH Shell*, this is a common Unix device. Many programs have a global configuration file that can be overridden by a user-specific configuration file. If no user-specific configuration file exists, the behavior of the program is determined by its global configuration file.

To start GNOME, type the command:

```
startx
```

You should see the GNOME desktop, as shown in Figure 6-1. The contents of your own desktop may be different, of course.

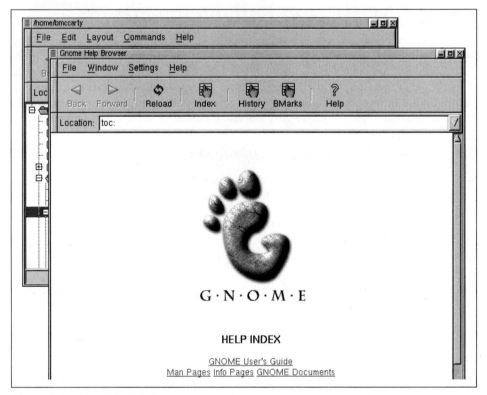

Figure 6-1. The GNOME desktop

Logging Out

To log out of GNOME, left click on the main menu, which resembles a foot, as shown in Figure 6-2. From the pop-up menu that appears, select the Log Out menu item. A Log Out dialog box, shown in Figure 6-3, appears and asks you to confirm your decision to log out. Selecting Yes terminates your GNOME session.

Parts of the Display

Figure 6-4 shows the parts of the GNOME display, which are described in the following sections.

Home directory icon

The home directory icon normally appears in the upper left corner of the display and resembles a file folder in appearance. The icon provides a convenient way to access the file manager: double clicking the icon by using the left mouse button

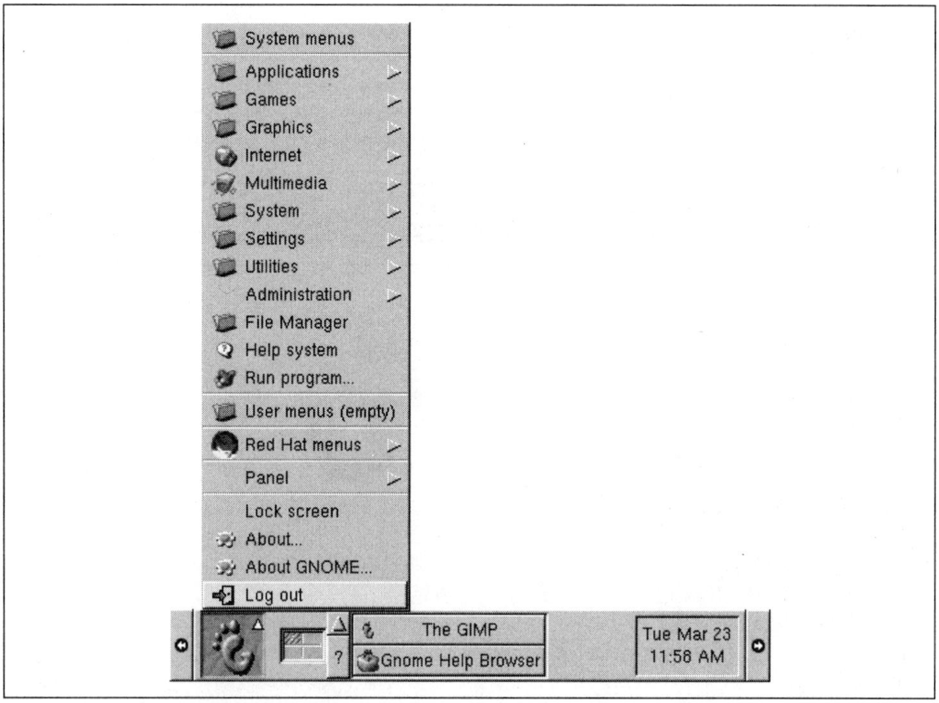

```
  System menus
  Applications        ▸
  Games               ▸
  Graphics            ▸
  Internet            ▸
  Multimedia          ▸
  System              ▸
  Settings            ▸
  Utilities           ▸
  Administration      ▸
  File Manager
  Help system
  Run program...
  User menus (empty)
  Red Hat menus       ▸
  Panel               ▸
  Lock screen
  About...
  About GNOME...
  Log out
```

Figure 6-2. Logging out of GNOME

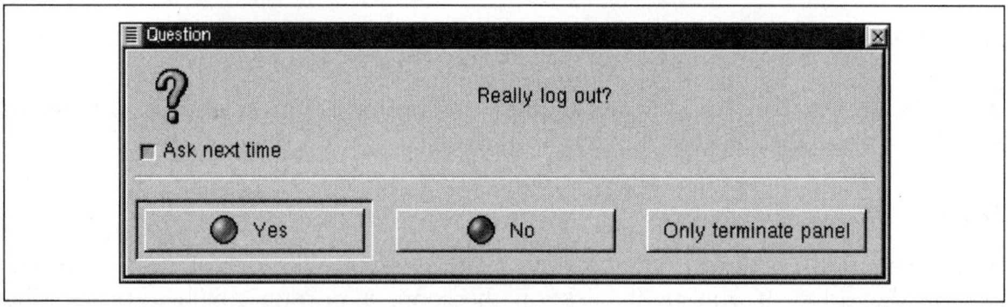

```
  Question                                          ×
    ?                        Really log out?

  ☐ Ask next time

     ●  Yes          ●  No        Only terminate panel
```

Figure 6-3. The log out dialog box

launches the file manager, which displays the contents of the user's home directory.

Desktop

The desktop is the empty area of the display, where no windows or icons appear. Clicking the desktop with the middle mouse button causes a pop-up menu to appear; the menu lets you conveniently launch popular applets and applications.

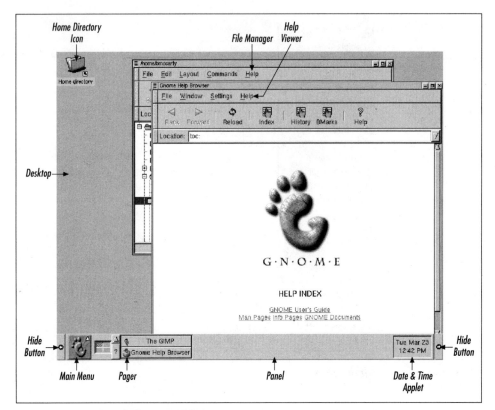

Figure 6-4. Parts of the GNOME desktop

Right clicking the desktop causes a different pop-up menu to appear; this menu lets you arrange the desktop windows and icons.

Drive icon

If you have permission to mount a drive, your desktop will include an icon representing the drive. If you right click on the icon, a pop-up menu appears. The menu lets you mount the device, eject the device's media, or open a file manager window to view the device.

Panel

The panel appears along the bottom edge of the display. However, if you prefer a different location, you can move the panel. The panel resembles the Windows 9x taskbar: You can use it to launch programs, switch from one program to another, and perform other tasks.

The panel normally contains the main menu, the pager, and two hide buttons. However, your panel may not initially display the pager.

The panel can also contain applets, programs represented as panel icons. Applets are typically small programs that display information or take action when clicked. For example, a launcher applet launches an application when clicked.

Date & time applet

The date and time applet displays your system's current date and time. If the date and time applet is not visible, you can add it to the panel in much the same way you add the pager to the panel. Simply select Panel → Add Applet → Utility → Clock from the main menu. Once you've added the clock applet to the panel, it will appear automatically the next time you start GNOME.

Main menu

The main menu resembles a big foot. Left clicking the main menu presents a menu from which you can choose a variety of programs. Several of the menu items are submenus; selecting such a menu item pops up a new menu to the side of the original menu item.

Pager

The pager lets you switch between running programs and navigate the desktop. If you don't see the pager on your panel, you can launch the pager by using the main menu, as shown in Figure 6-5: simply select Panel → Add Applet → Utility → Gnome Pager. Once you've launched the pager, it will automatically appear the next time you start GNOME.

The pager has two parts: The left part, which consists of a matrix of rectangles lets you navigate the desktop; the right part, which consists of a matrix of icons and text representing running tasks, lets you switch tasks. To switch to a task, left click the pager icon corresponding to the task.

Depending on your X configuration, GNOME may provide a virtual desktop larger than your monitor can display. In this case, the pager lets you switch between pages of the desktop. For example, Figure 6-4 shows that GNOME has provided a virtual desktop that has four pages, only one of which is visible at a time. The highlighted icon shows the page you're currently viewing as your desktop. To view a different page, simply left click the icon that represents the desktop page you want to view.

Hide button

You can hide and restore the panel by left clicking a hide button. Hiding the display is useful when you're using a window manager that likes to display a task bar or other information along the bottom of the screen.

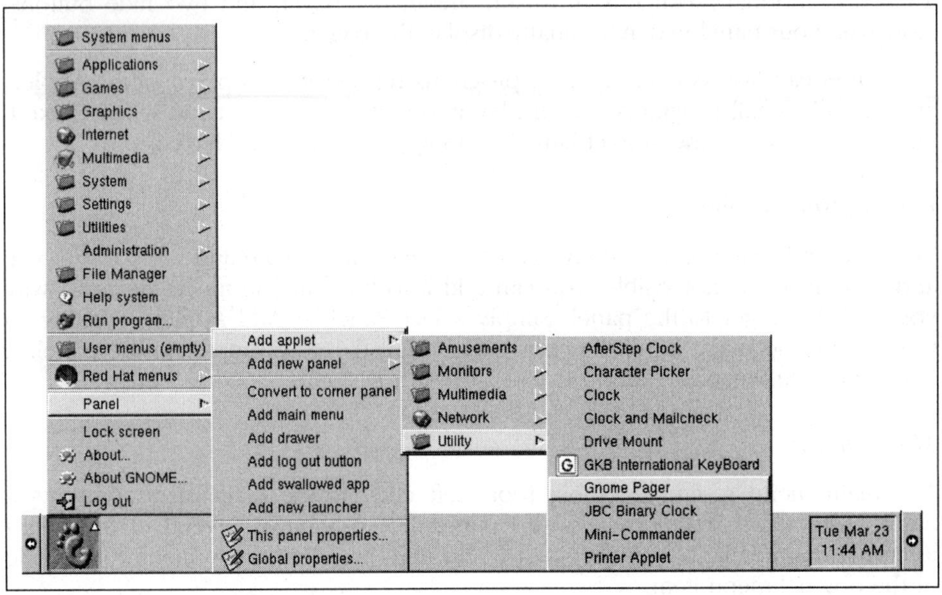

Figure 6-5. Launching the pager

Help viewer

The GNOME help viewer works much like a familiar web browser, except that you can use it to view primarily help information, not web pages. GNOME launches the help viewer whenever you select the Help menu item of an application or applet. You can also launch the help viewer by selecting the Help System menu item from the main menu.

The default home page of the help viewer includes a hyperlink that takes you to the GNOME User's Guide. The user's guide will help you discover additional useful GNOME features and capabilities.

File Manager

The file manager resembles the Windows 9x Explorer in both appearance and function. To launch the file manager, double click a directory or drive icon, or select File Manager from the main menu. The next section briefly explains the operation of the file manager.

Using the File Manager

Like the Microsoft Windows Explorer, the file manager window has two main panes.

As shown in Figure 6-6, the left file manager pane presents a hierarchical directory tree whereas the right pane shows the contents of the directory currently selected in the left pane. To select a directory, simply left click it.

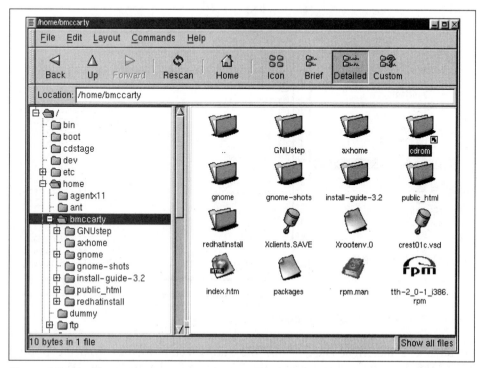

Figure 6-6. The file manager

The right pane can show an icon for each file or detailed information about each file, as shown in Figure 6-7. To switch from icon to detailed mode, left click the proper button on the file manager toolbar. You can also select custom mode, which lets you tailor the display appearance according to your own taste.

Like the Windows Explorer, the file manager can copy, move, rename, and delete files. To perform one of these operations, you must first select the file or files you want to copy, move, rename, or delete. You can select a single file by left clicking in the right file manager pane. To select additional files, hold down the **Ctrl** key as you select them. Alternatively, you can click and drag the cursor around a group of files. The Edit menu provides additional ways of selecting files.

To move a file, simply drag it to its new location. To copy a file, hold down **Shift** while dragging it. Alternatively, you can right click on a file and use the pop-up menu to specify the action you want to perform. The file manager then displays a dialog box that lets you specify additional options.

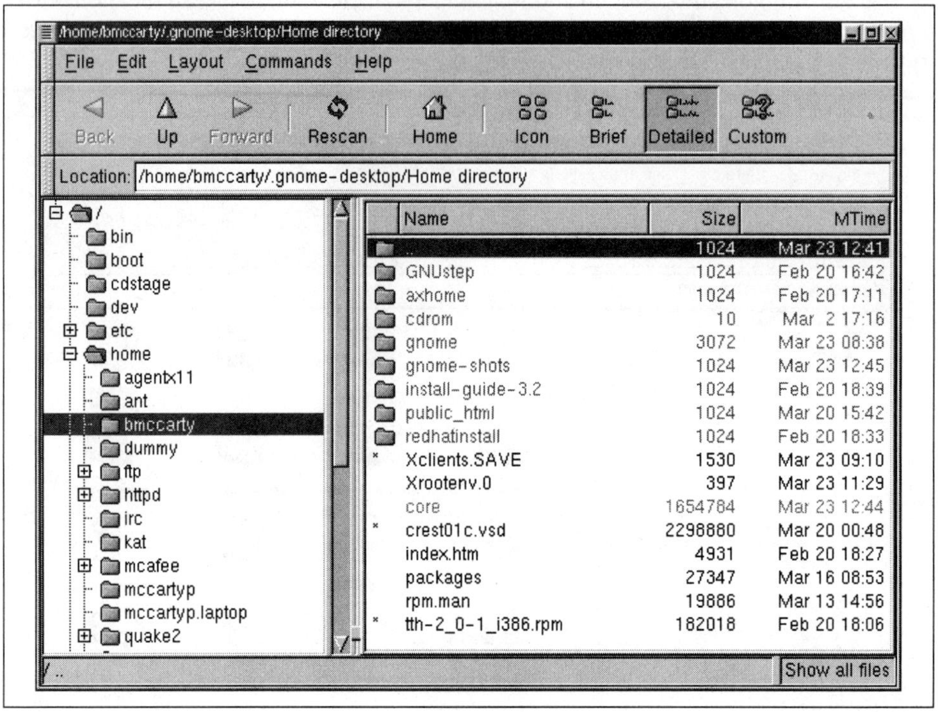

Figure 6-7. The file manager in detailed mode

To rename a file, right click on the file and select Properties from the pop-up menu. Simply type the new name in the File Name field and click on OK.

To delete a file, right click on the file and select Delete from the pop-up menu. A dialog box asks you to confirm your decision.

WARNING   Bear in mind that Linux provides no recycle bin for deleted files; once you delete a file you'll be unable to recover it except from a backup copy.

The file manager lets you double click on a file to launch the application associated with the file. Alternatively, you can right click on the file and select Open With from the pop-up menu. GNOME launches a dialog box that lets you specify the application that should be launched.

Many applications are GNOME compliant, supporting drag and drop operations like those supported by Windows 9x. For example, you can open two file manager windows and drag and drop files or directories between them.

The file manager menus provide additional functions, including the ability to configure the operation of the file manager. If you're familiar with the Windows Explorer, you'll find most of these functions and capabilities familiar. Consult the GNOME User's Guide for further information about the GNOME file manager.

Using GNOME Applets and Applications

The default GNOME installation includes several applets and applications. You can find additional applets and applications by visiting the GNOME app list at *http://www.gnome.org/applist/*. This section briefly explains two of the most popular GNOME programs, the GNOME terminal application and the GNOME CD Player applet.

GNOME Terminal

The GNOME terminal application, shown in Figure 6-8, provides a window in which you can type shell commands and view their output. To launch GNOME terminal, select Utilities → GNOME Terminal from the main menu. You can open multiple GNOME terminal windows if you like.

The Settings menu lets you configure the operation of GNOME terminal. For example, you may find that the default font is too large or too small for your liking. If so, select Settings → Preferences from the GNOME terminal window. A dialog box pops up. Select the General tab and left click the Browse button next to the Font field. A second dialog box pops up, from which you can select the font, font style, and font size you prefer.

To exit GNOME terminal, simply type `exit` on the command line and press **Enter**. Alternatively, select File → Close Terminal from the menu.

GNOME CD Player

Figure 6-9 shows the GNOME CD Player, which is represented by a window on the desktop and an icon on the panel. CD Player lets you play audio CDs though your computer's sound card. However, CD Player won't function unless you have read access to your CD-ROM's device file. If CD Player fails, log in as root and use the following command to give all users read access to the CD-ROM:

```
chmod a+r /dev/cdrom
```

This command assumes that the symbolic link */dev/cdrom* correctly refers to your CD-ROM device; if necessary, use a different argument that refers to your CD-ROM device.

The buttons that operate CD Player resemble those found on other CD Players, such as the one provided with Windows 9x. You can play, stop, or pause the CD Player, eject the CD, fast forward or rewind.

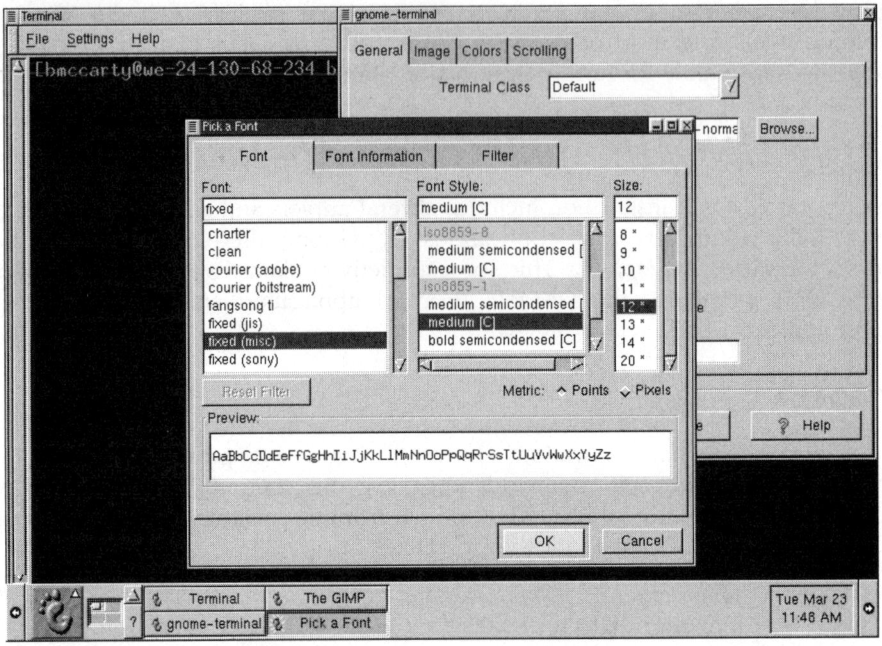

Figure 6-8. Editing terminal settings

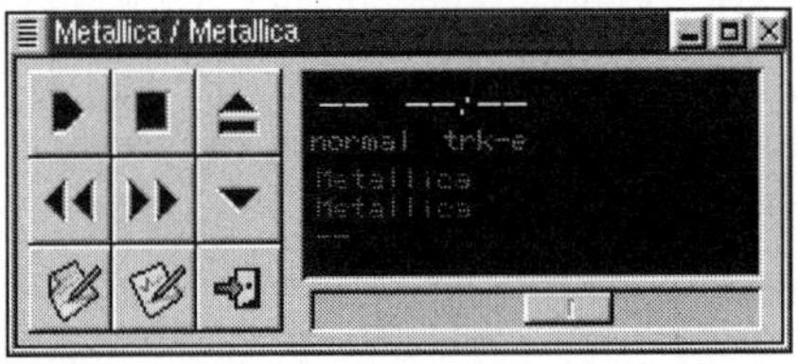

Figure 6-9. The GNOME CD Player

If your computer is connected to the Internet, CD Player can also access the database of CD information help on the CDDB Web site, *http://www.cddb.org/*. By doing so, CD Player can determine the artist and title of a CD and the titles of its tracks.

CD Player also lets you open a dialog box that lets you manually edit CD information. This is helpful if your computer is not connected to the Internet or if you find that the information on the CDDB database is incomplete or not to your liking.

Configuring GNOME

Like most GNOME applications, GNOME itself is highly configurable. You can configure GNOME's panel, its main menu, and its overall appearance and function. The following sections briefly show you how.

The GNOME Panel

You can add a launcher to the GNOME panel. Clicking on a launcher launches a predetermined application. To add a new launcher applet, right click on the panel and select Add New Launcher from the pop-up menu. The Create Launcher Applet dialog box appears, as shown in Figure 6-10.

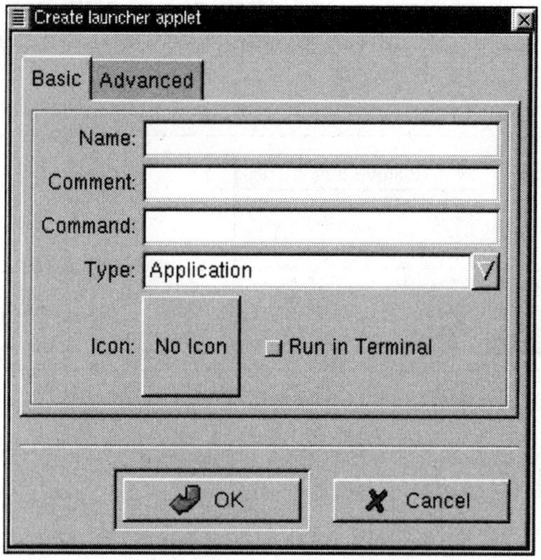

Figure 6-10. Creating a launcher applet

You can specify a name for the launcher, a comment, and the command that GNOME executes to launch the application. GNOME will automatically provide a default icon, but you can specify the icon of your choice by clicking the Icon button.

If an application is already on the main menu, you can quickly create a launcher for it. Simply right click on the application's menu item and select Add This Launcher To Panel from the pop-up menu.

If your panel contains many launchers, it may become crowded and confusing. To remedy this, you can create one or more drawers, like that shown in Figure 6-11. Drawers act like menus; you click on a drawer to open it and view the launchers it contains. Clicking an open drawer closes it and removes its contents from sight.

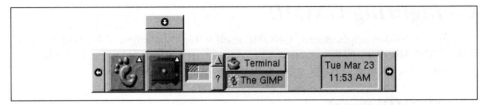

Figure 6-11. A drawer

To add a drawer, right click on the panel and select Add Drawer from the pop-up menu. To move a launcher into the drawer, right click on the launcher and select Move Applet from the pop-up menu. Move the cursor over the drawer and click the left mouse button.

If you add a launcher or drawer and later decide you don't want it, you can remove it from the panel. Simply right click on the unwanted applet and select Remove From Panel from the pop-up menu, as shown in Figure 6-12.

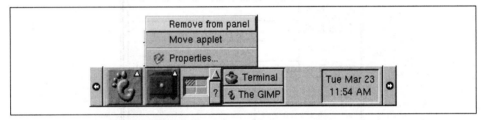

Figure 6-12. Removing a panel item

The GNOME Main Menu

You can configure GNOME's main menu by using the menu editor. To launch the menu editor, select Settings → Menu Editor from the main menu, as shown in Figure 6-13.

The menu editor window, shown in Figure 6-14, has two main panes. Its appearance and operation resemble that of the file manager. The left pane of the menu editor hierarchically displays the menu tree, whereas the right pane shows information pertaining to the currently selected menu item. You can use toolbar buttons to move the current menu item up or down the menu tree, add a new submenu or menu item, or delete the current menu item.

The GNOME Control Center

You can configure the appearance and operation of GNOME and GNOME-compliant applications by using the GNOME control center, shown in Figure 6-15. The function of Control Center resembles that of the Windows 9x control panel,

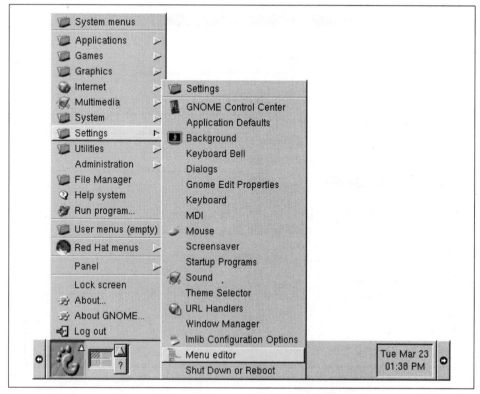

Figure 6-13. Launching the menu editor

though it looks different and works somewhat differently. To launch the control center, select System → Control Center from the GNOME main menu.

Like the Windows control panel, which uses small programs called applets to perform its functions, the GNOME control center uses small programs called capplets. However, the control center's user interface hides this detail from you, so you needn't normally be aware of what's happening behind the scenes. The control center user interface resembles that of file manager and menu editor: The left pane of the control center window presents a hierarchically structured set of configuration categories and the right pane displays information pertaining to the current choice.

Using control center, you can:

*   Select background properties
*   Configure a screen saver

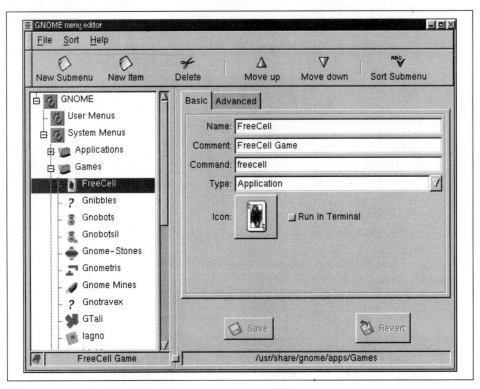

Figure 6-14. Using the menu editor

- Select a desktop theme

- Select a window manager

- Configure the default text editor

- Specify MIME types that control the handling of multimedia files

- Configure the keyboard bell and sounds

- Configure keyboard and mouse properties

- Specify applications that GNOME automatically launches when it starts

- Specify a variety of options governing the appearance of GNOME-compliant applications

Simply select the configuration category by clicking in the left pane. You can then revise the configuration parameters by specifying the desired values in the right pane. The buttons that appear in the right pane vary from capplet to capplet. The Try button lets you experiment without permanently altering the GNOME

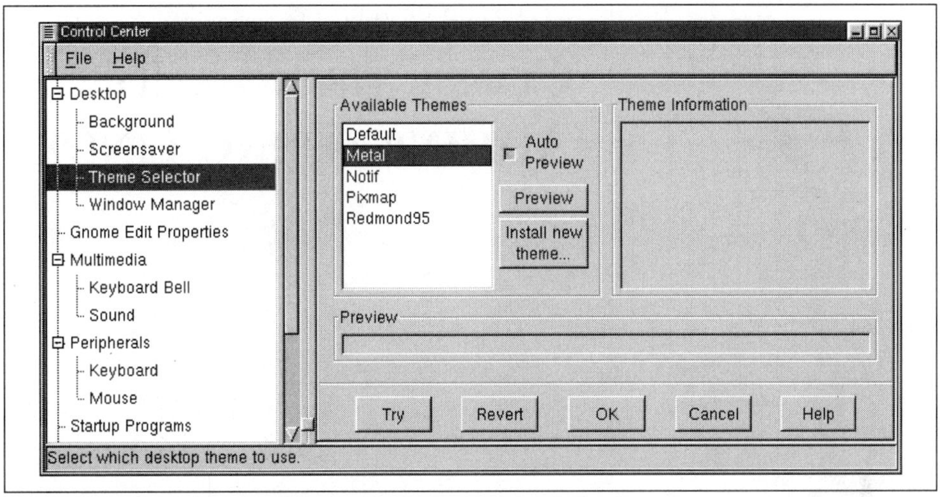

Figure 6-15. The GNOME Control Center

configuration. The OK button permanently updates the GNOME configuration whereas the Cancel button discards your changes.

CHAPTER SEVEN

CONFIGURING AND ADMINISTERING LINUX

This chapter equips you to perform common system administration tasks, focusing on tasks you can perform using *linuxconf*, a utility that provides a visual interface to system configuration information. By using *linuxconf*, you can override many configuration choices made during system installation. You'll learn how to add, delete, and modify user accounts, and how to add and delete groups and change their membership. You'll also learn how to configure swap space and how to cause Linux to automatically mount filesystems. This chapter shows how to configure LILO to load the kernel of your choice and how to use LILO to boot other operating systems. Finally, you'll learn how to use *linuxconf* to configure your system's TCP/IP networking facility.

Using linuxconf

linuxconf lets you view and modify system configuration information. Traditionally, system administrations have configured Unix systems by using a text editor to tweak files that hold configuration information, a complicated and error-prone process. *linuxconf* greatly simplifies Linux system administration: You don't have to recall what file holds what information or understand the format in which the configuration information is stored. Instead, *linuxconf* presents a menu of tasks, from which you simply choose the task you want to perform. Based on your choice, it then presents a dialog box that lets you view and change information.

148

Launching linuxconf

linuxconf supports several user interfaces: a text-based visual interface, a web interface, and a graphical user interface. The graphical user interface can't be used unless you've successfully installed and configured X and the web interface can't be used unless you've installed a web browser. This chapter focuses on the graphical user interface, which most *linuxconf* users prefer. However, the next subsection will show you how to launch both the X-based and text-based versions of the *linuxconf*. You can use the text-based version even if you haven't successfully installed X.

Launching X-based linuxconf

First, start X by typing the command:

```
startx
```

Next, select GNOME → Utilities → GNOME Terminal. When the terminal window opens, type the following commands:

```
su -
linuxconf &
```

When prompted, respond with the current password for the **root** user. The *linuxconf* utility will execute, displaying a screen like that shown in Figure 7-1.

The *su* command temporarily gives you superuser (**root**) privileges, which you must have in order to run *linuxconf*. These privileges disappear when you use the *exit* command to close the terminal. Moreover, they apply only to commands issued using this terminal.

Launching text-based linuxconf

To launch the text-based version of *linuxconf*, log in as **root**. Then type the command:

```
[root@desktop /root]# linuxconf
```

If you're already logged in, you can avoid having to log out and log in as **root**. Instead, use the *su* command, like this:

```
[user@desktop user]$ su -
Password:
[root@desktop user]#
```

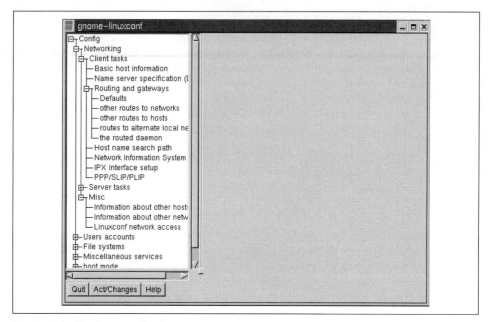

Figure 7-1. The linuxconf utility

The linuxconf Tree Menu

linuxconf presents a tree-like menu that works something like the Microsoft Windows Explorer. You can use the mouse to select an entry. If the current selection has a + at the left margin, the current selection is a menu. You can expand a selected menu by clicking the +, which causes *linuxconf* to display the menu's items, which it indents for clarity. For example, you can expand the Config item as shown in Figure 7-2. If a selected menu is currently expanded, clicking the – collapses (hides) the associated menu items. *linuxconf* provides many functions and so has many menus and submenus.

If the current item has no + at its left margin, it denotes an action you can request. Clicking the item launches a dialog box that lets you supply arguments to control the action. The dialog box appears to the right of the menu tree. For example, Figure 7-3 shows three actions:

- User accounts, which you can use to add, delete, and modify user accounts

- Group definitions, which you can use to add and delete groups, and to modify their membership

- Change root password, which you can use to change the `root` user's password

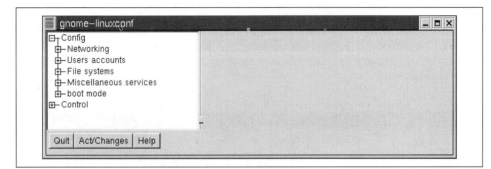

Figure 7-2. The config branch of the menu tree

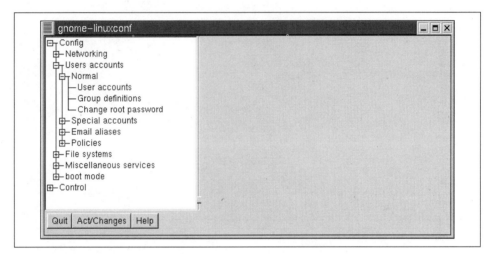

Figure 7-3. The users accounts menu tree

User and Group Administration

In this section, you'll learn how to use *linuxconf* to perform common administrative tasks affecting users and groups. You'll also learn more about the *linuxconf* user interface. Even if you're not currently interested in administering users and groups, you should read this section carefully: Subsequent sections, which focus on other administrative tasks, do not repeat the detailed information on the *linuxconf* user interface.

Configuring user accounts

To add, delete, or modify a user account, select Config → Users accounts → Normal → User accounts. In response, *linuxconf* displays the Users Accounts dialog box, shown in Figure 7-4. The Users Accounts dialog box presents the scrollable list of user accounts.

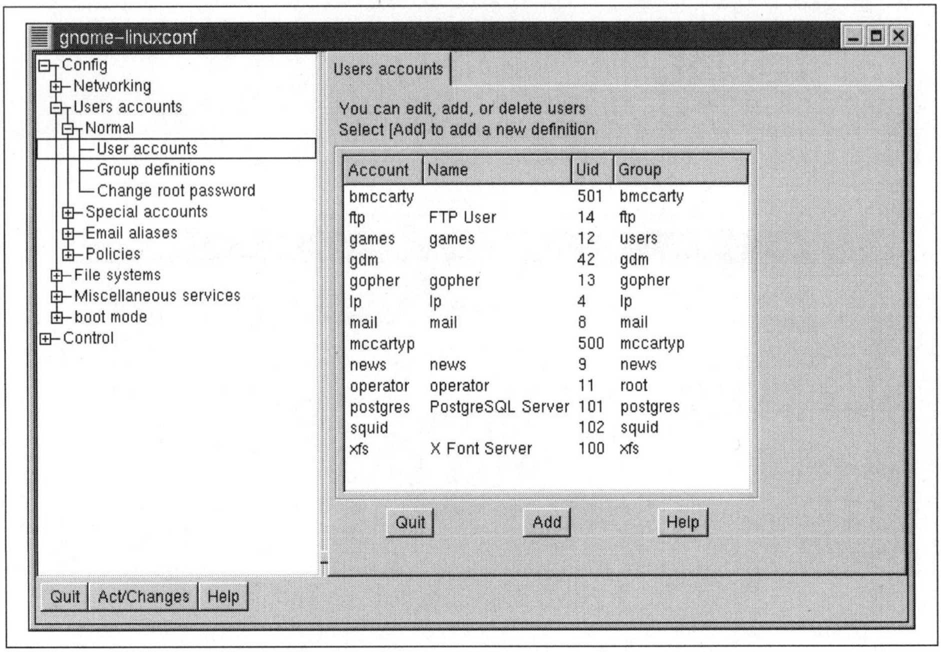

Figure 7-4. The Users accounts dialog box

You can modify or delete a user account by clicking on it. When you do so, the User Information dialog box, shown in Figure 7-5, appears. You can click Del to delete the user account; or, you can change the information associated with the user account and click Accept, which updates the configuration and returns you to the Users Accounts dialog box.

The other buttons of the User Information dialog box let you perform the following operations:

* The Cancel button exits the User Information dialog box, returning you to the Users Accounts dialog box.

* The Passwd button takes you to the Changing Password dialog box, which lets you change the password associated with the selected user account. For more information on changing passwords, see the section Changing the root password.

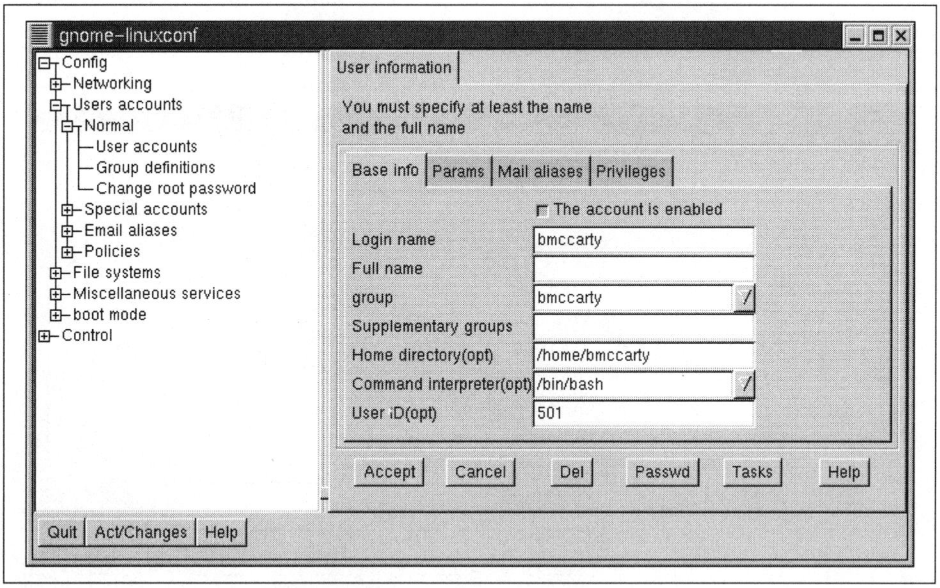

Figure 7-5. The User information dialog box

- The Tasks button takes you to the Schedule Job Definition dialog box. This dialog box lets you specify a command to be executed at a specified time or on a specified day of the week or month. For example, you can specify that a backup task will automatically run early in the morning, when your system won't be in use. See the *linuxconf* online help for more information on using the tasks facility.

- The Help button displays on-line help for the User Information dialog box, when available.

TIP   If your system is powered down, the commands queued from the Schedule Job Definition dialog won't run at the specified time. The tasks facility is more useful for servers, which are generally powered up 24 hours a day, than for desktop systems, which are generally powered up only during use.

To create a new user account, click Add on the Users Accounts dialog box. Doing so launches the User Account Creation dialog box, shown in Figure 7-6. When you create a new user account, you should always specify values for the login name and the full name. *linuxconf* provides reasonable default values for other fields, including the user ID. The user ID is a unique number which Linux uses to identify the user account. If you leave the user ID field blank, *linuxconf* will automatically assign an appropriate user ID when you select Accept.

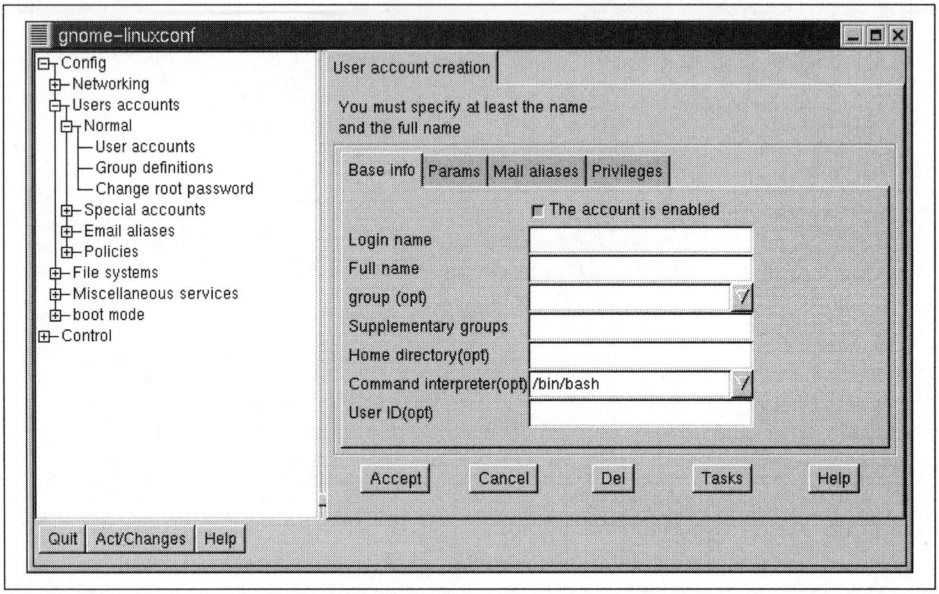

Figure 7-6. The User account creation dialog box

Configuring group definitions

Recall from Chapter 4, *Issuing Linux Commands*, that Linux uses groups to define a set of related user accounts that can share access to a file or directory. You probably won't often find it necessary to configure group definitions, particularly if you use your system as a desktop system rather than a server. However, when you wish, you can use *linuxconf* to create and delete groups and to modify their membership lists. To do so, select Config → Users accounts → Normal → Group definitions. The User Groups dialog box, shown in Figure 7-7, appears.

To modify or delete a group, click the group. The Group Specification dialog box, shown in Figure 7-8, appears. You can click Del to delete the current group. Or, you can change the group name and membership list and click Accept, which updates the configuration and returns you to the User Groups dialog box.

Changing the root password

From time to time, you should change your system's root password, particularly if your system is used as a server. To change the root password, select Config → Users accounts → Normal → Change root password. The Changing Password dialog box appears, as shown in Figure 7-9. This dialog box is the first of a series of three identically named dialog boxes that let you change the root password.

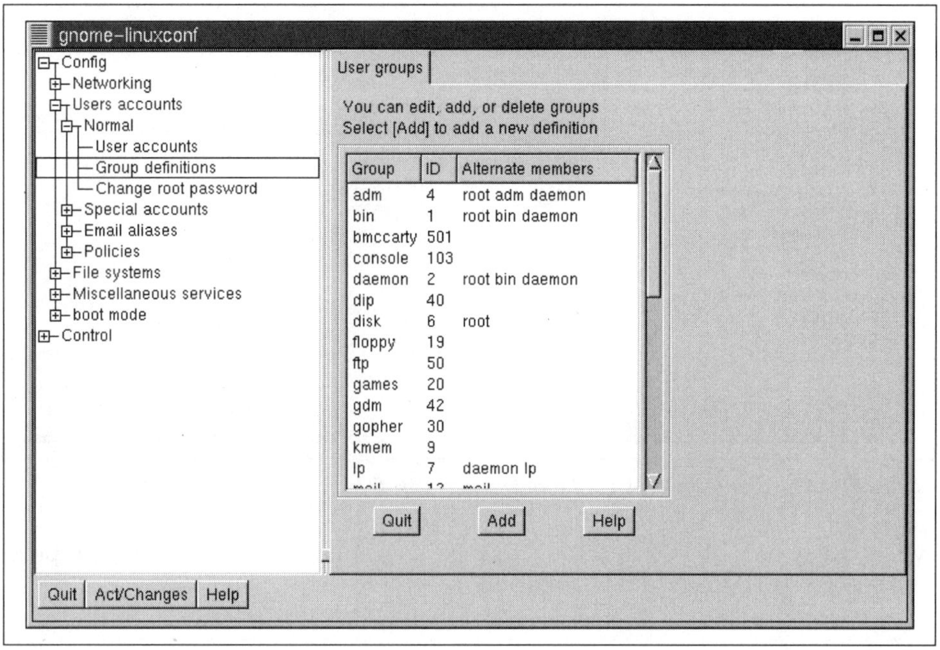

Figure 7-7. The User groups dialog box

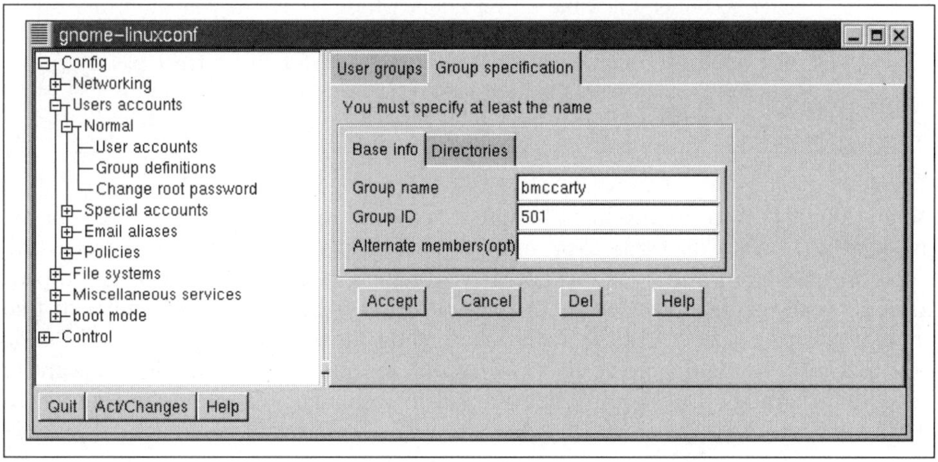

Figure 7-8. The Group specification dialog box

The first Changing Password dialog box prompts you to supply the current root password. Type the password and click Accept. *linuxconf* doesn't echo password characters as you type them, so that passersby won't inappropriately discover

155

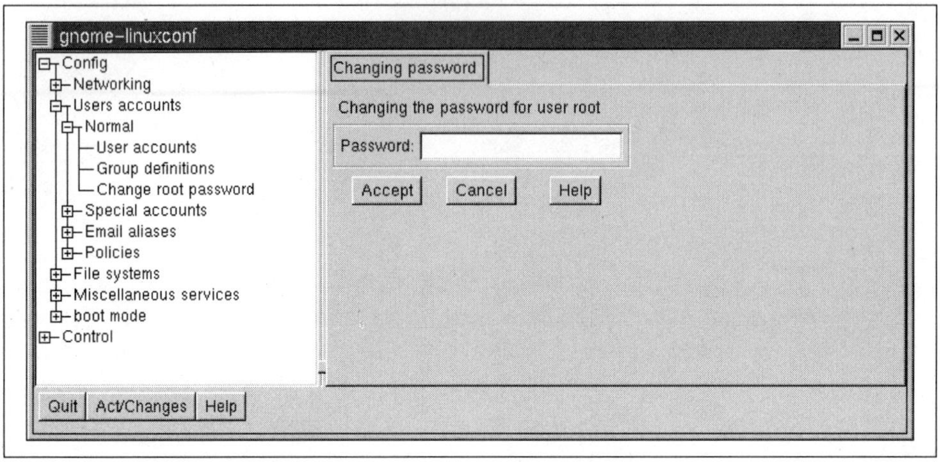

Figure 7-9. The Changing password dialog box—step 1

system passwords. If you become confused concerning what you've typed, press backspace several times and begin again.

TIP　　　The procedure for changing the password of a user account other than **root** is similar. Select Config → Users accounts → Normal → User accounts. Click the user account whose password you want to change. Then, click Passwd from the User Information dialog box that appears. *linuxconf* does not prompt you for the current password associated with the user account, because you have superuser (**root**) privileges.

When you click Accept, another Changing Password dialog box appears, as shown in Figure 7-10. This dialog box prompts you to supply the desired new password. Type the password and click Accept. If you type a password that doesn't appear to Linux to be sufficiently secure, *linuxconf* displays an error box, similar to that shown in Figure 7-11. Click Ok to proceed to the next Changing Password dialog box. Because you're the **root** user, *linuxconf* accepts your choice; if you want to heed the warning, you should click Cancel to terminate the procedure and then start over.

When you click Accept, the third and final Changing Password dialog box appears, as shown in Figure 7-12. This dialog box prompts you to retype the desired new password. Without this feature, you might type the desired password incorrectly and be unable to log in until you're able to successfully guess your error.

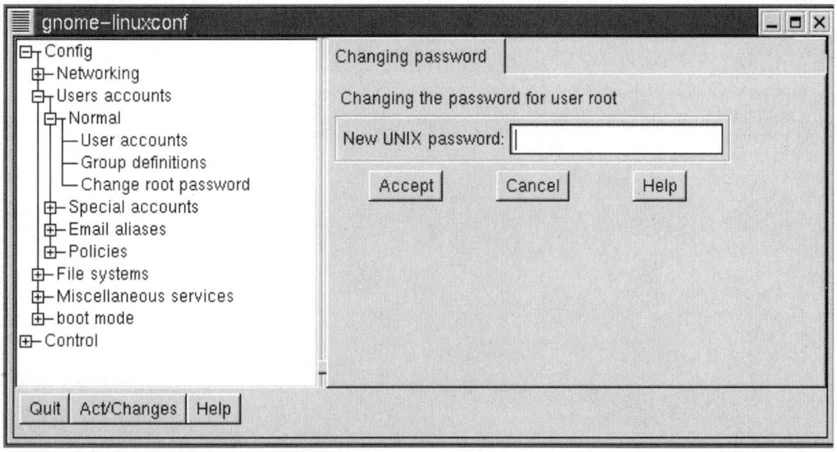

Figure 7-10. The Changing password dialog box—step 2

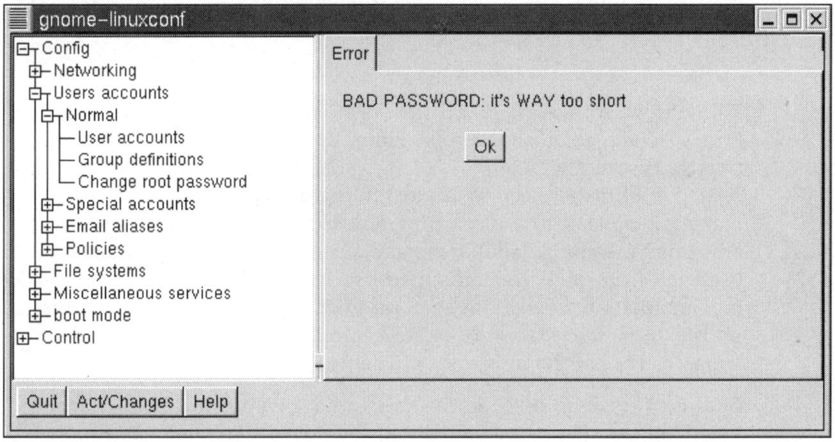

Figure 7-11. An error box

Carefully type the new password and click Accept. *linuxconf* exits the Changing Password dialog and updates the password.

Configuring password and account policies

You can adjust *linuxconf*'s policies governing passwords and accounts. For example, by default, *linuxconf* requires that passwords have a minimum length of six characters. You can easily raise or lower this value. To do so, or to change other

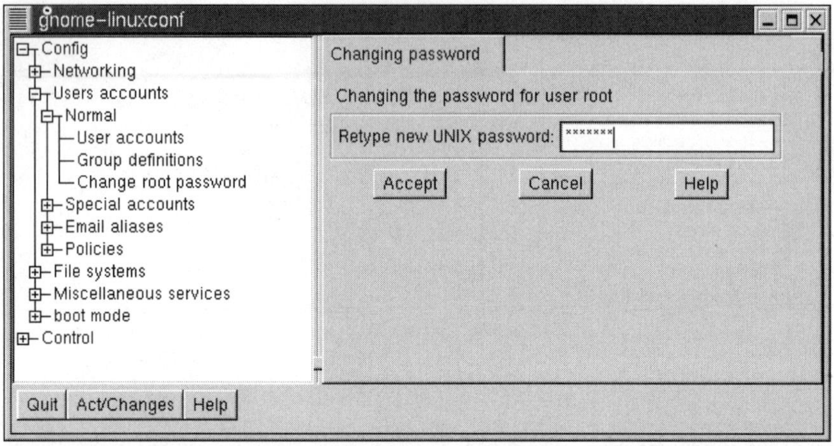

Figure 7-12. The Changing password dialog box—step 3

password or account policies, select Config $\to$ Users accounts $\to$ Policies. The Password/Account Setting Policies dialog box appears, as shown in Figure 7-13.

TIP   The current version of *linuxconf* does not cooperate with the PAM library, which contains the rules Linux uses to determine valid passwords. Historically, Linux systems scattered user- and password-related information across several files that used several formats, making it difficult to write a program that would work properly on any Linux system. A Linux program written using the PAM library is insulated from such concerns, because PAM does the work of finding information needed by the program. PAM also lets programs update user- and password-related information (assuming the program or user has the necessary privileges).

    Because *linuxconf* does not cooperate with PAM, using it to change the minimum password length or the minimum number of non-alphabetic password characters does not achieve the desired effect.

The dialog box also lets you specify whether *linuxconf* automatically creates a private group when you create a new user. If you or other users of your system frequently use groups to restrict access to files or directories, you may find it convenient to enable this facility.

The dialog box lets you change the default base directory for user home groups. Generally, the default choice, */home*, is satisfactory.

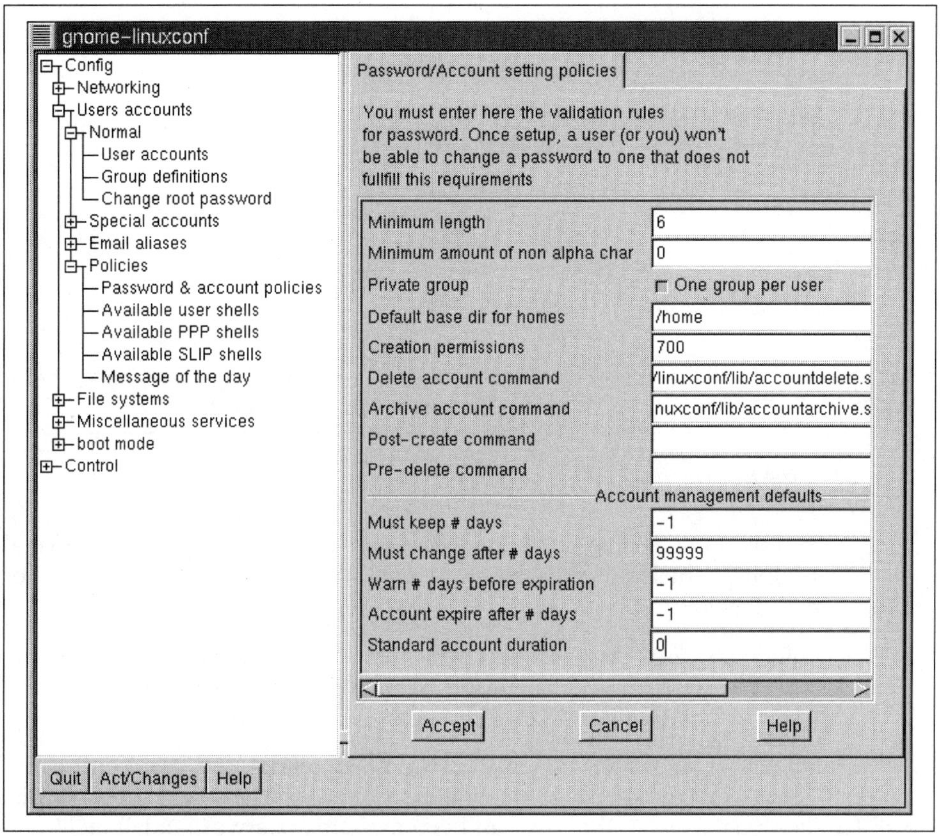

Figure 7-13. The Password/Account setting policies dialog box

The Password/Account Setting Policies dialog box lets you specify commands that *linuxconf* uses to archive or delete a user account. Generally, however, the default choice is satisfactory.

These options are useful when you request deletion of a user account. At such a time, *linuxconf* prompts you to specify how the account's data should be handled, by presenting a dialog box similar to that shown in Figure 7-14. You can:

• Archive the account's data, so that you can restore it if necessary.

• Delete the account's data, freeing disk space. In this case, you cannot restore the account's data.

• Leave the account's data in place, so that other users can access it.

You can select the desired choice by clicking it. Click Accept to delete the account.

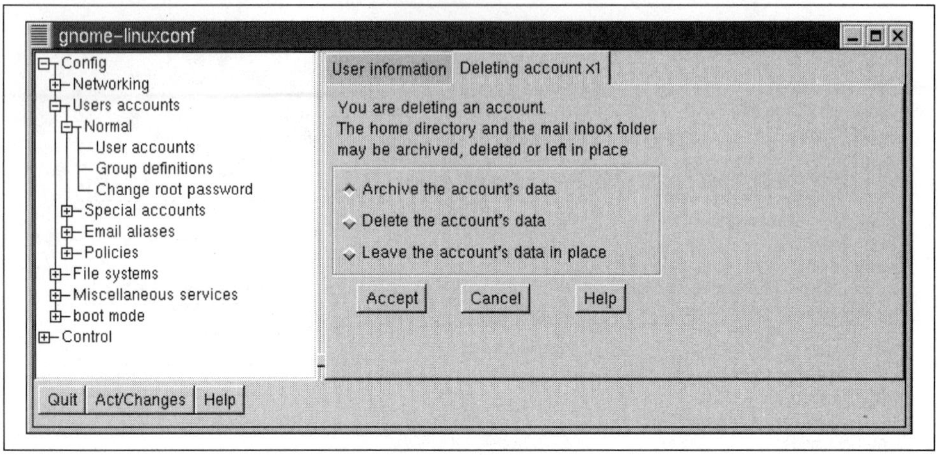

Figure 7-14. The Deleting account dialog box

The Password/Account Setting Policies dialog box also lets you specify several password options, which are applied by default when you create a new user account. These include:

- The number of days the password until the user is allowed to change the password; the user cannot change the password until this period expires. If you specify –1, the user can change the password at any time.

- The numbers of days after which the user must change the password; if the user fails to change the password when required, the account becomes disabled. If you specify –1, the user can keep the same password indefinitely.

- The number of days in advance of password expiration at which to begin warning the user to change the password. If you specify –1, the user receives no warning.

- The number of days after which to disable the account, once the password has expired. If you specify –1, the account remains enabled even after the password expires.

- The number of days until the account expires. If you specify –1, the account never expires.

Configuring special accounts

Besides user accounts, Linux supports several other kinds of accounts, including:

- PPP (point-to-point protocol) accounts, by means of which a remote host can connect to your system and establish a network connection. Most Internet Service Providers (ISPs) provide PPP accounts.

- SLIP accounts, by means of which a remote host can connect to a serial port (usually a modem) of your system and establish a network connection.

- UUCP accounts, by means of which a remote host can exchange data and email with your system, using a reliable, batch-oriented communications protocol.

- POP accounts, by means of which remote users can connect to your system and receive mail. You can also let POP users access files and printers.

Unless you operate your Linux system as a server, you won't need to configure special accounts. If you do operate your Linux system as a server, consult the *linuxconf* help facility for information on configuring these accounts.

Configuring available shells

The `bash` shell, which you met in Chapter 4, is the most popular, but not the only Linux shell. Others include:

- `ash`, a version of the `sh` shell that resembles the System V shell.

- `csh`, the C shell, favored by many users for interactive use.

- `sh`, the Bourne shell, a precursor of `bash`. Also known as the `bsh` shell.

- `tcsh`, an enhanced version of `csh`.

When you create a new user, you specify the shell (command interpreter) that Linux presents to the user when the user logs in. This shell must be on the list of available shells, which you can configure by using the Standard User Shells dialog box, which appears in Figure 7-15. To launch this dialog box, select Config → Users accounts → Policies → Available User Shells.

You must specify one shell on the list as the default shell. By default, this is the `bash` shell, which is generally a satisfactory choice. To add a new shell, use the Add button to create a new list entry and type the absolute pathname of the shell file. To change the list of available shells, use the cursor keys to select a shell and edit its name or use the backspace key to delete its name.

When a remote host connects to your system via PPP or SLIP, your system creates a session that runs a special shell. You can specify the shell by using the Available PPP Shells or the Available SLIP Shells dialog box; both dialog boxes work much like the Standard User Shells dialog box.

Filesystem Administration

You can use *linuxconf* to configure your system's filesystems. The File Systems menu, shown in Figure 7-16, lets you specify local filesystems and NFS volumes that the system should mount when it boots, configure swap space, set quota defaults, and check certain system files for proper permissions.

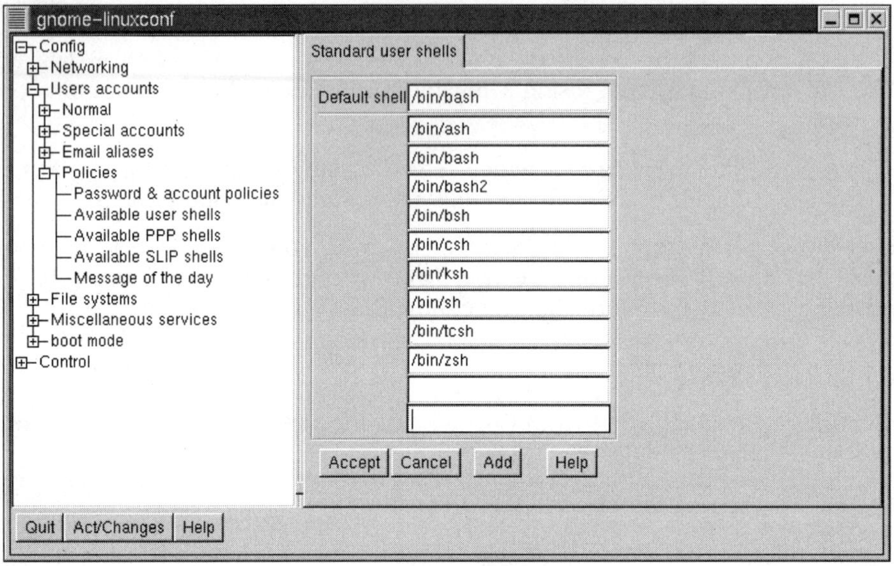

Figure 7-15. The Standard user shells dialog box

Configuring local drives

The Access Local Drive menu item launches the Local Volume dialog box, shown in Figure 7-17. This dialog box lets you specify the filesystems that Linux automatically mounts when it boots. To delete or change a local volume, click the desired entry; to add a new local volume, click Add.

In either case, the Volume Specification dialog box appears, as shown in Figure 7-18. This dialog box lets you specify the partition, the filesystem type and mount point of the local volume, as well as several options. To access the options, click Options. To toggle the state of an option, click it. When you've specified the necessary information and any desired options, click Accept to exit the dialog box and update the configuration.

Configuring NFS Volumes

An NFS (Network File System) volume is a volume that resides on another system, which makes the volume available to other systems via the network. You can mount an NFS volume as if it were a local volume by using the Access NFS Volume menu item to launch the NFS Volume dialog box. This dialog box resembles the Volume Specification dialog box; however, in addition to the information required by the Volume Specification dialog box, you must also specify the name of the server on which the NFS volume resides. NFS is a powerful and sophisticated facility that's generally beyond the scope of this book. You should consult

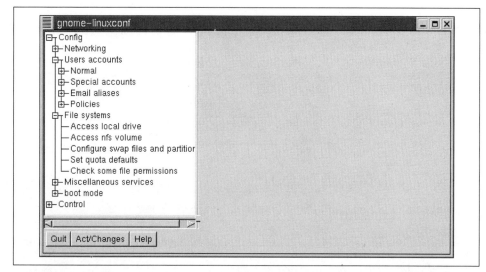

Figure 7-16. The file systems menu

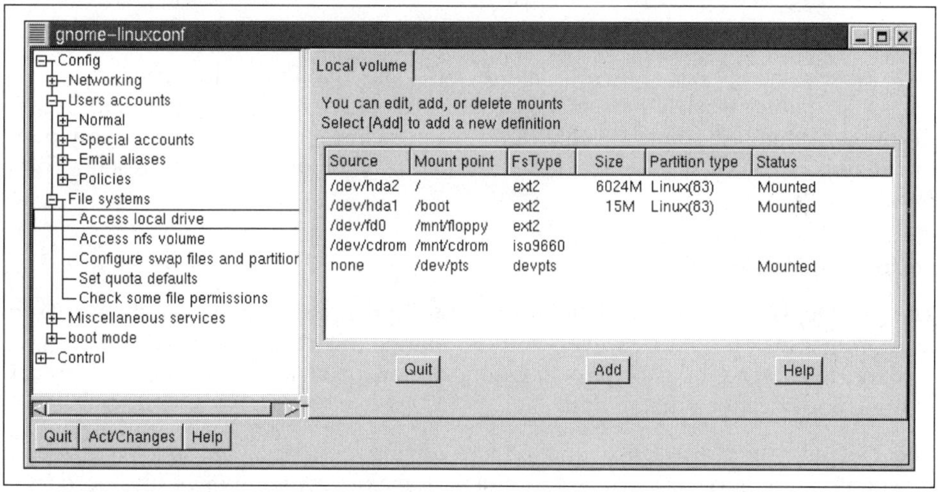

Figure 7-17. The Local volume dialog box

the Linux documentation or *Linux Network Administrator's Guide,* by Olaf Kirch
(O'Reilly & Associates, 1995).

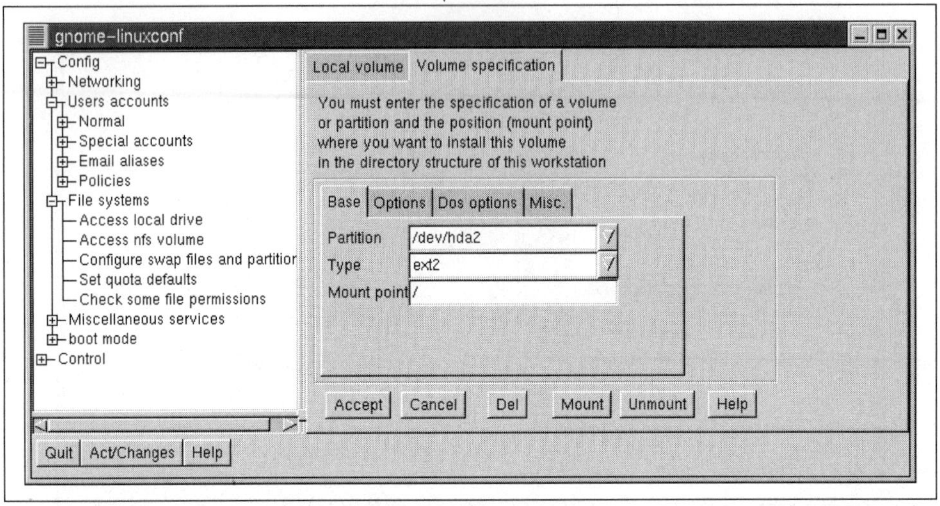

Figure 7-18. The Volume specification dialog box

Configuring swap files and partitions

You can use the Configure Swap Files and Partitions menu item to launch the Swap space dialog box, shown in Figure 7-19. This dialog box lets you view existing swap partitions, delete a swap partition, or add a new swap partition. If you properly configured your swap file during system installation, you'll probably need this dialog box only if you decide to restructure your hard drive or install a new hard drive.

Setting quota defaults

The Set Quota Defaults menu item lets you launch the Default Quota for Users and Groups dialog box. However, you can launch this dialog box only if you have enabled the User Quota or Group Quota option of at least one partition, in the Volume Specifications dialog box.

The Default Quota for Users and Groups dialog box lets you specify a default maximum amount of disk space and a default maximum number of files used by a user account or group of user accounts. This facility is generally of value only if you operate your system as a server; see the *linuxconf* help information for further details.

Checking file permissions

The Check Some File Permissions menu item launches a task that checks the ownership and access mode of several configuration files. If a file has incorrect ownership or access mode, the task will prompt you to allow it to correct the problem. If

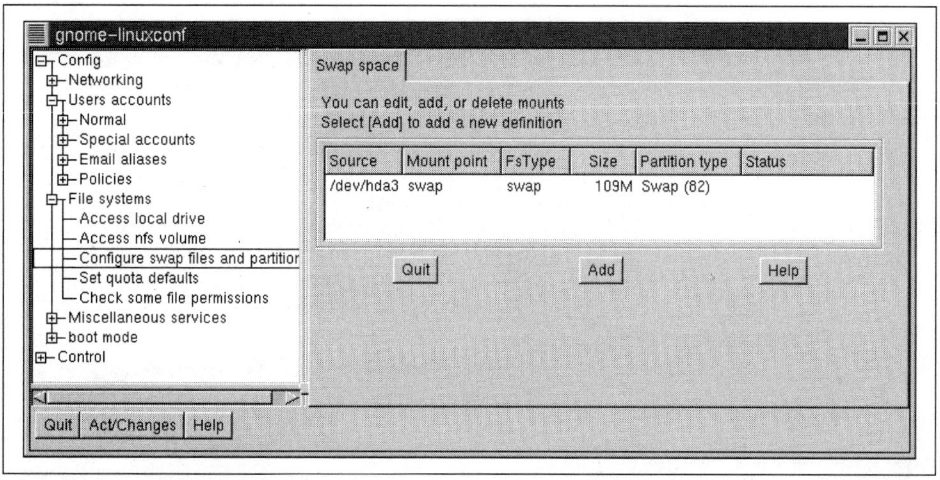

Figure 7-19. Swap space dialog box

you experience problems when you attempt to view or change configuration data, running this task may resolve the problem.

System Boot Administration

In addition to using *linuxconf* to configure user accounts and filesystems, you can use it to configure the way your Linux system boots. You can:

- Specify LILO (the Linux loader program) defaults

- Specify Linux partitions and kernels that can be booted

- Specify non-Linux operating system partitions that can be booted

- Select the default boot configuration

- Add a new kernel to an existing LILO configuration

Configuring LILO defaults

To configure LILO defaults, select Config → Boot Mode → Lilo → Lilo Defaults. The Lilo Defaults dialog box appears, as shown in Figure 7-20.

If you want to use LILO to boot your system, set the check box titled "LILO is used to boot this system"; otherwise, clear the check box. To use LILO to boot your system, LILO must reside on the boot sector of your system's boot drive; specify that device (usually */dev/hda*) as the location on which to install the boot sector.

The boot delay value instructs LILO to pause the specified number of seconds, allowing you to enter boot parameters, such as the partition you want to boot. If

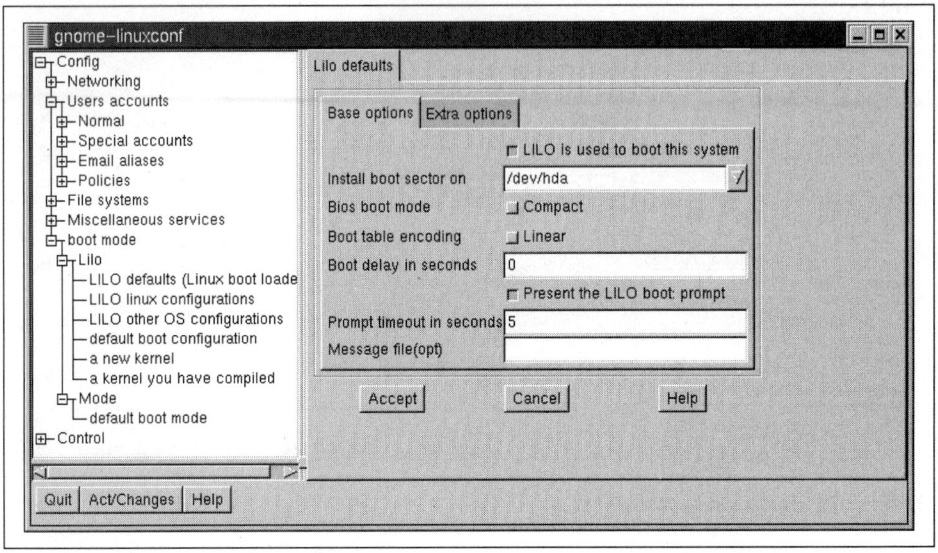

Figure 7-20. The Lilo defaults dialog box

you set the boot delay to 0, when LILO starts, it immediately boots the default Linux partition. The check box titled "Present the LILO boot: prompt" lets you enable or disable LILO's display of the boot prompt.

Generally, you need not specify any additional values. However, you may wish to set the Compact option if you boot your system from a floppy diskette; the Compact option tells LILO to read multiple sectors, when possible. Reading multiple sectors greatly reduces the time required to load a kernel from a floppy diskette.

The Linear option causes LILO to use linear addresses rather than cylinder/head/sector addresses. This option may be helpful when LILO has difficulty determining the geometry of a drive; however, it presents special problems when used with large disk drives (those having more than 1023 cylinders). Avoid it, if possible.

The Root Partition is the partition Linux will mount as / when it starts. If this option is not specified, Linux mounts the root partition specified by the kernel. Normally, the Boot Mode should be set to Read Only, letting Linux check the filesystem for errors before remounting it in read-write mode.

If you specify boot options, LILO passes these to the kernel. Boot options are useful for devices that Linux cannot properly auto-detect and devices that should not be auto-probed.

Configuring bootable Linux partitions

To configure bootable Linux partitions, select Config → Boot Mode → Lilo → Lilo Linux Configurations. The Lilo Linux Configurations dialog box, shown in Figure 7-21, appears.

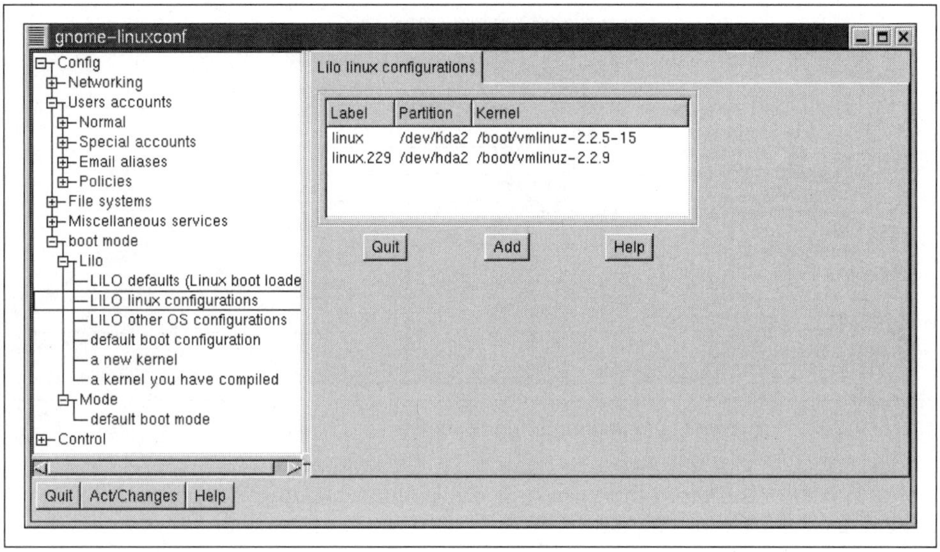

Figure 7-21. The Lilo Linux configurations dialog box

The dialog box lets you view the configured Linux partitions. You can load one of these by typing its label in response to the LILO `boot:` prompt. To modify an existing configuration, click it. The Linux Boot Configuration dialog box, shown in Figure 7-22, appears. To add a new configuration, click Add.

To modify an existing configuration, type the revised values and click Accept. To delete an existing configuration, click Del.

To create a new bootable configuration, specify a label, the kernel image file (for example, `/boot/vmlinuz`), and the root partition (for example, `/dev/hda1`). Generally, you don't need to specify additional values; however, you may need to specify boot options if Linux cannot auto-detect or should not auto-probe a system device. When you've specified all the necessary values, click Accept.

Configuring bootable non-Linux partitions

To configure a non-Linux bootable configuration (for example, a Microsoft Windows configuration), select Config → Boot Mode → Lilo → Lilo Other OSs Configurations. The Lilo Other OSs Configurations dialog box, shown in Figure 7-23, appears. If you have previously configured non-Linux bootable partitions, the

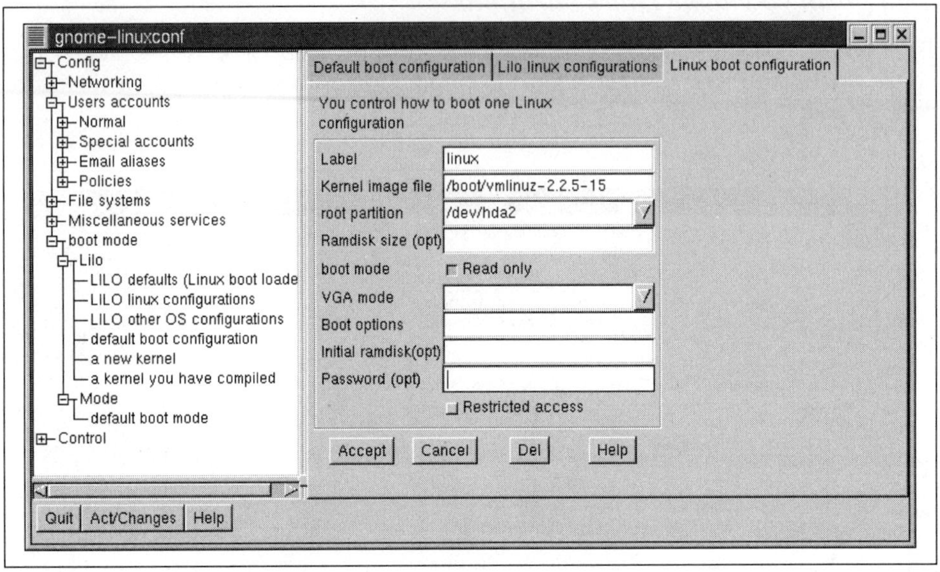

Figure 7-22. Linux boot configuration dialog box

dialog box shows them; otherwise only the column headings (Label and Partition) appear, as shown in the figure.

To modify an existing configuration, click it. The Other Operating System Setup dialog box, shown in Figure 7-24, appears. To add a new configuration, click Add. The Other Operating System Setup dialog box appears.

To modify an existing configuration, revise the Label or Partition to Boot field and click Accept. To delete an existing configuration, click Del.

To create a new bootable configuration, specify the label and the partition (for example, `/dev/hda1`), then click Accept.

Configuring the default boot configuration

As described in the section Configuring LILO defaults you can configure LILO to pause at boot time, waiting for you to specify the configuration that it should boot. You can also configure LILO to automatically boot a default operating system after a specified amount of time elapses. To specify the default configuration you use the Default Boot Configuration dialog box, shown in Figure 7-25. To launch this dialog box, select Config → Boot Mode → Lilo → Default Boot Configuration.

Use the cursor keys to select the desired default configuration, then click Accept to update the configuration.

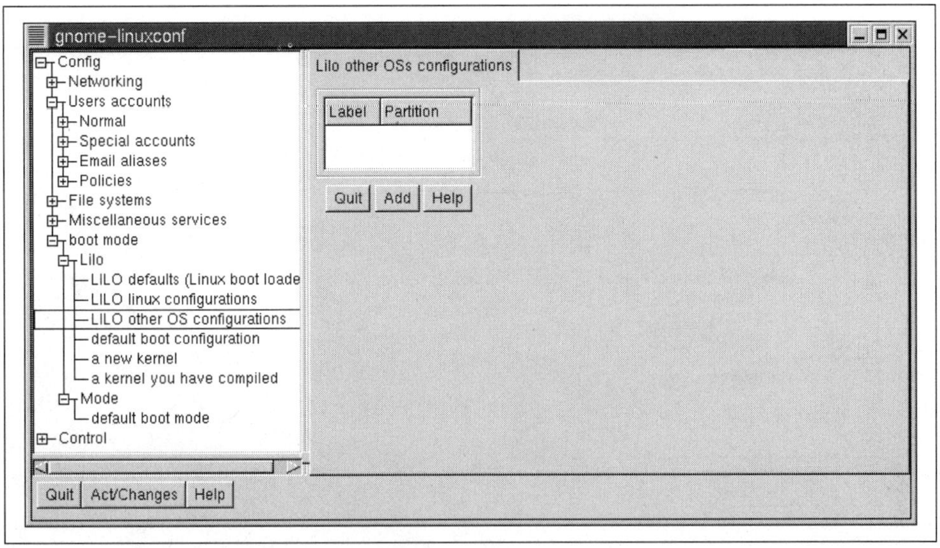

Figure 7-23. Lilo other OSs configurations dialog box

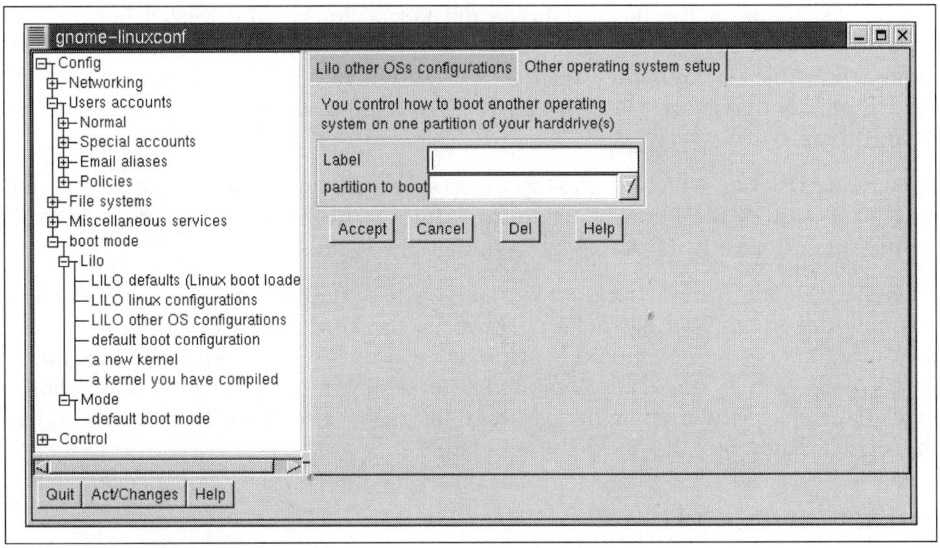

Figure 7-24. The Other operating system setup dialog box

Configuring a new kernel

You can use *linuxconf* to install a new Linux kernel. To do so, select Config →
Boot Mode → Lilo → A New Kernel. The Adding a New Kernel to LILO dialog
box appears, as shown in Figure 7-26.

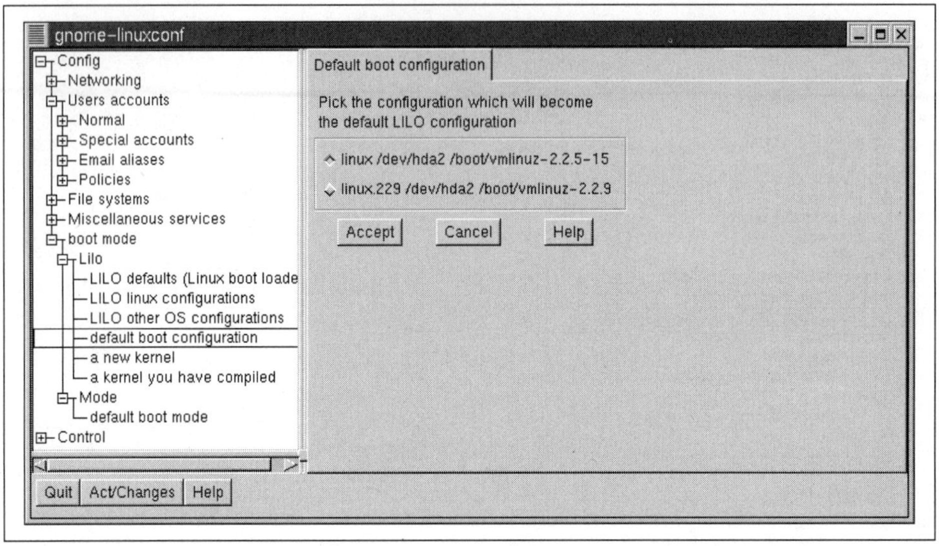

Figure 7-25. The Default boot configuration dialog box

Specify the name of the file that holds the kernel image (the Kernel Image File) and how you want to boot the kernel (How It Boots). You can create a new default bootable configuration, replace the current bootable configuration, or create a new configuration that you can boot by typing its label in response to the boot: prompt.

Specify the label by which to identify this configuration and the directory in which you want to store the kernel (Where to Copy the Kernel File). Specify other values as needed. Finally, click Accept to update the configuration.

If you've recently compiled a new kernel, you may find it more convenient to use a similar dialog box that has default values for the kernel image file and the directory in which the kernel should be stored. To do so, select Config → Boot Mode → Lilo → A Kernel You Have Compiled. The Adding a New Kernel to LILO dialog box appears, as shown in Figure 7-27. Use the dialog box n the same way you use the similar dialog box that lacks these defaults.

Configuring the boot mode

You can configure Linux to launch *linuxconf* as part of the boot process. To do so, select Config → Boot Mode → Mode → Default Boot Mode. The Boot Mode Configuration dialog box appears, as shown in Figure 7-28.

You can enable and disable the boot time menu that provides access to *linuxconf* and specify whether *linuxconf* runs in graphic or text mode. The Delay to Activate value specifies that a pause of specified duration (in seconds) should precede the

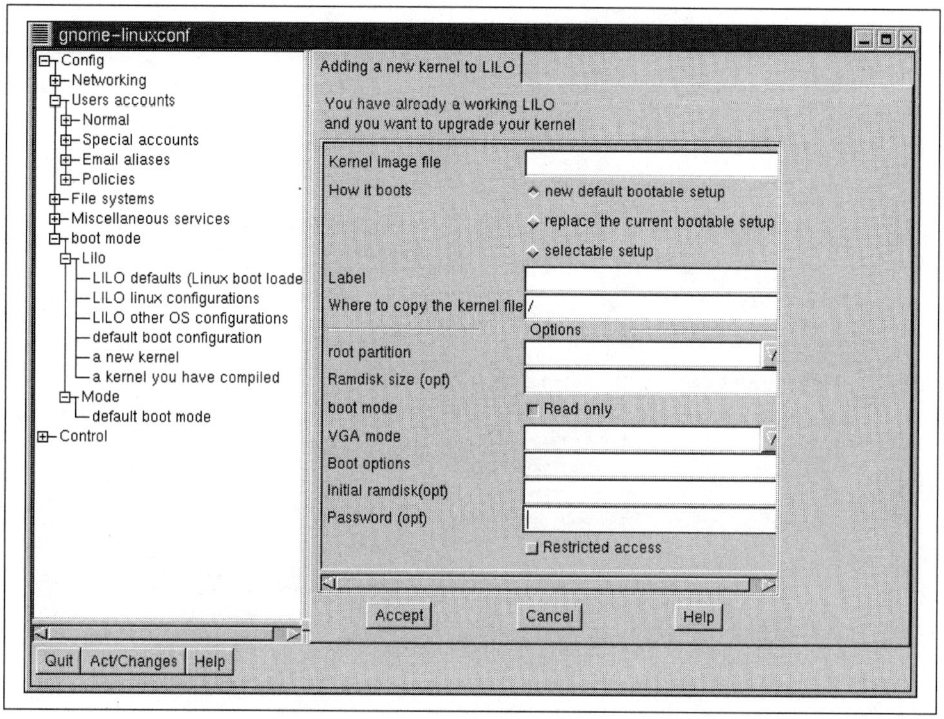

Figure 7-26. The Adding a new kernel to LILO dialog box

launch of *linuxconf*. Specifying a delay of 0 indicates that *linuxconf* should launch immediately.

The Prompt Timeout value specifies that, after the specified interval (in seconds), the default operation mode will be selected. Specifying a timeout of 0 causes *linuxconf* to wait indefinitely for a response.

Using the linuxconf Control Menu

The *linuxconf* Control menu tree includes:

- A control panel that lets you control and configure services and facilities

- A set of dialog boxes that let you control files and systems

- A set of dialog boxes that let you control system logs

- A dialog box that lets you set the date and time

- A dialog box that lets you configure *linuxconf* features

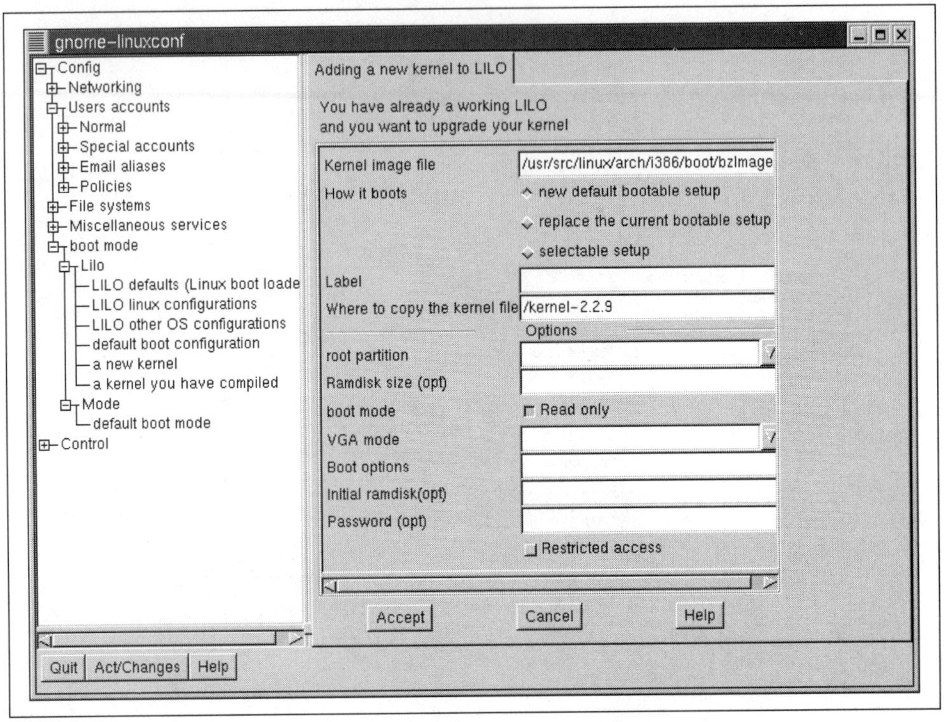

Figure 7-27. The Adding a new kernel to LILO dialog box with default values

The following sections briefly present the operation of these dialog boxes. Because you'll seldom (if ever) use them, the dialog boxes are not explained in detail. You can consult the *linuxconf* on-line help to learn more about them.

The Control Panel

Figure 7-29 shows the Control Panel menu tree, which includes the following items:

- Activate configuration, which restores the system configuration to the state recorded by *linuxconf*

- Shutdown/Reboot, which lets you shutdown and halt the system or reboot it (a task often easier to perform from the shell prompt)

- Control service activity, which lets you selectively enable and disable system services, temporarily or permanently

- Configure superuser scheduled tasks, which lets you specify tasks to be performed at predetermined times

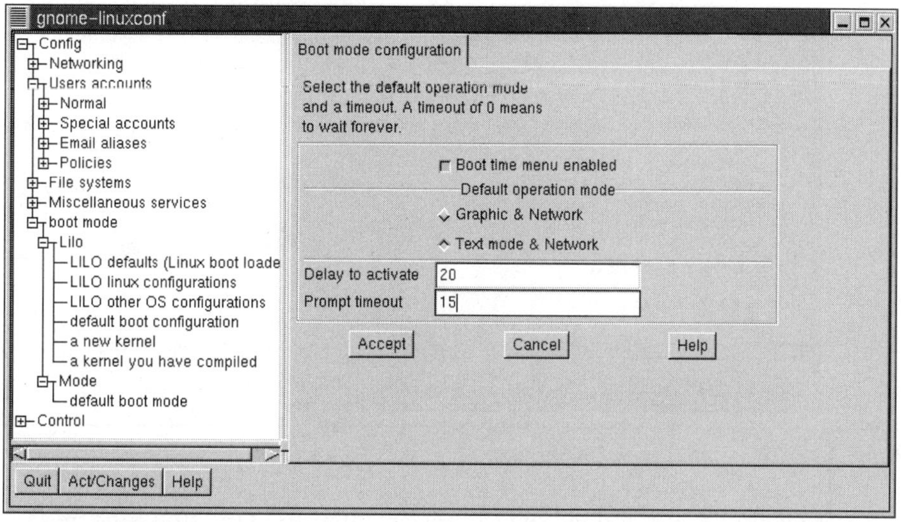

Figure 7-28. Boot mode configuration Dialog Box

- Archive configurations, which archives your system configuration information

- Switch system profile, which lets you manage and use multiple system configurations, switching between them by using this menu item

- Control PPP/SLIP/PLIP links, which lets you activate and deactivate PPP, SLIP, and PLIP links

Controlling Files and Systems

The Control Files and Systems submenu is shown in Figure 7-30. Its items include:

- Configure all configuration files, which describes the configuration files used by Linux and lets you assign them to different paths

- Configure all commands and daemons, which lets you change the way a background task is invoked, the path of the task's command file, and the task's command line arguments

- Configure file permission and ownership, which lets you change the permission settings of any file or directory managed by *linuxconf*

- Configure *linuxconf* modules, which lets you install new *linuxconf* modules that enhance its functionality

- Configure system profiles, which lets you define multiple versions of your system's configuration

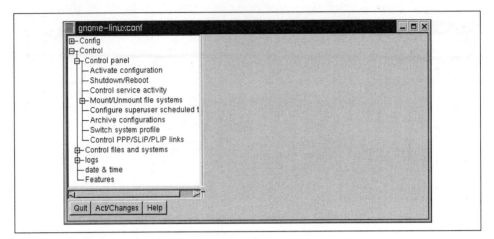

Figure 7-29. The Control panel menu tree

- Override *linuxconf* addons, which specify how to start, stop, and restart a package

- Create *linuxconf* addons, which lets you create your own addons to control packages

---

WARNING   The Control Files and Systems menu provides functions that can cause system instability if used improperly. For example, the Configure all configuration files function lets you specify a new path for a system configuration file; but, some programs may not correctly access the file at its new location. Use these functions only if you're confident that you know what you're doing and only if you have a reliable backup of your system.

Controlling systems messages and logs

linuxconf lets you view system messages and logs. The items of the Logs menu (shown in Figure 7-30) include:

- Boot messages, which lets you view boot messages. You can find these messages helpful in identifying and resolving system problems.

- *linuxconf* logs, which lets you view logs created whenever *linuxconf* issues a configuration command. You may find these messages helpful in troubleshooting problems with your configuration.

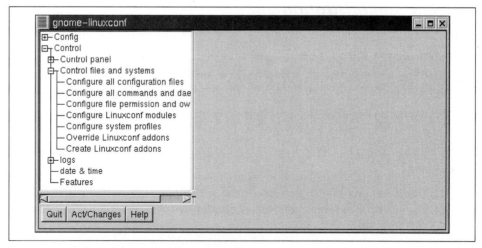

Figure 7-30. The Control files and systems menu tree

Controlling other facilities

linuxconf also lets you set the current date and time and define some special *linuxconf* behavior. To set the date and time, select Control → Logs → Date & Time. The Workstation Date and Time dialog box appears. This dialog box lets you:

- Select the proper timezone.

- Choose to store the date and time in CMOS (non-volatile) memory or obtain it from a specified time server.

- If you choose to store the date and time in CMOS, set the current date and time.

The Features menu item of the Logs menu lets you:

- Specify a custom keyboard mapping.

- Select the language in which *linuxconf* messages appear.

- Configure options that control the use of *linuxconf* via a web browser.

Consult the online help for more information about these specifications and options.

Network Administration

linuxconf's Config menu tree includes a Networking submenu that includes three submenus:

- The Client tasks submenu, which lets you configure basic networking facilities used by clients (see Figure 7-31).

- The Server tasks submenu, which lets you configure more sophisticated networking facilities used by servers (see Figure 7-32).

- The Misc submenu, which lets you configure other aspects of network operation.

The following sections briefly describe these submenus and the dialogs they provide. You'll learn more about network configuration in Chapter 11, *Getting Connected to the Internet.*

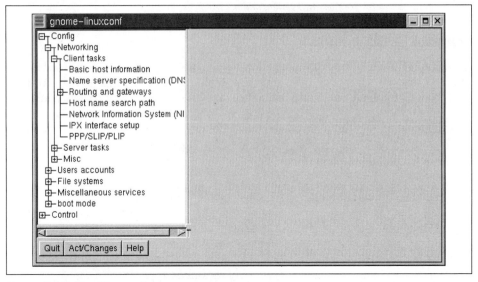

Figure 7-31. The Client tasks menu tree

The Client Tasks menu

The Client Tasks menu includes the following items and submenus:

- Basic host information, which lets you specify the host name of the system and configure the network adapters hosted by the system. For each adapter, you can specify how the adapter obtains its network configuration (manually, via DHCP, or via BOOTP), the IP address, the netmask, and so on.

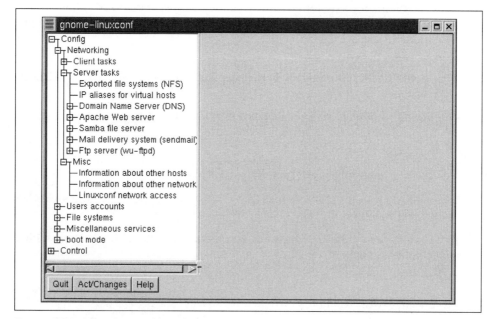

Figure 7-32. The Server tasks and Misc menu trees

- Name server specification (DNS), which lets you specify how the system translates host names into IP addresses.

- Routing and gateways. This submenu includes the following items:

  - Defaults, which lets you specify the address of the default gateway and whether your system is allowed to route packets.

  - Other routes to networks, which lets you specify routes to networks other than the local network that includes your system.

  - Other routes to hosts, which lets you specify routes to particular hosts outside the local network that includes your system.

  - Routes to alternate local nets, which lets you specify alternate routes to networks other than the local network that includes your system.

  - The routed Daemon, which lets you specify whether your system should export your default route and other routes.

- Host name search path, which lets you specify the order in which your system will access various information services when it needs to determine an IP address.

- Network Information System (NIS), which lets you specify an NIS domain and NIS server, if your system is part of an NIS domain. NIS is an auxiliary component of NFS.

- IPX Interface setup, which lets you configure IPX networking for compatibility with non-TCP/IP systems. IPX is the standard protocol used by Novell Netware systems.

- PPP/SLIP/PLIP, which lets you specify PPP, SLIP, or PLIP network interfaces.

The Server Tasks menu

The Server Tasks menu includes the following items and submenus:

- Exported file systems (NFS), which lets your system export directories via NFS (Network File System).

- IP aliases for virtual hosts, which lets you associate multiple IP numbers with a single network adapter.

- UUCP (Unix to Unix copy). This submenu lets you:

    - Specify UUCP configurations.

    - Specify UUCP devices.

    - Specify scheduled UUCP tasks.

The Misc menu

The Misc menu includes the following items:

- Information about other hosts, which lets you modify your system's *hosts* file.

- Information about other networks, which lets you modify your system's *networks* file.

- *linuxconf* network access, which lets you configure which hosts or networks are allowed to access *linuxconf* to configure your system.

CHAPTER EIGHT

USING LINUX
APPLICATIONS
AND CLIENTS

This chapter describes how you can use Linux to perform word processing and other common desktop computing tasks. The chapter introduces you to some of the most popular Linux desktop suites and applications, describing their capabilities and telling you where and how to obtain them. The chapter also introduces VMware, a program that lets you run Microsoft Windows and Linux simultaneously, and WINE, a program that lets you run some Microsoft Windows applications under Linux.

Linux Desktop Applications

Not long ago, running Linux meant abandoning your easy-to-use WYSIWYG word processor or configuring your system for dual boot, so that you could boot Microsoft Windows or IBM OS/2 to access friendly and familiar desktop applications. At that time, Linux supported no robust, full-featured graphical desktop suites.

Today, Linux supports several desktop suites; several more are under development. Apparently, if rumors are to be believed, even Microsoft is considering adapting their Office desktop suite to run under Linux. Whether or not Linux users can expect to soon run Microsoft Office for Linux (or whatever name Microsoft might give this potential product), Linux users who prefer to avoid other operating systems can now do so without compromising their ability to produce first-rate documents, spreadsheets, and graphics.

This section describes the three most popular desktop applications for Linux:

- Applix Applixware
- Corel WordPerfect for Linux
- Star Division's StarOffice

In addition, this section briefly describes other desktop options:

- Angoss SmartWare
- Axene Xclamation
- KOffice
- Lotus eSuite
- Quadratron Cliq
- TeX

The final section presents two entirely different approaches to desktop computing:

- The VMware virtual platform, which lets you run Windows and Linux simultaneously on a single computer
- WINE, which lets you run DOS and Windows programs under Linux

Applix Applixware

Applix distributes Applixware, a desktop suite available for a variety of platforms, including Microsoft Windows 9x, Microsoft Windows NT, and several varieties of UNIX, including Linux. Applixware is commercial software, but much less expensive than Microsoft Word. Currently, Applixware for Linux is priced at $99 (US); you can purchase it from the Applix web site, *http://www.applix.com/.* Print documentation and support programs are also available, at additional cost. If you prefer to try before buying, you can download a feature-disabled demo version; however, the download is quite large (over 38 MB) and therefore time-consuming (over 3 hours at 28.8 Kbps) unless you have a high-speed connection to the Internet.

Applixware includes eight main components:

- Words, a WYSIWYG word processor
- Spreadsheets, a graphical spreadsheet application
- Presents, a presentation graphics application
- Graphics, a drawing, charting, and graphics editing application

- Mail, an email client

- HTML Author, an application for authoring web documents

- Data, an application for accessing data held in Oracle, Informix, Sybase, or CA-Ingres databases

- Builder, an application development environment for decision support systems

Installing Applixware

To install Applixware from an Applixware distribution CD-ROM, log in as `root` (or use the *su* command to become the root user), mount the CD-ROM diskette, change to the directory that is the mount point of the CD-ROM device, and issue the `setup` command:

```
su
mount -t iso9660 /dev/cdrom /mnt/cdrom
cd /mnt/cdrom
./setup
```

The install program will guide you through the installation process.

Running Applixware

Once the installation is complete, you can run Applixware by starting X and using a terminal window to issue the following commands:

```
DISPLAY=localhost:0
/opt/applix/applix
```

If you installed Applixware to a directory other than */opt/applix*, you'll need to adapt the second command accordingly.

When Applixware starts up, it displays a window containing the Applixware main menu, shown in Figure 8-1. From the toolbar of the main menu, you can simply click to launch Words, Graphics and Presents, Spreadsheets, Mail, or Data. Alternatively, you can click on the asterisk icon, causing Applixware to display a menu, as shown in Figure 8-2.

Figure 8-3 shows the Words application. Words includes a spelling checker and supports document templates, tables, multimedia, and live links to Applixware and third-party documents. Moreover, it lets you import and export a variety of document formats, including Microsoft Word 2.0, 6.0, 7.0/95, and 97.

Figure 8-4 shows the Presents application, which lets you create presentations in a way that resembles that provided by Microsoft PowerPoint. Presents provides features such as transitions and animation, HTML export, and templates. Its drawing tools let you draw lines, curves, and shapes, and perform other operations, such as rotations and fills. Presents can also import and export PowerPoint presentations and a variety of other document types.

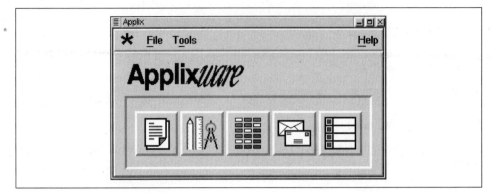

Figure 8-1. The Applixware main menu

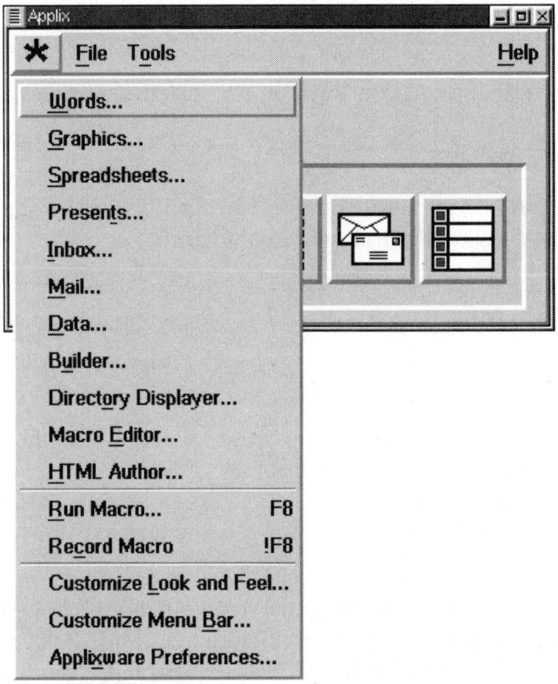

Figure 8-2. The Applixware application menu

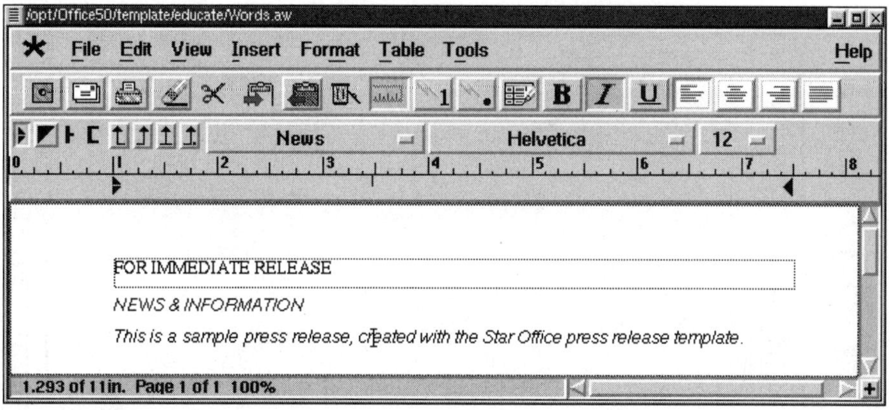

Figure 8-3. The Words application

TIP	Although a Linux application, such as Words or Presents, may be able to import a Microsoft Office document, the application may not be able to handle the full range of document and object types that can be embedded in an Office document. Some document and object types, for example, require access to a host application that runs only under Microsoft Windows.
	Moreover, some Linux applications do not currently support all the styles and options of their Office counterparts. For example, if a document uses Microsoft's Visual Basic for Applications, the document will probably not function correctly under Linux.
	If you plan on moving documents to and from Office, you may want to save your documents in a portable format (such as RTF), rather than a Microsoft proprietary format. This will significantly improve the chances that your document will work correctly both in Windows and Linux.

Figure 8-5 shows the Spreadsheets application, which provides functions similar to those of Microsoft Excel. Spreadsheets lets you create ordinary spreadsheets as well as 3D charts and sheets, and supports live links to objects created by Applixware and third-party applications, including Applix Data, which provides access to relational databases. Spreadsheets implements Applix's Extension Language Facility (ELF), which lets you add custom functions to the hundreds of built-in functions. Spreadsheets can import and export a variety of document types, including Lotus 1-2-3 (WKS, WK1, WK3, and WK4 files) and Microsoft Excel 3.0, 4.0, 5.0, 7.0/95, and 97.

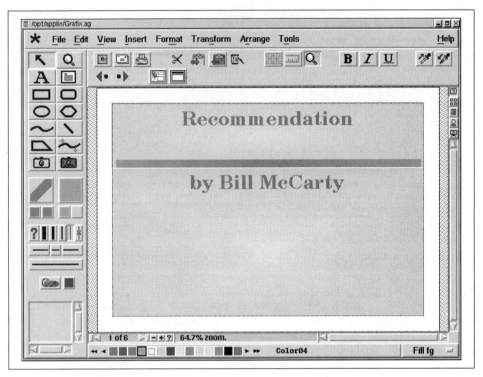

Figure 8-4. The Presents application

StarOffice

Another popular Linux desktop suite is StarOffice, a product of Star Division. StarOffice Personal Edition is available free of charge for non-commercial (home) use, from Star Division's web site, *http://www.stardivision.com/*. The download is about 70 MB, requiring over 6 hours at 28.8 Kbps. A deluxe edition is available on CD-ROM diskette. The deluxe edition provides a printed manual and additional templates, clipart files, and fonts; the deluxe edition is currently priced at $39.95 (US).

StarOffice includes an extensive range of applications, including:

- StarDesktop, a file manager and desktop

- StarWriter, a word processor

- StarCalc, a spreadsheet application

- StarDraw, a drawing application

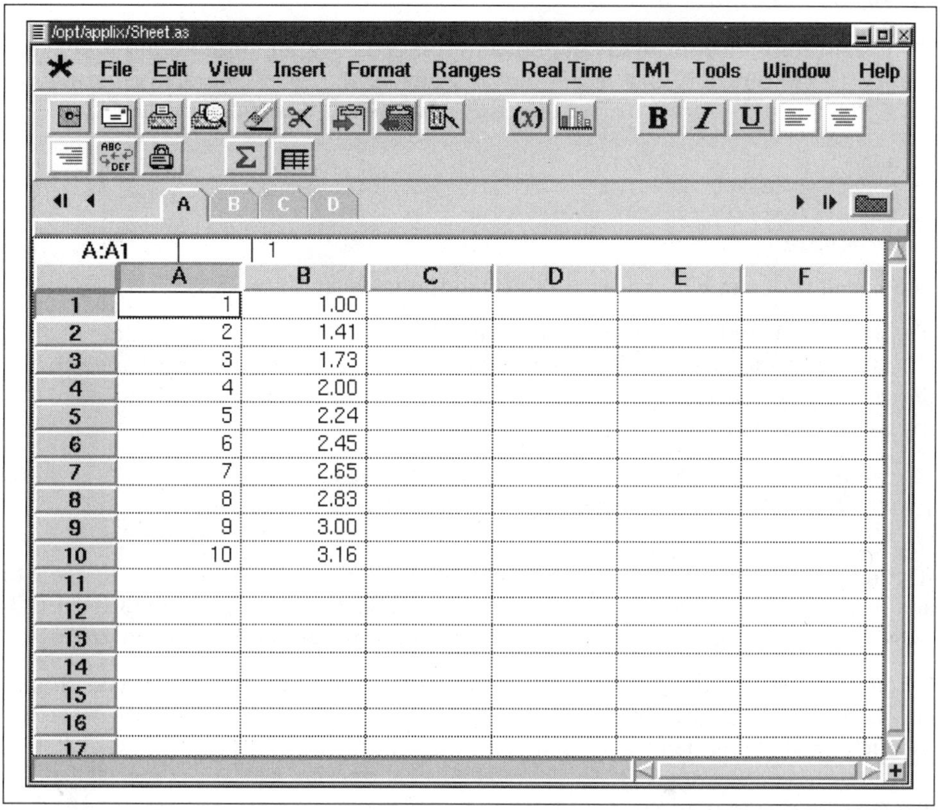

Figure 8-5. The Spreadsheets application

- StarImpress, a presentation graphics application

- StarBase, a relational database

- StarSchedule, a personal organizer that keeps track of events, tasks, contacts, and projects

- StarMail, an email client

- StarDiscussion, an Internet newsgroup reader

- SharChart, a business graphics application

- StarImage, an image editor that provides many special effects

- StarMath, a formula editor

Installing StarOffice

To install StarOffice from a StarOffice CD-ROM, log in, mount the CD-ROM, change to the directory that is the mount point of the CD-ROM device, change to the *Office50/english/prod_lnx* subdirectory, and issue the *setup* command:

```
su -
mount -t iso9660 /dev/cdrom /mnt/cdrom
cd /mnt/cdrom/Office50/english/prod_lnx
./setup
```

The install program will guide you through the installation process.

If you have downloaded the personal edition, you have a tar file, rather than a CD-ROM diskette. The tar file has a name similar to *so501_01.tar*. Change to the directory in which you saved the tar file (for example, */download*) and issue the following commands:

```
tar xvf so501_01.tar
cd so501_inst
./setup
```

If you saved your tar file using a name other than *so501_01.tar*, you'll need to adapt the first and second commands accordingly. As when you install from CD-ROM diskette, the install program will guide you through the installation process.

Whether you're installing from CD-ROM diskette or a downloaded file, you should check the *README* file in the *Office50* directory for additional information and instructions that will help you install and use StarOffice.

Running StarOffice

Once you have installed StarOffice, you can run it by starting X and using a terminal window to issue the following commands:

```
PATH=$PATH:/opt/Office50/bin
soffice
```

If you installed StarOffice into a directory other than */opt/Office50*, you'll need to adapt the first command accordingly.

When StarOffice loads, it automatically launches the StarDesktop application, as shown in Figure 8-6. StarDesktop resembles Windows Explorer and the GNOME File Manager. It lets you point, click, drag, and drop to open and manage document files and folders.

Figure 8-7 shows StarWriter, StarOffice's word processor. StarWriter provides PGP-encrypted email and other features not found in Microsoft Office 97. Like Applixware's Words, it imports and exports a variety of document types, including Microsoft Word 97.

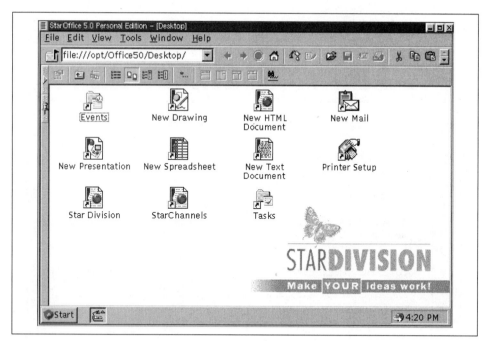

Figure 8-6. StarDesktop

Figure 8-8 shows StarImpress, the presentation graphics application included in StarOffice. Like Applixware's Presents, StarImpress imports and exports a variety of document types, including PowerPoint 97. StarImpress provides templates, animation and transitions, 3D effects, charts, and many other features.

Figure 8-9 shows StarDraw, StarOffice's drawing program. StarDraw provides a wide range of drawing tools and effects, and works with a variety of file types, including even Windows Metafile (WMF).

In addition to the bread-and-butter applications provided by Applixware, StarOffice provides several smaller, but quite useful, applications. For example, Figure 8-10 shows StarSchedule, which can help you keep track of the tasks on your to do list.

Corel WordPerfect for Linux

Another popular desktop application is Corel's WordPerfect for Linux, available free of charge for personal use from Corel's web site, *http://www.corel.com/*. WordPerfect is more a word processor than a complete desktop suite; for example, no spreadsheet application accompanies it. However, WordPerfect does provide many functions and features, including:

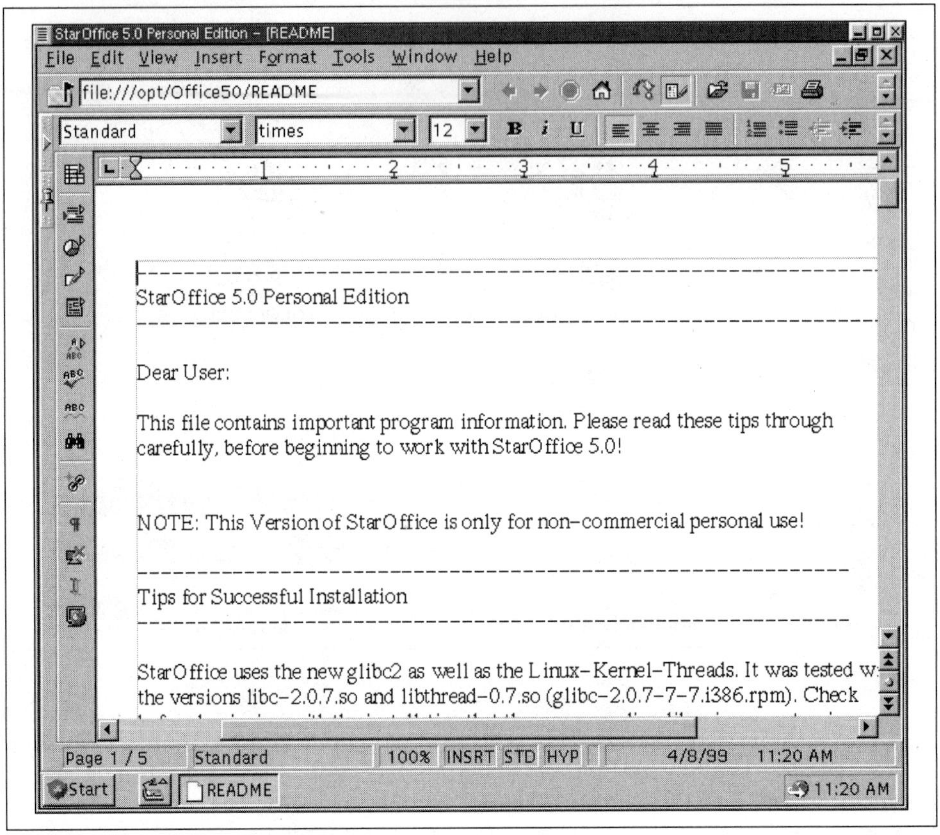

Figure 8-7. StarWriter

- a file manager
- drawing and charting
- spreadsheet functions in tables
- HTML authoring

A personal retail version (currently available for $69.95 (US)) adds such features as:

- advanced drawing and charting functions
- version control
- clipart images, photos, textures, templates, and fonts

The downloadable version is about 24 MB in size, about a 2 hour download at 28.8 Kbps.

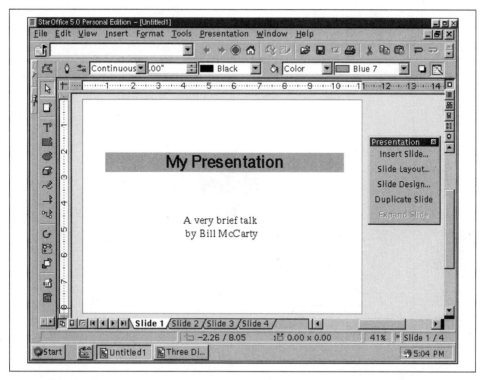

Figure 8-8. StarImpress

Installing WordPerfect for Linux

To install the downloaded version of WordPerfect for Linux, change to the directory that contains the downloaded file and issue the following command:

```
DISPLAY=localhost:0
```

Then start X, open a terminal window, and issue the following commands:

```
cd /download
tar zxvf wp.tgz
./Runme
```

If your downloaded file has a name other than *wp.tgz* or if it resides in a directory other than */download*, you'll need to adapt these commands accordingly.

The install program will guide you through the installation process.

To install the CD-ROM version of WordPerfect for Linux, follow the instructions that accompany the CD-ROM.

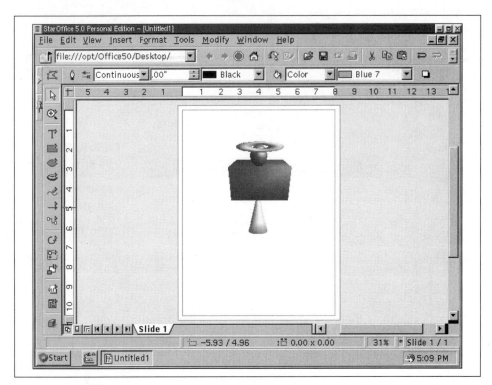

Figure 8-9. StarDraw

TIP   Some web sites, including the Corel web site, may provide WordPerfect for Linux as an uncompressed file. If the *tar* command fails with an error message indicating that the file is not in the gzip format, use the following command to unpack the file:

```
tar xvf wp.tgz
```

Running WordPerfect for Linux

Once you've installed WordPerfect for Linux, you can run it by starting X and using a terminal window to issue the command:

```
/opt/corelwp8/wpbin/xwp
```

Figure 8-11 shows WordPerfect for Linux in operation.

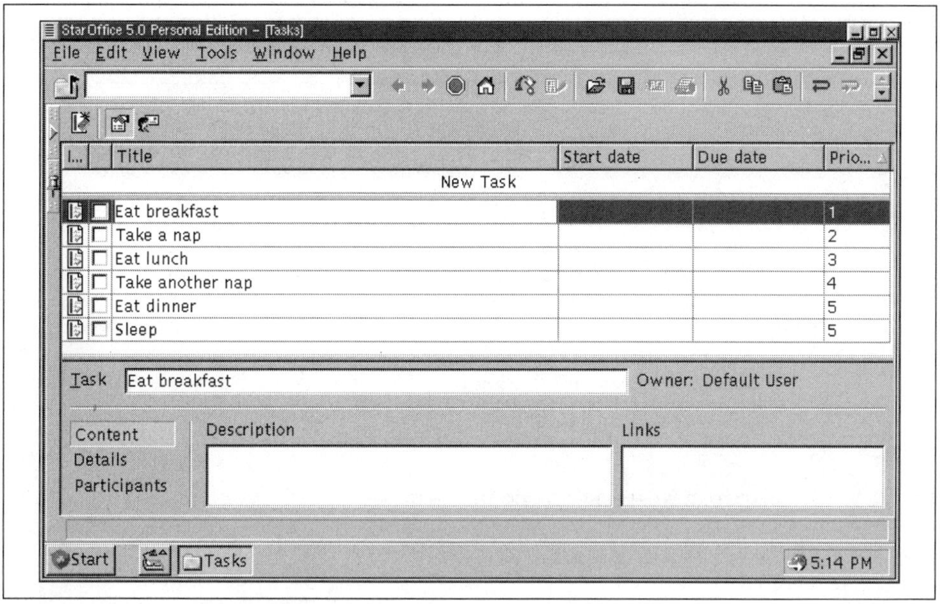

Figure 8-10. StarSchedule

Other Desktop Applications

Table 8-1 describes some other desktop applications available for Linux. Notable among these is TeX, a freely available desktop publishing package of unsurpassed power. Because of its powerful and sophisticated handling of formulas and mathematical notation, TeX is a favorite among scientists and mathematicians.

Table 8-1. Other Desktop Applications for Linux

Application	Web site	Description
Angoss SmartWare	*http://www.angoss.com/*	Includes a word processor, spreadsheet, and relational database. Print- and save-disabled demo version available for free download. Registration fee $50 (US).
Axene Office	*http://www.axene.com/*	Includes a word processor, desktop publishing application, and spreadsheet. Linux license $49 (US). Printed manuals $60 (US) per application.
KOffice	*http://koffice.kde.org/*	GPLed desktop suite. Currently in alpha release.

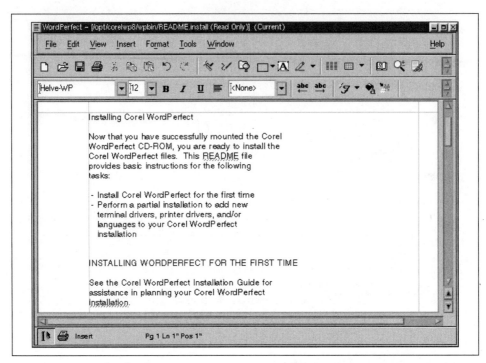

Figure 8-11. WordPerfect for Linux

Table 8-1. Other Desktop Applications for Linux (continued)

Application	Web site	Description
Lotus eSuite	*http://www.lotus.com/ home.nsf/tabs/esuite1*	Java applets that provide a word processor, spreadsheet, presentation graphics, project scheduler, chart, SQL/JDBC, and CGI gateway. Single-user license $127 (US).
Quadratron Cliq	*http://www.quad.com/*	Character-based desktop suite. Single-user license $49 (US).
TeX	*http://www.ctan.org/*	GPLed desktop publishing application. Sophisticated and powerful but somewhat cumbersome to use.

Other Approaches to Desktop Computing

If, after trying various desktop suites for Linux, you find yourself pining for your original Windows desktop suite, you can possibly coax your desktop suite to cooperate with Linux in either of two ways:

- the VMware virtual platform

- WINE

This section of the chapter explains these remaining options.

The VMware Virtual Platform

VMware, Inc. recently released a beta version of a product it calls VMware for Linux. The company promises a commercial release of the product that should be available by the time you read this. A related product, VMware for Windows NT, should also be available. For the latest information, check VMware's web site, *http://www.vmware.com/*.

As the names suggest, VMware for Linux runs under Linux whereas VMware for Windows NT runs under Microsoft Windows NT. Each product lets you run a so-called guest operating system alongside the host operating system. Supported guest operating systems include:

- FreeBSD

- Linux

- MS-DOS 6

- Solaris 7 Intel Edition

- Windows 2000 Professional Beta

- Windows 3.1

- Windows 95

- Windows 98

- Windows NT 4.0

For example, using VMware, your Linux system can launch and execute your favorite Windows 9x applications, including desktop suites. Preliminary experience with VMware suggests that it is a robust and efficient means of running legacy desktop applications under Linux.

A time-limited demo version of VMware for Linux is available on the company's web site. List price for both versions of VMware is $299 (US); once the product is released, it can be purchased from the company's web site. For VMware to operate, you must have copies of the guest operating system and any desired applications on the hard drive of your Linux system.

WINE

WINE (a recursive acronym for "WINE is not an emulator") takes a different approach to supporting legacy applications. WINE is a GPLed Unix implementation of the Windows 3.x and Win32 application programming interfaces (APIs). By installing WINE on your system, you can run MS-DOS and Windows applications under Linux. Because WINE implements the APIs themselves, you need not have a copy of MS-DOS or Windows on the hard drive of your Linux system.

The WINE project is an ongoing effort. Many MS-DOS and Windows applications run well under WINE, but others use functions that are as yet only partially implemented. The WINE Development HQ web site, *http://www.winehq.com/*, provides access to a database that records user evaluations of WINE's ability to run various applications. At the time of writing, the database contained 127 reports of applications scoring a perfect rating of 5.

Getting and installing WINE

WINE is frequently updated and improved and is not yet complete. Therefore, rather than installing WINE from this book's CD-ROM, you should obtain the latest version of WINE from the WINE Development HQ web site. WINE requires Mesa, a library of graphics rendering routines, which you can also obtain from the WINE Development HQ web site. To install WINE, download WINE and Mesa and issue the commands given in Appendix C, *The Red Hat Package Manager.*

Running WINE

If your Linux partition mounts your Windows partition (if any) as /c, you're ready to run WINE. Otherwise, you must first establish a simple directory structure. The easiest way to do so is to log in as root and issue the following commands:

```
mkdir -p /c/windows/system
> /c/windows/win.ini
```

WARNING   If your Linux system mounts your Windows partition as /c, these commands will damage your Windows configuration. Do not issue them; you don't require them in order to run WINE.

To prepare to run an MS-DOS or Windows application, copy the application and any necessary DLLs or other files to the */c/windows* directory. For example, to prepare to run the Minesweeper program, copy *winmine.exe* and *winmine.ini* to */c/windows*. To run the application, you must have started X. Simply issue the *wine* command, specifying the application as an argument. For example, to run the Minesweeper program, issue the command:

```
wine winmine.exe
```

Figure 8-12 shows the Minesweeper program running under WINE.

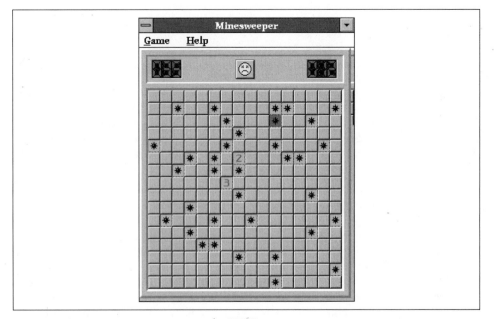

Figure 8-12. Minesweeper running under WINE

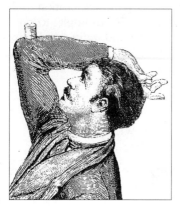

CHAPTER NINE

PLAYING LINUX GAMES

In the last chapter you learned how to use Linux to help you work; in this chapter you'll learn how to use Linux to help you play. A variety of challenging and exciting games are available for Linux; many of them are free. In addition, you can use WINE to run a variety of commercial games originally written for Microsoft Windows. Because most computer games include sound effects or music, this chapter also describes the procedure for configuring your sound card for operation under Linux.

Configuring Your Sound Card

If you recall playing computer games before computers were generally equipped with sound cards, you know firsthand why game players demand high-quality sound. A shoot-em-up game, for example, just isn't the same without the whizzing of bullets, no matter how sophisticated the graphics. Unfortunately, the Linux installation program does not automatically configure your computer's sound card. So, until you configure your sound card, you'll hear only the boring beep of your computer's speaker.

Fortunately, it's not difficult to configure Linux to work with most sound cards. In this section, you'll learn how to do so.

Early Linux Sound Support

At one time, configuring Linux to work with your sound card required you to compile a customized version of the Linux kernel. Today, Linux support for modular drivers lets you load (or unload) a sound driver without recompiling the kernel. You don't even need to reboot your system.

Compatible Sound Cards

Linux supports many sound cards, but not every sound card. You should check whether your sound card is supported before attempting to configure it. Cards supported at the time of writing are listed below.

WARNING   Many cards sold as compatible with a card supported by Linux will not function properly under Linux. Often the compatibility is provided by means of software emulation, which the manufacturer has not chosen to share with Linux developers.

Acer Notebook Sound
AdLib
Advance Logic ALS-007
Compaq Deskpro XL sound
Creative/Ensoniq Audio PCI 1371
Crystal CS423x sound chip
Ensoniq Audio PCI 1370 (SoundBlaster 64/128 PCI)
Ensoniq SoundScape
ESS1688 AudioDrive
ESS1868 AudioDrive
ESS688 AudioDrive
Gravis UltraSound
Gravis UltraSound MAX
Gravis UltraSound PnP
Logitech SoundMan 16
Logitech SoundMan Games (not SM16 or SM Wave)
MAD16 Pro (OPTi 82C929/82C930)
MediaTrix AudioTrix Pro
MediaVision Jazz16 (ProSonic, SoundMan Wave)
miroSOUND PCM12
Mozart/MAD16 (OPTi 82C928)
OPL3-SA1 or OPL3-SA2/3/x sound chip
Pro Audio Spectrum/Studio 16
PSS (Orchid SW32, Cardinal DSP16)
S3 SonicVibes
SoundBlaster
SoundBlaster 16/PNP
SoundBlaster AWE32/AWE64
SoundBlaster Pro
Turtle Beach MultiSound Classic/Monterey/Tahiti
Turtle Beach MultiSound Pinnacle/Fiji
Windows Sound System (AD1848/CS4248/CS4231)

The Sound Card Configuration Tool

Linux includes *sndconfig*, a utility that automatically configures modular sound card drivers. To use *sndconfig*, log in as `root` and type the command:

```
sndconfig
```

If you use *su*, rather than logging in as `root`, you'll probably need to type:

```
/usr/sbin/sndconfig
```

If your sound card supports Plug and Play, *sndconfig* should identify and configure it. If *sndconfig* cannot identify your sound card, it presents a list of supported sound cards. Highlight the entry that corresponds to your sound card, select the Ok button, and press **Space**. Then, specify your sound card's port, IRQ, and DMA settings in the dialog box that pops up. The information you collected in preparation for installing Linux should include these values. If not, obtain the information by following the procedures described in Chapter 2, *Preparing to Install Linux.*

If *sndconfig* pops up a dialog box informing you that */etc/conf.modules* already exists, select Ok and press **Space**.

Finally, *sndconfig* plays a sound, so that you can verify that your sound card is properly configured. If you can't hear the sound, consult the documentation in the */usr/doc/rhsound* directory.

A Survey of Linux Games

Linux includes several popular games. In addition, many Linux games are available on the Web. Table 9-1 lists some of the most popular sites offering Linux games and Table 9-2 describes some of the most popular Linux games.

Table 9-1. Popular Linux Game Web Sites

Web Site	URL
Freshmeat	*http://freshmeat.net/*
Linux Game Tome	*http://happypenguin.org/*
Linux Games Page	*http://www.linuxgames.com/*
Linux Quake Page	*http://www.planetquake.com/linux/*
linuxquake.com	*http://www.linuxquake.com/*
Loki Games	*http://www.lokigames.com/*
Slashdot	*http://www.slashdot.org/*

Table 9-2. Some Popular Linux Games

Game	Type	Description
BZFlag	Action	Multi-player tank battle game.
Civilization: Call To Power	Strategy	A commercial Linux version of the sequel to Micropose's Civilization. Supports network play.
CrossFire	Role Playing	Resembles Rogue. Supports multi-player network play.
DOOM	Action	Classic action game. Requires *doom.wad* file from licensed copy of game.
Freeciv	Strategy	Resembles Microprose's Civilization. Supports network play.
Illust Logic	Puzzle	A paint-by-numbers puzzle, wherein you strive to paint cells of a canvas.
Koules	Arcade	Multi-player action game. Supports console or X11 play.
NetHack	Role Playing	A quest game resembling Rogue. Supports console or X11 play.
Netrek	Arcade	Multi-player 2-D battle simulation with a Star Trek theme.
PySol	Card	Twenty different versions of solitaire.
Quake	Action	A Linux version of the commercial game Quake. Requires the PAK file from the game CD-ROM diskette. Supports console or X11 play.
Quake II	Action	In the opinion of many, the definitive multi-player 3D action shoot 'em up. Requires license fee. Supports console or X11 play.
Snes9X	Utility	A portable, freeware emulator of the Super Nintendo Entertainment System (SNES). Allows you to run Nintendo64 games on a PC.
Starcraft Linux-installation HOWTO	Document	Describes the procedures for installing and running the commercial game Starcraft on a Linux system using WINE.
XBomber	Arcade	Resembles the classic Bomberman game.
Xmame	Arcade	Emulator for popular arcade games. Requires ROM image from the original game.
XPat2	Card	An assortment of solitaire games.
XShipWars	Action	A graphical MUD (multi-user dungeon) with a space exploration theme.

As you can see, many types of games are available, including action games, arcade games, card games, puzzles, role playing games, and strategy games. Some Linux games can be played from the console; others require X. Many Linux games let multiple players compete at separate computers connected via a network, such as the Internet. Linux games may be freeware, shareware, or commercial software. In addition, Linux software such as Snes9X and WINE let you play games originally written for systems other than Linux.

Closeups of Some Popular Games

In this section, you'll get acquainted with three popular games you can run under Linux:

- DOOM, which runs on a console or under X

- Quake II, which runs on a console or under X

- StarCraft, which runs under X by using WINE

DOOM

Originally written for MS-DOS by id Software (*http://www.idsoftware.com/*), DOOM is the archetypal 3D action game. You play the role of a space marine, fighting your way through a series of bases on the moons of Mars that have been invaded by aliens. The game features real-time 3D graphics and stereo sound effects. Figure 9-1 shows a typical game screen.

Figure 9-1. A typical DOOM screen

If you prefer more cunning opponents, you can play the game in network mode, via modem, or an IPX or TCP/IP network. Network mode lets you match wits with two to four human opponents.

To run DOOM in a console, type the following command:

```
sdoom -warp 1 1
```

If you prefer to run DOOM under X, type the following command:

```
xdoom -warp 1 1
```

To call up DOOM's main menu, simply press **Esc**.

You can learn more about DOOM by visiting the DOOM Archives at *http://www.idsoftware.com/archives/doomarc.html* and the Linux DOOM FAQ at *http://jcomm.uoregon.edu/~stevev/Linux-DOOM-FAQ.html*. You might also enjoy lxDoom, a Linux port of Boom, which is an enhanced version of DOOM.

Quake II

Like DOOM, Quake II was also written by id Software. However, Quake II is a much more modern and sophisticated program than DOOM. For example, Quake II's multi-player mode lets as many as 32 players wander the planet of Stroggos. And, the single-player mode pits you against 18 artificially intelligent adversaries, who dodge your careless shots with agile ease. Figure 9-2 shows a typical Quake II game screen.

Figure 9-2. A typical Quake II screen

To run Quake II under X, change the working directory to the directory in which you installed Quake II, and issue the command:

```
./quake2 +set vid_ref softx
```

To run Quake II using a virtual console, issue the command:

```
./quake2 +set vid_ref soft
```

Once the game is running, you can access its main menu by pressing **Esc**.

Starcraft

Starcraft is a real-time strategy game published by Blizzard Entertainment, in which you participate as the leader of one of a group of humans exiled at the edge of galactic space. Your objective is to assemble a military force capable of dominating two other species, the Protoss and the Zreg. To do so, you must build bases, vehicles, and weapons, and train soldiers for combat.

Starcraft was not written for Linux; however, you can run it under Linux by using WINE. Assuming that you have WINE installed on your system, the following sections explain how to install and run Starcraft:

Installing Starcraft

If you have the commercial version of Starcraft, mount the CD-ROM diskette and locate the file *install.exe*. If you want to try the Starcraft demo, download the file *scdemo.exe*, which is a little over 28 MB in size. You can find the file on Blizzard's Web site (*http://www.blizzard.com/*) and elsewhere.

Change the current directory to the directory containing *install.exe* or *scdemo.exe* and use WINE to install Starcraft:

```
wine -display localhost:0 -winver win95 scdemo.exe
```

When asked if you want to install DirectX 5, highlight the No, But Continue option and click on OK. Choose the directory in which you want to install Starcraft (the default choice is generally acceptable) and click on OK. If the program asks if you want to register via the Internet, respond by clicking on No. Finally, click on Exit to terminate the install program.

Under Linux, Starcraft operates in 256-color 640×480 mode. Therefore, you must adjust your X configuration to provide this mode. Here's a quick way to do that. First copy the file */etc/X11/XF86Config* by issuing the following commands:

```
cd /etc/X11
cp XF86Config XF86Config.SAVE
cp XF86Config XF86Config.StarCraft
```

Now, edit the file *XF86Config.StarCraft* using the editor of your choice. Find the "Screen" section that specifies the X server (driver) you use and change the Depth parameter to 8 and the Modes parameter to "640x480". Delete any additional modes that appear. When you're done, the screen section should resemble the following:

```
Section "Screen"
   Driver      "svga"
   Device      "Millennium"
   Monitor     "Viewsonic17GS"
   Subsection "Display"
     Depth      8
     Modes      "640x480"
     ViewPort   0 0
     Virtual    640 480
   EndSubsection
EndSection
```

Playing Starcraft

To play Starcraft, replace your *XF86Config* file with the newly edited one:

```
cp XF86Config.StarCraft XF86Config
```

Then start X:

```
startx
```

Launch an X terminal, make the Starcraft installation directory the current directory, and start the Starcraft program:

```
# cd "/c/Program Files/Starcraft Shareware(ED)"
# wine -display localhost:0 -winver win95 -depth 8 \
> -geom 640x480 Starcraft.exe
```

If you installed Starcraft to a directory other than */c/Program Files/Starcraft Shareware(ED)*, you should adjust the commands accordingly.

Now, play Starcraft until you completely dominate the galaxy. The tutorial mission will help you learn how to do so. Of course, planning and executing a winning strategy will require practice.

Ending a Starcraft session

When you're done, press F10 to obtain a game menu, exit the current mission, and exit the game. Then, replace your original *XF86Config* file by entering the commands:

```
cd /etc/X11
cp XF86Config.SAVE XF86Config
```

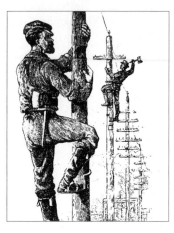

## CHAPTER TEN

SETTING UP A LINUX-BASED LAN

This chapter explains how to set up a local-area network (LAN) that includes a Linux Samba server, which lets Microsoft Windows and UNIX systems access shared files and printers hosted by your Linux system. The chapter also explains how to use *linuxconf* to administer a simple LAN and describes how to install, configure, and administer Samba servers and clients. Integrating your Linux system with an existing LAN is no more complicated than setting up your own LAN; the chapter also explains how to connect to an existing network. The chapter also explains how to use Linux backup and recovery utilities so that client systems can create and use backups stored on the server.

Introduction

One of the great strengths of Linux is its powerful and robust networking capabilities. The good news is that everything about Linux's networking setup is open to inspection and completely configurable. Nothing is hidden from the user, and no parameters are forced on you. The challenge is to get the most out of this setup for your needs.

Basic networking principles don't differ much between Windows and Linux, and indeed the principles aren't unfamiliar. This chapter starts with an overview of networking, and then looks in more detail at Linux networking on a Local Area Network (LAN). In the next two chapters, you'll learn about making a dialup Internet connection, and setting up Wide Area Network (WAN) services.

Most computers today handle network traffic much as the post office handles mail. Think, for example, of the steps involved in sending and receiving a letter. Your postal carrier must know where to drop off and where to pick up mail. So your home must have some kind of recognizable *interface*; we call this a mailbox. And whereas your postal carrier may know your neighborhood quite well, delivery in other areas will require other carriers. Mail is passed to these other carriers through a *gateway*; we call this the Post Office. Although you can think of the whole postal system as one big network, it's easier to understand if you think of it as a hierarchy of *subnetworks* (or *subnets*): the postal system is divided into states, states are divided by zip code, zip codes contain a number of streets, and each street contains unique addresses.

Computer networking mirrors this model. Let's trace an email message from you to a coworker. You compose the message and press Send. Your computer passes the message to a network interface. This interface may be a modem by which you dial up an ISP, or it may be an Ethernet card that connects you to a LAN. Either way, on the other side of the interface is a gateway machine. The gateway knows how to look at the address of the recipient on the email message, and interpret that message in terms of networks and subnets. Using this information, your gateway passes the message to other gateways until the message reaches the gateway for the destination machine. That gateway in turn delivers the message via a recognizable interface (such as modem or Ethernet card) to the recipient's inbox.

If you review this story, you can easily see what parts of networking you'll need to configure on your Linux system. You'll need to know the address of your machine. Just as the town name *Menlo Park* and the zip code *94025* are two different names for the same location, you may have both a name, called a *hostname*, and a number, called an *IP number*, that serve as the address for your machine.

To translate between these two notations, you may need to know the address of a *Domain Name Server*. This is a machine that matches IP numbers with hostnames. You'll also need to know the address of a gateway machine through which network traffic will be routed. Finally, you'll need to be able to bring up an interface on your system for networking, and you'll need to assign a route from that interface to the gateway.

While all of this can seem complex, it really isn't any more complex than the postal system, and functions in much the same way. Fortunately, Linux comes with tools to help you automate network configuration. In this chapter you'll look at networking on a LAN, and we'll start by looking at *linuxconf* to set up LAN networking.

Network Administration Using linuxconf

In Chapter 5, *Installing and Configuring the X Window System*, you were introduced to *linuxconf*, which is analogous to the Microsoft Windows Control Panel. However, that chapter touched only briefly on the Linux configuration options that pertain to networking. This section describes these options in more detail. By following the instructions in this section you should be able to configure your system to connect to a local area network, the Internet, or both.

Basic Host Information

Basic host information includes the Internet name of your system and information on your system's network adapter cards. To specify these, launch *linuxconf* by starting X, launching an xterm, and typing the commands:

```
su -
linuxconf
```

Because you're likely to use the *linuxconf* program often, you may want to include it as a menu item or shortcut in your desktop manager.

Once the *linuxconf* window appears, select the Config → Networking → Client Tasks → Basic Host Information subtree. Figure 10-1 shows the Basic Host Information dialog box that appears.

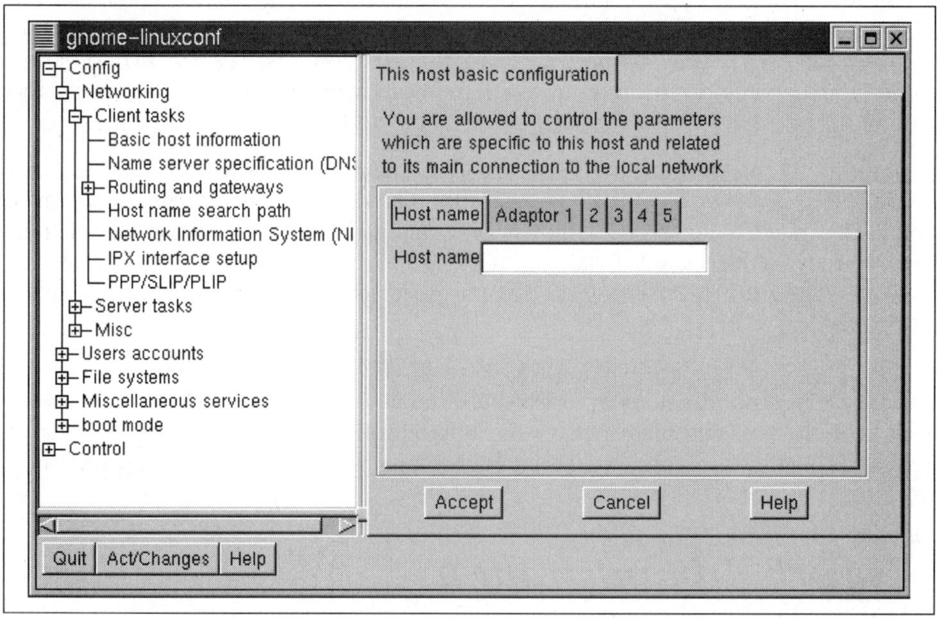

Figure 10-1. The basic host information dialog box

Every computer attached to the Internet has at least one hostname, which generally consists of three words separated by dots; for example, *www.oreilly.com.* If your ISP provides you with a hostname for your system, you should enter it here. Otherwise, you can choose your own hostname, so long as you choose a name that won't conflict with an Internet host you'd like to access. No one outside your LAN will use, or need to use, your made-up hostname, so a simple one-word hostname such as *server* will suffice.

Next, you must specify information pertaining to your system's network adapter card (or cards, if you have more than one). Click on the Adapter 1 tab; Figure 10-2 shows the dialog box that appears. Table 10-1 describes the available options. You should choose a Configuration Mode and specify your card's net device and kernel module. If you select Manual as the Configuration Mode, you should also specify the card's Primary Name and IP address. You may optionally specify other parameters. If your system has multiple adapters, you should specify a configuration for each of them.

TIP	Many peripheral devices, such as Ethernet cards, have a Linux device driver written as a loadable module. Loadable modules can be dynamically loaded and unloaded; when loaded, they integrate with the kernel, effectively becoming part of the kernel. Loadable modules avoid the hassle of older versions of Linux, which required you to compile a special version of the kernel containing a device driver for each of your system's peripherals. Because loadable modules must be loaded before they're operational, configuring a device supported by a loadable modules requires you to identify the associated module.

Table 10-1. Network Adapter Options

Option	Description
Enabled	Specifies whether the adapter is enabled.
Config mode	Specifies how the adapter's IP address and other information are specified; manually specifies that the information is specified using this dialog box; DHCP specifies that the information is obtained from a DHCP server when the connection is established; BOOTP specifies that the information is obtained from a BOOTP server when the connection is established.
Primary name + domain	The hostname associated with the adapter.
Aliases	Other hostnames associated with the adapter (optional).
IP address	The IP address associated with the adapter. You need not—and should not—specify this option for adapters configured to use DHCP or BOOTP. Otherwise, specify the IP address provided by your ISP as four numbers separated by dots; for example, 192.168.1.1.

Table 10-1. Network Adapter Options (continued)

Option	Description
Netmask	The netmask, which identifies the portion of the IP address that specifies the network and the portion that specifies the host. You need not—and should not—specify this option for adapters configured to use DHCP or BOOTP. Otherwise, specify the netmask provided by your ISP as four numbers separated by dots; for example, 255.255.255.0. If you're uncertain of the proper value, leave this field blank; *linuxconf* will determine a default value that will probably work. (optional)
Net device	Specify `ethn`, where *n* is the number of the adapter. If your system has only one adapter, specify `eth0`.
Kernel module	Specify the name of the kernel module that supports your adapter card. If you can't find an exact match, pick the closest available entry. If that fails, seek technical assistance.
I/O port	The Linux kernel can automatically detect most adapter cards. However, if it cannot detect your card, you can specify the card's I/O port explicitly. Consult the documentation that accompanies your card to determine the I/O port it uses. (optional)
IRQ	The Linux kernel can automatically detect most adapter cards. However, if it cannot detect your card, you can specify the card's IRQ explicitly. Consult the documentation that accompanies your card to determine the IRQ it uses. (optional)

Name Server Specification

After you specify the basic host information, you should specify the name server information. Select the Config → Networking → Client Tasks → Name Server Specification subtree. The dialog box shown in Figure 10-3 appears.

Here you must specify the IP address of at least one server that translates host-names to IP addresses. Your ISP should provide you with the proper IP address or addresses.

If you frequently access other hosts on your ISP's network, you should specify a default domain; for example, *mediaone.net*. Doing so would let you refer to the host *abc.mediaone,net* as simply *abc*.

Generally, you should not specify search domains, which override the default domain in sometimes confusing ways.

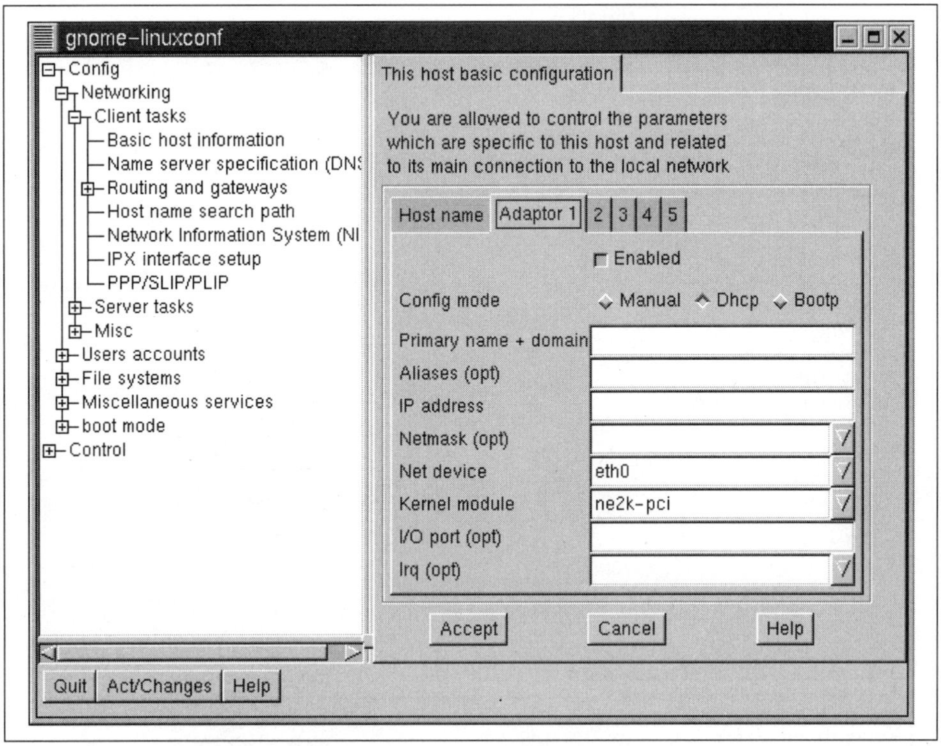

Figure 10-2. The network adapter options dialog box

Routing and Gateways

When your system is connected to the Internet, the packets of data it sends must be directed to a gateway that forwards the packets to the intended destination host. If your system connects to the Internet via PPP, the packets will be automatically directed to the appropriate gateway. In that case, you can generally omit the options described in this subsection.

TIP   PPP (point-to-point protocol) is the most popular protocol for connecting a host to the Internet via a dialup modem. Most Internet Service Providers support PPP. You'll learn more about PPP in the next chapter.

However, if your computer is connected to the Internet via a local area network, you must specify the IP address of the system on your local area network that acts as your gateway to the Internet. The administrator of your network should provide

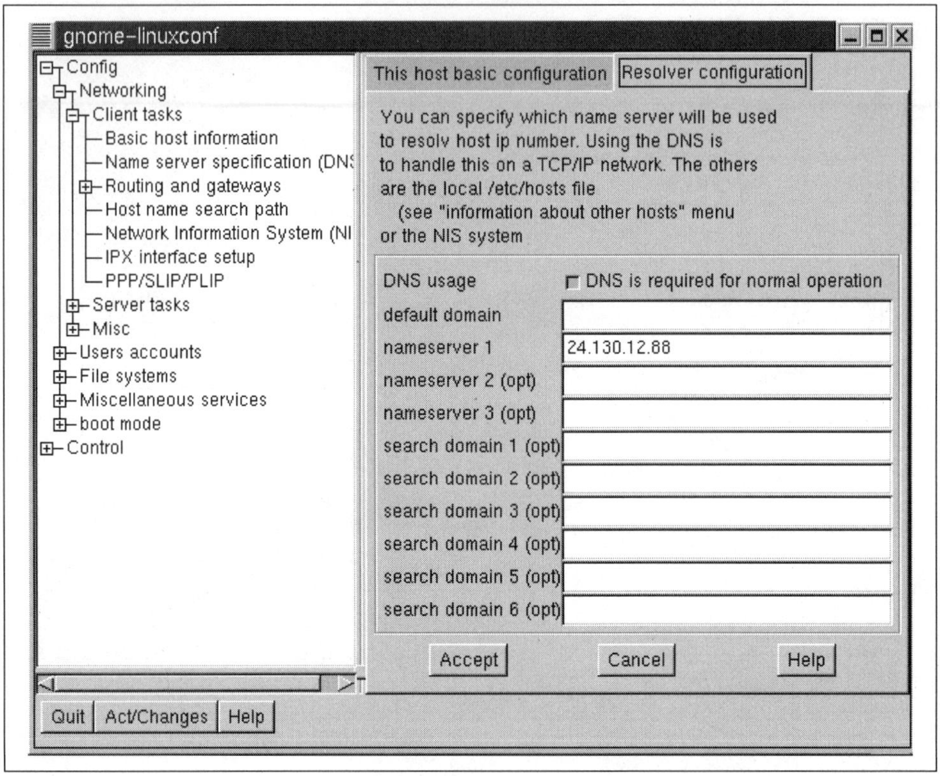

Figure 10-3. The name server options dialog box

this information, which consists of four numbers separated by dots; for example, 192.168.1.1. Figure 10-4 shows the dialog box by which you specify the default gateway option.

If your system is part of a group of local area networks, you should specify routes to reach the other local networks. You can do so using the dialog box shown in Figure 10-5. For each network, you must specify the IP address of the network, the netmask, and the IP address of the gateway system. Your network administrator should provide you with these values.

If your system has access to remote hosts other than via the Internet, you should specify routes to reach each such host. You can do so using the dialog box shown in Figure 10-6. You must specify the IP address of each host and the IP address of the gateway system. Your network administrator should provide you with these values.

If your system is part of a group of IP networks that share the same physical network, you should specify routes to reach the other networks. You can do so using

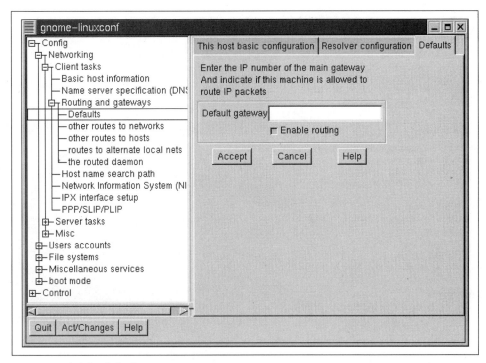

Figure 10-4. The default gateway option

the dialog box shown in Figure 10-7. For each network, you must specify the IP address of the network, the netmask, and the interface (that is, the adapter) that provides access to the network. Your network administrator should provide you with these values.

Your system can act as a gateway (router), providing other systems with access to hosts and networks to which it's connected. The *routed* daemon provides this service.

Figure 10-8 shows the dialog box used to enable routing. If you want your system to provide routing, select the Export Your Default Route option. Most users should not select this option.

Hostname Search Path

Your Linux system can use as many as three methods to determine the IP address that corresponds to a hostname:

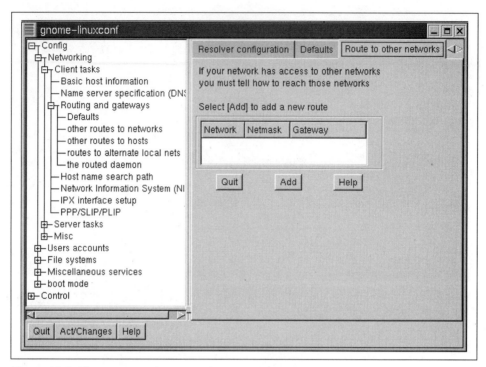

Figure 10-5. The routes to other networks option

- It can query a DNS server (you configured your system's DNS client earlier)

- It can read the contents of the file */etc/hosts*, known as the *hosts file*

- It can query an NIS (Network Information System) server

Using the Name Service dialog box, which is shown in Figure 10-9, you can specify which of these methods your system uses and the order in which your system will use them.

Unless your system is part of a sophisticated local area network, it's unlikely that an NIS server is available to you. So, most users should choose the "hosts, dns" entry or the "dns, hosts" entry. Generally, it's better to choose the "hosts, dns" entry. Doing so will cause your system to consult the local hosts file before consulting the DNS server; this arrangement can provide improved performance when accessing hosts specified in the hosts file. You'll learn how to use the hosts file in the next subsection.

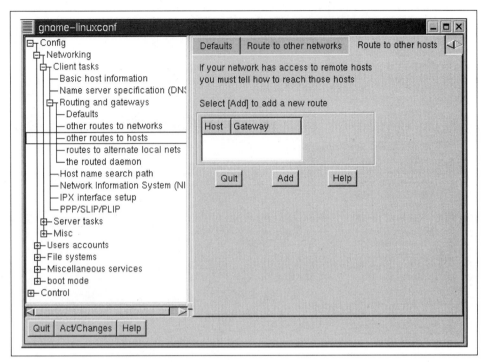

Figure 10-6. The routes to other hosts option

Miscellaneous Network Configuration Options

The Host Information dialog box, shown in Figure 10-10, lets you maintain the contents of your system's hosts file, */etc/hosts*. Entries in the file have two parts:

- an IP address

- a hostname, or a list of hostnames separated by spaces

The hosts file associates an IP address with one or more hostnames, so the system can determine the IP number that corresponds to a hostname. By default, the hosts file contains an entry that associates the hostname *localhost* with the IP address 127.0.0.1. Using the Host Information dialog box, you can add other entries to the file. Generally, it's not necessary that you do so. However, by including the appropriate entries in the hosts file, you can access frequently used hosts by hostname even if your DNS server is unavailable.

The Network Information dialog box, shown in Figure 10-11, lets you maintain the file */etc/networks*, known as the networks file. This file performs a function similar to that of the hosts file; whereas the hosts file associates hostnames with IP addresses, the networks file associates networks' names with network IP

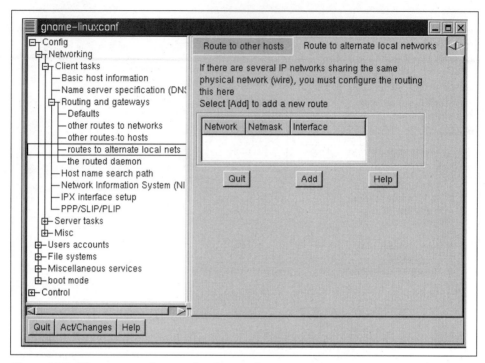

Figure 10-7. The routes to alternate local networks option

addresses. Generally, it's not necessary that you add entries to the networks file. However, by doing so, you can access frequently used networks by name even if your DNS server is unavailable.

Samba

Available since version 3.11 of Microsoft Windows, printer and file sharing are two of Window's most useful features. For example, outfitting each computer in a large office with a laser printer would be quite expensive. But printer sharing lets you reduce the cost of providing every user with printing capability; with printer sharing, each computer system in the office can print to a single printer.

Just as printer sharing lets your computer access a printer attached to another computer, file sharing lets your computer access files stored on another computer. File sharing makes it quick and easy to transfer data from one system to another and avoids the confusion that results when everyone has their own—possibly out of date or inconsistent—copy of important data files they could not otherwise access.

To provide printer and file sharing, Microsoft Windows uses a facility known as SMB (Server Message Block). This same facility is sometimes known as NetBIOS or

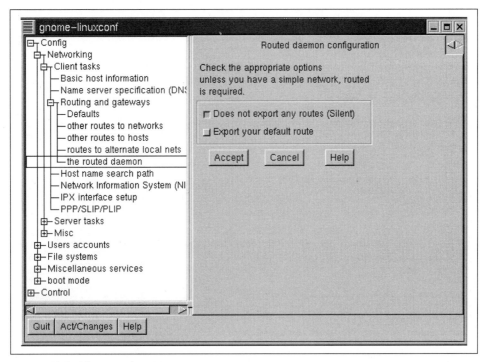

Figure 10-8. The routed options

LanManager. Thanks to Andrew Tridgell and others, Linux systems provide support for SMB via a package known as Samba. Like SMB, Samba lets you:

- Share printers and files among Microsoft Windows, OS/2, Netware, and Unix systems

- Establish a simple nameserver for identifying systems on your local area network

- Backup PC files to a Linux system and restore them

- Administer users and passwords

Samba has proven its reliability and high performance in many organizations. According to the online survey at *http://www.samba.org/pub/samba/survey/ssstats.html*, Bank of America is using Samba in a configuration that includes about 15,000 clients, and Hewlett-Packard is using Samba in a configuration that includes about 7,000 clients.

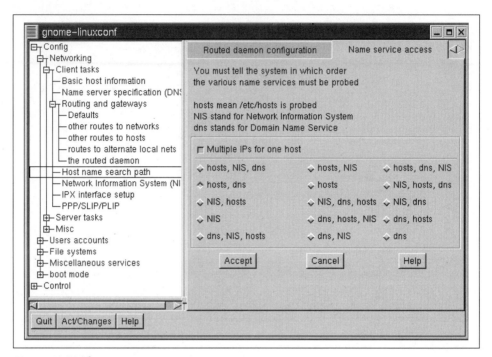

Figure 10-9. The name service options

Samba Server Installation

If you've never installed and configured a network server, Samba is a good place to begin; its installation and configuration are generally simple and straightforward.

Samba includes the *smbd* program, which runs as a daemon, several utility programs, man pages and other documentation, and two configuration files: */etc/smbusers* and */etc/smb.conf.* The */etc/smbusers* file associates several userids that are special to Samba with Linux userids; for example, it associates the Samba userids `administrator` and `admin` with `root`. Generally, you don't need to make changes to */etc/smbusers.* You'll learn how to configure the */etc/smb.conf* file shortly.

Starting Samba

To start Samba, you must add three lines to the file */etc/inet.d.* Using your favorite text editor, add these lines at the bottom of the file:

```
#SAMBA NetBIOS services
netbios-ssn stream tcp nowait root /usr/sbin/smbd smbd
netbios-ns  dgram  udp wait  root /usr/sbin/nmbd nmbd
```

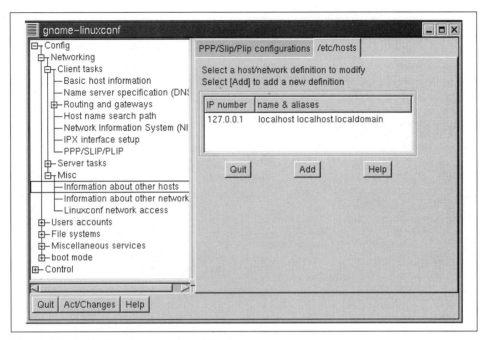

Figure 10-10. The host information dialog box

Samba should start the next time you boot your system. However, you can start and stop Samba without rebooting. Change to the directory */etc/rc.d/init.d* and issue the following command:

```
./smb start
```

As you might expect, you can stop Samba by issuing the similar command:

```
./smb stop
```

Configuring Samba

The */etc/smb.conf* file lets you specify a variety of options that control Samba's operation. You can edit the file by using your favorite text editor; however, Samba includes a tool called *swat* that lets you view and change options by using your Web browser, which is generally much easier than using a text editor. The *swat* tool verifies the values of parameters you enter and provides online help. To access *swat*, point your browser to port 901 of your system. For example, you can use the URL *http://localhost:901/.* Your web browser will prompt you for a userid and password; specify `root` as the userid and give the appropriate password. Figure 10-12 shows *swat*'s main menu, accessed by using the system's IP address in place of its hostname.

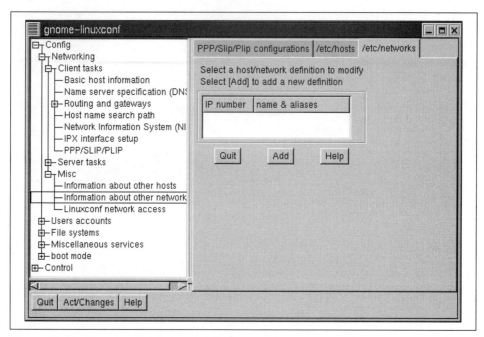

Figure 10-11. The network information dialog box

To configure your Samba server, you click on simulated tool bar entries:

- Globals lets you configure global Samba variables (options)

- Shares lets you configure file shares

- Printers lets you configure shared printers

- Status lets you view the status of the Samba server

- View lets you view the *smb.conf* file

- Password lets you add and delete users and change user password

The main menu also provides convenient access to Samba documentation.

Configuring global variables

To configure global options, click on the Globals button on the tool bar. Figure 10-13 shows the Global Variables page and Table 10-2 describes the most important options. You can access additional options by clicking on Advanced View. To change an option, select or type the desired value. When you've changed all the options you want to change, click on Commit Changes, which causes the changes to take effect.

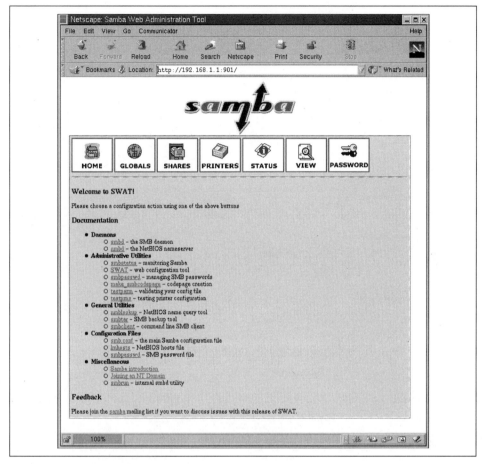

Figure 10-12. The Samba main menu

Table 10-2. Samba Global Variables

Option group	Option	Description
Base	workgroup	The workgroup name displayed when the server is queried by a client.
	netbios name	The name by which the server is known to the NetBIOS nameserver.
	server string	The text string displayed to describe the server.

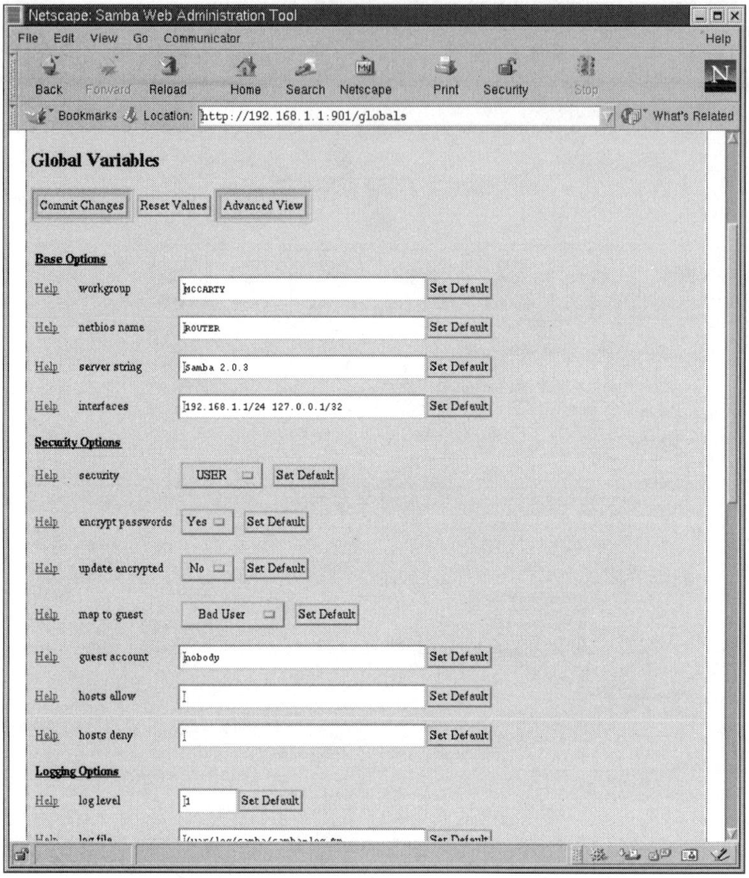

Figure 10-13. Samba global variables

Table 10-2. Samba Global Variables (continued)

Option group	Option	Description
Base (cont.)	interfaces	The IP address of the interface or the IP addresses of the interfaces through which Samba should listen. Each IP address is followed by a forward slash and a number that specifies the number of bits that pertain to the network portion of the IP address (usually 24). If this option is not set, Samba attempts to locate and automatically configure a primary interface.

Table 10-2. Samba Global Variables (continued)

Option group	Option	Description
Security	security	Specifies how Samba authenticates requests for access to shared resources. The default value, **user**, is helpful when the Samba server and its clients have many common userids. The value **share** can be useful when few common userids exist. The value **system** lets another SMB server perform authentication on behalf of the server. You should generally use the default value; see the Samba documentation for details.
	encrypt passwords	Specifies whether Samba will negotiate encrypted passwords, which are expected by Windows NT 4.0 SP3 and Windows 98.
	update encrypted	Allows automatic updating of an encrypted password when a user logs on using a non-encrypted password. This option is useful when migrating to encrypted passwords and should otherwise be set **off**.
	map to guest	Specifies Samba's action when a user attempts to log on using an invalid password. The **Bad User** option is generally appropriate.
	guest account	The Linux account used to provide services for guest users.
	hosts allow	A list of hosts that can access the server. If not specified, all hosts are permitted access.
	hosts deny	A list of hosts that cannot access the server.
Logging	log level	An integer that specifies the verbosity of log messages. A low value (such as 0) specifies that few messages are written to the log.
	log file	Specifies the name of Samba's log file.
	max log size	The maximum size of the log file in kilobytes (kb). When the specified size is exceeded, Samba begins a new log file. A value of zero lets the log file grow indefinitely large.
Tuning	read prediction	Specifies whether Samba will attempt to pre-read data from files, in order to speed data transfer. This code is disabled in Samba 2.0.
	socket options	Specifies TCP options that can improve performance. See the Samba documentation for details.

Table 10-2. Samba Global Variables (continued)

Option group	Option	Description
Printing	printcap name	Specifies the name of the *printcap* file used by the server.
	printing	Specifies how Samba interprets printer status information. Generally, SYSV is an appropriate choice for a Linux system.
Logon	logon script	Specifies the path of a BAT file that is downloaded from the server and run when a user logs on to Samba.
	domain logons	Specifies whether Samba will serve Windows 9x domain logons for its workgroup. Note: Samba cannot yet serve Windows NT domain logons, which require a Primary Domain Controller (PDC).
Browse	os level	Specifies the level at which Samba advertises itself for browse elections. A high number makes it more likely that Samba will be selected as the browser. The value 65 will cause clients to prefer Samba to a Windows NT server.
	preferred master	Specifies whether the NetBIOS name server is the preferred master browser for its workgroup.
	local master	Specifies whether the NetBIOS name server will bid to become the local master browser on a subnet.
	domain master	Specifies collation of browse lists across a wide-area network (WAN). May result in strange behavior when a workgroup includes a Windows NT Primary Domain Controller (PDC).
WINS	wins server	Specifies the IP address of the WINS server with which the NetBIOS nameserver should register itself, if any.
	wins support	Specifies that the NetBIOS nameserver should act as a WINS server. Useful when the network includes several subnets. Do not specify this option for multiple systems of a single network.
Locking	strict locking	Specifies whether the server will automatically lock files and check locks when files are accessed. Enabling this option may slow performance.

You probably won't need to make many changes to Samba's global variables. Setting the `workgroup` and `netbios name` is sufficient for most users. If your system has more than one network adapter card, you'll also need to set the interfaces variable.

WARNING   If your system is attached to a cable modem or other interface that makes it available to other network users, you should consider specifying security options that prevent unauthorized users from accessing your files or printer. Like other Samba users, the author has had a rogue system (in Pakistan) repeatedly attempt to access his shared files. To ensure that such attempts are unsuccessful, you might (for example) use the `hosts allow` option to restrict the hosts allowed to access your Samba server.

Configuring file share parameters

To establish and maintain file shares, you use the Shares button on the tool bar. Figure 10-14 shows the Share Parameters page.

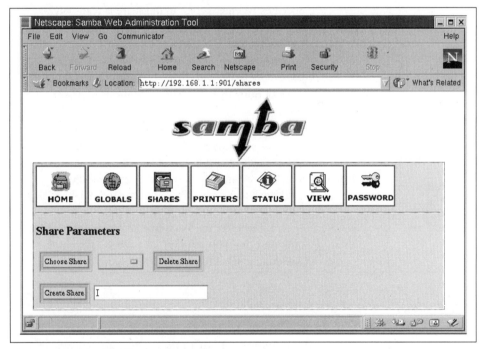

Figure 10-14. Samba file share parameters

You can create a new share by typing its name and clicking on Create Share. To delete a share, choose it from the drop-down list, and click on Delete Share. To work with an existing share, choose it from the drop-down list, and click on

Choose Share. When you click on Choose Share, the page shown in Figure 10-15 appears. This page lets you view and change a variety of share options. Table 10-3 describes the available share options. You can access additional options by clicking on Advanced View. As with the global options, you may not need to change many (if any) share options. Likely candidates for change are the `comment`, `path`, `read only`, and `create mask` options.

Table 10-3. Samba File Share Options

Option Group	Option	Description
Base	comment	The description displayed when the file share is queried by a client.
	path	The path (directory or file) that is shared by the server.
Security	guest account	The Linux account used to provide services for guest users.
	read only	Specifies whether access to the share is read-only.
	create mask	The default mode assigned to a newly created file within a shared directory.
	guest ok	Specifies whether guest access (access without a password) is allowed.
	hosts allow	A list of hosts that can access the file share. If not specified, all hosts are permitted access.
	hosts deny	A list of hosts that cannot access the file share.
Browse	browseable	Specifies whether the file share is visible in the list of shares made available by the server.
Locking	strict locking	Specifies whether the server will automatically lock files and check locks when files are accessed. Enabling this option may slow performance.
Miscellaneous	available	Specifies whether the share is available; by setting this option to "no" you can prevent access to the share.
	volume	The volume label returned for the share.

Configuring printer share parameters

You configure printer share parameters in much the same way you configure shares. Begin by clicking on the Printers tool bar button. The page shown in Figure 10-16 appears. You can use the page to create a new printer share, delete a printer share, or modify an existing printer share.

If you select a printer from the drop-down list and click on Choose Printer, the page shown in Figure 10-17 appears. Table 10-4 describes the available print share options. You can access additional options by clicking on Advanced View. As with the global options and file share options, you may not need to change many (if

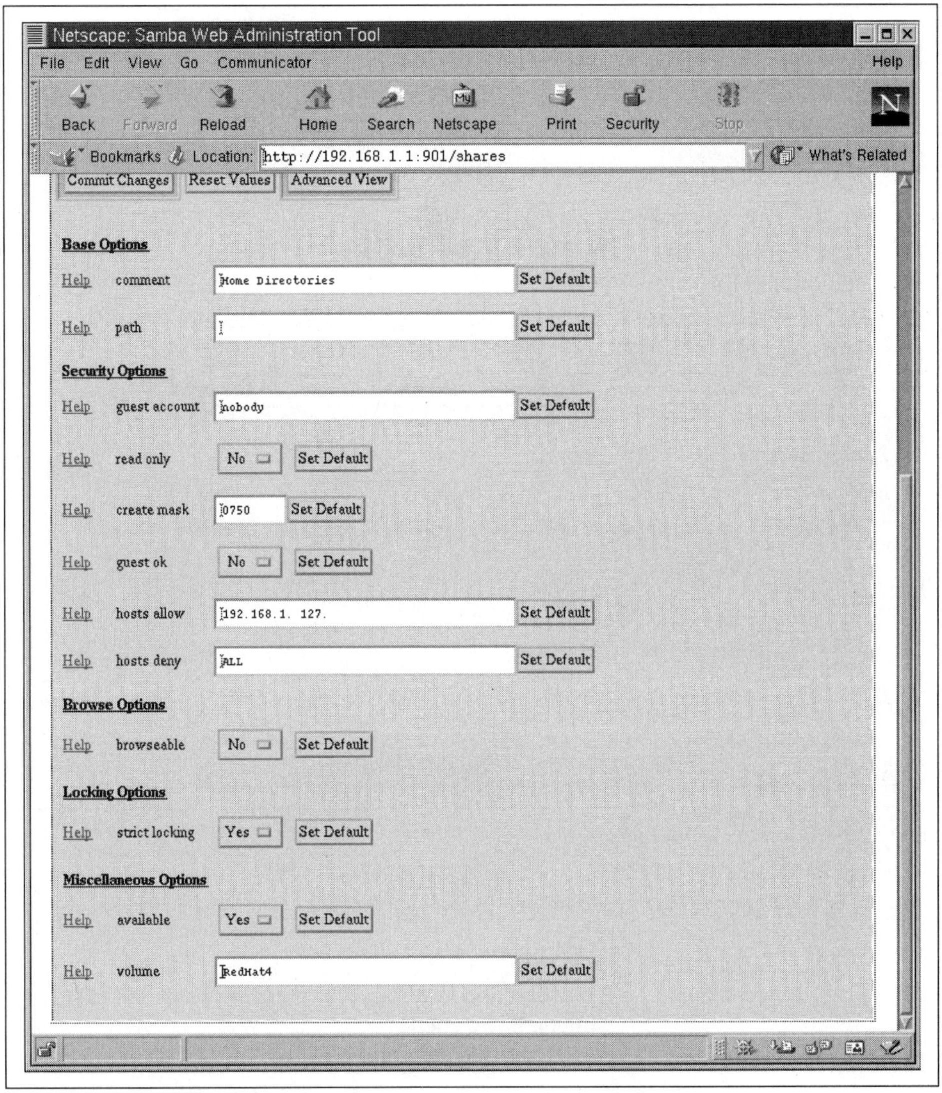

Figure 10-15. Samba file share parameters

any) printer share options. Likely candidates for change are the `comment`, `path`, `read only`, and `create mask` options.

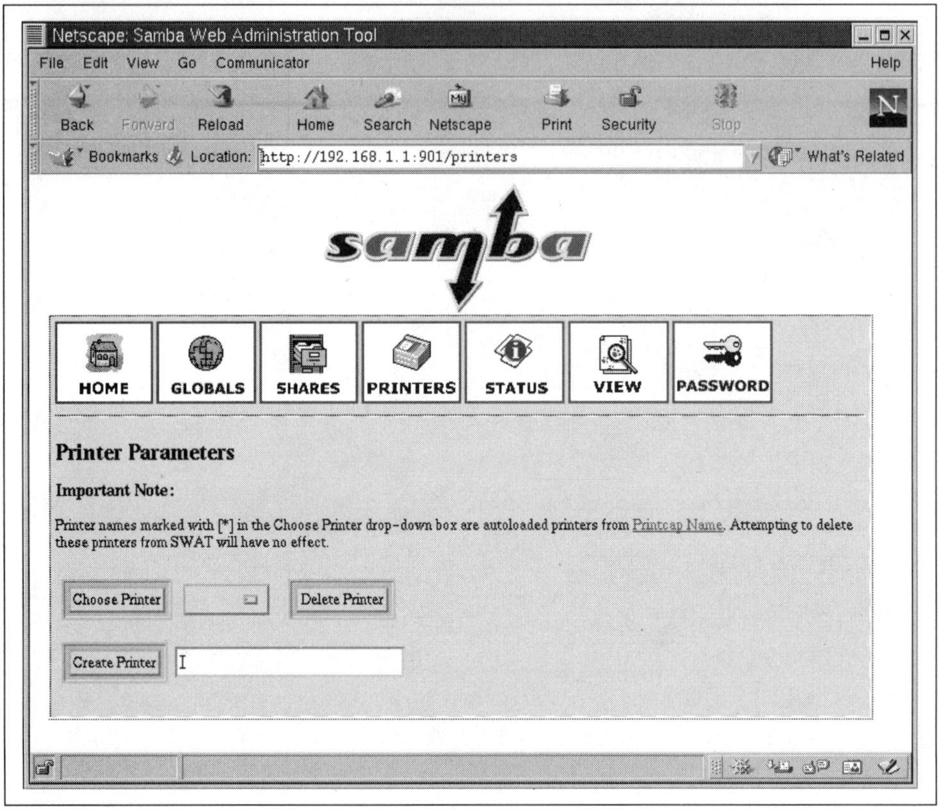

Figure 10-16. Samba printer parameters

Table 10-4. Samba Print Share Options

Option Group	Option	Description
Base	*comment*	The description displayed when the printer share is queried by a client.
	path	The print spooling directory.
Security	*guest account*	The Linux account used to provide services for guest users.
	guest ok	Specifies whether guest access (access without a password) is allowed.
	hosts allow	A list of hosts that can access the printer share. If not specified, all hosts are permitted access.
	hosts deny	A list of hosts that cannot access the printer share.

Table 10-4. Samba Print Share Options (continued)

Option Group	Option	Description
Printing	*print ok*	Specifies whether printing is permitted. If this option is set to "no," clients may still be able to browse the printer share.
	printing	Specifies the type of printer interface used, which determines what commands Samba issues to control the printer. "BSD" is generally a good choice.
	printer name	Specifies the name of the printer to which the printer share corresponds; "lp" is generally a good choice.
Browse	*browseable*	Specifies whether the printer share is visible in the list of shares made available by the server.
Miscellaneous	*available*	Specifies whether the printer share is available; by setting this option to "no" you can prevent access to the printer share.

Viewing Samba Server Status

The Status button on *swat*'s tool bar lets you view the status of the Samba server. Figure 10-18 shows the page that appears when you click on Status. The page shows:

- the status of the server daemons (*smbd* and *nmbd*) and the version of Samba
- active connections
- active file and printer shares
- open files

Using the controls on the page, you can refresh the page contents, set the auto refresh interval, start and stop either daemon, or kill an active connection.

Viewing Samba Server Configuration

The View button on *swat*'s tool bar lets you view the Samba server's main configuration file, */etc/smb.conf.* Figure 10-19 shows the page that appears when you click on View. By default, the page shows only the basic configuration options; clicking on Full View causes *swat* to display every configuration option.

Managing Users and Passwords

You can create userids for accessing Samba resources by clicking on *swat*'s Password tool bar button. Figure 10-20 shows the Password page that appears.

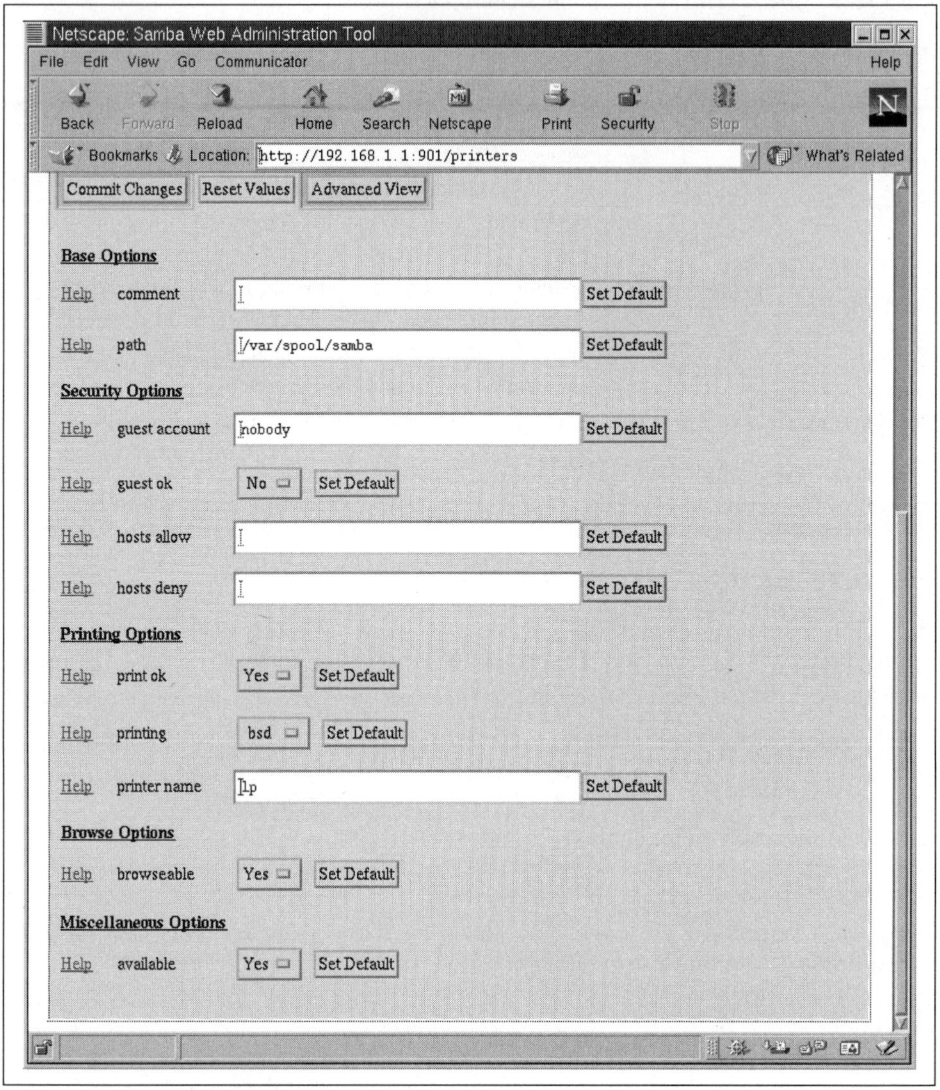

Figure 10-17. Samba printer parameters

The top part of the page, titled Server Password Management, lets you:

- Create a new userid

- Delete a userid

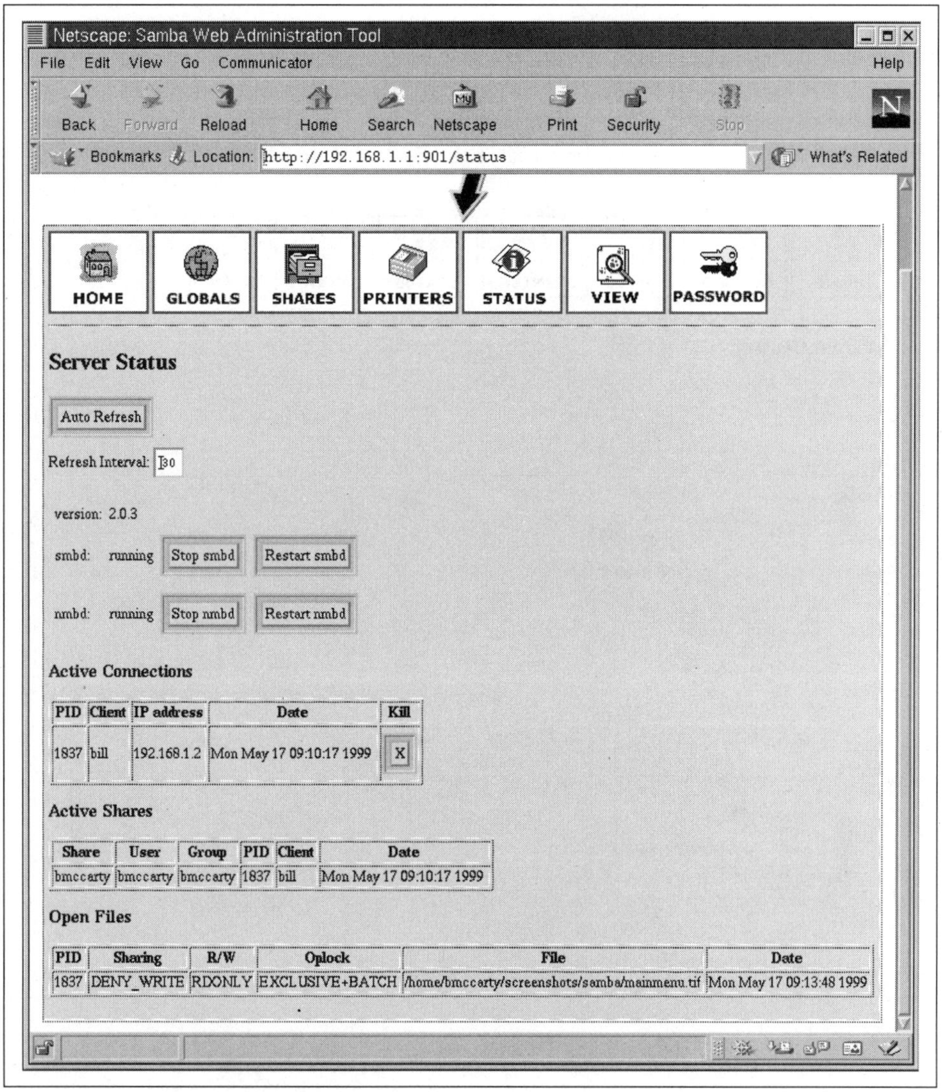

Figure 10-18. Samba status page

- Change the password associated with a userid

- Enable or disable a userid

The userids you specify using Server Password Management are those that your Samba server recognizes as authorized to access its resources.

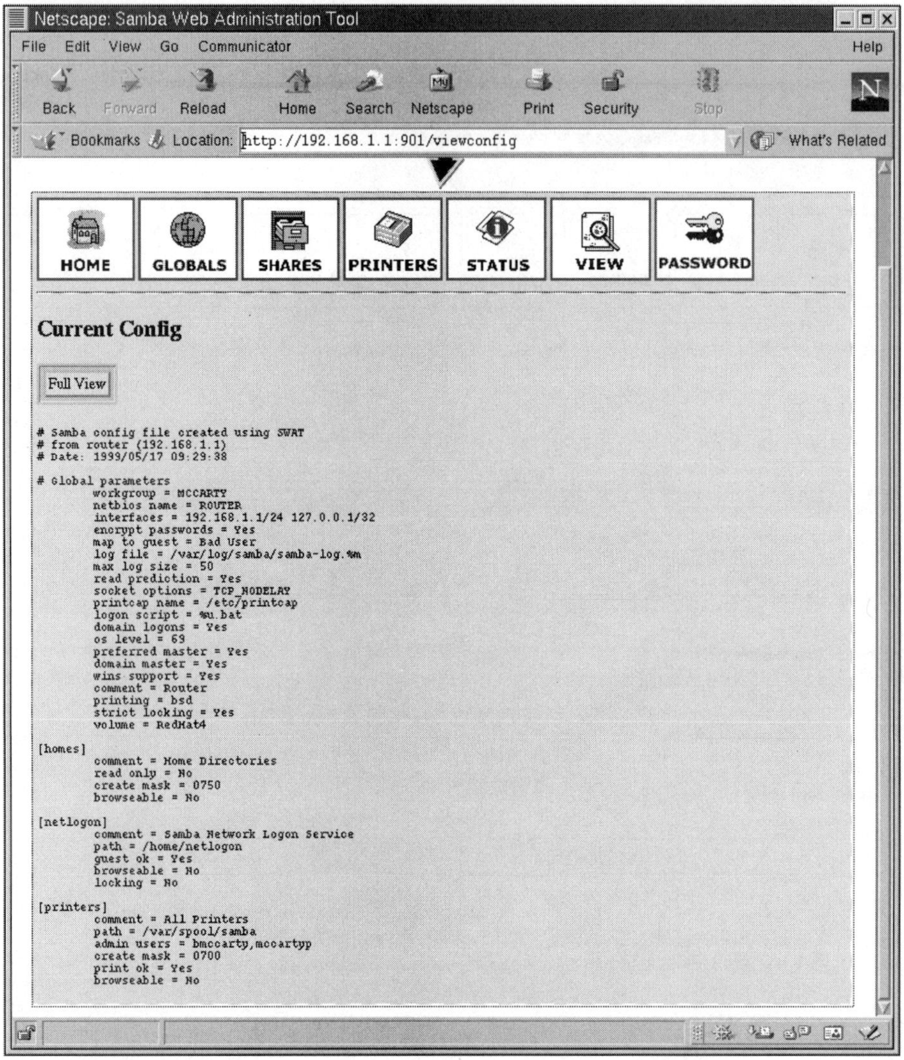

Figure 10-19. The Samba /etc/smb.conf file

The bottom part of the page, titled Client/Server Password Management, lets you change the password associated with a userid on a remote system running Samba or SMB. Changing a password by using Client/Server Password Management is often more convenient than logging in to the remote host and using its password change facility.

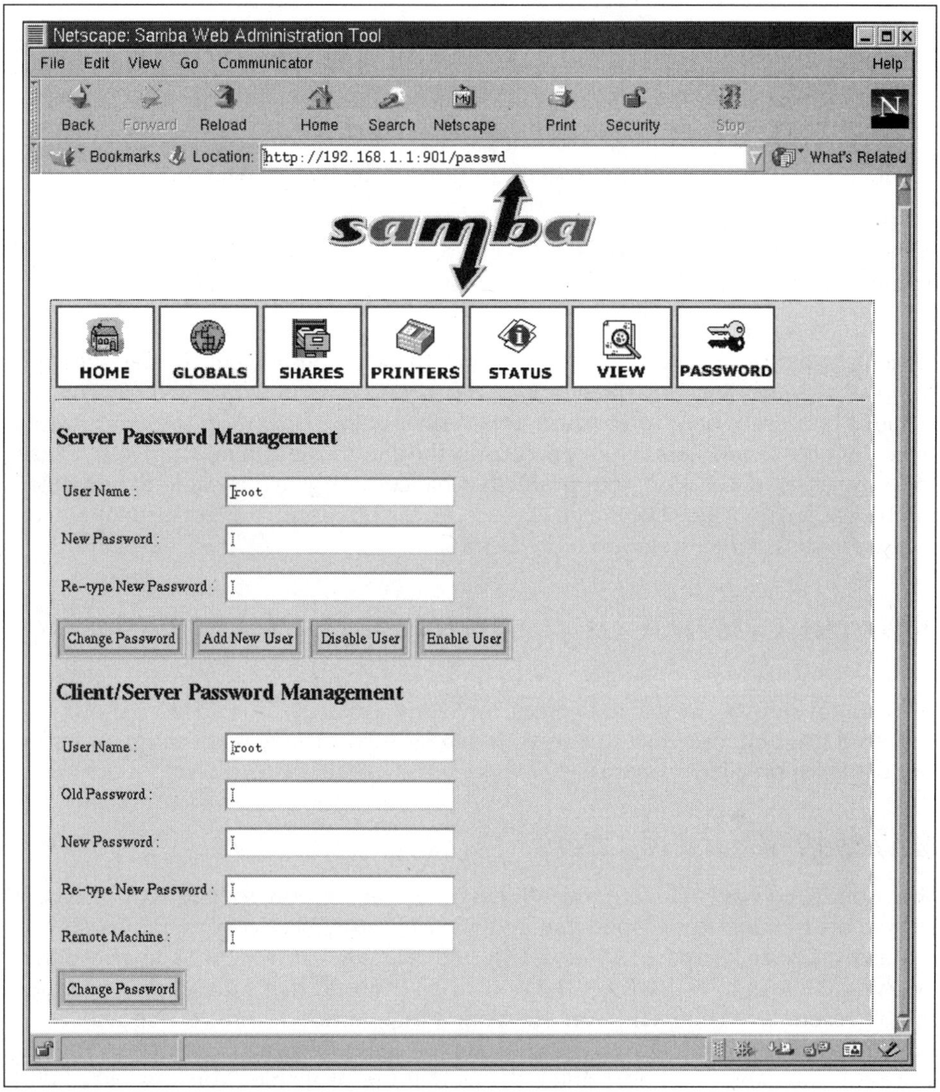

Netscape: Samba Web Administration Tool

File   Edit   View   Go   Communicator

Back   Forward   Reload   Home   Search   Netscape   Print   Security   Stop

Bookmarks   Location: http://192.168.1.1:901/passwd   What's Related

samba

HOME   GLOBALS   SHARES   PRINTERS   STATUS   VIEW   PASSWORD

Server Password Management

User Name :   root

New Password :

Re-type New Password :

Change Password   Add New User   Disable User   Enable User

Client/Server Password Management

User Name :   root

Old Password :

New Password :

Re-type New Password :

Remote Machine :

Change Password

Figure 10-20. The password page

Troubleshooting Samba

Like any network server, Samba provides a wealth of options and facilities. If you thoroughly explore these facilities, you're likely to break your server. To avoid problems, you should keep a backup copy of your */etc/smb.conf* file. Doing so can be as easy as issuing the following command after Samba is up and running:

```
cp /etc/smb.conf /etc/smb.conf.SAVE
```

Then, if your server ceases to work, you can restore your old configuration by issuing the command:

```
cp /etc/smb.conf.SAVE /etc/smb.conf
```

You'll also need to restart your system (or at least the Samba daemons).

On the other hand, you may have difficulty in getting Samba to operate correctly in the first place. Or, you may need to change Samba's configuration and therefore be unwilling to simply restore its previous status.

In such cases, you can consult the documentation that accompanies Samba. In particular, peruse the file *DIAGNOSIS.txt*, which should be in the */usr/doc/ Samba-2.0.3/docs/textdocs* directory, or its equivalent on your system. This file includes a step-by-step procedure for verifying the operation of your Samba server. When a step fails, you can consult the file to determine the likely causes and how to go about fixing the problem. Chances are, you'll be able to administer Samba without outside help; but, if you can't, you'll find the participants of the *comp.protocols.smb* newsgroup to be helpful.

Samba Client Configuration and Use

Once you've got your Samba server up and running, you can access it via Microsoft Windows, Linux, and other operating systems. This section shows you how to do so and also how to use your Samba server to create backups of important data files on client systems.

Microsoft Windows Client

Microsoft Windows 3.11, 9x, and NT have built-in support for the SMB protocol, so systems running these operating systems can easily access your Samba server's resources. Under Microsoft Windows 9x and NT, you can access Samba resources by using the Windows Explorer. Log on using a userid that's authorized to access Samba resources. Then click on Network Neighborhood and you should see a subtree that corresponds to your Samba server. By expanding the subtree, you can see the browseable file and printer shares that are available. You can easily drag and drop files to and from a shared directory, assuming your userid is permitted the necessary access.

To use a shared printer, click on Start → Settings → Printers and then double click on Add Printer. The wizard will guide you through the setup procedure. Simply choose the Network Printer option and then browse to select the desired printer. If you configured the printer share without the browseable option, you cannot browse and therefore must type the name of the printer share. To do so, type two backward slashes, followed by the name of your Samba server, followed by a single backslash, followed by the name of the printer share. For example, if you want to access a printer share named *lp* on the Samba server known as *SERVER*, you'd type *\\SERVER\lp*.

You can map a file share to a drive letter by using the Tools → Map Network Drive menu item of the Windows Explorer. Simply select an available drive letter and type the name of the file share, which consists of two backward slashes, followed by the name of your Samba server, followed by a single backslash, followed by the name of the file share. For example, if you want to access a file share named *db* on the Samba server known as *SERVER*, you'd type *\\SERVER\db*.

If you have difficulty connecting to your Samba server, follow the procedure given in the preceding section on troubleshooting.

Other Clients

Of course, an SMB client is available for Linux; you'll learn about it in the next subsection. SMB clients are also available for most popular operating systems, including IBM OS/2 and Mac OS. You shouldn't expect to have trouble getting them to work with Samba. If your client seems not to work, simply follow the procedure given in the troubleshooting section.

Linux Client

The Samba package includes a simple SMB client that can access your Samba server and other SMB servers accessible to your system. To demonstrate that your client and server are working, log on using a userid that has Samba authorization and issue the following command:

```
smbclient -L localhost
```

You should see a list of the browseable shares available on your server. To query a different SMB server, issue the following command:

```
smbclient -L server
```

where *server* is the name of the SMB server you want to contact. Rather than log on using a authorized userid, you can explicitly specify a userid by using this command form:

```
smbclient -L server -U userid
```

To actually access resources via SMB, use the following command form:

```
smbclient -L service -U userid
```

where *service* specifies the name of the SMB host and share and *userid* specifies the userid to be used. The name of the SMB host should be preceded by two backward slashes and followed by one backward slash.

If the SMB server accepts your request, the client displays a special prompt:

    smb: *dir>*

where *dir* indicates the current working directory on the SMB server. To download a file from the server, issue the command:

    get *file*

where *file* specifies the name of the file. To upload a file to the server, issue the command:

    put *file*

where *file* specifies the name of the file. To list the contents of the current directory, issue the command:

    dir

where *file* specifies the name of the file. To enter a subdirectory, issue the command:

    cd *dir*

where *dir* specifies the name of the subdirectory. You can return to the parent directory by issuing the command:

    cd ..

To exit the SMB client, issue the command *exit*. You can obtain a list of commands by issuing the command *help* or obtain help on a particular command by issuing the command:

    help *command*:

where *command* specifies the command for which you want help.

Ivan Volosuk has written an X11 interface for **smbclient**, which you may find easier to use. You can learn more about it from his web page, available at *http://www.rt.mipt.ru/frtk/ivan/*.

You can use *smbprint* script included in the Samba package to print Linux files by using a printer share. However, you'll probably have to do some tweaking of configuration files and adjusting of shell scripts to get *smbprint* to work. This might be a good project for you to tackle after you've read Chapter 13, *Conquering the BASH Shell*.

Using the Linux Samba Client for File Backup and Recovery

One of the most practical uses of the Linux SMB client is creating backup copies of files stored on a Microsoft Windows system. To do so, simply share the drive or directory containing the files you want to backup: using the Windows Explorer, right click on the drive or directory, click on Properties, click on the Sharing tab, and select the desired share options. Then, access the share from Linux using *smb-client*. Once you have the SMB prompt, move to the directory you want to backup, and issue the following SMB command:

```
tar c backup.tar
```

The files of the current directory and all its subdirectories will be backed up and stored in the file *backup.tar* on your Linux system. Of course, you can specify a filename other than *backup.tar*, if you wish. Once you've created the backup file, you can write it to a tape, a writable CD-ROM, or other media, if you need an off-site copy. If your backup requirements are meager, it may be sufficient merely to have a copy of the file on both your Windows system and your Linux system.

To restore a backup, move to the directory to which you want the files restored and issue the following SMB command:

```
tar x backup.tar
```

The SMB client restores each file from the tar file. Of course, you must have write access to the shared directory in order to be able to write the restored files.

CHAPTER ELEVEN

GETTING CONNECTED TO THE INTERNET

This chapter explains how to use Linux to connect to remote servers. First, it explains how to use *wvdial*, a program that makes it easy to connect to the Internet via a PPP connection provided by an ISP. Then, the chapter explains basic TCP/IP network concepts that you must know in order to administer a Linux system connected to the Internet or a local area network. So that you can use your knowledge of TCP/IP effectively, the chapter explains how to use *linuxconf* to configure and administer a system that connects to a local area network and to a remote server via PPP. Next, the chapter describes several popular network client applications available under Linux, including a web browser and an FTP client. The chapter then describes the use of *minicom* and *seyon*, which provide dial-out capabilities like those of Window's *hyperterminal*. Finally, the chapter shows how to make a PPP connection manually, by using *minicom*.

Connecting to the Internet

Most Internet service providers (ISPs) offer two primary types of service: shell accounts and PPP (point-to-point protocol) accounts. Shell accounts were more popular before the advent of the Web. A shell account lets you use your computer much as if it were a virtual console associated with a remote computer. You can type commands, which are interpreted by the remote computer, and view the resulting output on your computer. Although a few web browsers, such as Lynx, can operate via a shell account, they don't generally support the highly graphical, multimedia pages which web surfers have come to expect.

In contrast, a PPP account connects your computer directly to the Internet. While your computer is connected to the Internet, you can use it to surf the Web with your favorite browser. If your ISP allows, you can even run a web server, providing pages that can be viewed by others around the world.

You can compare the two types of Internet accounts—shell and PPP—with two kinds of postal service. Imagine that no mail carrier actually comes to your home to pick and deliver mail. Instead, every time you want to conduct postal business, you go to the post office. This resembles a shell account: The computer that connects you to the Internet is remote, and every time you want to do something on the Internet you must open a terminal, or telnet, session to that computer. PPP, on the other hand, is like home delivery: The Internet comes right to your doorstep, and your computer is literally placed on the Internet by the machine at your ISP that you connect to.

Under Microsoft Windows, you use *hyperterminal* to access a shell account and Dial-Up Networking to access a PPP account. Under Linux, you can choose from among several programs that let you access a shell account. The most commonly used programs are *minicom* and *seyon*. To access a PPP account under Linux, you use the PPP daemon, *pppd*. The next section describes how to use *wvdial* to make the process of establishing a PPP connection simple.

Configuring Your Modem

Your modem is a peripheral device to Linux, like a CD-ROM drive, hard drive, or a mouse. Your modem will be connected to a serial port, which means that one of the serial devices in the */dev* directory actually points to your modem. You'll notice that there's also a file, */dev/modem*, which serves as a placeholder for your modem. Initially this file doesn't point to anything. To simplify your operations, so that applications like `minicom` and *seyon* need only refer to */dev/modem*, you can create a symbolic link from the serial device connected to your modem to */dev/modem*. The easiest way to do so is to use *modemtool*.

To use *modemtool*, start X. Then launch an xterm and issue the following commands:

```
su
export DISPLAY=:0
modemtool
```

You'll have to correctly respond to `su`'s request for the `root` password.

Figure 11-1 shows the dialog box that *modemtool* displays. Simply click on the device that corresponds to your modem (usually *ttyS1*) and click on Ok. The program creates the required symbolic link on your behalf.

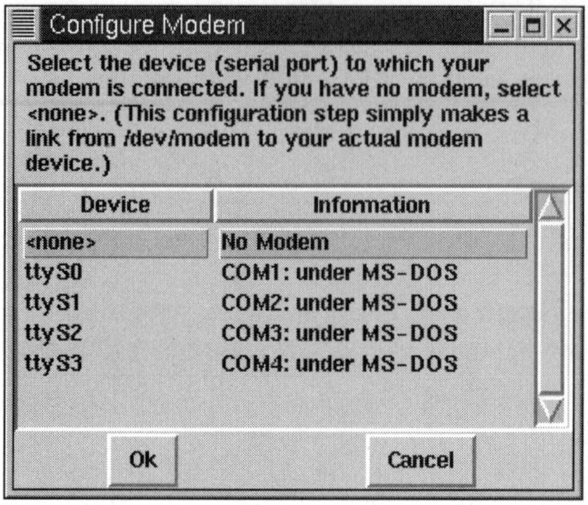

Figure 11-1. Using modemtool to configure a modem

Alternatively, from the console or an xterm, you can issue the command:

```
ln -s /dev/ttySX /dev/modem
```

where *X* is replaced by the number corresponding to the serial device that points to your modem.

TIP   Conventions about numbering devices differ on different systems. On Windows, device numbers begin with 1, so your modem is likely to be either COM1 or COM2. On Linux, device numbers begin with 0, so COM1 corresponds to ttyS0 and COM2 corresponds to ttyS1.

Using wvdial

ISPs use a variety of dialogs to make a PPP connection. Often the most difficult part of configuring your computer to make a PPP connection is specifying dialog options consistent with those required by your ISP, which may not be especially helpful in explaining the necessary options to you.

For example, most ISPs use one of three PPP login procedures: PAP (Password Authentication Protocol), CHAP (Challenge-Handshake Authentication Protocol), or ordinary user/password authentication. PAP is currently the most popular of the three procedures. If you ask the tech support person at your ISP what login procedure your ISP uses, the tech support person may have no idea what you're talking about, because most users run Microsoft Windows, and Windows Dial-Up Networking handles the login procedure transparently.

The *wvdial* program transparently establishes a PPP connection in much the same way as Windows Dial-Up Networking. It understands a variety of possible dialogs used by ISPs. In most cases, it will analyze data sent by your ISP and respond with the proper data in the format required by the ISP.

To install *wvdial*, follow the instructions given in Appendix C, *The Red Hat Package Manager*. Then, issue the following command:

```
/usr/local/bin/wvdialconf /etc/wvdial.conf
```

This command analyzes your system and creates a template configuration file, */etc/wvdial.conf.* You must edit this file to specify the userid and password your ISP expects. The contents of the template file will look something like this:

```
[Dialer Defaults]
Modem = /dev/ttyS1
Baud =   115200
Init1 = ATZ
Init2 = ATQ0 V1 E1 &C1 &D2 +FCLASS=0
; Phone = Target Phone Number
; Username = Your Login Name
; Password = Your Password
```

Edit the last three lines of the file, deleting the leading semi-colon and space and substituting the proper phone number, userid, and password required to connect to your ISP. Then, after the line that specifies the phone number, add a line that reads:

```
New PPPD
```

When you're done, your file should resemble this one:

```
[Dialer Defaults]
Modem = /dev/ttyS1
Baud =   115200
Init1 = ATZ
Init2 = ATQ0 V1 E1 &C1 &D2 +FCLASS=0
Phone = 15625551100
New PPPD
Username = bill100
Password = donttell
```

Next, be sure that you've established your name server configuration, as described in Chapter 10, *Setting Up a Linux-Based LAN*.

Now, you're ready to make a connection. Issue the following commands:

```
route del default
/usr/local/bin/wvdial &
```

The second command generates quite a bit of output, which makes further use of this virtual terminal distracting. The simplest solution is to switch to another virtual terminal, by pressing **Alt-***n*, where *n* stands for the virtual terminal (1–7).

Alternatively, you can direct the output of the command to a file, by typing this command in place of the one given earlier:

```
/usr/local/bin/wvdial 2>/tmp/wvdial.messages &
```

Of course, you'll need to consult the file if something goes wrong with *wvdial*. Do so by using the *more* command:

```
more /tmp/wvdial.messages
```

Once your connection is up, you can browse the Web and access other Internet services, as described later in this chapter. For now, simply verify that your connection is working by issuing the command:

```
ping www.oreilly.com
```

The *ping* command should report that echo packets were successfully received from the server. If not, check your name server configuration.

When you want to log off your ISP, issue the following command:

```
killall /usr/local/bin/wvdial
```

PPP Client

The Linux PPP client lets your Linux system connect to the Internet via a PPP server, much the same way Dial-Up Networking lets your Microsoft Windows system do so. Behind the scenes, *wvdial* calls on the services of the PPP client to connect to a PPP server. However, it's possible to use the Linux PPP client directly, without the aid of *wvdial*. Doing so gives you access to the many options provided by PPP, which can prove helpful if your networking needs are too sophisticated to be met by *wvdial's* simple fire-and-forget mechanism. Even if you're content with *wvdial*, you'll benefit from understanding the PPP client. For example, you'll find it much easier to troubleshoot PPP problems if you understand the functions performed by the PPP client on behalf of *wvdial*.

The PPP/SLIP/PLIP Configuration dialog box, shown in Figure 11-2, lets you specify one or more connection configurations. The dialog box also lets you specify SLIP and PLIP connections, though these are used much less frequently than PPP. With the advent of PPP, SLIP and PLIP have fallen by the wayside; PPP is really all you need to know about.

When you click on Add, the PPP Interface dialog box, shown in Figure 11-3, appears. This dialog box contains four tabs; the figure shows the Hardware tab.

The default options on the Hardware tab are generally acceptable. You should specify hardware flow control and instruct PPP to abort the connection when any of a set of defined errors is detected. If you experience problems in transmitting and receiving data via PPP, you can specify that transmitted control characters should be escaped; doing so may stop your modem from garbling transmissions.

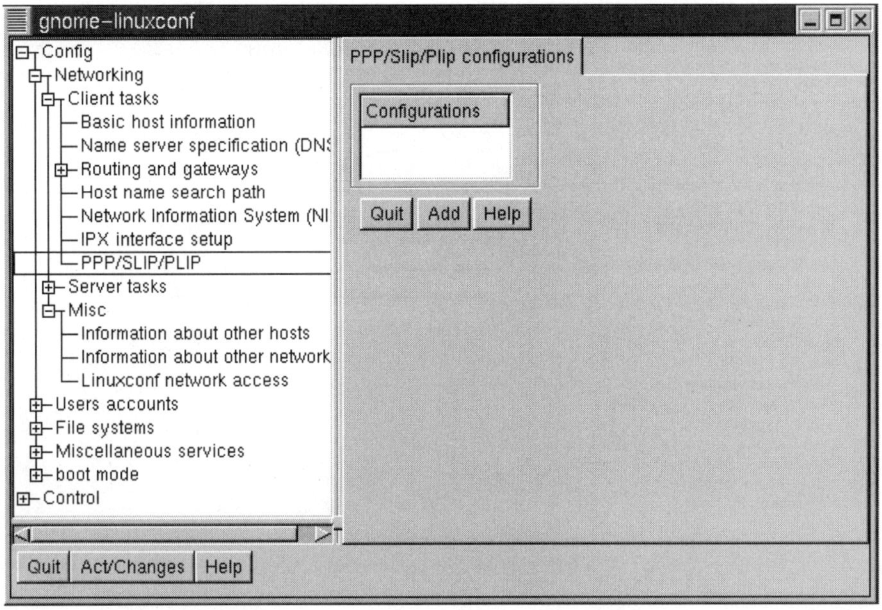

Figure 11-2. PPP configuration options

Generally, you should specify the highest line speed supported by your modem; the default option, 115200, baud is generally a good choice. You should specify the device file that corresponds to your modem. If you've used *modemtool* to configure your modem (as described later in this chapter), you can simply specify */dev/modem.*

When you've specified the hardware options, move on to the communication tab, shown in Figure 11-4. Generally, all you need to specify is the phone number of your ISP. However, if your ISP's PPP server requires a special sequence of commands in order to establish your connection, you can specify those commands using this dialog box.

The Networking tab, shown in Figure 11-5, lets you specify options related to PPP networking. Generally, the default options are acceptable. However, if you want your system to automatically establish a PPP connection when it's booted, you should specify the Activate Interface at Boot Time option.

Most PPP servers prompt for a userid and password before establishing a connection. Use the PAP tab, shown in Figure 11-6, to specify the userid and password required to access your PPP server.

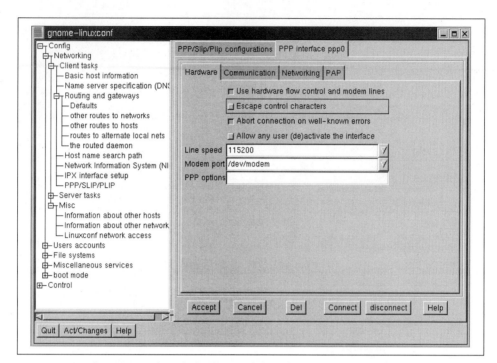

Figure 11-3. The PPP interface dialog box and the PPP hardware options

Once you've completely specified your PPP options, you can click Act/Changes to activate your changes. Then, you're ready to establish a PPP connection. Select the Config → Networking → Client Tasks → PPP/SLIP/PLIP subtree and click Connect on the dialog box that appears. You can monitor the progress of the operation by issuing the following command:

```
tail -f /var/log/messages
```

This command continually displays messages as they're posted to the system log file. Because PPP writes log entries that describe its progress, the command lets you see what PPP is doing. When you're done viewing log entries, type **Ctrl-C** to exit the *tail* command.

You can verify that the PPP connection has been established by issuing the following command:

```
ifconfig
```

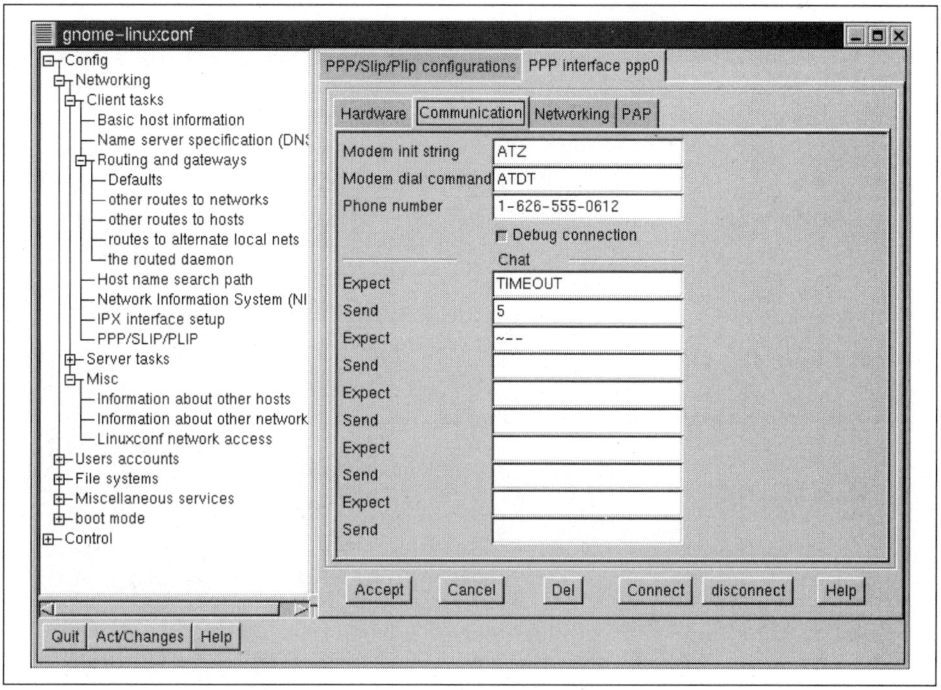

Figure 11-4. PPP communication options

If the output of the command includes a description of a PPP connection, the connection was successfully established. To verify that the connection is operational, issue the *ping* command:

```
ping www.oreilly.com
```

If your connection failed, you should check the following before contacting your ISP or other Linux users for support:

* Did you correctly specify your ISP's phone number?

* Did you correctly specify your userid and password?

* Did you correctly specify your modem's device file and line speed?

* Is your modem properly connected to your telephone line?

* Is your telephone line operational?

When you want to terminate the PPP connection, you can click on the Disconnect button of the dialog box you used to establish the connection.

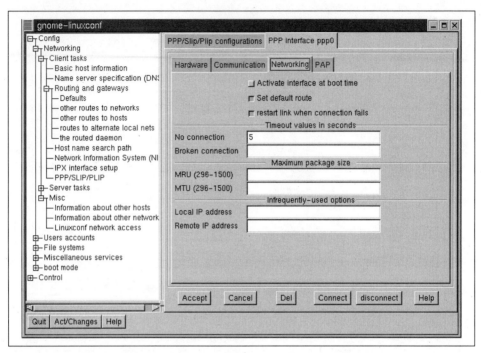

Figure 11-5. PPP networking options

Web Browser

Once you've established a PPP connection to the Internet, whether via *wvdial* or *pppd*, you can surf the Web using a Linux browser. In addition to browsers written specifically for Unix and Linux, you can use the popular Netscape Navigator web browser, which includes a mail client, newsgroup client, HTML editor, and other features.

As you can see in Figure 11-7, the Linux version of Navigator is very similar to the Microsoft Windows version. So, if you've used the Microsoft Windows version of Navigator, you'll find configuring and using Navigator to be quite straightforward. To configure Navigator, click on Edit → Preferences. Then specify your identity and that of your mail and newsgroup servers, along with any other special preferences you desire.

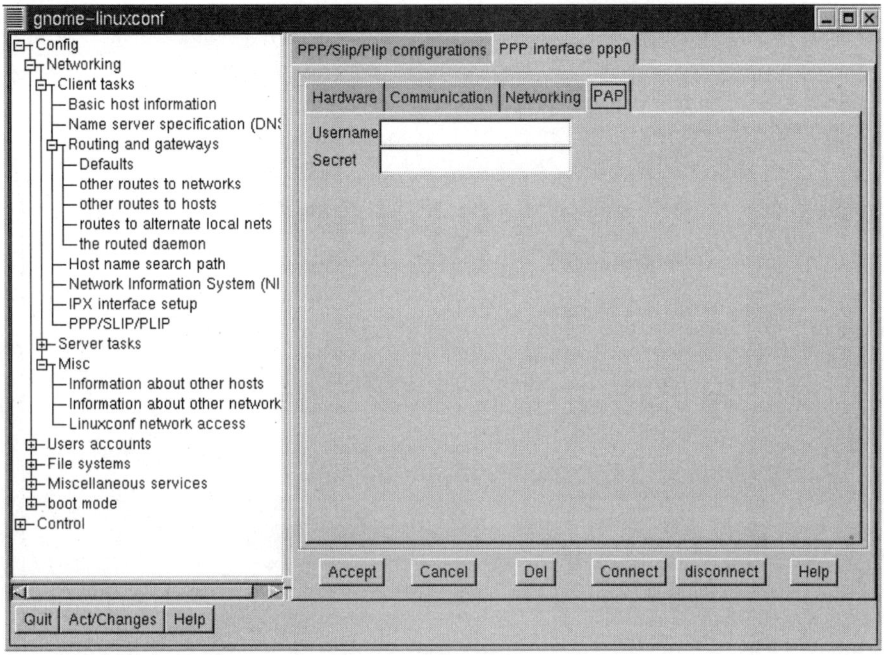

Figure 11-6. PPP PAP options

gFTP FTP Client

You can use your web browser to download files from an FTP server, but to upload files you need an FTP client. The gFTP client, included on the Linux CD-ROM, is an excellent choice, because its user interface resembles that of popular Microsoft Windows FTP clients, such as WS-FTP.

Figure 11-8 shows the *gFTP* client. To connect to a remote system, click on Remote → Connect, identify the system's hostname, specify any necessary userid or password, and click on Connect. To upload a file, click on the name of the file in the local list box at the left of the window and then click on →. To download a file, click on the name of the file in the list box at the right of the window and then click on ←. When you've transferred all your files, click on Remote → Disconnect.

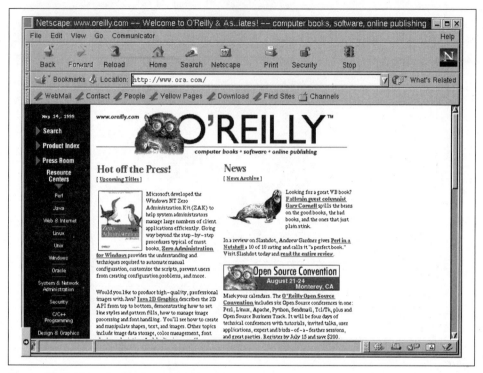

Figure 11-7. Netscape Navigator for Linux

Using minicom and seyon

Some ISPs provide a choice of a PPP account or a shell account. The two most popular Linux programs for accessing a shell account are *minicom*, a graphical program that runs in a virtual console, and *seyon*, which runs under X. Although *seyon* has the more modern user interface, most Linux users prefer *minicom*, which supports more options than does *seyon*.

Using seyon

Once you've configured your modem, you're ready to run *seyon*. To do so, start X and issue the command:

```
seyon
```

Figure 11-9 shows the main *seyon* window. The top row contains several labels that indicate the status of your modem:

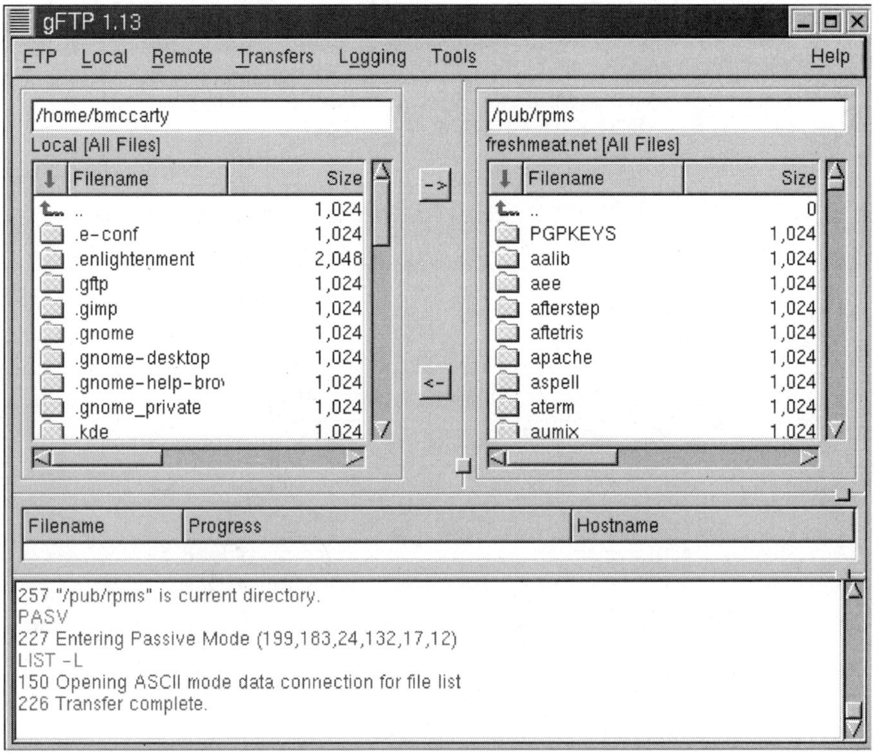

Figure 11-8. The gFTP FTP client

DTR

> Indicates that your computer is ready to send and receive data

DSR

> Indicates that the modem is ready to send and receive data

RTS

> Indicates that your computer has requested to send data

CTS

> Indicates that the modem is ready to receive data

RNG

> Indicates that the modem has detected a ring signal on the telephone line

The second row contains several programmable buttons, which have no associated default action. The remaining buttons, in the third, fourth, and fifth rows, let you operate *seyon*. For example, to make a connection, you click on the Dial button, which pops up *seyon*'s Dialing Directory dialog box, shown in Figure 11-10.

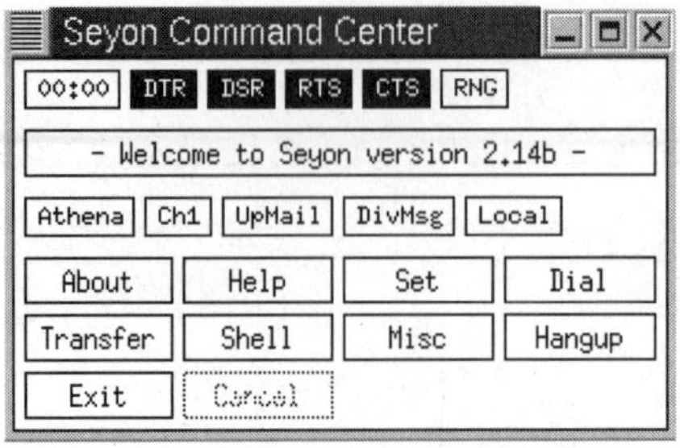

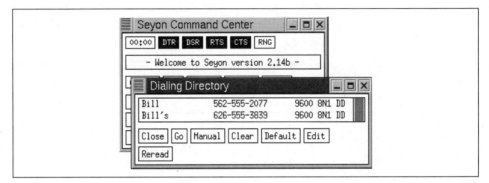

Figure 11-9. The main seyon window

Figure 11-10. The seyon Dialing Directory

However, the Dialing Directory dialog box will not appear until you create a file named *phonelist* in the *.seyon* subdirectory of your home directory. To do so, issue the following commands:

```
cd
mkdir .seyon
> .seyon/phonelist
```

The third command uses a clever trick to create an empty file: it redirects the output of a null command to the file. Now, when you click on Dial, the Dialing Directory dialog box appears, although no entries will be shown. To create an entry, click on Edit and an edit window appears. Type the name of the entry and the phone number, separated by a space. If you like, you can specify other options, such as the desired connection speed, the number of bits per character, the data parity, and the number of stop bits associated with a character. However, usually such options are not required. Clicking on Help on *seyon*'s main menu will pop up a window that describes *seyon* and its operation, including the contents of the *phonelist* file.

To initiate a connection, simply highlight the entry in the Dialing Directory dialog box and click on Go. When the connection has been established, the Dialing Directory dialog box will disappear. You can click Hangup to abruptly terminate a connection or Exit to exit *seyon*.

Using minicom

Despite a user interface less modern than that of *seyon*, *minicom* is the more popular Linux communications program. Before launching *minicom*, you must configure it. To do so, login in as **root** and issue the command:

```
minicom -s
```

Figure 11-11 shows the Configuration dialog box that *minicom* presents. Like the Linux install program, *minicom* does not support use of the mouse. Instead, you use tab and cursor keys to navigate the screen. For example, you can use the up and down arrow keys to highlight various items on the configuration menu. To select an item, highlight it and press **Enter**.

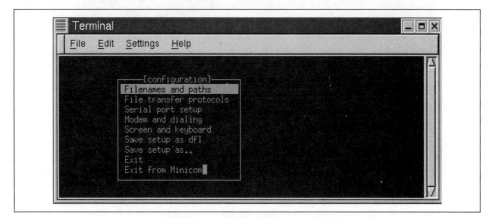

Figure 11-11. The minicom configuration dialog box

Generally, the default configuration options are acceptable. You can simply highlight Save Setup As Dfl, press **Enter**, then highlight Exit From Minicom, and press **Enter**. However, the next several subsections briefly describe the available options just in case you may need to change them.

Configuring filenames and paths

The *minicom* dialog box for configuring filenames and paths is shown in Figure 11-12. Using it, you can configure the default directories used by *minicom* for downloads, uploads, and scripts. You can also configure the name of the program used to process *minicom* scripts and the path for *kermit* (a program used to perform file transfers) though it's unlikely you'll want to do so.

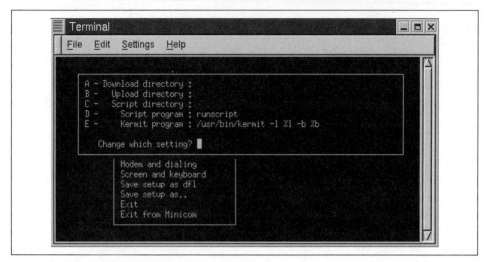

Figure 11-12. Configuring filenames and paths

To change an option, type the letter that appears to the left of the option, type the desired value of the option, and press **Enter**. No changes are stored until you select a Save item from the main menu.

Configuring file transfer protocols

The *minicom* dialog box for configuring file transfer protocols is shown in Figure 11-13. For each supported protocol, you can specify the path and command line arguments used to perform uploads and downloads. You can also specify how ASCII uploads are performed and set several transfer options.

The columns have the following meanings:

- Name specifies whether the program requires a filename as an argument
- U/D specifies whether a given row specifies an upload protocol (U) or download protocol (D)
- FullScr specifies whether the program runs in its own window

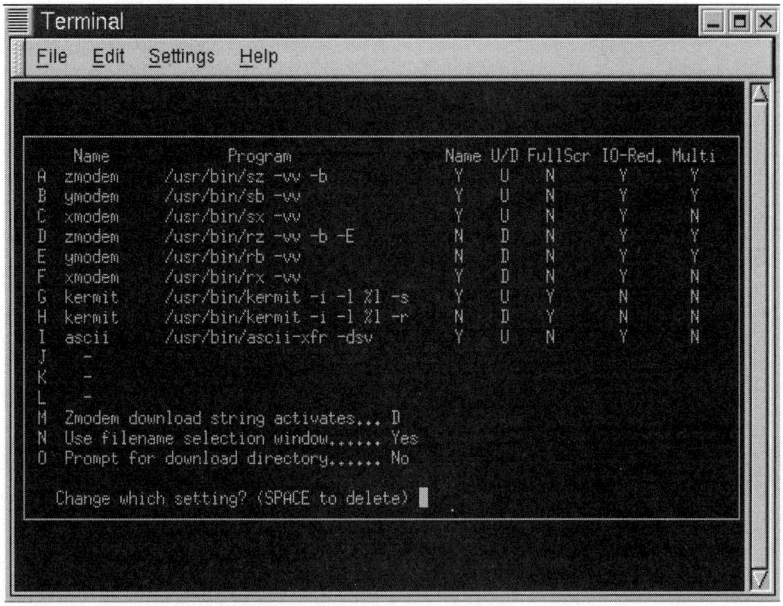

Figure 11-13. Configuring file transfer protocols

- IO-Red. specifies whether the program obtains its input from the standard input stream and directs its output to the standard output stream

- Multi specifies whether multiple files can be transferred by a single command

As mentioned, you probably won't need to change any file transfer options. However, you can change an option by typing the letter that appears to its left, typing the desired value of the option, and pressing **Enter**. No changes are stored until you select a Save item from the main menu.

Configuring the serial port

The *minicom* dialog box for configuring the serial port is shown in Figure 11-14. If you have a high-speed modem, you may obtain faster data transfers by increasing the data rate from the default 38400 bps to 57600 bps or 115200 bps. You can change this and other options in the same way you change filename and path options and file transfer protocol options.

Configuring modem and dialing options

The *minicom* dialog box for configuring modem and dialing options is shown in Figure 11-15. If your modem uses standard (Hayes-compatible) commands, you'll probably find the default options satisfactory. However, the default options will

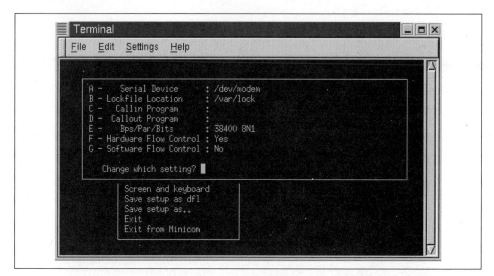

Figure 11-14. Configuring the serial port

probably not take advantage of special capabilities afforded by your modem. You can consult your modem documentation and revise the command strings to incorporate the codes that activate your modem's special features.

Configuring screen and keyboard options

The *minicom* dialog box for configuring screen and keyboard options is shown in Figure 11-16. Many users prefer screen colors other than those provided by default. You can separately specify the foreground and background colors of the menu, terminal window, and status line.

Saving your changes

After you've made changes to *minicom*'s options, use the Save Setup As Dfl item on the main menu to save your new configuration as the default configuration. To do so, highlight the Save Setup As Dfl item, press **Enter**, then highlight Exit From Minicom, and press **Enter**.

Running minicom

Once you've configured *minicom*, you're ready to launch it. To do so, issue the command:

```
minicom -c on
```

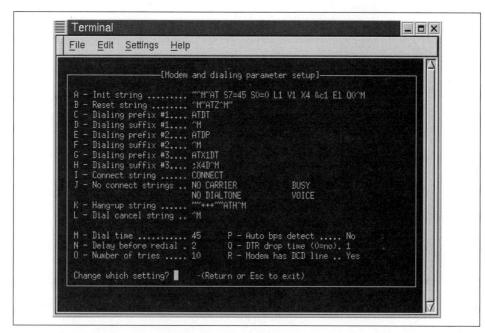

Figure 11-15. Configuring modem and dialing options

The arguments specify that *minicom* should present a color display; without them, its output is monochrome. Figure 11-17 shows *minicom* 's terminal window and status line.

To operate *minicom,* you use single letter commands that you call up by typing **Ctrl-A** and then the command. For example, typing **Ctrl-A** followed by Z produces the command summary shown in Figure 11-18.

To access *minicom*'s Dialing Directory dialog box, type **Ctrl-A** followed by D. Figure 11-19 shows this dialog box. The menu at the bottom of the dialog box lets you dial the selected entry, find an entry that contains a specified text string, add a new entry, edit an existing entry, or remove an entry. You can also manually dial a number that's not in the directory.

Once you've mastered *minicom*'s basic functions, you might enjoy learning how to write scripts. Using scripts, you can (for example) automate logging into your shell account, eliminating the need for you to recall your userid and password. Consult the files in */usr/doc/minicom-1.82/doc* and */usr/doc/minicom-1.82/demos* to learn how *minicom*'s scripting language works and how to write your own scripts.

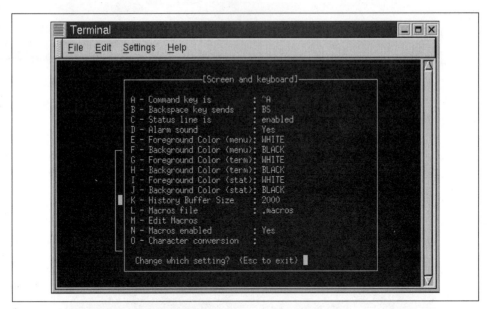

Figure 11-16. Configuring screen and keyboard options

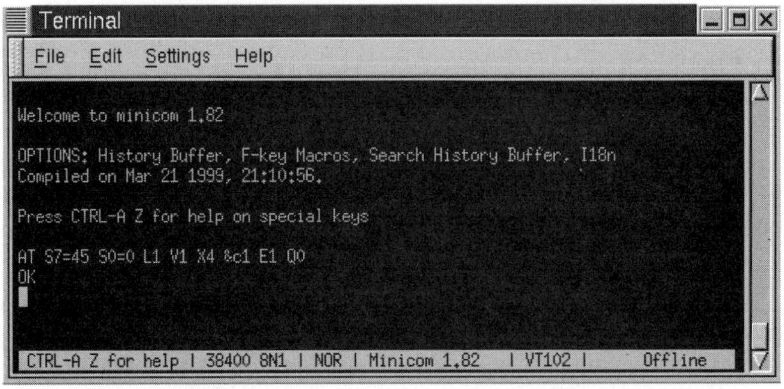

Figure 11-17. The minicom main window

Making a PPP Connection Manually

Sometimes you may have difficulty making a PPP connection by using *wvdial* or *linuxconf*. In such a case, it's helpful to know how to make a PPP connection manually. Once you make a connection, you can use email and Usenet newsgroups to seek the help you need to resolve your problem in using *wvdial* or *linuxconf*.

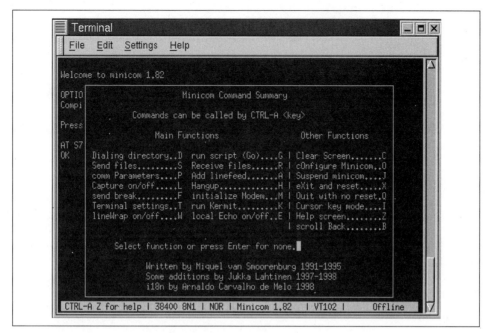

Figure 11-18. The minicom Command Summary

Before making the PPP connection, you must have:

- Established the name server configuration, as described in Chapter 10.

- Established the PAP configuration, as described earlier in this chapter.

If you're unsure whether you've performed these operations, do them again, just to be safe.

To make a PPP connection manually, log in as `root`, launch *minicom* and dial your ISP. If your ISP prompts for a userid or password, reply appropriately. Most ISPs now use automatic authentication, so it isn't usually necessary to enter your user information. Once authentication is complete, nonsense characters should begin to appear on *minicom*'s screen. Type **Ctrl-A** then J to suspend *minicom* and launch a shell. At the shell prompt, issue the commands:

```
route del default
pppd -detach defaultroute /dev/modem 38400 &
```

In a short while, the PPP connection should be made. To verify that the connection is working, use a web browser to contact a remote server. If this doesn't work, check your configuration carefully.

Figure 11-19. The minicom Dialing Directory

To shut down the PPP connection, issue the command:

```
ppp -off
```

After a short pause, the modem will hang up. To resume *minicom*, type the command:

```
fg
```

You can then exit *minicom* normally.

CHAPTER TWELVE

SETTING UP A
LINUX-BASED WAN

In the last chapter, you learned how to connect your Linux system to a local-area network or, via an Internet Service Provider, to the Internet. By doing so, you were able to access a plethora of services provided by others, including file transfers via FTP, web pages, email, and telnet. In this chapter you'll learn how to set up several Linux wide-area network servers, including an FTP server, a web server (Apache), an email (SMTP/POP) server, and a dial-in shell server. These applications let you and others access data on your Linux system from anywhere in the world via the Internet. These applications will be most useful if your system is connected to the Internet 24 hours a day, 7 days a week. But, even if your connection is intermittent, you and others can access the services these applications provide whenever the connection is active.

Installing and Configuring an FTP Server

An FTP server lets you transfer files from one system to another, via a network. When two computers are connected to the Internet, you can use FTP to transfer files from one to the other even though the computers are not directly connected.

An FTP server attempts to authenticate users that request to use it. You can configure your FTP server to accept requests only from users who have an account on the system running the FTP server. Alternatively, you can configure the FTP server to accept requests from anyone, via a facility known as *anonymous FTP*. It's fairly simple to install and configure an anonymous FTP server; however, hackers regularly exploit vulnerabilities in anonymous FTP servers, breaking into systems and causing manifold mischief. Because it's difficult to protect a system running anonymous FTP from attack, this section does not describe the process for installing and configuring anonymous FTP.

Configuring the FTP Server

To configure your FTP server, you must add a line to the */etc/inetd.conf* file:

```
ftp     stream tcp     nowait root     /usr/sbin/tcpd in.ftpd -l -a
```

This line starts the FTP server process whenever an FTP client requests a connection. To cause the new configuration to take effect, you must reboot your system. Alternatively, you can use the following command to cause the `inetd` daemon to re-read its configuration file:

```
killall -HUP inetd
```

Testing the FTP Server

To test your FTP server, start an FTP client by issuing the following command:

```
ftp localhost
```

The FTP server should prompt you for a login userid and password. If you correctly supply them, you should see the FTP prompt that lets you know the FTP server is ready to execute FTP subsystem commands. Type `quit` and press **Enter** to exit the FTP client. Or, if you'd like to transfer some files, you can use the FTP subsystem commands described in Table 12-1.

Table 12-1. Important FTP Subsystem Commands

Command	Function
`!command`	Invokes a shell on the local system. You can use this command, for example, to obtain a listing of the current directory on the local system by issuing the command `!ls`, for a Unix system, or `!dir`, for a Microsoft system.
`ascii`	Specifies that files will be transferred in ASCII mode.
`binary`	Specifies that files will be transferred in binary mode, which performs no translation.
`cd directory`	Changes to the specified directory of the remote system.
`delete file`	Deletes the specified file from the remote system.
`dir`	Displays the contents of the current directory of the remote system.
`get file`	Retrieves the specified file from the remote system.
`help`	Displays command help information.

Table 12-1. Important FTP Subsystem Commands (continued)

Command	Function
`lcd` *directory*	Changes to the specified directory of the local system.
`mkdir` *directory*	Creates the specified directory on the remote system.
`put` *file*	Stores the specified local file on the remote system.
`pwd`	Displays the current working directory on the remote system.
`quit`	Exits the FTP subsystem.
`rmdir` *directory*	Removes the specified directory from the remote system.

If your FTP fails to respond properly, check the line you added to the *inetd.conf* file. If you're unable to find an error, reboot your system. If that fails to solve the problem, post a message to the *comp.os.linux.setup* newsgroup.

Once your FTP server is working, try contacting it from a remote system. If you have a Microsoft Windows system, you can contact your server by using the built-in FTP client that works similarly to the Linux FTP client, interpreting the same FTP subsystem commands. Open an MS-DOS Prompt window and type the command:

```
ftp server
```

where *server* specifies the hostname or IP address of your Linux server. Generally, once the FTP subsystem prompt is available, you should immediately issue the **binary** command. This command specifies that files will be transferred verbatim; without it, executable files, documents, and other files that contain binary data will be scrambled when transferred.

Most Windows users prefer to use a graphical FTP client. Many such clients, including WS-FTP, are freely available and make FTP access easy for even novice Windows users. FTP provides a very fast and reliable way for a Linux server to share files with Windows clients, without the need to install and configure Samba.

Installing and Configuring a Web Server

Installing and configuring a web server is not much more difficult than installing an FTP server. Once your web server is up and running, other Internet users can view documents you publish on your Linux system.

Configuration

Configuring a web server can be as easy or as difficult as you choose. Like other web servers, Apache provides seemingly countless options. Fortunately, you probably need to set only one option; with luck, you may not need to set even that option. Of course, you can set other options if you like.

Apache's configuration files reside in the directory */etc/httpd/conf.* For historical reasons that no longer apply, Apache has three configuration files:

access.conf
> Specifies what hosts and users are allowed access to what documents and services

httpd.conf
> Specifies options that govern the operation of the *httpd* daemon

srm.conf
> Specifies how your server's documents and organized and formatted

Currently, you can place Apache configuration commands in any of these files. However, each of these files must exist, even if it is empty; otherwise, the *httpd* daemon will refuse to run. As distributed, the files contain a default configuration. Before starting the web server, you should revise the `ServerName` option of the *httpd.conf* file. The three following subsections describe other options that you may wish to specify. You can scan them to see what options are available and specify options that interest you. A more complete description of the options is available in Apache's online documentation. Also, the Apache web site (*http://www.apache.org/*) provides a tutorial on Apache configuration. To change an option, simply open the related file by using your favorite text editor, change the file as you wish, and save the file.

TIP   The subsections assume some familiarity with HTML and web servers. If you find that some options are obscure, don't fret; your web server will serve ordinary HTML pages even if you set no options other than `ServerName`.

The access.conf file

The *access.conf* file specifies a default set of permissions that govern access to documents and services. It then specifies sets of permissions that override the default permissions for particular documents and services. The usual practice is to specify a quite restrictive set of default permissions, relaxing these permissions to provide access to particular documents and services.

The file contains a mixture of comments (lines beginning with #) and directives. Comments are ignored by the server.

The default permissions are specified as follows:

```
<Directory />
Options None
AllowOverride None
</Directory>
```

The paired tags `<Directory>` and `</Directory>` enclose a list of options that pertain to the / directory, the directory specified in the `<Directory>` tag. The options are:

- `Options None`, which specifies that no special server features are enabled for the specified directory or its subdirectories.

- `AllowOverride None`, which specifies that access specifications cannot be overridden by an *.htaccess* file.

Table 12-2 describes special server features that are available.

Table 12-2. Special Server Features

Option	Description
`ExecCGI`	Execution of CGI scripts is permitted in this directory.
`FollowSymLinks`	The server will follow symbolic links in this directory.
`Includes`	Server-side includes are permitted.
`IncludesNOEXEC`	Server-side includes, except `#exec` and `#include`, are permitted in this directory.
`Indexes`	If the directory contains no index file (for example, *index.html*), the server will prepare a formatted index.
`MultiViews`	Content-negotiated MultiViews are permitted in this directory. MultiViews permit, for example, a client browser to select a document in a particular language from a set of documents.
`SymLinksIfOwnerMatch`	The server will follow symbolic links for which the target file or directory has the same owner as the link.

Unless the specification for a directory specifies `AllowOverride None`, you can override the specified options by placing an *.htaccess* file in the directory or one of its subdirectories. The *.htaccess* file can contain specifications of the same sort as the *access.conf* file; the server applies the specifications in the *.htaccess* file in preference to those specified in the *access.conf* file.

After the restrictive default specifications come some more relaxed specifications:

```
<Directory /home/httpd/html>
Options Indexes Includes FollowSymLinks
AllowOverride None
order allow,deny
allow from all
</Directory>
```

These specifications apply to the directory */home/httpd/html* and its subdirectories.

Here, the `Indexes`, `Includes`, and `FollowSymLinks` options are specified. As for the root directory, use of *.htaccess* files is forbidden, via `AllowOverride None`. Here, unlike the specification for the root directory, the hosts allowed to access documents are services are specified. The `order allow, deny` directive specifies that any `deny` directives will be applied after any `allow` directives, and will therefore take precedence. No `deny` directives appear in this specification; the `allow from all` directive permits any host to access documents and services within the */home/httpd/html* directory and its subdirectories.

Another specification allows execution of CGI scripts within the */home/httpd/cgi-bin* directory and its subdirectories:

```
<Directory /home/httpd/cgi-bin>
AllowOverride None
Options ExecCGI
</Directory>
```

The final specification in the default configuration lets the local host access HTML documents within the */usr/doc* directory and its subdirectories:

```
<Directory /usr/doc>
order deny,allow
deny from all
allow from localhost
Options Indexes FollowSymLinks
</Directory>
```

The srm.conf File

The *srm.conf* file specifies the organization and format of documents provided by your web server. As was the case with the *access.conf* file, you don't need to make any changes to the *srm.conf* file, though you may wish to do so.

The `DocumentRoot` directive specifies the directory that contains your HTML files. When a web client accesses the root directory, the server actually fetches files from the directory specified as `DocumentRoot`:

```
DocumentRoot /home/httpd/html
```

The UserDir directive specifies the name of the subdirectory that the server appends to a user's home directory when a client makes a ˜*user* request:

```
UserDir public_html
```

This directive specifies that a reference to ˜*user* will be translated to a reference to */home/user/public_html.*

The `DirectoryIndex` directive specifies the name of the file (or names of the files) used a directory indexes:

```
DirectoryIndex index.html index.shtml index.cgi
```

The `FancyIndexing` directive specifies whether icons are used to produce fancy directory indexes:

```
FancyIndexing on
```

The `AddIcon` and `AddIconByType` directives associate icons with files of given types:

```
AddIconByType (TXT,/icons/text.gif) text/*
AddIcon /icons/binary.gif .bin .exe
```

The default configuration includes many such directives. If you wish to add support for a new type of file, you may want to add a directive associating an icon with the new file type.

The DefaultIcon directive specifies the icon used for file types not explicitly associated with an icon:

```
DefaultIcon /icons/unknown.gif
```

The `ReadmeName` directive specifies the name of a file used by the server to produce readme entries:

```
ReadmeName README
```

The server will first look for the file README.html and then for the file README.

The similar `HeaderName` directive specifies the name of a file that the server will prepend to a generated index:

```
HeaderName HEADER
```

The `IndexIgnore` directive specifies a set of file names that should not be included in a generated index. These are often specified by using wildcard characters:

```
IndexIgnore .??* *~ *# HEADER* README* RCS
```

The `AccessFileName` directive specifies the name of the file that, if present, overrides access control specifications for a directory:

```
AccessFileName .htaccess
```

The `TypesConfig` directive identifies the *mime.types* file, which describes multimedia files:

```
TypesConfig /etc/mime.types
```

The `DefaultType` directive specifies the default MIME type for documents:

```
DefaultType text/plain
```

The `AddEncoding` directive instructs compatible browsers to uncompress information as it's downloaded:

```
AddEncoding x-compress Z
AddEncoding x-gzip gz
```

The `Redirect` directive lets you provide a forwarding address for documents that have moved. The default configuration includes no `Redirect`s, which have this simple form:

```
Redirect old-URL new-URL
```

The `Alias` directive lets you refer to a directory by using an alias. For example, the following directive provides a more convenient way of referring to the */home/httpd/icons* directory:

```
Alias /icons/ /home/httpd/icons/
```

The `ScriptAlias` directive lets users refer to the CGI directory as simply */cgi-bin/*:

```
ScriptAlias /cgi-bin/ /home/httpd/cgi-bin/
```

The following sets of specifications work around problems with several browsers. First, two directives that disable `keepalive` for browsers that do not support it:

```
BrowserMatch "Mozilla/2" nokeepalive
BrowserMatch "MSIE 4\.0b2;" nokeepalive downgrade-1.0 force-response-1.0
```

The final directives force use of HTTP version 1.0 responses for several browsers that do not support HTTP 1.1:

```
BrowserMatch "RealPlayer 4\.0" force-response-1.0
BrowserMatch "Java/1\.0" force-response-1.0
BrowserMatch "JDK/1\.0" force-response-1.0
```

The *httpd.conf* File

The *httpd.conf* file specifies options related to the *httpd* daemon. You should specify the `ServerName` option before starting your web server.

The `ServerType` directory specifies whether the web server is started via *inetd* or standalone:

```
ServerType standalone
```

The `port` directive specifies the port on which the web server listens for client requests:

```
Port 80
```

The `HostnameLookups` directive specifies whether clients are logged by IP address (off) or hostname (on):

```
HostnameLookups off
```

The `User` and `Group` directives specify the userid and group under which the *httpd* daemon runs. The daemon initially runs as `root` and then switches to the specified userid and group. The default configuration specifies the userid as `nobody`, a standard Unix userid that has very limited permissions. A user or process running as `nobody` can access files only in ways permitted to all users; generally, this means the user or process cannot modify files. The group `nobody` has similarly constrained privileges:

```
    User nobody
    Group nobody
```

The `ServerAdmin` directive specifies the email address of the server administrator:

```
ServerAdmin root@localhost
```

The `ServerRoot` directive specifies the directory that contains the configuration, error, and log files:

```
ServerRoot /etc/httpd
```

The `BindAddress` directive provides for virtual hosts. It specifies the IP address to which the server should listen. It is normally disabled by a comment token:

```
#BindAddress *
```

The `ErrorLog` directive specifies the location of the error log file:

```
ErrorLog logs/error_log
```

The `LogLevel` directive specifies the verbosity of the server log. Possible values include `debug`, `info`, `notice`, `warn`, `error`, `crit`, `alert`, and `emerg`:

```
LogLevel warn
```

The `LogFormat` directive specifies format names that can be used with the `CustomLog` directive:

```
LogFormat "%h %l %u %t \"%r\" %>s %b \"%{Referer}i\" \"%{User-Agent}i\""
combined LogFormat "%h %l %u %t \"%r\" %>s %b" common
LogFormat "%{Referer}i -> %U" referer
LogFormat "%{User-agent}i" agent
CustomLog logs/access_log common
```

For more information about `LogFormat` and `CustomLog`, see the Apache documentation.

The `PidFile` directive specifies the file in which the server should log its process id:

```
PidFile /var/run/httpd.pid
```

The `ScoreBoardFile` directive specifies the name of the file used to store internal server process data:

```
ScoreBoardFile /var/run/httpd.scoreboard
```

The `LockFile` directive specifies the file used to providing locking. You'll need to change this option only if you NFS mount the directory used by the server for logging:

```
#LockFile /var/lock/httpd.lock
```

The `ServerName` directive specifies the hostname of the system on which your server runs. Depending on your network configuration, you may not need to specify this directive:

```
ServerName host.domain.com
```

The `UseCanonicalName` directive specifies whether the server will return a canonical URL formed from the `ServerName` and `Port` directives (on) or the hostname and port supplied by the client (off):

```
UseCanonicalName on
```

The `CacheNegotiatedDocs` directive instructs browsers not to cache documents; it is usually disabled by prefixing it with a comment token (#):

```
#CacheNegotiatedDocs
```

The `Timeout` directive specifies the maximum number of seconds the server will wait for certain responses, such as the next packet in a sequence of TCP packets:

```
Timeout 300
```

The `KeepAlive` directive specifies that connections are persistent; that is, that a client can make multiple requests per connection:

```
KeepAlive On
```

The `MaxKeepAliveRequests` directive specifies the maximum number of requests permitted during a persistent connection:

```
MaxKeepAliveRequests 100
```

The value 0 denotes an unlimited number of requests.

The `KeepAliveTimeout` directive specifies the maximum number of seconds during which the server will wait for the next request:

```
KeepAliveTimeout 15
```

The `MinSpareServers` and `MaxSpareServers` directives respectively fix the minimum and maximum number of spare server processes the server will create. Having an available server expedites handling of an incoming request:

```
MinSpareServers 8
MaxSpareServers 20
```

The `StartServers` directive specifies the initial number of server processes:

```
StartServers 10
```

The `MaxClients` directive specifies the maximum number of simultaneous server processes. When this number is reached, requests from additional clients are locked out:

```
MaxClients 150
```

The default values of these options are higher than necessary for most workstation users. Your system will perform more efficiently (and perhaps more reliably) if you change the directives to specify the following values:

```
MinSpareServers 3
MaxSpareServers 6
StartServers 3
MaxClients 20
```

The `MaxRequestsPerChild` directive specifies the number of requests a child process can handle before expiring. This ensures that processes are periodically recreated, minimizing problems due to software errors such as memory leaks:

```
MaxRequestsPerChild 100
```

The `ProxyRequests` directive specifies whether the proxy server is enabled; it is normally disabled:

```
#ProxyRequests On
```

When the proxy server is active, the following directives specify various caching options. They are normally disabled:

```
#CacheRoot /var/cache/httpd
#CacheSize 5
#CacheGcInterval 4
#CacheMaxExpire 24
#CacheLastModifiedFactor 0.1
#CacheDefaultExpire 1
#NoCache a_domain.com another_domain.edu joes.garage_sale.com
```

The `Listen` directive lets your bind Apache to a specific IP address or port, in addition to the default IP address and port. It is generally disabled:

```
#Listen 3000
#Listen 12.34.56.78:80
```

The `<VirtualHost>` and `</VirtualHost>` tags enclose a series of options that establish a virtual host, useful if your system has multiple IP addresses. The options can include any of the options described in this subsection. The tags and options are normally disabled:

```
#<VirtualHost host.some_domain.com>
#ServerAdmin webmaster@host.some_domain.com
#DocumentRoot /www/docs/host.some_domain.com
#ServerName host.some_domain.com
#ErrorLog logs/host.some_domain.com-error_log
#TransferLog logs/host.some_domain.com-access_log
#</VirtualHost>
```

Startup and Use

Once you've configured your web server, you can start it by rebooting your system. Alternatively, you can start it manually by logging in as `root` and issuing the following commands:

```
cd /etc/rc.d/init.d
./httpd start
```

You can verify that the web server has started by issuing the command:

```
./httpd status
```

which should report that one or more processes are running.

If you installed the lynx browser, you can use it to test your web server. Issue the command:

```
lynx http://localhost
```

You should see a screen that resembles Figure 12-1.

If you prefer, you can view the start page by using Netscape Navigator, which supports the graphics embedded in the page. The result should resemble Figure 12-2.

Once you can access your web server locally, try accessing it from a remote computer. This should be as simple as forming a URL that includes the fully qualified hostname of your system (that is, the host and domain names); for example, *http://mysystem.mydomain.*

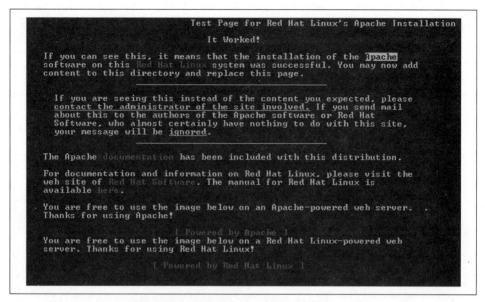

Figure 12-1. The Apache start page viewed by lynx

Configuring a Mail Server

Does your Internet service provider prohibit email message attachments larger than 1 MB or impose other restrictions that you find cumbersome? Your Linux system can provide an email server that you can configure any way you like.

The *sendmail* package provides a powerful mail transfer agent (MTA), which transfers email from one system to another.

TIP   Don't confuse **sendmail** and other MTAs with mail clients, which merely let you read email.

Once you've installed *sendmail*, you must configure its operation. To do so, log on as **root** and use your favorite text editor to add the following two lines to the */etc/inetd.conf* file:

```
pop-3   stream  tcp     nowait  root    /usr/sbin/tcpd          ipop3d
imap    stream  tcp     nowait  root    /usr/sbin/tcpd          imapd
```

Now, you must reboot your system. Alternatively, you can cause the *inetd* daemon to re-read its configuration file and you can start the *sendmail* process manually. To do so, issue the following commands:

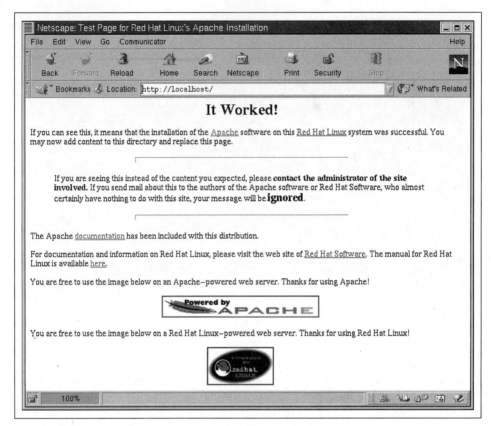

Figure 12-2. The Apache start page viewed by Netscape Navigator

```
killall -HUP inetd
./sendmail start
```

To verify that *sendmail* is running, issue the following command:

```
./sendmail status
```

The output of the command should report that the process is running.

You should now be able to send email to users on other systems, and to receive email sent by them to you. Simply reconfigure your favorite mail client to specify your own system as your mail server. For example, if you're using Netscape Navigator, select Edit → Preferences → Mail Servers. Make a note of the existing mail server settings, just in case something goes wrong. Then, change the incoming and outgoing mail server options to specify your Linux machine.

TIP   If you want to continue receiving mail on another mail server, but want to read it from your Linux system, you might consider using *fetchmail*, a package that can retrieve email messages from the server (by using POP, IMAP, or just about any other remote mail protocol) and forward them to your Linux system.

Configuring a Secure Shell Server

A secure shell server lets you connect to a system from another system, via TCP/IP, and obtain a shell prompt, from which you can issue commands and view output. You may not be familiar with secure shell servers, but familiar with Telnet, which works similarly. A secure shell server differs from a Telnet server in that the conversation between a secure shell server and its clients is sent in encrypted form so that hackers cannot easily discover private information, including userids and passwords.

The secure shell client and server cannot be distributed on a CD, because they utilize advanced encryption techniques; U.S. law currently forbids general distribution of such software. Therefore, you must download the client and server from SSH Protocols' web site in Finland, *http://www.ssh.fi/sshprotocols2/*. At the time of this writing, you could somewhat more conveniently download the client and server from Replay Associate's web site, *http://www.replay.com/redhat/ssh.html*. Replay Associate's web site includes RPM files, making it easy to complete the installation. The secure shell client and server are free for non-commercial and educational use.

To start the secure shell server, you must reboot your system. Alternatively, you can log in as **root** and issue the command:

```
/etc/rc.d/init.d/sshd start
```

You can verify that the server has properly started by issuing the command:

```
/etc/rc.d/init.d/sshd status
```

The command's output should report that the server is running.

Using a Secure Shell Client

To verify that the server is properly running, you can access it via a client on the local system. Issue the following command:

```
ssh localhost
```

The client will attempt to log you onto the local system by using your current userid, and should prompt you for your password. If you supply the correct password, you should see a shell prompt, indicating that the client and server are functioning correctly. Type **exit** and press **Enter** to exit the secure shell provided by the client.

Using a Secure Server from a Remote System

To log onto your Linux system from a remote system via the secure shell server, you must install a secure shell client on the remote system. A suitable client for Microsoft Windows 9x systems is *ttssh*, available from Robert O'Callahan's web site, *http://www.zip.com.au/~roca/ttssh.html*. Simply download and install *ttssh* on your Windows system, specify the hostname or IP address of your Linux system and your userid and password, and *ttssh* will log you onto your Linux system.

Configuring a Dial-In Shell Server

A dial-in server lets you connect to a system via a modem and phone line, and obtain a shell prompt, from which you can issue commands and view output. Using a dial-in server is a great deal like using Telnet or a secure shell server, except that your connection to the server is via a phone line. The *mgetty* package provides a simple-to-use dial-in server.

Configuration

To configure *mgetty* to answer incoming modem calls, use your favorite text editor to find the following lines in the file */etc/inittab*:

```
# Run gettys in standard runlevels
1:2345:respawn:/sbin/mingetty tty1
2:2345:respawn:/sbin/mingetty tty2
3:2345:respawn:/sbin/mingetty tty3
4:2345:respawn:/sbin/mingetty tty4
5:2345:respawn:/sbin/mingetty tty5
6:2345:respawn:/sbin/mingetty tty6
```

Then, add the following line after the last of these lines:

```
7:2345:respawn:/sbin/mgetty modem
```

Notice that the added line invokes *mgetty*, not *mingetty*. The final argument specified on the added line assumes that your modem is configured as */dev/modem*. If your modem is configured as a different device, you must adjust the added line accordingly. The Chapter 11, *Getting Connected to the Internet* described the use of *modemtool* to configure your modem; if you followed its instructions, */dev/modem* refers to your modem.

To cause your configuration change to take effect, you must reboot your system. Alternatively, you can cause the *init* process to re-examine the *inittab* file. To do so, issue the following command:

```
/sbin/telinit q
```

The *mgetty* process should begin monitoring your modem, awaiting an incoming call.

Using the Dial-In Server

To use the dial-in server, launch a program such as Microsoft Windows' Hyperterminal and place a call to the phone line to which your Linux system's modem is connected. Your Linux system should answer the call and provide you with a login prompt. Respond with your userid and password and you should receive a shell prompt, at which you can enter commands and view their output.

TIP   If you have only a single phone line, you'll be unable to place a call to your Linux system. You'll have to call from some other location.

## CHAPTER THIRTEEN

CONQUERING THE BASH SHELL

This chapter describes the powerful BASH shell, providing a much more detailed explanation than that provided in Chapter 4, *Issuing Linux Commands*. The chapter also briefly explains shell variables, shell scripts, and shell aliases, preparing you for an in-depth, continuing study of Linux.

The Linux Shell

You met the Linux command interpreter, or shell, early in this book. Like an MS-DOS Prompt window, the shell lets you issue commands that it interprets, or executes. By means of the shell, you use and control your system.

A Variety of Shells

The MS-DOS shell has been fairly consistent over time; for example, the differences between MS-DOS v3 and MS-DOS v7 are few. The Unix shell, however, has experienced significantly more evolutionary development than MS-DOS. Today, you find both versions and variants of the Unix shell. The Unix shell variants have much in common, but each has a different authorship and history, and each reflects a different view of how users should interact with Unix.

Linux includes the most popular Unix shells, as shown in Table 13-1. The most popular Linux shell is the BASH shell (the "Bourne Again SHell"), based on the original Unix Bourne shell. The BASH shell is largely compliant with the POSIX standard, which specifies the syntax and operation of a standard Unix shell and which has been widely implemented. Because of the popularity of the POSIX standard and the obvious advantage of working with a shell that's consistent across a variety of computing platforms, this chapter focuses on the BASH shell. Most Linux systems are configured to automatically start a BASH shell on your behalf when you log in; so, you don't generally need to be much concerned about choosing a shell. However, for information about the other available shells, you can consult the Linux man pages.

Table 13-1. Common Linux Shells

Shell name	Program name(s)	Description
ASH shell	*/bin/ash* */bin/bsh*	Resembles the shell used by AT&T's System V Unix.
BASH shell	*/bin/bash* */bin/bash2*	The standard shell for Linux, based on the original Unix Bourne shell. According to its man page, BASH is "ultimately intended" to be POSIX compliant.
C shell	*/bin/csh* */bin/tcsh*	The second Unix shell. Designed to facilitate interactive use, it added many new features and functions. Its syntax resembles that of the C programming language.
Korn shell	*/bin/ksh*	The third Unix shell, added many of the features of the C shell to the original Bourne shell.
Z shell	*/bin/zsh*	A feature-packed shell based on the Korn shell.

Why Learn to Use the Shell?

If you're accustomed to the point-and-click world of graphical user interfaces, you may question the value of learning to use the Linux shell. Many users initially find the shell cumbersome, and some retreat to the familiar comfort of the graphical user interface, avoiding the shell whenever possible.

While it's true that the shell is an older style of interacting with a computer than the graphical user interface, the graphical user interface is actually the more primitive interface. The graphical user interface is easy to learn and widely used, but the shell is vastly more sophisticated. Using a graphical user interface is somewhat like communicating in American Indian sign language. If your message is a simple one, like "we come in peace," you can communicate it by using a few gestures. However, if you attempted to give Lincoln's Gettysburg address—a notably short public discourse—by means of American Indian sign language, you'd find your task quite formidable.

American Sign Language, used to communicate with those who have a hearing impairment, is a much richer language than American Indian sign language. Unfortunately, programmers have not yet risen to the challenge of creating graphical user interfaces that are equally sophisticated. The designer of a program that provides a graphical user interface must anticipate all the possible ways in which the user will interact with the program and provide ways to trigger the appropriate program responses by means of pointing and clicking. Consequently, the user is constrained to working only in predicted ways. The user is therefore unable to adapt the graphical user interface program to accommodate unforeseen tasks and circumstances. In a nutshell, that's why many system administration tasks are performed using the shell: system administrators, in fulfilling their responsibility to keep a system up and running, must continually deal with and overcome the unforeseen.

The shell reflects the underlying philosophy of Unix, which provides a wide variety of small, simple tools (that is, programs), each performing a single task. When a complex operation is needed, the tools work together to accomplish the complex operation as a series of simple operations, one step at a time. Many Unix tools manipulate text and, since Unix stores its configuration data in text form rather than in binary form, the tools are ideally suited for manipulating Unix itself. The shell's ability to freely combine tools in novel ways is what makes Unix powerful and sophisticated. Moreover, as you'll learn, the shell is extensible: You can create shell scripts that let you store a series of commands for later execution, saving you the future tedium of typing or pointing and clicking to recall them.

The contrary philosophy is seen in operating systems such as Microsoft Windows, which employ elaborate, monolithic programs that provide menus, submenus, and dialog boxes. Such programs have no way to cooperate with one another to accomplish complex operations that weren't anticipated when the programs were designed. They're easy to use so long as you remain on the beaten path, but once you step off the trail you find yourself in a confusing wilderness.

Of course, not everyone shares this perspective. The USENET newsgroups, for example, are filled with postings debating the relative merits of graphical user interfaces. Some see the Unix shell as an arcane and intimidating monstrosity. But, even if they're correct, it's inarguable that when you learn to use the shell, you begin to see Unix as it was intended (whether that's for better or for worse).

The author's perspective is pragmatic: When performing common, routine operations, a graphical user interface that minimizes typing can be a relief; but, when faced with a complex, unstructured problem that requires creative solution, the shell is more often the tool of choice. By creating solutions in the form of shell scripts, solutions can be stored for subsequent reuse. Perhaps even more important, shell scripts can be studied to quickly bone up on forgotten details, expediting the solution of related problems.

Using the Shell

This book introduced you to the shell in Chapter 4. However, many important details were omitted in that chapter, which was aimed at helping you to get your Linux system up and running as quickly as possible. This section revisits the shell, providing you with information that will help you use the shell efficiently and effectively.

Typing Shell Commands

When typing shell commands, you have access to a mini-editor that resembles the DOSKEYS editor of MS-DOS. Table 13-2 summarizes some useful keystroke commands interpreted by the shell. The keystroke commands let you access a list of recently executed commands, called the *history list*. To re-execute a command, you can press the Up key several times until you locate the command and then merely press **Enter** to execute the command.

Table 13-2. Useful Editing Keystrokes

Keystroke(s)	Function
Up	Move back one command in the history list.
Down	Move forward one command in the history list.
Left	Move back one character.
Right	Move forward one character.
Esc f	Move forward one word.
Esc b	Move back one word.
Ctrl-A	Move to beginning of line.
Ctrl-E	Move to end of line.
Ctrl-D	Delete current character.
Backspace	Delete previous character.
Esc d	Delete current word.
Ctrl-U	Delete from beginning of line.
Esc k	Delete to end of line.
Ctrl-Y	Retrieve last item deleted.
Esc .	Insert last word of previous command.
Ctrl-L	Clear the screen, placing the current line at the top of the screen.
Tab	Attempt to complete the current word, interpreting it as a filename, username. variable name, hostname, or command as determined by the context.
Esc ?	List the possible completions.

One of the most useful editing keystrokes, **Tab**, can also be used when typing a command. If you type the first part of a filename and press **Tab**, the shell will attempt to locate files with names matching the characters you've typed. If exactly one such file exists, the shell fills out the partially typed name with the proper characters. You can then press **Enter** to execute the command or continue typing other options and arguments. This feature, called either filename completion or command completion, makes the shell much easier to use.

In addition to keystrokes for editing the command line, the shell interprets several keystrokes that control the operation of the currently executing program. Table 13-3 summarizes these keystrokes. For example, typing **Ctrl-C** generally cancels execution of a program. This keystroke command is handy, for example, when a program is taking too long to execute and you'd prefer to try something else.

Table 13-3. Useful Control Keystrokes

Keystroke	Function
Ctrl-C	Sends an interrupt signal to the currently executing command, which generally responds by terminating itself.
Ctrl-D	Sends an end of file to the currently executing command. Use this keystroke to terminate console input.
Ctrl-Z	Suspends the currently executing program.

Several other special characters control the operation of the shell, as shown in Table 13-4. The # and ; characters are most often used in shell scripts, which you'll learn about later in this chapter. The & character is useful for running a command as a background process.

Table 13-4. Other Special Shell Characters

Character	Function
#	Marks the command as a comment, which the shell ignores.
;	Separates commands, letting you enter several commands on a single line.
&	Placed at the end of a command, causes the command to execute as a background process, so that a new shell prompt appears immediately after the command is entered.

Commands and Arguments

As you already know, the general form a shell command line is this:

```
command options arguments
```

The command determines what operation the shell will perform and the options and arguments customize or fine-tune the operation. Sometimes the command specifies a program file that will be launched and run; such a command is called an *external command.* Linux generally stores these files in */bin, /usr/bin,* or */usr/local/bin.* System administration commands are generally stored in */sbin* or */usr/sbin.* When a command specifies a program file, the shell passes any specified arguments to the program, which scans them and interprets them, adjusting its operation accordingly.

However, some commands are not program files; instead they are built-in commands interpreted by the shell itself. One important way in which shells differ is the built-in commands that they support. Later in this section, you'll learn about some commands built into the BASH shell.

Filename Globbing

Before the shell passes arguments to an external command or interprets a built-in command, it scans the command line for certain special characters and performs an operation known as *filename globbing.* Filename globbing resembles the processing of wildcards used in MS-DOS commands, but it's much more sophisticated. Table 13-5 describes the special characters used in filename globbing, known as *filename metacharacters.*

Table 13-5. Filename Metacharacters

Metacharacter	Meaning
*	Matches a string of zero or more characters
?	Matches exactly one character
[abc . . .]	Matches any of the characters specified
[a-z]	Matches any character in the specified range
[!abc . . .]	Matches any character other than those specified
[!a-z]	Matches any character not in the specified range
~	The home directory of the current user
~userid	The home directory of the specified user
~+	The current working directory
~-	The previous working directory

In filename globbing just as in MS-DOS wildcarding, the shell attempts to replace metacharacters appearing in arguments in such a way that arguments specify filenames. Filename globbing makes it easier to specify names of files and sets of files.

For example, suppose the current working directory contains the following files: *file1*, *file2*, *file3*, and *file04*. Suppose you want to know the size of each file. The following command reports that information:

```
ls -l file1 file2 file3 file04
```

However, the following command reports the same information and is much easier to type:

```
ls -l file*
```

As Table 13-2 shows, the * filename metacharacter can match any string of characters. Suppose you issued the following command:

```
ls -l file?
```

The ? filename metacharacter can match only a single character. Therefore, *file04* would not appear in the output of the command.

Similarly, the command:

```
ls -l file[2-3]
```

would report only *file2* and *file3*, because only these files have names that match the specified pattern, which requires that the last character of the filename be in the range 2-3.

You can use more than one metacharacter in a single argument. For example, consider the following command:

```
ls -l file??
```

This command will list *file04*, because each metacharacter matches exactly one filename character.

Most commands let you specify multiple arguments. If no files match a given argument, the command ignores the argument. Here's another command that reports all four files:

```
ls -l file0* file[1-3]
```

TIP   Suppose that a command has one or more arguments that include one or more metacharacters. If none of the arguments matches any filenames, the shell passes the arguments to the program with the metacharacters intact. When the program expects a valid filename, an unexpected error may result.

Another metacharacter lets you easily refer to your home directory. For example, the following command:

```
ls ~
```

lists the files in the user's home directory.

Filename metacharacters don't merely save you typing. They let you write scripts that selectively process files by name. You'll see how that works later in this chapter.

Shell Aliases

Shell aliases make it easier to use commands by letting you establish abbreviated command names and by letting you pre-specify common arguments. To establish a command alias, issue a command of the form:

```
alias name='command'
```

where *command* specifies the command for which you want to create an alias and *name* specifies the alias. For example, suppose you frequently type the MS-DOS command *Dir* when you intend to type the Linux command *ls*. You can establish an alias for the *ls* command by issuing this command:

```
alias dir='ls -l'
```

Once the alias is established, if you mistakenly type *Dir*, you'll nevertheless get the directory listing you want. If you like, you can establish similar aliases for other commands.

Your default Linux configuration probably defines several aliases on your behalf. To see what they are, issue the command:

```
alias
```

If you're logged in as **root**, you may see the following aliases:

```
alias cp='cp -i'
alias dir='ls -l'
alias ls='ls --color'
alias mv='mv -i'
alias rm='rm -i'
```

Notice how several commands are self-aliased. For example, the command *rm –i* is aliased as *rm*. The effect is that the *–i* option appears whenever you issue the *rm* command, whether or not you type the option. The *–i* option specifies that the shell will prompt for confirmation before deleting files. This helps avoid accidental deletion of files, which can be particularly hazardous when you're logged in as

root. The alias ensures that you're prompted for confirmation even if you don't ask to be prompted. If you don't want to be prompted, you can issue a command like:

```
rm -f files
```

where *files* specifies the files to be deleted. The *–f* option has an effect opposite that of the *–i* option; it forces deletion of files without prompting for confirmation. Because the command is aliased, the command actually executed is:

```
rm -i -f files
```

The *–f* option takes precedence over the *–i* option, because it occurs later in the command line.

If you want to remove a command alias, you can issue the *unalias* command:

```
unalias alias
```

where *alias* specifies the alias you want to remove. Aliases last only for the duration of a log in session, so you needn't bother to remove them before logging off. If you want an alias to be effective each time you log in, you can use a shell script. The next subsection shows you how to do so.

Shell Scripts

A shell script is simply a file that contains commands. By storing commands as a shell script you make it easy to execute them again and again. As an example, consider a file named *deleter*, which contains the following lines:

```
echo -n Deleting the temporary files...
rm -f *.tmp
echo Done.
```

The echo commands simply print text on the console. The *–n* option of the first *echo* command causes omission of the trailing newline character normally written by the *echo* command, so both *echo* commands write their text on a single line. The *rm* command removes from the current working directory all files having names ending in *.tmp*.

You can execute this script by issuing the *sh* command:

```
sh deleter
```

TIP   If you invoke the *sh* command without an argument specifying a script file, a new interactive shell is launched. To exit the new shell and return to your previous session, issue the *exit* command.

If the *deleter* file were in a directory other than the current working directory, you'd have to type an absolute path, for example:

```
sh /home/bill/deleter
```

You can make it a bit easier to execute the script by changing its access mode to include execute access. To do so, issue the following command:

```
chmod ugo+x deleter
```

This gives you, members of your group, and everyone else the ability to execute the file. To do so, simply type the absolute path of the file, for example:

```
/home/bill/deleter
```

If the file is in the current directory, you can issue the following command:

```
./deleter
```

You may wonder why you can't simply issue the command:

```
deleter
```

In fact, this still simpler form of the command will work, so long as *deleter* resides in a directory on your search path. You'll learn about the search path later.

Linux includes several standard scripts that are run at various times. Table 13-6 identifies these and gives the time when each is run. You can modify these scripts to operate differently. For example, if you want to establish command aliases that are available whenever you log in, you can use a text editor to add the appropriate lines to the *.profile* file that resides in your home directory. Recall that, since the name of this file begins with a dot, the *ls* command won't normally show the file. You must specify the *−a* option in order to see this and other hidden files.

Table 13-6. Special Scripts

Script	Function
/etc/profile	Executed when the user logs in
~/.profile	Executed when the user logs in
~/.bashrc	Executed when BASH is launched
~/.bash_logout	Executed when the user logs out

TIP   If you want to modify one of the standard scripts that should reside in your home directory, but find that your home directory does not contain the indicated file, simply create the file. The next time you log in, log out, or launch BASH (as appropriate) the shell will execute your script.

Input/Output Redirection and Piping

The shell provides three standard data streams:

stdin
> The standard input stream

stdout
> The standard output stream

stderr
> The standard error stream

By default, most programs read their input from stdin and write their output to stdout. Because both streams are normally associated with a console, programs behave as you generally want, reading input data from the console keyboard and writing output to the console screen. When a well-behaved program writes an error message, it writes the message to the stderr stream, which is also associated with the console by default. Having separate streams for output and error messages presents an important opportunity, as you'll see in a moment.

Although the shell associates the three standard input/output streams with the console by default, you can specify input/output redirectors that, for example, associate an input or output stream with a file. Table 13-7 summarizes the most important input/output redirectors.

Table 13-7. Input/Output Redirectors

Redirector	Function
>*file*	Redirects standard output stream to specified file
2>*file*	Redirects standard error stream to specified file
>>*file*	Redirects standard output stream to specified file, appending output to the file if the file already exists
2>>*file*	Redirects standard error stream to specified file, appending output to the file if the file already exists
&>*file*	Redirects standard output and error streams to the specified file
<*file*	Redirects standard input stream to the specified file
<<*text*	Reads standard input until a line matching *text* is found, at which point end of file is posted
cmd1 | *cmd2*	Takes the standard input of *cmd2* from the standard output of *cmd1* (also known as the *pipe redirector*)

To see how redirection works, consider the *wc* command. This command takes a series of filenames as arguments and prints the total number of lines, words, and characters present in the specified files. For example, the command:

```
wc /etc/passwd
```

might produce the output:

```
    22      26     790 /etc/passwd
```

which indicates that the file */etc/passwd* contains 22 lines, 26 words, and 790 characters. Generally, the output of the command appears on console. But, consider the following command, which includes an output redirector:

```
wc /etc/passwd > total
```

If you issue this command, you'll see no console output, because the output is redirected to the file *total*, which the command creates (or overwrites, if the file already exists). If you execute the pair of commands:

```
wc /etc/passwd > total
cat total
```

you can see the output of the *wc* command on the console.

Perhaps you can now see the reason for having the separate output streams **stdout** and **stderr**. If the shell provided a single output stream, error messages and output would be mingled. Therefore, if you redirected the output of a program to a file, any error messages would also be redirected to the file. This might make it difficult to notice an error that occurred during program execution. Instead, because the streams are separate, you can choose to redirect only **stdout** to a file. When you do so, error messages sent to **stderr** appear on the console in the usual way. Of course, if you prefer, you can redirect both **stdout** and **stderr** to the same file or redirect them to different files. As usual in the Unix world, you can have it your own way.

A simple way of avoiding annoying output is to redirect it to the null file, */dev/null*. If you redirect the **stderr** stream of a command to */dev/null*, you won't see any error messages the command produces.

Just as you can direct the standard output or error stream of a command to a file, you can also redirect a command's standard input stream to a file, so that the command reads from the file instead of the console. For example, if you issue the *wc* command without arguments, the command reads its input from **stdin**. Type some words and then type the end of file character (Ctrl-D) and *wc* will report the number of lines, words, and characters you entered. You can tell *wc* to read from a file, rather than the console, by issuing a command like:

```
wc </etc/passwd
```

Of course, this isn't the usual way of invoking *wc*. The author of *wc* helpfully provided a command-line argument that lets you specify the file from which *wc* reads. However, by using a redirector, you could read from any desired file even if the author had been less helpful.

TIP   Some programs are written to ignore redirectors. For example, the
               passwd command expects to read the new password only from the
               console, not from a file. You can compel such programs to read
               from a file, but doing so requires techniques more advanced than
               redirectors.

When you specify no command-line arguments, many Unix programs read their input from `stdin` and write their output to `stdout`. Such programs are called *filters*. Filters can be easily fitted together to perform a series of related operations. The tool for combining filters is the *pipe*, which connects the output of one program to the input of another. For example, consider this command:

```
ls -l ~ | wc -l
```

The command consists of two commands, joined by the pipe redirector (|). The first command lists the names of the files in the users home directory, one file per line. The second command invokes *wc* by using the *-1* option, which causes *wc* to print only the total number of lines, rather than printing the total number of lines, words, and characters. The pipe redirector sends the output of the *ls* command to the *wc* command, which counts and prints the number of lines in its input, which happens to be the number of files in the user's home directory.

This is a simple example of the power and sophistication of the Unix shell. Unix doesn't include a command that counts the files in the user's home directory and doesn't need to do so. Should the need to count the files arise, a knowledgeable Unix user can prepare a simple script that computes the desired result by using general-purpose Unix commands.

Shell Variables

If you've studied programming, you know that programming languages resemble algebra. Both programming languages and algebra let you refer to a value by a name. And both programming languages and algebra include elaborate mechanisms for manipulating named values.

The shell is a programming language in its own right, letting you refer to variables known as *shell variables* or *environment variables*. To assign a value to a shell variable, you use a command that has the following form:

```
variable=value
```

For example, the command:

```
DifficultyLevel=1
```

assigns the value 1 to the shell variable named `DifficultyLevel`. Unlike algebraic variable, shell variables can have non-numeric values. For example, the command:

```
Difficulty=medium
```

assigns the value `medium` to the shell variable named `Difficulty`.

Shell variables are widely used within Unix, because they provide a convenient way of transferring values from one command to another. Programs can obtain the value of a shell variable and use the value to modify their operation, in much the same way they use the value of command-line arguments.

You can see a list of shell variables by issuing the *set* command. Usually, the command produces more than a single screen of output. So, you can use a pipe redirector and the *more* command to view the output one screen at a time:

```
set | more
```

Press the **Space** bar to see each successive page of output. You'll probably see several of the shell variables described in Table 13-8 among those printed by the *set* command. The values of these shell variables are generally set by one or another of the startup scripts described earlier in this chapter.

Table 13-8. Important Environment Variables

Variable	Function
DISPLAY	The X display to be used; for example, `localhost:0`
HOME	The absolute path of the user's home directory
HOSTNAME	The Internet name of the host
LOGNAME	The user's login name
MAIL	The absolute path of the user's mail file
PATH	The search path (see next subsection)
SHELL	The absolute path of the current shell
TERM	The terminal type
USER	The user's current username; may differ from the login name if the user executes the *su* command

You can use the value of a shell variable in a command by preceding the name of the shell variable by a dollar sign ($). To avoid confusion with surrounding text, you can enclose the name of the shell variable within curly braces ({}); it's good practice (though not necessary) to do so consistently. For example, you can change the current working directory to your home directory by issuing the command:

```
cd ${HOME}
```

Of course, issuing the *cd* command with no argument causes the same result. However, suppose you want to change to the *work* subdirectory of your home directory. The following command accomplishes exactly that:

```
cd ${HOME}/work
```

An easy way to see the value of a shell variable is to specify the variable as the argument of the *echo* command. For example, to see the value of the HOME shell variable, issue the command:

```
echo ${HOME}
```

To make the value of a shell variable available not just to the shell, but to programs invoked by using the shell, you must export the shell variable. To do so, use the *export* command, which has the form:

```
export variable
```

where *variable* specifies the name of the variable to be exported. A shorthand form of the command lets you assign a value to a shell variable and export the variable in a single command:

```
export variable=value
```

You can remove the value associated with a shell variable by giving the variable an empty value:

```
variable=
```

However, a shell variable with an empty value remains a shell variable and appears in the output of the *set* command. To dispense with a shell variable, you can issue the *unset* command:

```
unset variable
```

Once you unset the value of a variable, the variable no longer appears in the output of the *set* command.

The Search Path

The special shell variable PATH holds a series of paths known collectively as the *search path*. Whenever you issue an external command, the shell searches paths that comprise the search path, seeking the program file that corresponds to the command. The startup scripts establish the initial value of the PATH shell variable, but you can modify its value to include any desired series of paths. You must use a colon (:) to separate each path of the search path.

For example, suppose that PATH has the following value:

```
/usr/bin:/bin:/usr/local/bin:/usr/bin/X11:/usr/X11R6/bin
```

You can add a new search directory, say */home/bill*, by issuing the following command:

```
PATH=${PATH}:/home/bill
```

Now, the shell will look for external programs in */home/bill* as well as the default directories. However, it will look there last. If you prefer to check */home/bill* first, issue the following command instead:

```
PATH=/home/bill:${PATH}
```

The *which* command helps you work with the PATH shell variable. It checks the search path for the file specified as its argument and prints the name of the matching path, if any. For example, suppose you want to know where the program file for the *wc* command resides. Issuing the command:

```
which wc
```

will tell you that the program file is */usr/bin/wc*, or whatever other path is correct for your system.

Quoted Strings

Sometimes the shell may misinterpret a command that you've written, globbing a filename or expanding a reference to a shell variable that you hadn't intended. Of course, it's actually your interpretation that's mistaken, not the shell's. Therefore, it's up to you to rewrite your command so that the shell's interpretation is congruent with what you intend.

Quote characters, described in Table 13-9, can help you do so, by controlling the operation of the shell. For example, by enclosing a command argument within single quotes, you can prevent the shell from globbing the argument or substituting the argument with the value of a shell variable.

Table 13-9. Quote Characters

Character	Function
'	Characters within a pair of single quotes are interpreted literally; that is, their metacharacter meanings (if any) are ignored. Similarly, the shell does not replace references to shell or environment variables with the value of the referenced variable.
"	Characters within a pair of double quotes are interpreted literally; that is, their metacharacter meanings (if any) are ignored. However, the shell does replace references to shell or environment variables with the value of the referenced variable.
`	Text within a pair of back quotes is interpreted as a command, which the shell executes before executing the rest of the command line. The output of the command replaces the original back-quoted text.
\	The following character is interpreted literally; that is, its metacharacter meaning (if any) is ignored. The backslash character has a special use as a line continuation character. When a line ends with a backslash, the line and the following line are considered part of a single line.

To see this in action, consider how you might cause the *echo* command to produce the output $PATH. If you simply issue the command:

```
echo $PATH
```

the echo command will print the value of the PATH shell variable. However, by enclosing the argument within single quotes, you obtain the desired result:

```
echo '$PATH'
```

Double quotes have a similar effect. They prevent the shell from globbing a filename but permit the expansion of shell variables.

Back quotes operate differently; they let you execute a command and use its output as an argument of another command. For example, the command:

```
echo My home directory contains `ls ~ | wc -l` files.
```

prints a message that gives the number of files in the user's home directory. The command works by first executing the command contained within back quotes:

```
ls ~ | wc -l
```

This command, as explained earlier, computes and prints the number of files in the user's directory. Because the command is enclosed in back quotes, its output is not printed; instead the output replaces the original back quoted text.

The resulting command becomes:

```
echo My home directory contains 22 files.
```

When executed, this command prints the output:

```
My home directory contains 22 files.
```

The Power of the Linux Shell

You may now begin to appreciate the power of the Linux shell: by including command aliases in your *bashrc* script, you can extend the command repertoire of the shell. And, by using filename completion and the history list, you can reduce the amount of typing necessary. Once you grasp how to properly use it, the Linux shell is a powerful, fast, and easy to use interface that avoids the limitations and monotony of the more familiar point-and-click graphical interface.

But, the shell has additional features that extend its capabilities even further. As you'll see in the next section, the Linux shell includes a powerful programming language that provides argument processing, conditional logic, and loops.

Understanding Shell Scripts

This section explains how more advanced shell scripts work. The information is also adequate to equip you to write many of your own useful shell scripts. The section begins by showing how to process a script's arguments. Then it shows how to perform conditional and iterative operations.

Processing Arguments

You can easily write scripts that process arguments, because a set of special shell variables holds the values of arguments specified when your script is invoked. Table 13-10 describes the most popular such shell variables.

Table 13-10. Special Shell Variables Used in Scripts

Variable	Meaning
$#	The number of arguments.
$0	The command name.
$1, $2, ... ,$9	The individual arguments of the command.
$*	The entire list of arguments, treated as a single word.
$@	The entire list of arguments, treated as a series of words.
$?	The exit status of the previous command. The value 0 denotes successful completion.
$$	The process id of the current process.

For example, here's a simple one-line script that prints the value of its second argument:

```
echo My second argument has the value $2.
```

Suppose you store this script in the file *second*, change its access mode to permit execution, and invoke it as follows:

```
./second a b c
```

The script will print the output:

```
My second argument has the value b.
```

Notice that the shell provides variables for accessing only nine arguments. Nevertheless, you can access more than nine arguments. The key to doing so is the *shift* command, which discards the value of the first argument and shifts the remaining values down one position. Thus, after executing the *shift* command, the shell variable $9 contains the value of the tenth argument. To access the eleventh and subsequent arguments, you simply execute the *shift* command the appropriate number of times.

Exit Codes

The shell variable $? holds the numeric exit status of the most recently completed command. By convention, an exit status of zero denotes successful completion; other values denote error conditions of various sorts.

You can set the error code in a script by issuing the *exit* command, which terminates the script and posts the specified exit status. The format of the command is:

```
exit status
```

where *status* is a non-negative integer that specifies the exit status.

Conditional Logic

A shell script can employ conditional logic, which lets the script take different action based on the values of arguments, shell variables, or other conditions. The *test* command lets you specify a condition, which can be either true or false. Conditional commands (including the *if*, *case*, *while*, and *until* commands) use the *test* command to evaluate conditions.

The test command

Table 13-11 describes some commonly used argument forms used with the *test* command. The *test* command evaluates its arguments and sets the exit status to 0, which indicates that the specified condition was true, or a non-zero value, which indicates that the specified condition was false.

Table 13-11. Commonly Used Argument Forms of the test Command

Form	Function
-d *file*	The specified file exists and is a directory.
-e *file*	The specified file exists.
-r *file*	The specified file exists and is readable.
-s *file*	The specified file exists and has non-zero size.
-w *file*	The specified file exists and is writable.
-x *file*	The specified file exists and is executable.
-L *file*	The specified file exists and is a symbolic link.
f1 -nt *f2*	File *f1* is newer than file *f2*.
f1 -ot *f2*	File *f1* is older than file *f2*.
-n *s1*	String *s1* has nonzero length.
-z *s1*	String *s1* has zero length.
s1 = *s2*	String *s1* is the same as string *s2*.
s1 != *s2*	String *s1* is not the same as string *s2*.
n1 -eq *n2*	Integer *n1* is equal to integer *n2*.
n1 -ge *n2*	Integer *n1* is greater than or equal to integer *n2*.
n1 -gt *n2*	Integer *n1* is greater than integer *n2*.
n1 -le *n2*	Integer *n1* is less than integer *n2*.
n1 -lt *n2*	Integer *n1* is less than or equal to integer *n2*.
n1 -ne *n2*	Integer *n1* is not equal to integer *n2*.
!	The **not** operator, which reverses the value of the following condition.
-a	The **and** operator, which joins two conditions. Both conditions must be true for the overall result to be true.
-o	The **or** operator, which joins two conditions. If either condition is true, the overall result is true.
\(. . . \)	You can group expressions within the *test* command by enclosing them within \(and \).

To see the *test* command in action, consider the following script:

```
test -d $1
echo $?
```

This script tests whether its first argument specifies a directory and displays the resulting exit status, a zero or a non-zero value that reflects the result of the test.

Suppose the script were stored in the file *tester*, which permitted read access. Executing the script might yield results similar to the following:

```
$ ./tester /
0
$ ./tester /missing
1
```

These results indicate that the / directory exists and that the */missing* directory does not exist.

The *if* command

The *test* command is not of much use by itself, but combined with commands such as the *if* command, it is useful indeed. The *if* command has the following form:

```
if command
then
   commands
else
  commands
fi
```

Usually the command that immediately follows the word *if* is a *test* command. However, this need not be so. The *if* command merely executes the specified command and tests its exit status. If the exit status is 0, the first set of commands is executed; otherwise the second set of commands is executed. An abbreviated form of the *if* command does nothing if the specified condition is false:

```
if command
then
   commands
fi
```

When you type an *if* command, it occupies several lines; nevertheless it's considered a single command. To underscore this, the shell provides a special prompt (called the *secondary prompt*) after you enter each line. Often, scripts are entered by using a text editor; when you enter a script using a text editor you don't see the secondary prompt, or any other shell prompt for that matter.

As an example, suppose you want to delete a file `file1` if it's older than another file `file2`. The following command would accomplish the desired result:

```
if test file1 -ot file2
then
   rm file1
fi
```

You could incorporate this command in a script that accepts arguments specifying the filenames:

```
if test $1 -ot $2
then
  rm $1
  echo Deleted the old file.
fi
```

If you name the script *riddance* and invoke it as follows:

```
riddance thursday wednesday
```

the script will delete the file *thursday* if that file is older than the file *wednesday*.

The case command

The *case* command provides a more sophisticated form of conditional processing:

```
case value in
  pattern1) commands ;;
  pattern2) commands ;;
  ...
esac
```

The *case* command attempts to match the specified value against a series of patterns. The commands associated with the first matching pattern, if any, are executed. Patterns are built using characters and metacharacters, such as those used to specify command arguments. As an example, here's a *case* command that interprets the value of the first argument of its script:

```
case $1 in
  -r) echo Force deletion without confirmation ;;
  -i) echo Confirm before deleting ;;
   *) echo Unknown argument ;;
esac
```

The command echoes a different line of text, depending on the value of the script's first argument. As done here, it's good practice to include a final pattern that matches any value.

The while command

The *while* command lets you execute a series of commands iteratively (that is, repeatedly) so long as a condition tests true:

```
while command
do
  commands
done
```

Here's a script that uses a *while* command to print its arguments on successive lines:

```
echo $1
while shift 2> /dev/null
do
  echo $1
done
```

The commands that comprise the *do* part of a *while* (or another loop command) can include *if* commands, *case* commands, and even other *while* commands. However, scripts rapidly become difficult to understand when this occurs often. You should include conditional commands within other conditional commands only with due consideration for the clarity of the result. Include a comment command (#) to clarify difficult constructs.

The until command

The *until* command lets you execute a series of commands iteratively (that is, repeatedly) so long as a condition tests false:

```
until command
do
 commands
done
```

Here's a script that uses an *until* command to print its arguments on successive lines, until it encounters an argument that has the value *red*:

```
until test $1 = red
do
  echo $1
  shift
done
```

For example, if the script were named *stopandgo* and stored in the current working directory, the command:

```
./stopandgo green yellow red blue
```

would print the lines:

```
green
yellow
```

The for command

The *for* command iterates over the elements of a specified list:

```
for variable in list
do
  commands
done
```

Within the commands, you can reference the current element of the list by means of the shell variable $*variable*, where *variable* is the name specified following the *for*. The list typically takes the form of a series of arguments, which can incorporate metacharacters. For example, the following *for* command:

```
for i in 2 4 6 8
do
   echo $i
done
```

prints the numbers 2, 4, 6, and 8 on successive lines.

A special form of the *for* command iterates over the arguments of a script:

```
for variable
do
   commands
done
```

For example, the following script prints its arguments on successive lines:

```
for i
do
   echo $i
done
```

The break and continue commands

The *break* and *continue* commands are simple commands that take no arguments. When the shell encounters a *break* command, it immediately exits the body of the enclosing loop (*while*, *until*, or *for*) command. When the shell encounters a *continue* command, it immediately discontinues the current iteration of the loop. If the loop condition permits, other iterations may occur; otherwise the loop is exited.

Periscope: A Useful Networking Script

Suppose you have a free email account such as that provided by Yahoo! You're traveling and find yourself in a remote location with Web access. However, you're unable to access files on your home machine or check email that has arrived there. This is a common circumstance, especially if your business requires that you travel.

If your home computer runs Microsoft Windows, you're pretty much out of luck. You'll find it extraordinarily difficult to access your home computer from afar. However, if your home computer runs Linux, gaining access is practically a piece of cake.

In order to show the power of shell scripts, this subsection explains a more complex shell script, *periscope*. At an appointed time each day, *periscope* causes your computer (which you must leave powered on) to establish a PPP connection to your ISP, which is maintained for about one hour. This provides you enough time to connect to an ISP from your hotel room or other remote location and then connect via the Internet with your home Linux system, avoiding long distance charges. Once connected, you have about an hour to view or download mail and perform other work. Then, *periscope* breaks its PPP connection, which it will re-establish at the appointed time the next day.

Example 13-1 shows the *periscope* script file, which is considerably larger than any script you've so far encountered in this chapter. Therefore, we'll disassemble the script, explaining it line by line. As you'll see, each line is fairly simple in itself and the lines work together in a straightforward fashion.

Example 13-1: Periscope

```
PATH=${PATH}:/usr/local/bin
route del default
wvdial &
sleep 1m
ifconfig | mail userid@mail.com
sleep 1h
killall wvdial
sleep 2s
killall -9 wvdial
killall pppd
sleep 2s
killall -9 pppd
echo "/root/periscope" | at 10:00
```

The first line of the script augments the search path for the script to include */usr/local/bin*, the directory that contains the *wvdial* external command. Some versions of the startup scripts may not include this path in the search path, so explicitly placing it there avoids a possible problem.

```
    PATH=${PATH}:/usr/local/bin
```

The next line is perhaps the most complex line of the entire script:

```
    route del default
```

The *route* command is normally issued by the system administrator. You've probably never issued the command yourself, because *linuxconf* or another network configuration program has issued it on your behalf. The effect of the command is to delete the default network route, if any. The default route is the one along which TCP/IP sends packets when it knows no specific route to their specified destination. It's necessary to delete the default route because the *wvdial* program, which the script uses to establish its PPP connection, will not override an existing default route.

```
wvdial &
```

The next line launches the *wvdial* program. As specified by the ampersand (&), the program runs in the background, so the script continues executing while *wvdial* starts up and runs. The next line pauses the script for one minute, giving *wvdial* time to establish the PPP connection:

```
sleep 1m
```

The next line runs the *ifconfig* command and mails its output to the specified user (you must replace *userid@mail.com* with your own email address, which you can access remotely):

```
ifconfig | mail userid@mail.com
```

The *ifconfig* command produces output that looks something like this:

```
ppp0    Link encap:Point-Point Protocol
        inet addr:10.144.153.105  P-t-P:10.144.153.52 Mask:255.255.255.0
        UP POINTOPOINT RUNNING  MTU:552  Metric:1
        RX packets:0 errors:0 dropped:0 overruns:0
        TX packets:0 errors:0 dropped:0 overruns:0
```

You'll probably see other sections describing your Ethernet interface (*eth0*) and a loopback device (*lo*). The **inet addr** given in the command output (10.144.153.105) is the IP address of your computer. By mailing the output to yourself, you provide a simple way to discover your computer's IP address, which is likely to be different each time it connects to your ISP.

The next line causes the script to pause for an interval of one hour:

```
sleep 1h
```

You can easily change this interval to something more appropriate to your own needs.

The connection interval now having elapsed, the next line terminates all executing instances of the **wvdial** program:

```
killall wvdial
```

TIP   Appendix E, *Linux Command Quick Reference*, briefly describes the *killall* command and other possibly unfamiliar commands employed in this script.

The script then pauses for two seconds, to ensure that *wvdial* has completely terminated:

```
sleep 2s
```

Under some circumstances, a program will ignore a termination request. The next line deals with this possibility by sending a special code that compels a reluctant program to terminate without further delay:

```
killall -9 wvdial
```

Behind the scenes, *wvdial* launches a program known as *pppd*, which actually established and manages the PPP connection. Another *killall* command is designed to terminate *pppd* if *wvdial* has failed to do so:

```
killall pppd
```

Again, the script pauses for a few seconds:

```
sleep 2s
```

And, again the script uses the −9 option to specify that any remaining instances of *pppd* should terminate immediately:

```
killall -9 pppd
```

Finally, the script uses the *at* command to schedule itself for execution at 10:00 tomorrow:

```
echo "/root/periscope" | at 10:00
```

The *at* command reads one or more commands from its standard input and executes them at the time specified as an argument.

To try the script for yourself, you must have installed the *wvdial* program, as explained in Chapter 11, *Getting Connected to the Internet*. Place the script in the file */root/periscope*. Of course, you'll probably want to customize the script to specify an appointment time and duration of your own choosing. To start *periscope*, log in as root and issue the command:

```
(echo "/root/periscope" | at 10:00)&
```

When 10:00 (or such other time as you specified) comes around, your Linux system should obediently dial your ISP and maintain the connection for the specified interval of time.

Using periscope

At the appointed time, fire up your computer and access your email account. You should find a mail message that contains the *ifconfig* output giving your computer's current IP address. Now you can use *telnet* or an *ssh* client—your choice corresponds to the server you're running on your Linux system—to contact your computer and work for the remainder of the specified connection time. At the end of the connection time, your Linux system will sever its PPP connection and begin counting down until it's again time to connect.

Continuing Onward

Because it's quite a simple script, *periscope* doesn't do full justice to the capabilities of Linux. For example, suppose you want to establish connections at varying times or on varying days of the week. Or, suppose you want to schedule the next connection each time you log in.

Linux is able to answer such challenges in a variety of ways. For example, the *cron* program, though more complicated to use than the *at* command, provides the ability to specify program launch times very flexibly. For example, *cron* can let you establish a connection at 10:00 in the morning of the third Friday of each month.

You can learn more about Linux from Appendix E, which summarizes many useful Linux commands that you can use and include in shell scripts. A good way to continue learning about Linux is to peruse Appendix E and try each of the commands described there. Read their man pages and learn more about them. Ask yourself how the commands might be used in scripts that would facilitate your use of Linux.

If you truly catch the Linux bug, as many have, you'll want to peruse other Linux works, such as:

- *Running Linux*, 3rd edition, by Matt Welsh, Kalle Dalheimer, and Lar Kaufman (Sebastopol, CA: O'Reilly & Associates, 1999).

- *Learning the bash Shell*, 2nd edition, by Cameron Newham and BIll Rosenblatt (Sebastopol, CA: O'Reilly & Associates, 1998).

- *Linux Network Administrator's Guide*, by Olaf Kirch (Sebastopol, CA: O'Reilly & Associates, 1995).

- *Learning the vi Editor*, 6th edition, by Linda Lamb and Arnold Robbins (Sebastopol, CA: O'Reilly & Associates, 1998).

You'll also find a wealth of useful information on the Web sites described in Chapter 1, *Why Run Linux?* and in periodicals such as *Linux Journal* and *Linux Magazine*.

However, don't merely read about Linux; work with it. Write, test, and debug your own scripts. Share scripts you've written with others and study scripts written by others. Above all, read, communicate, and share what you've learned and what you want to learn. These activities are the foundation of the Linux culture and they are means whereby Linux users—and Linux itself—grow and develop.

LINUX DIRECTORY TREE

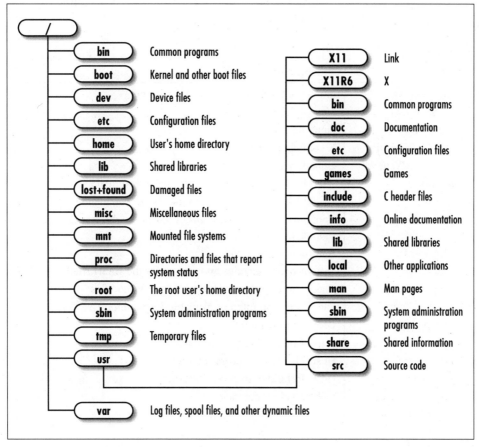

Figure A-1. The Red Hat Linux directory tree

Figure A-1 shows the typical structure of the Linux directory tree. Only the principal directories are shown.

PRINCIPAL LINUX FILES

Table B-1 describes the principal Linux files. You can use it, for example, to help you locate configuration files quickly.

Table B-1. Principal Linux Files

File	Description
/boot/module-info	Module information for the Linux kernel
/boot/System.map	Map of the Linux kernel
/boot/vmlinuz	Linux kernel
/etc/X11/XF86Config	X configuration file
/etc/X11/xinit/Xclients	Default script for *xinit*
/etc/at.allow	Userids of users allowed to use the *at* command
/etc/at.deny	Userids of users forbidden to use the *at* command
/etc/auto.master	Configuration file for the *autofs* daemon, which automatically mounts filesystems
/etc/auto.misc	Automounter map file
/etc/bashrc	System-wide functions and aliases for the BASH shell
/etc/conf.modules	Aliases and options for loadable kernel modules
/etc/fstab	Filesystems mounted or available for mounting
/etc/group	Group information
/etc/hosts	Map of IP numbers to hostnames
/etc/hosts.allow	Hosts allowed to access Internet services
/etc/hosts.deny	Hosts forbidden to access Internet services
/etc/httpd/access.conf	Web server configuration file
/etc/httpd/httpd.conf	Web server configuration file
/etc/httpd/srm.conf	Web server configuration file
/etc/inetd.conf	Configuration for the *inetd* daemon, which controls access to Internet services
/etc/inittab	Configuration for the *init* daemon, which controls executing processes
/etc/issue	Linux kernel and distribution version

Table B-1. Principal Linux Files (continued)

File	Description
/etc/lilo.conf	Loader (*lilo*) configuration file
/etc/login.defs	Options for *useradd* and related commands
/etc/minicom.users	Userids allowed to use *minicom*
/etc/mtab	Mounted filesystems
/etc/passwd	User account information
/etc/pine.conf	Configuration of *pine* mail reader
/etc/printcap	Printer options and capabilities
/etc/profile	Default environment for users of BASH shell
/etc/rc.d	Scripts for system and process startup and shutdown
/etc/shadow	Secure user account information
/etc/skel	Skeleton files used to establish new user accounts
/etc/smb/smb.conf	Configuration of *smb* (Samba) daemon
/etc/smb/smbpasswd	Account information for Samba users
/etc/smb/smbusers	User mappings for Samba
/etc/termcap	Terminal capabilities and options
/var/log/cron	Log of *cron* activity
/var/log/httpd/access_log	Log of web server access
/var/log/httpd/error_log	Log of web server errors
/var/log/messages	System log

APPENDIX C

THE RED HAT PACKAGE MANAGER

This appendix introduces you to the Red Hat Package Manager (RPM), a tool that facilitates installing, uninstalling, and upgrading Linux software. Suppose, for example, that after installing Linux, you discover you need an application that you omitted; you can find the missing application's package and use RPM to quickly and easily install the application. Similarly, when a new version of an application becomes available, RPM helps you upgrade painlessly, by preserving the application's configuration files. RPM also lets you query the status of your systems, helping you determine whether important files have been deleted.

Packages

An RPM package (or more simply, an RPM or a package) is a file that contains files necessary to install an application or software unit. RPM packages are generally named using a convention that lets you determine the name of the package, the version of the software, the release number of the software, and the system architecture for which the application is intended. Figure C-1 shows how the components of a package name are arranged.

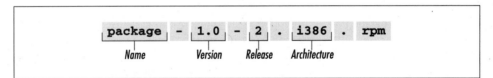

Figure C-1. The structure of a package name

Installing a Package

To install a package, log in as **root** and issue the following command from a shell prompt:

    rpm -ivh *package*

In the command, *package* specifies the name of the file that contains the package.

TIP   Strictly speaking, it's not necessary that you log in as `root`; however, your userid must be authorized to create and access the files and directories required by the package. Generally, the easiest way to ensure such access is by logging in as `root`.

The switches used in this command have the following meanings:

−i This switch specifies that RPM should install the package or packages given as arguments.

−v This switch, the verbose switch, specifies that RPM should print messages that summarize its actions and progress.

−b This switch specifies that RPM should print hash marks (#) as it installs the package, as a visible indication of progress.

Generally, RPM will successfully install the specified package. However, several sorts of error can occur:

- RPM may report that the package is already installed.

- RPM may report that a package file conflicts with a file from another package.

- RPM may report a failed dependency.

The next three sections explain how to resolve these errors.

Package Already Installed

If a package has already been installed, RPM will not overwrite the package without your permission:

```
# rpm -ivh bad-1.0-1.i386.rpm
bad package bad-1.0-1 is already installed
```

If you want to overwrite the package, add the *−−replacepkgs* switch to your command:

```
rpm -ivh --replacepkgs package
```

It may be more appropriate to update the package. Updating the package leaves its configuration files intact, whereas overwriting the package replaces the configuration files with files containing default options. An upcoming section shows you how to update a package.

Of course, it's also possible that you should do nothing. You may have attempted to install the package without first checking whether it's already installed and operational. In such a case, you can use RPM to verify that the package is installed correctly, and update or overwrite the package only if RPM reports problems.

To verify a package, issue the following command from a shell prompt:

```
rpm -Vp package
```

In the command, *package* specifies the name of the file that contains the package. If RPM detects no discrepancies, no output appears. Otherwise, RPM displays a line for each file that differs from the original package contents. Figure C-2 shows the structure of such a line. The first 8 characters of such a line report discrepancies; each character has the meaning described in Table C-1. Following the list of discrepancies, you may see the letter *c*, which denotes that the file is a configuration file. Finally, the filename appears.

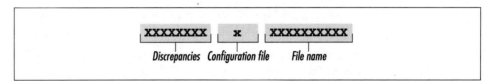

Figure C-2. The structure of RPM's discrepancy report

Table C-1. Package File Discrepancy Codes

Code	Meaning
.	No discrepancy
5	MD5 checksum discrepancy
D	Device discrepancy
G	Group discrepancy
L	Symbolic link discrepancy
M	Access mode or file type discrepancy
S	File size discrepancy
T	File modification time discrepancy
U	User discrepancy

The configuration files associated with a package are generally modified during installation and use, so it's not unusual for the contents of configuration files to differ from that of the original files. You can normally ignore MD5 checksum and file size discrepancies that pertain to configuration files.

Another form of the *rpm* command lets you verify packages that contain a specified file:

```
rpm -Vf path
```

In this form, *path* specifies the absolute pathname of the file. The output of this command is the same as that given earlier.

Conflicting File

If you instruct RPM to install a package and RPM finds that one or more of the package files conflict with existing files, RPM reports the conflict and terminates without installing the package:

```
# rpm -ivh bad-1.0-1.i386.rpm
bad /bin/badfile conflicts with file from good-1.0-1
```

In its report, RPM gives the name of the file and the name of the package that originally installed the file. You can force RPM to install the package, by using the *--replacefiles* switch:

```
rpm -ivh --replacefiles package
```

In response, RPM overwrites the conflicting files. Before overwriting a file, you should consider verifying the status of the package that originally installed it. You can use the -*Vf* switch or -*Vp* switch to perform the verification.

Failed Dependency

Packages are not always self-contained: Some packages require that other packages be installed before they operate correctly. RPM can identify such dependencies. If you attempt to install a package before you install other packages it requires, RPM reports a "failed dependency" and terminates without installing the package:

```
# rpm -ivh bad-1.0-1.i386.rpm
failed dependencies:
    mefirst is needed by bad-1.0-1
```

To resolve a failed dependency, you should install the missing package (or packages) and then install the desired package.

You can force *rpm* to install the package by specifying the *--nodeps* switch:

```
# rpm -ivh --nodeps bad-1.0-1.i386.rpm
```

However, the package will probably not operate correctly until you install the package (or packages) on which it depends. Therefore, you'll not often need to use this switch.

Uninstalling a Package

To uninstall a package, type a command like this one:

```
rpm -e package
```

In this command, **package** is the name of the package, not the name of the package file.

If you attempt to uninstall a package on which another package depends, *rpm* will report a dependency error and terminate without uninstalling the package. You can force *rpm* to uninstall the package, by using the *--nodeps* switch:

```
rpm -e --nodeps package
```

However, doing so will probably cause the depending package to cease working properly. Therefore, you'll not often need to use the *--nodeps* switch.

Updating a Package

When you update (upgrade) a package, RPM installs the new version of the software but attempts to leave your existing configuration files intact. You can update a package by using the *-U* switch of the *rpm* command:

```
rpm -Uvh package
```

When you update a package, RPM automatically uninstalls the old version of the package before installing the new one.

TIP   If no old version of the specified package exists, RPM simply installs
           the new version. Therefore, you can use the *-U* switch to install or
           update a package; many Linux users avoid the *-i* switch, always
           using the *-U* switch instead.

If RPM determines that your existing configuration files may be incompatible with those of the new version of the package, RPM will save a copy of the existing files. In such a case, you need to examine the old and new files and determine what the proper configuration should be. The documentation that accompanies the package should assist you in this process.

If you attempt to update an existing package using an older version of the package, RPM will report an error and terminate without performing the update. To force RPM to perform the update, use the *--oldpackage* switch:

```
rpm -Uvh --oldpackage package
```

Querying Your System's RPM Database

You can query RPM's database that describes the packages installed on your system. For example, to display a simple description of a package, use a command like this one:

```
rpm -q package
```

In this command, `package` is the name of the package you want RPM to describe. In response, RPM prints the package name, version, and release number.

Rather than use the *–q* option and the package name, you can use any of the following alternative options:

–a Causes RPM to display information about all installed packages

–f file
> Causes RPM to display information about the package that owns *file*

–p packagefile
> Causes RPM to display information about the package contained in *packagefile*

You can also tailor the output of an RPM query, by specifying one or more of the following options:

–i Causes RPM to display the package name, description, release number, size, build date, install date, vendor, and other information

–l Causes RPM to display the list of files that the package owns

–s Causes RPM to display the state of all the files in the package, which is *normal, not installed,* or *replaced*

–d Causes RPM to display a list of documentation files included in the package

–c Causes RPM to display a list of configuration files included in the package

For example, the command:

```
rpm -q -i -d rhide
```

displays information about the *rhide* package, including a list of documentation files included in the package.

Advanced RPM Techniques

Because you invoke the *rpm* command by using the shell, just as you do any other program, you can combine options and arguments to perform a variety of useful tasks. Consider the following examples:

rpm -Va
> This command verifies every installed package. You might find this command useful if you accidentally deleted some files. The output of the command would help you determine what packages, if any, suffered damage.

rpm -qf /usr/bin/mystery

This command displays the name of the package that owns the specified file.

rpm -Vf /usr/bin/mystery

This command verifies the package that owns the file */usr/bin/mystery*.

rpm -qdf /usr/bin/puzzle

This command lists the documentation files associated with the package that owns the file */usr/bin/puzzle*. This could be helpful, for example, if */usr/bin/puzzle* is a program you're having difficulty using.

Finding Interesting Packages

A good place to look for interesting packages is the RPM Repository, *http://rufus.w3.org/linux/RPM/*. Mirror sites are available for speedy access throughout North America and Europe. At the time of writing, the main site hosted 33,707 packages.

The RPM Repository uses *rpm2html*, a utility that automatically generates Web pages that describe a set of packages. This utility helps the site administrator keep the list of packages up to date. A related utility, *rpmfind*, can help you locate and download packages. Simply download the *rpmfind* package and install it on your system.

To use *rpmfind*, type a command like this one:

```
rpmfind --apropos borland
```

The command will search the RPM database on *rufus.w3.org*, reporting the name of each package having a description that includes the word *borland*:

```
Loading catalog to /tmp/fullIndex.rdf.gz
Searching the RPM catalog for borland ...
1: ftp://rpmfind.net/linux/contrib/libc5/SRPMS/rhide-1.3-1.src.rpm
   rhide : Rhide is a very nice IDE exactly like Borland's

Found 1 packages related to borland
```

To download and install a package, type a command like this one, which installs the *rhide* package found by the previous command:

```
# rpmfind rhide
Installing rhide will require 3810 KBytes

### To Transfer:
ftp://rpmfind.net/linux/contrib/libc5/i386/rhide-1.3-1.i386.rpm
Do you want to download these files to /tmp [Y/n/a] ? :
```

The *rpmfind* utility prompts you to authorize download and installation of the files. If you decide you don't want to download the files, simply respond by typing *n*.

GnoRPM

If you've installed the GNOME desktop environment, you can install the GnoRPM utility, which provides a graphical interface to the *rpm* command. To do so, issue the following commands:

```
cd /mnt/cdrom/oreilly
rpm -ivh gnorpm-0.7-*.rpm
```

Launch GnoRPM by clicking on GNOME → System → GnoRPM. Soon, the GnoRPM utility's window appears, as shown in Figure C-3.

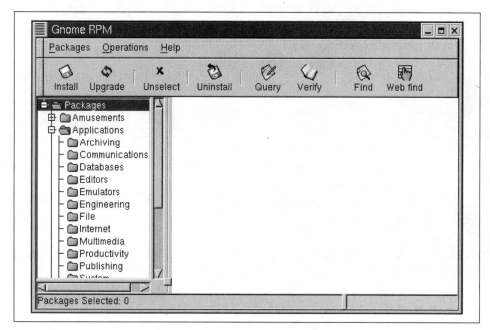

Figure C-3. GnoRPM

The left half of the window contains a tree that represents the package hierarchy, which is organized by subject. If you click on a subtree, the right half of the GnoRPM window displays the packages that reside in the subtree, as shown in Figure C-4.

If you right click on an icon representing a package, a pop-up menu lets you query, uninstall, or verify the package. If you select the query item, the Package Info window appears, as shown in Figure C-5. As you can see, this window shows the same information as that provided by the *–l* option of the *rpm* command.

You can also use GnoRPM to query packages by their attributes and to install packages. To query a package by its attributes, click on the Find icon on the

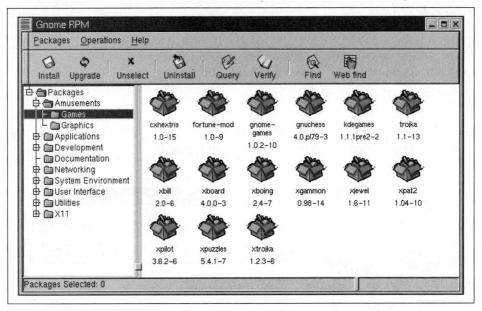

Figure C-4. Selecting a package subtree

toolbar. The Find Packages window, shown in Figure C-6 appears. You can select the type of query you want to perform (for example, finding packages that contain a specified file) and provide the name of a file, group, or package. Clicking Find starts the query; the results appear in the text area.

To install a package, click the Install icon on the toolbar. This launches a file selection dialog that lets you choose the package files you want to install.

Package Contents and Installation Commands

Some packages referred to in the book are not part of the standard Red Hat Linux distribution. Where distribution terms permit, such packages have been placed on the Linux CD-ROM in the */oreilly* directory.

The X Window System Packages (Chapter 5)

If Red Hat's installation process has installed X for you, then you'll find that the packages listed in Table C-3 are already installed on your system. You can verify this by running *rpm* with the query option on these package names. If you didn't

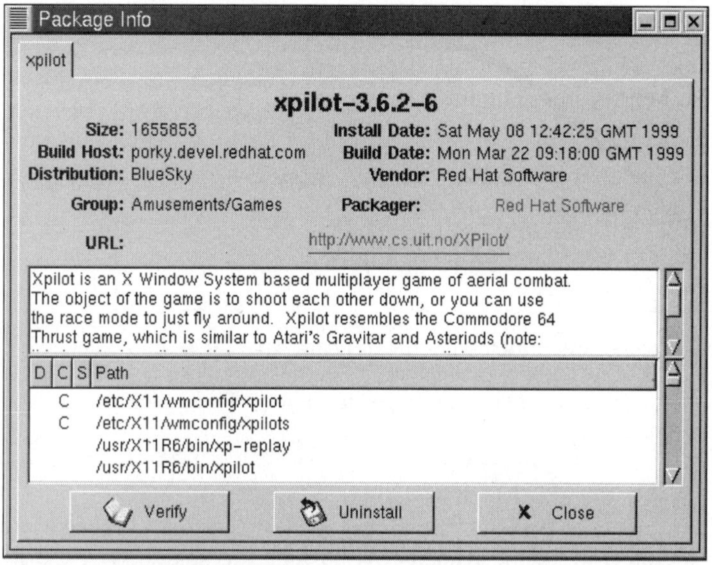

Figure C-5. The Package Info window

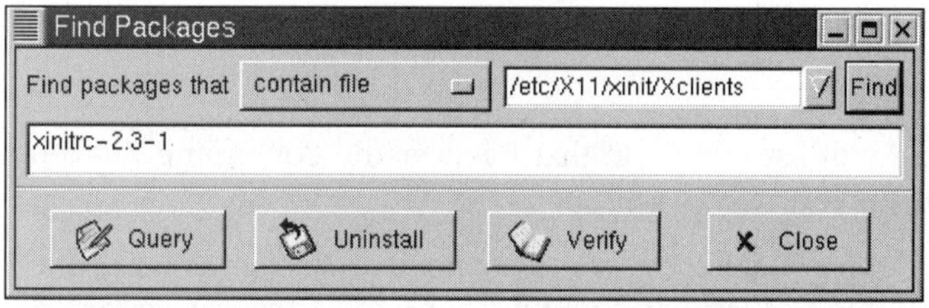

Figure C-6. The Find Packages window

install X during initial Red Hat installation, you can still use *rpm* to install the needed packages. Some of these packages are dependent on others, so you must install them in this order:

XFree86-75dpi-fonts
> Fonts used by X (if you have a monitor that supports resolutions of 1024x768 or greater, you may prefer to install *XFree86-100dpi-fonts*)

XFree86-libs
> Shared libraries used by X and X programs

XFree86
> Basic files needed by X

Xconfigurator
> Tool that helps you configure X

Xaw3d
> Library of 3D controls used by many X programs

X11R6-contrib
> Assortment of useful contributed X programs

TIP	Because the contents of the X-related packages may change from release to release, you may find that this sequence fails; if so, simply inspect the RPM error messages to identify the missing packages and install them.

Because the name of a package file includes the version and release numbers and the system architecture of the package, you'll need to search your CD-ROM to find each package and specify the proper filename as an argument of the *rpm* command. For example, you may find that the full name of the *XFree86-libs* package file is *XFree86-libs-3.3.2.3-25.i386.rpm*. An easy way to discover the package names is to go to the */RedHat/RPMS* directory and issue the command:

```
ls *X*
```

This command will list every file that has a name containing *X*—among these will be each package you need to install.

In addition to these packages, you also need to install at least one X server that supports your graphics card and monitor. The most basic X servers are these:

XFree86-Mono, the monochrome server
> A server that supports monochrome (black and white) monitors. The server runs with standard VGA graphics cards and supports a resolution of 640x480 or better.

XF86_VGA16, the VGA server
> A server that supports standard VGA cards and monitors, providing the standard 16 VGA colors. This server works with nearly all VGA and SVGA cards, but only in low resolution and with few colors.

XF86_SVGA, the SVGA server

A server that supports most SVGA cards, including the Trident 8900 and 9400, Cirrus Logic, C&T, ET4000, S3 ViRGE, and others.

However, XFree86 also includes a variety of servers for accelerated graphics cards, as shown in Table C-2. If you install an accelerated server, you should generally install one of the basic servers as well; the basic servers are easier to install and configure and can be helpful in troubleshooting configuration problems.

TIP   The list of available Linux drivers for advanced graphics cards expands rapidly. For a complete list, check relevant online resources, such as those at *http://www.xfree86.org/*.

Table C-2. X Servers for Accelerated Graphics Cards

Package	Server	Supported cards and chipsets
XFree86-8514	*XF86_8514*	IBM 8514/A and other compatible cards.
XFree86-AGX	*XF86_AGX*	All AGX cards
XFree86-I128	*XF86_I128*	#9 Imagine 128 (including Series II) cards
XFree86-Mach32	*XF86_Mach32*	ATI cards using the Mach32 chipset
XFree86-Mach64	*XF86_Mach64*	ATI cards using the Mach64 chipset
XFree86-Mach8	*XF86_Mach8*	ATI cards using the Mach8 chipset
XFree86-P9000	*XF86_P9000*	Diamond Viper and other P9000 cards (excluding cards using the 9100)
XFree86-S3	*XF86_S3*	#9 cards, most Diamond cards, some Orchid cards, and others
XFree86-S3V	*XF86_S3V*	Cards using the S3 ViRGE chipset, including the DX, GX, and VX
XFree86-W32	*XF86_W32*	ET4000/W32 cards, excluding standard ET4000 cards

Table C-3 describes several X-related packages. You may find the information it contains helpful if you choose to install X manually.

Table C-3. X-Related Packages

Package	Contents
XFree86	X Window System servers and basic programs
XFree86-libs	X11R6 shared libraries
Xconfigurator	Red Hat X Window System Configuration tool
XFree86-XF86Setup	Graphical configuration tool for XFree86

Table C-3. X-Related Packages (continued)

Package	Contents
XFree86-SVGA	SVGA server (*XF86_SVGA*)
XFree86-VGA16	VGA16 server (*XF86_VGA16*)
XFree86-Mono	Mono server (*XF86_Mono*)
XFree86-S3	S3 server
XFree86-S3V	S3 Virge server
XFree86-W32	W32 server
XFree86-Mach32	Mach32 server
XFree86-Mach64	Mach64 server
XFree86-Mach8	Mach8 server
XFree86-8514	8514 server
XFree86-AGX	AGX server
XFree86-I128	#9 Imagine 128 Server
XFree86-P9000	P9000 server
XFree86-Xnest	Xnest, an X server that runs in an X window
XFree86-Xvfb	Xvfb server, a X server that doesn't require a graphics card and therefore lets you run X programs in batch mode
XFree86-75dpi-fonts	X11R6 75-dpi fonts (needed only by server, not client)
XFree86-100dpi-fonts	X11R6 100-dpi fonts (needed only by server, not client)
XFree86-ISO8859-2	ISO-8859-2 (Central European) System Fonts for X11
XFree86-ISO8859-2-Type1-fonts	Type 1 (scalable) ISO8859-2 X11 system fonts
XFree86-ISO8859-9	Turkish X terminal fonts and modmaps
XFree86-ISO8859-9-75dpi-fonts	75-dpi Turkish X fonts
XFree86-ISO8859-9-100dpi-fonts	100-dpi Turkish X fonts

TIP   Only packages used to run X are shown. Packages used to develop X programs, or applications that require X to run do not appear.

Linux Applications and Clients (Chapter 8)

Applications and clients are updated frequently. For packages like WINE its always a good idea to check online for the current version.

The TeX RPM Package Files

Table C-4 describes several packages related to TeX.

Table C-4. Principle TeX-Related Packages

Package file	Contents
tetex-0.9-6.i386.rpm	TeX program
tetex-afm-0.9-6.i386.rpm	Adobe font metrics fonts and utilities
tetex-doc-0.9-6.i386.rpm	Documentation
tetex-dvilj-0.9-6.i386.rpm	HP PCL conversion program
tetex-dvips-0.9-6.i386.rpm	Postscript conversion program
tetex-latex-0.9-6.i386.rpm	LaTeX, a TeX macro package
tetex-xdvi-0.9-6.i386.rpm	X program for viewing TeX output

Installing the Mesa and WINE packages

You can download the latest versions of Mesa and WINE from the WINE Head-quarters at *http://www.winehq.com/*. Install Mesa and WINE by issuing the following command from the directory containing the downloaded packages:

```
rpm -ivh Mesa-*.rpm wine-*.rpm
```

Linux Games (Chapter 9)

While doom is easy to install, the installation process for Quake is complex.

Installing the doom package

Install *doom* by issuing the following commands:

```
cd /mnt/cdrom/oreilly
rpm -ivh doom-*.rpm
```

Installing the quake2 Package

To install Quake II under Linux, you'll need the RPM file and the official game data from id Software. You can obtain the RPM file from id Software's FTP server, *ftp://ftp.idsoftware.com/*. You can obtain the game data in any of several ways. The best way is by purchasing the retail Quake II CD-ROM diskette. However, if you want merely to try out the game, you can download the Windows 9x demo file.

To install Quake II, first login as **root** and create the directory */usr/local/games/quake2*. Then make the new directory your current working directory:

```
su
mkdir /usr/local/games/quake2
cd /usr/local/games/quake2
```

Installing from the Quake II CD-ROM

If you have the Quake II CD-ROM, mount it and copy the files in the *Install/Data* directory (and all its subdirectories) to the current working directory. To copy the subdirectories, use the *−r* option:

```
mount -t iso9660 /dev/cdrom /mnt/cdrom
cp -r /mnt/cdrom/Install/Data/* .
```

Now you can delete some unneeded files:

```
rm -f /usr/local/quake2/*.dll
rm -f /usr/local/quake2/quake2.exe
rm -f /usr/local/quake2/baseq2/gamex386.dll
```

Installing from the Quake II demo

If you have the self-extracting demo file (*q2-314-demo-x86.exe* or a similarly named file) rather than the CD-ROM, place the file in the current working directory and use the *unzip* utility to extract its contents:

```
unzip q2-314-demo-x86.exe
```

If your file has a different name, adjust the command accordingly.

Then, rearrange some files and delete others:

```
rm -rf Splash Setup.exe
mv Install/Data/baseq2 .
mv Install/Data/DOCS docs
rm -rf Install
rm -f baseq2/gamex86.dll
```

Installing the Linux Quake binaries

To install the Linux Quake binaries, issue the command:

```
rpm -ivh quake2-*.rpm
```

The *rpm* utility may complain that it cannot find *libglide2x.so*, a file needed to run Quake II with Voodoo video hardware acceleration. If your video card doesn't support Voodoo hardware acceleration (or if you don't plan to use acceleration), you can override the error by specifying the *−−nodeps* argument:

```
rpm -ivh quake2-*.rpm --nodeps
```

Using Voodoo hardware acceleration presents several challenges. For example, you must download and install the Glide library, which you can obtain at *http://glide.xxedgexx.com/3DfxRPMS.html*, and the Mesa library, which you can obtain at *http://www.mesa3d.org/*. Then you can retry the installation of the *quake2* package. However, you'll need to perform special configuration steps to complete the installation. For further details, see the Linux Quake HOWTO online at *http://www.linuxquake.com/howto/Quake-HOWTO.html*.

LAN-Related Packages (Chapter 10)

To install *samba*, issue the following commands:

```
cd /mnt/cdrom/RedHat/RPMS
rpm -ivh samba-*.rpm
```

Internet-Related Packages (Chapter 11)

wvdial isn't a standard Red Hat package, but it is readily available. Current versions of Navigator are available from the Netscape FTP site, but not in *rpm* format.

Installing the wvdial package

To install *wvdial*, issue the following commands:

```
cd /mnt/cdrom/oreilly
rpm -ivh wvdial-*.rpm
```

Installing the netscape-navigator package

To install Netscape Navigator, issue the following commands:

```
cd /mnt/cdrom/RedHat/RPMS
rpm -ivh netscape-navigator-*.rpm
```

Installing the seyon package

To install *seyon*, issue the following commands:

```
cd /mnt/cdrom/oreilly
rpm -ivh seyon-*.rpm
```

Installing the minicom package

To install *minicom*, issue the following commands:

```
cd /mnt/cdrom/RedHat/RPMS
rpm -ivh minicom-*.rpm
```

WAN-Related Packages (Chapter 12)

U.S. law forbids the export of strong cryptography software. Consequently the secure shell packages cannot be included on this CD-ROM.

Installing the wu-ftpd package

To install the Washington University FTP daemon, issue the following commands:

```
cd /mnt/cdrom/RedHat/RPMS
rpm -ivh wu-ftpd-*.rpm
```

Installing the apache Package

To install the Apache web server, issue the following commands:

```
cd /mnt/cdrom/RedHat/RPMS
rpm -ivh apache-*.rpm
```

Installing the sendmail and imap packages

To install *sendmail* and *imap*, issue the following commands:

```
cd /mnt/cdrom/RedHat/RPMS
rpm -ivh sendmail-[0-9]*.rpm
rpm -ivh sendmail-doc*.rpm   # optional documentation
rpm -ivh sendmail-cf-*.rpm   # optional configuration files
rpm -ivh imap-*.rpm          # optional support for pop and imap
```

Installing the ssh client and server package

The Secure Shell client and server are available from *http://www.ssg.fi/*. Once you've downloaded them, you can install them by issuing the following commands:

```
rpm -ivh ssh-*.rpm           # base package
rpm -ivh ssh-clients-*.rpm   # client
rpm -ivh ssh-server-*.rpm    # server
rpm -ivh ssh-extras-*.rpm    # extras
```

Installing the mgetty dial-in server package

To install the Dial-In Server, issue the following commands:

```
cd /mnt/cdrom/RedHat/RPMS
rpm -ivh mgetty-*.rpm
```

MANAGING THE BOOT PROCESS

In this appendix, you'll learn more about how to boot a Linux system; in particular, you'll learn more about configuring your computer system to boot any of several operating systems. The chapter focuses on *lilo* and *loadlin*, the most popular utilities for booting Linux systems, explaining their capabilities and options in considerable detail.

Booting Linux

When you boot a PC, you cause it to execute a small program known as a *boot loader*. The purpose of the boot loader is to locate and read into memory the first stage of an operating system and transfer control to it. The operating system then locates and reads its remaining components as needed.

The simplest way to boot Linux is by using a floppy diskette. By doing so, you're able to leave the boot information on your hard drive untouched, ensuring that you can still boot Microsoft Windows or another operating system stored on the same hard drive. Moreover, some operating systems and virus protection programs prevent modification of the boot information on your hard drive. By booting from a floppy diskette, you avoid several potential problems.

However, many users find booting from a floppy diskette slow or inconvenient. You don't have to boot Linux from a floppy diskette; you can boot Linux in any of several other ways. The two most popular alternatives are by using *lilo*, which replaces the boot loader stored on your hard drive, or *loadlin*, which lets you first boot DOS and then boot Linux from DOS.

This chapter cannot describe the entire range of issues involved in booting Linux. Much of the information in this chapter is taken from several Linux HOWTOs that contain additional useful information on booting Linux:

- BootPrompt-HOWTO

- CD-Writing-HOWTO

- CDROM-HOWTO

- Ethernet-HOWTO

- Ftape-HOWTO

- Hardware-HOWTO

- Multi-Disk-HOWTO

- PCI-HOWTO

- PCMCIA-HOWTO

Boot Disks

Even if you don't want to boot Linux from a floppy diskette, you should create and keep on hand a Linux boot floppy. If something goes wrong with your system, preventing you from booting in the normal way, you may be able to boot your system by using the floppy diskette. Then, you can diagnose and repair the problem and get back to business as usual.

Creating a Boot Disk

The Red Hat install program gives you the option of creating a boot diskette when you install Linux. You should exercise this option each time you install Linux, so that you have a fresh boot disk containing software consistent with that stored on your hard drive.

However, you can easily create a boot diskette after the installation is complete. To do so, insert a blank floppy diskette into your system's floppy drive. Log on as `root` and issue the following command:

```
/sbin/mkbootdisk version
```

For *version*, supply the version number of your kernel. If you don't recall the version, simply access an unused virtual console. There you'll see the default Red Hat log in prompt, which includes the version number of the kernel; for example, 2.0.36.

The *mkbootdisk* command creates a boot disk that uses the same kernel running when the command is issued. It also configures the boot diskette to load any necessary SCSI modules, so that your SCSI drives will be accessible after booting from the floppy.

Using a Boot Disk

Insert the boot disk into your system's floppy drive. If your system is turned off, power up your system. If your system is turned on, first shut down the active operating system in the proper manner, then restart the system. Linux should then boot from the floppy diskette.

TIP   To use your boot disk, your system's CMOS must be configured to allow booting from the floppy drive. If your system boots from its hard drive even when the boot floppy is present, you must change your system's CMOS configuration. The relevant option is generally named Boot Sequence, Boot Order, or something similar. The value you want is generally labeled A:,C: or something similar. Consult your system's documentation for further information.

The lilo Loader

Most PCs can be booted from a floppy drive or hard drive; many recently manufactured PCs can be booted from a CD-ROM drive. The first sector of a disk, diskette, or partition is known as the *boot sector*. The boot sector associated with a disk or diskette (the first sector of the disk or diskette) is know as the *master boot record*. In order for a diskette or disk to be bootable, it must contain a boot loader, which can reside in:

• The boot sector of the floppy diskette.

• The master boot record (MBR) of the first hard disk or the first CD-ROM drive, if the PC supports booting from a CD-ROM diskette.

• The boot sector of a Linux file system partition on the first hard disk.

• The boot sector of an extended partition on the first hard disk.

The *lilo* loader, or simply *lilo*, is a simple boot loader that can load Linux, Microsoft Windows 3.x and 9x, and other popular operating systems. Most users install *lilo* on the MBR of their system's first hard disk. That way, when the system is started, it boots *lilo*, which can be used to load Linux, Microsoft Windows, or another operating system.

The Red Hat Linux installation procedure automatically installs *lilo*. Therefore, you don't need to install *lilo*; you merely need to configure it.

However, before configuring *lilo*, you should make a fresh startup diskette for your system. If you have more than one operating system on your hard drive, make a startup diskette for each. Then, test each startup diskette. If you have a startup diskette for each operating system on your hard drive, you'll be able to start each operating system even if the MBR becomes damaged.

The easiest way to configure *lilo* is by using *linuxconf*, as described in Chapter 5, *Installing and Configuring the X Window System*. The *linuxconf* utility makes it easy to specify what operating systems are present and whether and how *lilo* should boot them. You can specify boot options, which control the booting of your system, in the Linux Boot Configuration dialog box. You'll learn more about the most popular and useful boot options later in this chapter.

If you prefer, you can edit *lilo*'s configuration file, */etc/lilo.conf*, by using your favorite text editor. The *lilo* User's Guide, found in the */usr/doc/lilo-0.21/doc* directory, describes the format of the configuration file directives.

After revising the configuration file, you run *lilo* by issuing the command:

```
/sbin/lilo
```

This causes *lilo* to update the master boot record or boot sector, according to the information in its configuration file. Then, you can boot your system according to the latest *lilo* specifications.

To boot your system, *lilo* uses your system's BIOS, which may not be able to load a Linux kernel (or other program) stored beyond cylinder 1023 of your hard drive. If you're installing Linux to a preexisting hard drive, you may not be able to place your Linux kernel in an appropriate location. In that case, you won't be able to use *lilo* to boot your system.

The loadlin Loader

Another way of booting Linux is by using *loadlin*, an MS-DOS program that can load a Linux kernel. To load Linux, *loadlin* relies on MS-DOS rather than your system's BIOS; therefore, *loadlin* can load a kernel stored beyond cylinder 1023. More generally, it can load a kernel from any filesystem or location accessible to MS-DOS.

However, *loadlin* cannot be run from a DOS Prompt Window within Windows 3.x or 9x. You must start your system in MS-DOS mode in order for *loadlin* to work. By making the proper entries to your *config.sys* file, you can create a convenient boot menu that lets you boot MS-DOS, Windows, or Linux.

Installing loadlin

The *loadlin* program is found in the */dosutils* directory of the Red Hat Linux CD-ROM. The *loadlin* program must have access to the file containing the Linux kernel you want to boot. The easiest way to get this file onto your Windows system is to boot Linux, make sure the Windows filesystem that corresponds to the Windows C: drive is mounted, and copy the kernel file. The following commands assume that your Windows filesystem is mounted as */mnt/c* and that you want to store the kernel in the directory *c:\linux*.

```
mkdir /mnt/c/linux
cp /boot/vmlinuz /mnt/c/linux/vmlinuz
```

The *loadlin* program needs to know the identity of your Linux root partition. To learn the name of the root partition, issue the command:

```
mount
```

The command reports all the mounted devices:

```
/dev/hda2 on / type ext2 (rw)
none on /proc type proc (rw)
/dev/hda1 on /boot type ext2 (ro)
none on /dev/pts type devpts (rw,mode=0622)
/dev/hdc on /mnt/cdrom type iso9660 (ro)
```

The root partition is the partition mounted as /. Here, it's **/dev/hda2**. Make a note of the partition name. Then, boot your Microsoft Windows system and copy the file *loadlin.exe* from the */dosutils* directory to a convenient location on your hard drive.

Using loadlin

To test *loadlin*, restart your Windows system in MS-DOS mode, by clicking on Start → Shut Down, choosing Restart in MS-DOS Mode from the Shut Down Windows dialog box that appears, and clicking on OK. When the MS-DOS prompt appears, change to the directory containing *loadlin* and issue the command:

```
loadlin c:\linux\vmlinuz root=/dev/hdxn ro
```

where **/dev/hdxn** is the root partition of your Linux system, which you earlier recorded. If your Linux files are stored in a directory other than *\linux*, you must adjust the command's first argument appropriately. Your Linux system should boot. If it does not, check your work and try again.

Configuring loadlin

Once you're satisfied that *loadlin* works with your system, you can configure your system to make using *loadlin* more convenient. Microsoft Windows supports a simple boot menu that will let you decide whether to boot Linux or Windows. To create such a boot menu, boot Microsoft Windows and use *Notepad* to add the following lines to the top of your *config.sys* file:

```
[menu]
menuitem=Linux, Boot Linux
menuitem=Win95, Boot Windows 95
```

```
menudefault=Linux, 15

[linux]
shell=c:\linux\loadlin.exe @c:\linux\bootopts.txt

[win95]
```

If you're using Windows 3.x or Windows 98 rather than Windows 95, change the file accordingly.

TIP   The *config.sys* file is located in the root directory of the *C:* drive. If your system has no *config.sys* file, create one using the lines given.

Now, add the following lines to the top of your *autoexec.bat* file:

```
goto %config%
:win95
```

TIP   The *autoexec.bat* file is located in the root directory of the *C:* drive. If your system has no *autoexec.bat* file, create one using the lines given.

Finally, use *Notepad* to create the file *bootopts.txt* in the *linux* directory. The file should have the contents similar to the following:

```
c:\linux\vmlinuz root=/dev/hdxn ro
```

Be sure to substitute the name of your Linux root partition for the placeholder /dev/hdxn. You can specify additional options if you like. The next section introduces you to the most popular ones.

Now, when you boot your system, you'll see a convenient menu that lets you type a digit to choose which operating system you want to boot.

TIP   Another convenient way to use *loadlin* with Windows 95 (but not Windows 98) is to create a program shortcut that switches your system to MS-DOS mode and runs *loadlin*. Launch the dialog box for creating the shortcut by right clicking on the desktop and clicking on New → Shortcut. The dialog lets you specify the contents of the *autoexec.bat* and *config.sys* files. The former should be empty and the latter should contain the line:

```
shell=c:\linux\loadlin.exe @c:\linux\bootopts.txt
```

Boot Parameters

When you boot your system by using *loadlin*, you specify several parameters that control the boot process. Such parameters are sometimes needed to take advantage of unusual hardware devices, large amounts of RAM (more than 128 MB), and so on. Similarly, when you boot by using *lilo*, you can also boot parameters to control the boot process; you can specify *lilo*'s boot parameters by using *linuxconf* or by editing *lilo*'s configuration file. You can also specify boot parameters to *lilo* by typing them in response to *lilo*'s prompt.

Boot parameters are specified using a three-part directive that includes:

- the name of the parameter

- an optional list of options, which consists of an equals sign (=) followed by a comma-separated list of option values

No spaces may appear in the directive. As an example, the following directive specifies the identity of the Linux root partition:

```
root=/dev/hda1
```

You can specify multiple directives by separating them with a space. For example, the following specifies the identity of the Linux root partition and specifies that the root partition is initially mounted read-only, so that a thorough check of its filesystem can be performed:

```
root=/dev/hda1 ro
```

Most directives are interpreted by the kernel, though *lilo* is also capable of processing directives. If you specify a directive that neither the kernel nor *lilo* understands (assuming you're using *lilo*), a directive that includes an equals sign is passed to the *init* process as an environment variable. You've learned about environment variables in Chapter 13, *Conquering the BASH Shell*. A non-kernel directive that doesn't include an equals sign is passed to the *init* process. An example of this usage is specifying the directive *single*, which causes *init* to start your system in single-user mode:

```
root=/dev/hda1 ro single
```

This directive is especially useful when booting your system using *lilo*; by specifying the single directive in response to *lilo*'s command prompt, you can boot your system in single-user mode.

General Boot Arguments

Table D-1 describes some of the most popular and useful boot arguments. These arguments apply to your system as a whole; in subsequent sections you'll learn about other boot arguments that apply to specific devices or functions. In addition to boot arguments previously introduced, the table describes the *reserve* argument, which is helpful in avoided system memory conflicts.

Table D-1. Selected General Boot Arguments

Argument	Description and options
`init=`	Specifies arguments passed by the kernel to the *init* process.
`mem=`	Specifies the amount of physical memory available to Linux; lets you instruct Linux to avoid high memory areas used by some systems for BIOS or caching. You can specify the amount as a hexadecimal number, or as a decimal number followed by k or M, denoting kilobytes or megabytes, respectively.
`reserve=`	Specifies I/O ports that must not be probed. The port number is specified by using a hexadecimal number and the range is specified by using a decimal number. For example, `reserve=0x320,32` specifies the I/O ports `320-33f` must not be probed.
`ro`	Initially mount the root filesystem in read-only mode, so that a more effective filesystem check can be done.
`root=`	Identifies the root filesystem: • `/dev/fdn`, floppy disk *n* (0 or 1) • `/dev/hdxn`, partition *n* of IDE drive *x* (a to d) • `/dev/sdxn`, partition *n* of SCSI drive *x* (a to e)
`rw`	Initially mount the root filesystem in read-write mode; do not perform a filesystem check.
`vga=`	Specifies the default display mode set before booting. Specifying `vga=ask` will cause *lilo* to list the available video modes. You can then specify the desired mode in place of ask. Note: This argument is interpreted by *lilo* and will have no effect if another loader is used.

RAM Disk Boot Arguments

Table D-2 describes several boot arguments used in working with RAM disks. You won't likely need to specify any of these; but knowing about them may help you understand boot specifications written by others, including those used by Red Hat Linux.

Table D-2. Selected RAM Disk Arguments

Argument	Description and options
`load_ramdisk=`	Specifies that a ramdisk is not to be loaded (0) or is to be loaded (1).
`prompt_ramdisk=`	Specifies whether to provide a prompt instructing the user to insert a floppy containing a ramdisk (1) or provide no such prompt (0).
`ramdisk_size=`	Specifies the amount of RAM to be allocated to a ramdisk. If not specified, the default value is 4 MB.
`ramdisk_start=`	Specifies the offset (in disk blocks from the start of the boot media) of the ramdisk data; lets a kernel and ramdisk data occupy the same floppy disk.

SCSI Host Adapter Boot Arguments

Table D-3 describes the most often used boot arguments related to SCSI host adapters. Table D-4 describes the options used by the SCSI host adapter boot arguments and other boot arguments.

Table D-3. Selected SCSI Host Adapter Arguments

Argument	Description and options
`advansys=`	Advansys SCSI host adapter: *iobase*, [*iobase*, [*iobase*, [*iobase*]]]
`aha152x=`	Adaptec aha151x, ada152x, aic6260, aic6360, and SB16-SCSI SCSI host adapters: *iobase*[,*irq*[, *scsi_id*[,*reconnect*[,*parity*]]]]
`aha1542=`	Adaptec aha154x SCSI host adapter: *iobase*[,*buson*,*busoff*[,*dmaspeed*]]
`aic7xxx=`	Adaptec aha274x, aha284x, aic7xxx SCSI host adapters: *extended*,*no_reset*
`AM53C974=`	AMD AM53C974-based SCSI host adapters: *scsi-id*,*dev_id*,*dmaspeed*,*offset* See the file *linux/drivers/scsi/README.AM53C974*.

Table D-3. Selected SCSI Host Adapter Arguments (continued)

Argument	Description and options
`buslogic=`	BusLogic SCSI controller:
	Many options are available. See the BootPrompt-HOWTO.
`eata=`	EATA SCSI host adapter:
	$iobase,[iobase,[iobase,[iobase]]]$
`fdomain=`	Future Domain SCSI controller:
	$iobase,irq[,scsi\_id]$
`in2000=`	Always SCSI host adapter:
	The driver for the Always SCSI controller accepts options in somewhat different format than other drivers. See the BootPrompt-HOWTO.
`max-scsi-luns=`	Specifies the maximum number of SCSI logical units to be probed; lets you avoid probing devices that might lock up the SCSI bus.
`ncr5380=`	NCR 5380-based SCSI host adapters:
	$iobase,irq,dma$ $membase,irq,dma$
`ncr53c400=`	NCR 53c400-based SCSI host adapters:
	$iobase,irq$ $membase,irq$
`ncr53c406a=`	NCR 53c406a-based SCSI host adapters:
	$iobase,irq,pio$ $membase,irq,pio$
`ppa=`	IOMEGA parallel port SCSI adapter for ZIP drive:
	$iobase,speed\_high,speed\_low,nybble$
`pas16=`	Pro Audio Spectrum SCSI host adapter:
	$iobase,irq$
`st0x=`	Seagate ST-0x SCSI host adapter:
	$membase,irq$

Table D-3. Selected SCSI Host Adapter Arguments (continued)

Argument	Description and options
`t128=`	Trantor T128 SCSI host adapter: *membase, irq*
`tmc8xx=`	Future Domain TMC-8xx and TMC-950 SCSI host adapters: *membase, irq*
`u14-34f=`	Ultrastor SCSI host adapter: *iobase,*[*iobase,*[*iobase,*[*iobase*]]]
`wd7000=`	Western Digital WD7000 SCSI host adapter: *irq, dma, iobase*

For example, from Table D-3 you can learn that Adaptec aha154x SCSI host adapters use a boot argument having the form:

    iobase[*,buson,busoff*[*,dmaspeed*]]

Table D-4 helps you understand the form of the *iobase* option and the other italicized options. The *iobase* option, for example, lets you specify the I/O port associated with the SCSI host adapter. Don't include the square brackets in your boot argument; they merely indicate which options must be present. For example, you can specify a boot argument for an Adaptec aha154x SCSI host adapter by writing only an *iobase* option; the remaining options are optional. However, as indicated by the square brackets, if you include a *buson* option, you must include a *busoff* option. Similarly, to include the *dmaspeed* option, you must include each of the other options. Here's an example of a complete boot argument:

    aha1542=0x300,11,4

Table D-4. Selected Boot Prompt Options

Option	Description and options
busoff	The interval (number of microseconds) during which the device will relinquish the ISA bus, specified as a decimal integer; for example, 4.
buson	The interval (number of microseconds) during which the device will dominate the ISA bus, specified as a decimal integer; for example, 11.

Table D-4. Selected Boot Prompt Options (continued)

Option	Description and options
ctl	The I/O port used for control, specified as a hexadecimal number; for example, 0x300.
cyl,head,sect	The geometry of the storage device, specified as three integers denoting the number of cylinders, heads, and sectors, respectively.
dev_id	A SCSI device with which the host adapter communicates, specified as a decimal integer; for example, 2.
dma	The DMA (direct memory access) channel by used by the device, specified as a decimal integer; for example, 3.
dmaspeed	The rate (in MB/sec.) at which DMA transfers are performed, specified as a decimal integer; for example, 5.
extended	Specifies whether extended translation for large disks is enabled (1) or not (0).
magic_number	Specifying the value 79 causes the driver to attempt to work, even if the firmware version is unknown; other values are ignored.
no_reset	Specifies whether the driver should reset the SCSI bus when setting up the host adapter at boot (1) or not (0).
iobase	An I/O port, specified as a hexadecimal number; for example, 0x300.
irq	A hardware interrupt number, specified as a decimal integer; for example, 5.
is_pas_card	Specifies whether a Pro Audio Spectrum card is used (PAS); otherwise, do not specify this option.
membase	The base address of a memory region used for memory-mapped I/O, specified as a hexadecimal number; for example, 0x2000.
parity	Specifies whether the SCSI host adapter uses parity (1) or does not use parity (0).
pio	Specifies whether insl and outsl multi-byte instructions (1) or inb and outb single-byte instructions (0) are used.
reconnect	Specifies whether the SCSI host adapter is allowed to disconnect and reconnect (1) or holds a connection until the operation is complete (0).
scsi_id	The ID by which the SCSI host adapter identifies itself, specified as a decimal integer; for example, 7.

To determine a proper value for options described in Table D-4, you must often know something about the hardware structure of your system. The procedures described in Chapter 2, *Preparing to Install Linux* will help you.

IDE Hard Drive and CD-ROM Boot Arguments

Table D-5 describes the most commonly used boot arguments associated with IDE hard rives and CD-ROM drives. Refer to Table D-6 to determine the form of the italicized options.

Table D-5. Selected IDE Hard Drive Arguments

Argument	Description and Options
`hdx=`	IDE hard drive or CD-ROM (*x* denotes the physical device, and must be a letter from *a* to *h*):
	• `autotune`, which specifies that the driver should attempt to tune the interface to the fastest possible mode and speed.
	• `cdrom`, which specifies that the drive is a CD-ROM drive.
	• `cyl,head,sect`, which specifies the geometry of the drive.
	• `none`, which specifies that the drive is not present—do not probe.
	• `noprobe`, which specifies that the driver should not probe for the device.
	• `nowerr`, which specifies that the **WRERR_STAT** bit should be ignored on this drive.
`ide0=`	IDE hard drive or CD-ROM:
	• `ali14xx`, probe for, and support, the alil4xx interface.
	• `cmd640_vlb`, probe for, and support, the cmd640 chip (required for controllers using a VLB interface).
	• `dtc2278`, probe for, and support, the dtc2278 interface.
	• `ht6560b`, probe for, and support, the ht6560b interface.
	• `qd6580`, probe for, and support, the qd6580 interface.
	• `umc8672`, probe for, and support, the umc8672 interface.
`idex=`	IDE hard drive or CD-ROM (*x* specifies the physical device, and must be a digit from 0 to 3):
	• `autotune`, which specifies that the driver should attempt to tune the interface to the fastest possible mode and speed.
	• `iobase`, which specifies the I/O port used by the drive.
	• `iobase,ctl`, which specifies the I/O port and control port used by the drive.
	• `iobase,ctl,irq`, which specifies the I/O port, control port, and IRQ used by the drive.
	• `noautotune`, which specifies that the driver should not attempt to tune the interface for fastest mode and speed.

Table D-5. Selected IDE Hard Drive Arguments (continued)

Argument	Description and Options
	• `noprobe`, which specifies that the driver should not probe for the device.
	• `serialize`, which specifies that I/O operations should not be overlapped.

Non-IDE CD-ROM Drive Boot Arguments

Table D-6 describes the most common boot arguments for non-IDE CD-ROM drives. Refer to Table D-4 to determine the form of the italicized options.

Table D-6. Selected CD-ROM Arguments

Argument	Description and Options
`aztcd=`	Aztech CD-ROM: *iobase*[,*magic_number*]
`cdu31a=`	Sony CDU-31A or CDU-33A CD-ROM: *iobase*,[*irq*[,*is_pas_card*]]
`sonycd535=`	Sony CDU-535 CD-ROM: *iobase*[,*irq*]
`gscd=`	Goldstar CD-ROM: *iobase*
`isp16=`	ISP16 CD-ROM: [*port*[,*irq*[,*dma*]]][[,]*drive_type*]
`mcd=`	Mitsumi CD-ROM: *iobase*,[*irq*[,*wait_value*]]
`optcd=`	Optical Storage CD-ROM: *iobase*

Table D-6. Selected CD-ROM Arguments (continued)

Argument	Description and Options
cm206=	Phillips CD206 CD-ROM: *[iobase]* *[,irq]*
sjcd=	Sanyo CD-ROM: *iobase[,irq[,dma_channel]]*
sbpcd=	SoundBlaster Pro CD-ROM: *iobase,type*

Floppy Drive Boot Arguments

A few systems require special boot arguments to make best use of their floppy drives. Table D-7 describes the most common boot arguments related to floppy drives. The file *README.fd* in *linux/drivers/block* describes additional arguments. Floppy drives that are not well behaved may malfunction if you specify the **daring** option, which you should use only with care.

Table D-7. Selected Floppy Disk Arguments and Options

Argument and Option	Description
floppy=asus_pci	Specifies that only units 0 and 1 are allowed, to work around problem with BIOS of certain ASUS motherboards.
floppy=daring	Specifies that the floppy controller is well behaved, allowing more efficient operation.
floppy=0,daring	Specifies that the floppy controller may not be well behaved (default).
floppy=thinkpad	Specifies that the system is an IBM Thinkpad.
floppy=no_unexpected_interrupts or floppy=L40SX	Specifies that a message should be printed when an unexpected interrupt is received. This is required by IBM L40SX laptops in certain video modes.

Bus Mouse Boot Arguments

Two boot arguments provide bus mouse support. The first supports the Microsoft bus mouse:

```
msmouse=irq
```

The second supports any non-Microsoft bus mouse:

```
bmouse=irq
```

Each argument accepts a single option specifying the IRQ associated with the mouse.

Parallel Port Printer Boot Arguments

The Linux printer driver claims all available parallel ports. If you want to access a device other than a printer attached to a parallel port, you must instruct the printer driver to reserve only the ports associated with printers. To do so, use the `lp` boot argument, which takes as its options a list of ports and IRQs use to support printers. For example, the following boot argument specifies two printers:

```
lp=0x3bc,0,0x378,7
```

The first printer is on port `0x3bc` and the second is on port `0x378`. The first printer uses a special IRQ-less mode known as polling, so its IRQ is specified as 0. The second printer uses IRQ 7.

To disable all printers, specify `lp=0`.

Using Loadable Ethernet Drivers

Early versions of Linux used a so-called monolithic kernel. At that time, Linux distributions typically included several kernels, offering support for a variety of devices that might be needed to boot and install a Linux system. Devices not needed to boot and install a system—so-called special devices—had second-class status. To access special devices, users had to compile customized kernels that included support for those devices. When a user added a device to a system, it was often necessary to compile a new kernel, which was something of an inconvenience.

More recent versions of Linux feature a modular kernel, which allows drivers to be dynamically loaded on command. This makes it much easier than before to configure your Linux system to support Ethernet cards and other special devices. Red Hat Linux is generally able to configure your primary Ethernet card automatically, by probing for it during installation of Linux.

However, the autoprobe doesn't always succeed. Moreover, if you have more than one Ethernet card, the installation program setups up only the first card it finds. To set up additional cards, you need to know a bit about Linux's loadable modules.

Dynamically Loading a Modular Driver

To dynamically load a modular driver, you issue the following command:

```
insmod driver
```

Where *driver* specifies the module to be loaded. Table D-8 lists modular Ethernet drivers and the cards they support. As an example, the command:

```
insmod ne2k-pci
```

loads the modular driver for the PCI-based NE2000 Ethernet card.

Table D-8. Modular Ethernet Drivers and Supported Cards

Driver	Cards
3c501	3Com 3c501
3c503	3Com EtherLink II
3c505	3Com EtherLink Plus
3c507	3Com EtnerLink 16
3c509	3Com EtherLink III
3c515	3Com EtherLink XL
8390	National Semiconductor NS8390
a2065	Commodore/Ameristar A2065
ac3200	Ansel Communications AC3200 (EISA)
apricot	Apricot 82596
arcnet	ARCnet COM9026 and COM20020
ariadne	Village Tronic Ariadne
at1700	Allied Telesis AT1700
atari_bionet	Atari BIONET-100
atari_pamsnet	Atari PAMsNet
atarilance	Atari VME Lance
cops	LocalTalk PC
de4x5	EtherWORKS DE425, DE434, DE435, DE450, DE500, DC21040, DC21041, DC21142, DC21143
de600	D-Link DE-600
de620	D-Link DE-620
depca	DEPCA/EtherWORKS DEPCA, DE100, DE101, DE200, DE201, DE202, DE210, DE422

Table D-8. Modular Ethernet Drivers and Supported Cards (continued)

Driver	Cards
dgrs	Digi RightSwitch SE-X
e2100	Cabletron E2100
eepro	Intel EtherExpress Pro/10
eepro100	Intel EtherExpress Pro/100
eexpress	Intel EtherExpress
epic100	SMC 83c170 EPIC/100
eth16i	ICL EtherTeam 16i, EtherTeam 32 (EISA)
ewrk3	EtherWORKS DE203, DE204, DE205
hp-plus	HP PCLAN/Plus
hp	HP LAN
hp100	HP J2585A, J2585B, J2970, J2973, J2573Compex ReadyLink ENET100-VG4Compex FreedomLine 100/VG
hydra	Hydra Amiganet
ibmtr	IBM token ring
lance	Allied Telesis AT1500HP J2405ANE 2100, 2500
ne	NE1000, NE2000 (non-PCI)
ne2k-pci	NE2000 (PCI)
ni52	Rascal-Interlan NI5210
ni65	Rascal-Interlan NI6510
pcnet	AMD PCnet32- and PCnetPCI-based cards
rtl8139	Cards based on the RTL8129 and RTL8139 PCI Ethernet chips, such as:
	ALFA GFC2206
	Allied Telesyn AT2550
	Genius GF100TXR (RTL8139)
	NDC Communications NE100TX-E
	SiS 900 (PCI)
	SMC 1211TX (PCI)
smc-ultra	SMC Ultra, UltraEZ, Ultra32
smc9194	SMC 9000
tlan	Various Compaq and Olicom cards

Table D-8. Modular Ethernet Drivers and Supported Cards (continued)

Driver	Cards
`tulip`	Cards based on the DEC 21040/21041/21140/21142/21143, such as:
	Accton EtherDuo PCI, EN1207
	Adaptec ANA6901/C, ANA6911/TX
	C-NET CNE-935
	Cogent EM100, EM110, EM400, EM960, EM964 Quartet
	Danpex EN-9400P3
	D-Link DFE500-Tx, DE-530CT, DFE-540TX
	Linksys EtherPCI
	Kingston EtherX KNT40T, EtherX KNE100TX
	Netgear FX310 TX 10/100
	SMC EtherPower, 8432BT, EtherPower10/100, EtherPower10/100
	Surecom EP-320X
	Thomas Conrad TC5048
	Znyx ZX312 EtherAction, ZX314, ZX315 EtherArray, ZX342, ZX344, ZX345, ZX346, ZX348, ZX351
`wavelan`	AT&T/NCR GIS WaveLAN
`wd`	WD8003, WD8013
`yellowfin`	Packet Engines G-NIC

When a driver is loaded, it generally probes to locate the supported device. In case an autoprobe fails, most drivers let you specify the I/O port and IRQ by using a command like the following:

```
insmod ne2k=pci io=0x280 irq=11
```

Some cards support additional options; these are documented in the file */usr/src/linux/Documentation/networking/net-modules.txt.*

Loading Modular Drivers at Boot Time

The Linux kernel automatically loads modules specified in the module configuration file, */etc/conf.modules*. So, once you've determined the proper module and options required by your Ethernet card, you can add a line or two to the module configuration file so that your card will be made ready to operate each time you boot your system.

The *alias* directive associates a logical module name with an actual module. Logical module names specify types of devices; for example, eth0 specifies the first Ethernet card in a system and eth1 specifies the second Ethernet card in a system. Suppose your system includes two Ethernet cards: a non-PCI-based NE2000 and an SMC EtherPower, which is based on DEC's TULIP chip. You could use the following directives to automatically load these modules at boot time:

```
alias eth0 ne
alias eth1 tulip
```

If a driver requires options, you can specify them by using an options directive, which has the following form:

```
options driver argument=value[,value,...]
              argument=value[,value,...] ...
```

For example, you might specify the I/O port and IRQ used by the NE2000 card like this:

```
options ne io=0x280 irq=12
```

Most ISA modules accept parameters like io=0x340 and irq=12 on the insmod command line. You should supply these parameters to avoid probing for the card. Unlike PCI and EISA devices, ISA devices sometimes cannot be safely auto-probed.

Administering Modular Drivers

The lsmod command, which takes no arguments, lists the loaded modular drivers. To unload a modular driver, specify the driver as the argument of the rmmod command. For example, to remove the **ne** driver, issue the command:

```
rmmod ne
```

By specifying the -a argument, you can cause rmmod to unload every unused module; that is, every module not associated with an operational device:

```
rmmod -a
```

You can't remove a module that's in use; therefore, you must shut down the device before removing it. To shut down an Ethernet device, you can use linux-config. Or, you can issue the following command:

```
ifconfig ethn down
```

where eth*n* specifies the logical device (for example, eth0 or eth1).

LINUX COMMAND QUICK REFERENCE

The following list describes some of the most useful and popular Linux commands. Consult the man page for each command to learn about additional arguments and details of operation.

adduser *userid*

Creates a new userid, prompting for necessary information (requires `root` privileges).

apropos *keyword*

Searches the manual pages for occurrences of the specified keyword and prints short descriptions from the beginning of matching manual pages.

at *time*

at -f *file time*

Executes commands entered via `stdin` (or, by using the alternative form, the specified file) at the specified time. The time can be specified in a variety of ways; for example, in hour and minute format *hh:mm* or in hour, minute, month, day, and year format *hh:mm mm/dd/yy*.

atq

Prints descriptions of jobs pending via the *at* command.

atrm *job*

Cancels execution of a job scheduled via the *at* command. Use the *atq* command to discover the identities of scheduled jobs.

bg

bg *jobs*

Places the current job (or, by using the alternative form, the specified jobs) in the background, suspending its execution so that a new user prompt appears immediately. Use the *jobs* command to discover the identities of background jobs.

cal *month year*
> Prints a calendar for the specified month of the specified year.

cat *files*
> Prints the contents of the specified files.

cd
cd *directory*
> Changes the current working directory to the user's home directory or the specified directory.

chgrp *group files*
chgrp -R *group files*
> Changes the group of the specified files to the specified group. The alternative form of the command operates recursively, changing the group of subdirectories and files beneath a specified directory. The group must be named in the */etc/groups* file, maintained by the *newgroup* command.

chmod *mode files*
chmod -R *mode files*
> Changes the access mode of the specified files to the specified mode. The alternative form of the command operates recursively, changing the mode of subdirectories and files beneath a specified directory.

chown *userid files*
chown -R *userid files*
> Changes the owner of the specified files to the specified userid. The alternative form of the command operates recursively, changing the owner of subdirectories and files beneath a specified directory

clear
> Clears the terminal screen.

cmp *file1 file2*
> Compares two files, reporting all discrepancies. Similar to the *diff* command, though the output format differs.

cp *file1 file2*
cp *files directory*
cp -R *files directory*
> Copies a file to another file or directory, or copies a subdirectory and all its files to another directory.

date
date *date*
> Displays the current date and time or changes the system date and time to the specified value, of the form *MMddhhmmyy* or *MMddhhmmyyyy*.

df Prints the amount of free disk space on each mounted filesystem.

diff *file1 file2*
> Compares two files, reporting all discrepancies. Similar to the cmp command, though the output format differs.

dmesg
> Prints the messages resulting from the most recent system boot.

du
du *directories*
> Prints the amount of disk space used by the current directory (or the specified directories) and its (their) subdirectories.

echo *string*
echo -n *string*
> Prints the specified text on the standard output stream. The *–n* option causes omission of the trailing newline character.

fdformat *device*
> Formats the media inserted in the specified floppy disk drive. The command performs a low-level format only; it does not create a filesystem. To create a filesystem, issue the *mkfs* command after formatting the media.

fdisk *device*
> Edits the partition table of the specified hard disk.

fg
fg *jobs*
> Brings the current job (or the specified jobs) to the foreground.

file *files*
> Determines and prints a description of the type of each specified file.

find *path* -name *pattern* -print
> Searches the specified path for files with names matching the specified pattern (usually enclosed in single quotes) and prints their names. The *find* command has many other arguments and functions; see the online documentation.

finger *users*
> Prints descriptions of the specified users.

free
> Displays the amount of used and free system memory.

ftp *hostname*
> Opens an FTP connection to the specified host, allowing files to be transferred. The FTP program provides subcommands for accomplishing file transfers; see the online documentation.

`grep` *pattern files*
`grep -i` *pattern files*
`grep -n` *pattern files*
`grep -v` *pattern files*
> Search the specified files for text matching the specified pattern (usually enclosed in single quotes) and print matching lines. The *−i* option specifies that matching is performed without regard to case. The *−n* option specifies that each line of output is preceded by the file name and line number. The *−v* option reverses the matching, causing non-matched lines to be printed.

`gzip` *files*
`gunzip` *files*
> Compress (or expand) the specified files. Generally, a compressed file has the same name as the original file, followed by *.gz*.

`head` *files*
> Prints the first several lines of each specified file.

`hostname`
`hostname` *name*
> Displays (or sets) the name of the host.

`info`
> Launches the GNU Texinfo help system.

`init` *run_level*
> Changes the system run level to the specified value (requires `root` privileges).

`insmod` *module*
> Dynamically loads the specified module (requires `root` privileges).

`jobs`
> Displays all background jobs.

`ispell` *files*
> Checks the spelling of the contents of the specified files.

`kill` *process_ids*
`kill -signal process_ids`
`kill -l`
> Kills the specified processes, sends the specified processes the specified signal (given as a number or name), or prints a list of available signals.

`killall` *program*
`killall -signal program*
> Kills all processes that are instances of the specified program or sends the specified signal to all processes that are instances of the specified program.

`ln old new`
`ln -s old new`

Creates a hard (or soft) link associating a new name with an existing file or directory.

`locate pattern`

Locates files with names containing the specified pattern. Uses the database maintained by the *updatedb* command.

`lpq`

Prints the entries of the print queue.

`lpr files`

Prints the specified files.

`lprm job`

Cancels printing of the specified print queue entries. Use *lpq* to determine the contents of the print queue.

`ls`
`ls files`
`ls -a files`
`ls -l files`
`ls -lR files`

Lists (non-hidden) files in the current directory or the specified files or directories. The *−a* option lists hidden files as well has non-hidden files. The *−l* option causes the list to include descriptive information, such as file size and modification date. The *−R* option recursively lists the subdirectories of the specified directories.

`mail`

Launches a simple mail client that permits sending and receiving email messages.

`man title`
`man section title`

Prints the specified man page.

`mkdir directories`
`mkdir -p directories`

Creates the specified directories. The *−p* option causes creation of any parent directories needed to create a specified directory.

`mkfs -t type device`

Creates a file system of the specified type (such as **ext2** or **msdos**) on the specified device (requires **root** privileges).

mkswap *device*

Creates a Linux swap space on the specified hard disk partition (requires root privileges).

more *file*

Lets the user peruse a file too large to be displayed as a single screen (page) of output. The *more* command provides many subcommands that let the user navigate the file. For example, the **Space** key moves forward one page, the **b** key moves back one page, and the **q** key exits the program.

mount
mount *device directory*
mount -o *option* -t *type device directory*

Prints the mounted devices or mounts the specified device at the specified mount point (generally a subdirectory of */mnt*). The mount command consults */etc/fstab* to determine standard options associated with a device. The command generally requires root privileges. The −*o* option allows specification of a variety of options; for example, ro for read-only access. The −*t* option allows specification of the filesystem type (for example, ext2, msdos, or iso9660, the filesystem type generally used for CD-ROMs).

mv *paths target*

Moves the specified files or directories to the specified target.

newgroup *group*

Creates the specified group.

passwd
passwd *user*

Changes the current user's password, or that of the specified user (requires root privileges). The command prompts for the new password.

ping *host*

Sends an echo request via TCP/IP to the specified host. A response confirms that the host is operational.

pr *files*

Formats the specified files for printing, by inserting page breaks and so on. The command provides many arguments and functions.

ps
ps -Aux

Displays the processes associated with the current userid or displays a description of each process.

pwd
>   Prints the absolute path corresponding to the current working directory.

reboot
>   Reboots the system (requires root privileges).

reset
>   Clears the terminal screen and resets the terminal status.

rm *files*
rm -i *files*
rm -f *files*
rm -if *files*
rm -rf *files*
>   Deletes the specified files or (when the $-r$ option is specified) recursively deletes all subdirectories of the specified files and directories. The $-i$ option causes the command to prompt for confirmation; the $-f$ option suppresses confirmation. Because deleted files cannot generally be recovered, the $-f$ option should be used only with extreme care, particularly when used by the root user.

rmdir *directories*
rmdir -p *directories*
>   Deletes the specified empty directories or (when the $-p$ option is specified) the empty directories along the specified path.

shutdown *minutes*
shutdown -r *minutes*
>   Shuts down the system after the specified number of minutes elapses (requires root privileges). The $-r$ option causes the system to be rebooted once it has shut down.

sleep *time*
>   Causes the command interpreter to pause for the specified number of seconds.

sort *files*
>   Sorts the specified files. The command has many useful arguments; see the online documentation.

split *file*
>   Splits a file into several smaller files. The command has many arguments; see the online documentation.

su

su *user*

su –

su – *user*

> Changes the current userid to root or to the specified userid (the latter requires root privileges). The – option establishes a default environment for the new userid.

swapon *device*

> Enables use of the specified device for swapping (requires root privileges).

swapoff *device*

> Disables use of the specified device for swapping (requires root privileges).

sync

> Completes all pending input/output operations (requires root privileges).

tail *file*

tail -n *file*

tail -f *file*

> Prints the last several lines of the specified files. The *–n* option specifies the number of lines to be printed. The *–f* option causes the command to continuously print additional lines as they are written to the file.

talk *user*

> Launches a program that allows a chat-like dialog with the specified user.

tar cvf *tar_file files*

tar zcvf *tar_file files*

> Creates a tar file with the specified name, containing the specified files and their subdirectories. The z option specified that the tar file will be compressed.

tar xvf *tar_file*

tar zxvf *tar_file*

> Extracts the contents of the specified tar file. The z option specified that the tar file has been compressed.

telnet *host*

> Opens a login session on the specified host.

top

> Prints a display of system processes that's continually updated until the user presses the q key.

`traceroute` *host*
> Uses echo requests to determine and print a network path to the host.

`umount` *device*
> Unmounts the specified filesystem (generally requires `root` privileges).

`uptime`
> Prints the system uptime.

`w`   Prints the current system users.

`wall`
> Prints a message to each user except those who've disabled message reception. Type **Ctrl-D** to end the message.

`wc` *files*
> Prints the number of characters, words, and lines in the specified files.

Table E-1 identifies Linux commands that perform functions similar to MS-DOS commands. The operation of the Linux command is not generally identical to that of the corresponding MS-DOS command. See the index to this book or the Linux online documentation for further information about Linux commands.

Table E-1. MS-DOS Commands and Related Linux Commands

MS-DOS	Linux
ATTRIB	chmod
CD	cd
CHKDSK	df, du
DELTREE	rm -R
DIR	ls -l
DOSKEY	(built-in; no need to launch separately)
EDIT	pico, vi, and so on
EXTRACT	tar
FC	cmp, diff
FDISK	fdisk
FIND	grep
FORMAT	fdformat
MORE	more
MOVE	mv
SORT	sort
START	at, bg
XCOPY, XCOPY32	cp

GLOSSARY

Absolute Path
See Path.

Access Mode
An attribute of a file or directory, which determines what operations a user may perform on the file or directory.

Alias
An alternative name for a command.

Argument
A parameter that controls the operation of a program or command.

Background
A background program is temporarily suspended from execution and does not interact with the user. See Foreground.

BIOS (Basic Input/Output System)
The program built into a computer to control its operation, especially the booting of an operating system. Most computers let the user configure various BIOS options by means of a special screen or set of screens.

Boot diskette
A diskette that contains the parts of an operating system needed to start the operating system.

Boot Sector
A sector that contains a loader program for starting an operating system.

Browser
A client program that operates under user control, especially a web client.

Client
A program that makes a request (generally via a network) of a server.

Command Interpreter
A program that accepts commands and executes (interprets) them.

Daemon
A program that runs in the background; that is, without user interaction.

Desktop
A work environment provided by a graphical user interface, generally including a video monitor background, a screen saver, and one or more taskbars and icons.

Distribution
A combination of a Linux kernel, a suite of UNIX-like command programs, and other software for installing and maintaining a Linux system.

DNS (Domain Name Server)
A computer that translates hostnames to IP addresses on behalf of requesting clients.

Dotted Quad Notation
A form of representing a 32-bit IP address, consisting of 4 numbers from 0 to 255, each separated from the others by a dot.

EIDE (Enhanced Integrated Drive Electronics)
An incremental improvement of the IDE standard for hard drives, designed to better accommodate large capacity drives.

Ethernet
A standard for sending data packets across networks, focused on the electronic signaling issues.

Foreground
A foreground program runs and interacts with the user. See Background.

FTP (File Transfer Protocol)
A protocol for transferring data files across a TCP/IP network.

GNU
GNU stands for "GNU's not Unix," and refers generally to software distributed under the GNU Public License (GPL).

GPL (GNU Public License)
The GNU Public License provides for free access to software published under its glossterms. Users are allowed to copy, modify, and redistribute GPL software, provided that the GPL is maintained.

Graphical User Interface (GUI)
A graphical user interface is a program that lets the user interact with a computer system in a highly visual manner, with a minimum of typing. Graphical user interfaces usually require a high-resolution display and a pointing device, such as a computer mouse.

Hidden File
A file having a name that begins with a dot (.). Such files are not listed by the *ls* command unless a special argument (*–a*) is specified.

Home Directory
A directory provided for the personal files and directories of a user.

Host
A computer attached to a network.

Hostname
A name by which a host is known to other hosts on a network.

HTML
Hypertext Markup Language is the form in which web documents are transmitted and interpreted by browsers.

IDE
A popular standard for internal hard drives and CD-ROM drives of IBM-compatible systems.

Internet
A relatively loose federation of computer networks that permits data to be widely transferred among computers.

IP Number
A number that identifies a host, corresponding to a network interface associated with the host.

Kernel
The part of an operating system that contains the most primitive functions upon which other, more sophisticated functions depend.

Kill
To terminate a process.

LILO
A program often used to load the Linux kernel from a hard drive or boot diskette.

Man Page
A document that describes a Unix command or file, readable by using the *man* command.

Master Boot Record (MBR)
The first sector of a hard drive, which by convention contains a loader program for starting an operating system.

Mount
To make a filesystem available for use.

Operating System
A program that provides a user interface and an application interface (which makes it possible for application programs to run) and manages computer system resources.

Option
A command argument that takes one of a small number of values. Command arguments that specify files (for example) are not options.

Package
A file that contains a set of related files that can be installed as a unit.

Partition
An area of a hard disk, generally allocated to a specific operating system (though perhaps usable by multiple operating systems).

Path
A path denotes the location of a file or directory. The path is an absolute path if it gives the complete path, beginning with the root directory and including every subdirectory. Otherwise, the path is a relative path.

PPP
Point-to-point protocol, the most popular way of connecting a computer to the Internet via a dialup modem.

Process
An instance of a running program.

Prompt
A character or series of characters displayed by a command interpreter to inform the user that execution of a command has been completed and the interpreter is ready to accept a new command.

Relative Path
See Path.

root
The specially privileged userid used to perform Unix system administration.

Root Directory
The unique directory that has no parent directory. All other directories are child of the root directory or its subdirectories.

Route
A path along which data packets move from host to host across a network.

Run Level
The operating mode of a UNIX system; for example, single-user, multi-user without networking, or multi-user with networking.

Script
A series of commands, stored in a file for subsequent or repeated execution.

SCSI
A popular standard for internal and external hard drives and other peripherals.

Search Path
A series of directories automatically searched by a command interpreter in order to locate the program file that corresponds to a command to be executed.

Server
A program that responds to client requests, which are generally transmitted over a network.

Shell
A command interpreter.

Swap File
A disk file or partition used to temporarily store information when system memory runs low.

Symbolic Link
A filesystem entity that lets you associate an alternative name with a file or directory.

System Administrator
The user who installs, configures, and otherwise maintains the software (and possibly the hardware) associated with a computer system.

TCP/IP (Transmission Control Protocol/Internet Protocol)
A standard method of sending data packets across a computer network, focused on the routing and connection issues.

Terminal
A combination of a keyboard and monitor, which together provide the capability to interact with a computer system.

Text Editor
A program that lets you create and modify the contents of text files.

Telnet
A protocol for establishing a login session via TCP/IP on a remote system.

Userid
The unique identifier associated with a system user.

Window Manager
A program that manages a graphical user interface, determining the appearance of windows (by providing standard elements such as title bars, for example) and determining the response to operations such as clicking on the desktop.

Working Directory
The directory that is implicitly combined with a relative path reference to determine the corresponding absolute path reference.

X Server
A program that implements X for some platform and type of video hardware.

X
A sophisticated and powerful graphical user interface implemented on a variety of computer platforms.

INDEX

routing/routes, 177, 209-211
  enabling, 211
  network route, deleting, 298
RPM files, 271
RPM (Red Hat Linux Package Manager),
  306-322
RTF file format, 182
RTS (modem indicator), 247
running programs, 99
  search path and, 289

S

safety via passwords, 62
safety/security, specifying options for, 223
Samba, 214-215
  resources for further information, 215
Samba server
  backups, 231
  client configuration, 232-235
  configuring, 217-227
  global variables, configuring, 218-223
  installing, 216
  netbios name option, 222
  print share options for, 218-227
  printer share parameters, configuring,
    224-227
  starting/stopping, 216
  troubleshooting, 231
  verifying operation of, 232
  version of, viewing, 227
  viewing configuration, 227
  viewing status of, 227
  workgroup option, 222
saving changes (partitions), 48
savings changes (minicom program), 252
/sbin file, 279
/sbin directory, 78
ScanDisk utility, 30, 32
schedulers, 192
  StarSchedule, 187
scientists, 2
screen options, configuring (minicom program), 252
screen output
  viewing directories, 90
  viewing files, 92
  viewing tar files, 95

screen savers, 78
  GNOME control center, 145
screens (see monitors)
script file (periscope), 298
scripts, 249, 253
  modifying standard, 283
  shell scripts, 282, 286
    advanced, 291-302
    periscope, 297-300
  standard included with Linux, 283
scroll bars, 129
SCSI adapters, 42
  configuration information for, 21
search domains, caution with, 208
search engine for Linux information, 15
search path, 289, 298
  hostnames, 177
searching by keywords, 82
secondary name server, 56
secondary prompt, 294
sector addresses, 166
sectors, 25
secure shell client, 272
secure shell server
  configuring, 271
  secure shell client on, 272
security
  via passwords, 62
  specifying options for, 223
selecting
  components, 49
  installation method, 41
  installation options, 41-43
  keyboard type, 39
  language for installation process, 39
  packages, 49-51
  PCMCIA support, 40
sendmail package, 269
serial port, configuring (minicom program),
  251
server administrator, email address of, 265
server daemons, 227
server installation, 42
server installation type, 23
server logs
  web server, 265
Server Message Block (SMB), 214, 232
server processes (web server), 267

About the Author

Bill McCarty is associate professor of management information systems in the School of Business and Management of Azusa Pacific University, Azusa, California, and was previously associate professor of computer science, in which capacity he taught for ten years in Azusa Pacific's Master of Applied Computer Science program.

Bill holds a Ph.D. in the management of information systems from the Claremont Graduate University, Claremont, California, and worked for 15 years as a software developer and manager.

Colophon

Our look is the result of reader comments, our own experimentation, and feedback from distribution channels. Distinctive covers complement our distinctive approach to technical topics, breathing personality and life into potentially dry subjects.

The cover image of a man wearing a wide-brimmed hat is adapted from a 19th-century engraving from *Marvels of the New West: A Vivid Portrayal of the Stupendous Marvels in the Vast Wonderland West of the Missouri River*, by William Thayer (The Henry Bill Publishing Co., Norwich, CT, 1888).

David Futato was the production editor and copyeditor for *Learning Red Hat Linux*; Ellie Cutler was the proofreader; Kimo Carter provided production assistance; Sarah Jane Shangraw, Jeff Holcomb, and Claire Cloutier LeBlanc provided quality control. Robert Romano and Rhon Porter created the illustrations using Adobe Photoshop 5 and Macromedia FreeHand 8. Brenda Miller wrote the index.

The cover layout was designed by Hanna Dyer and produced by Kathleen Wilson with QuarkXPress 3.32 and Adobe Photoshop 5 software, using the ITC Garamond Condensed font. The interior layouts were designed by Alicia Cech, based on a series design created by Edie Freedman and Jennifer Niederst and modified by Nancy Priest. Chapter opening graphics are from the Dover Pictorial Archive and *Marvels of the New West*.

Whenever possible, our books use RepKover™, a durable and flexible lay-flat binding. If the page count exceeds RepKover's limit, perfect binding is used.

Interior fonts are Adobe ITC Garamond and Adobe ConstantWillison. Text was prepared in SGML using the DocBook 2.1 DTD. The print version of this book was created by translating the SGML source into a set of gtroff macros using a filter developed at O'Reilly by Norman Walsh. Steve Talbott designed and wrote the underlying macro set on the basis of the GNU *gtroff –gs* macros; Lenny Muellner adapted them to SGML and implemented the book design. The GNU groff text formatter version 1.09 was used to generate PostScript output; this output was distilled to PDF for use at press.

Linux in a Nutshell, 2nd Edition

By Ellen Siever &
the Staff of O'Reilly & Associates
2nd Edition February 1999
628 pages, ISBN 1-56592-585-8

This complete reference covers the core
commands available on common Linux
distributions. It contains all user, programming,
administration, and networking commands with
options, and also documents a wide range of
GNU tools. New material in the second edition includes popular LILO
and Loadlin programs used for dual-booting, a Perl quick-reference,
and RCS/CVS source control commands.

Linux Multimedia Guide

By Jeff Tranter
1st Edition September 1996
386 pages, ISBN 1-56592-219-0

Linux is increasingly popular among
computer enthusiasts of all types, and one
of the applications where it is flourishing
is multimedia. This book tells you how to
program such popular devices as sound cards,
CD-ROMs, and joysticks. It also describes the best free software
packages that support manipulation of graphics, audio, and video
and offers guidance on fitting the pieces together.

Linux Network Administrator's Guide

By Olaf Kirch
1st Edition January 1995
370 pages, ISBN 1-56592-087-2

One of the most successful books to come
from the Linux Documentation Project,
Linux Network Administrator's Guide touches
on all the essential networking software
included with Linux, plus some hardware
considerations. Topics include serial connections, UUCP, routing
and DNS, mail and News, SLIP and PPP, NFS, and NIS.

Running Linux, 3rd Edition

By Matt Welsh, Matthias Kalle Dalheimer &
Lar Kaufman
3rd Edition August 1999
752 pages, ISBN 1-56592-469-X

This book explains everything you need to
understand, install, and start using the Linux
operating system. It includes an installation
tutorial, system maintenance tips, document
development and programming tools, and guidelines for network,
file, printer, and Web site administration. New topics in the third
edition include KDE, Samba, PPP, and revised instructions for
installation and configuration (especially for the Red Hat, SuSE
and Debian distributions).

Linux Device Drivers

By Alessandro Rubini
1st Edition February 1998
442 pages, ISBN 1-56592-292-1

This practical guide is for anyone who
wants to support computer peripherals
under the Linux operating system or who
wants to develop new hardware and run it
under Linux. It shows step-by-step how to
write a driver for character devices, block devices, and network
interfaces, illustrated with examples you can compile and run.
Focuses on portability.

Learning the bash Shell, 2nd Edition

By Cameron Newham & Bill Rosenblatt
2nd Edition January 1998
336 pages, ISBN 1-56592-347-2

This second edition covers all of the features
of bash Version 2.0, while still applying to
bash Version 1.x. It includes one-dimensional
arrays, parameter expansion, more pattern-
matching operations, new commands, security
improvements, additions to ReadLine, improved configuration and
installation, and an additional programming aid, the bash shell
debugger.

Linux

Using Samba

By Peter Kelly, Perry Donham & David Collier-Brown
1st Edition October 1999 (est.)
420 pages (est.), Includes CD-ROM
ISBN 1-56592-449-5

Samba turns a UNIX or Linux system into a file and print server for Microsoft Windows network clients. This complete guide to Samba administration covers basic 2.0 configuration, security, logging, and troubleshooting. Whether you're playing on one note or a full three-octave range, this book will help you maintain an efficient and secure server. Includes a CD-ROM of sources and ready-to-install binaries.

MySQL & mSQL

By Randy Jay Yarger, George Reese & Tim King
1st Edition July 1999
506 pages, ISBN 1-56592-434-7

This book teaches you how to use MySQL and mSQL, two popular and robust database products that support key subsets of SQL on both Linux and UNIX systems. Anyone who knows basic C, Java, Perl, or Python can write a program to interact with a database, either as a stand-alone application or through a Web page. This book takes you through the whole process, from installation and configuration to programming interfaces and basic administration. Includes ample tutorial material.

Programming with GNU Software

By Mike Loukides & Andy Oram
1st Edition December 1996
260 pages, Includes CD-ROM
ISBN 1-56592-112-7

This book and CD combination is a complete package for programmers who are new to UNIX or who would like to make better use of the system. The tools come from Cygnus Support, Inc., and Cyclic Software, companies that provide support for free software. Contents include GNU Emacs, gcc, C and C++ libraries, gdb, RCS, and make. The book provides an introduction to all these tools for a C programmer.

Programming with Qt

By Matthias Kalle Dalheimer
1st Edition April 1999
384 pages, ISBN 1-56592-588-2

This indispensable guide teaches you how to take full advantage of Qt, a powerful, easy-to-use, cross-platform GUI toolkit, and guides you through the steps of writing your first Qt application. It describes all of the GUI elements in Qt, along with advice about when and how to use them. It also contains material on advanced topics like 2D transformations, drag-and-drop, and custom image file filters.

Open Sources: Voices from the Open Source Revolution

Edited by Chris DiBona, Sam Ockman & Mark Stone
1st Edition January 1999
280 pages, ISBN 1-56592-582-3

In Open Sources, leaders of Open Source come together in print for the first time to discuss the new vision of the software industry they have created, through essays that explain how the movement works, why it succeeds, and where it is going. A powerful vision from the movement's spiritual leaders, this book reveals the mysteries of how open development builds better software and how businesses can leverage freely available software for a competitive business advantage.

UNIX Tools

UNIX Power Tools, 2nd Edition

By Jerry Peek, Tim O'Reilly & Mike Loukides
2nd Edition August 1997
1120 pages, Includes CD-ROM
ISBN 1-56592-260-3

Loaded with practical advice about almost every aspect of UNIX, this second edition of UNIX Power Tools addresses the technology that UNIX users face today. You'll find thorough coverage of POSIX utilities, including GNU versions, detailed bash and tcsh shell coverage, a strong emphasis on Perl, and a CD-ROM that contains the best freeware available.

UNIX Tools

The UNIX CD Bookshelf

By O'Reilly & Associates, Inc.
1st Edition November 1998
444 pages, Includes CD-ROM
ISBN 1-56592-406-1

The UNIX CD Bookshelf contains six books from O'Reilly plus the software from UNIX Power Tools – all on a convenient CD-ROM. A bonus hard-copy book, UNIX in a Nutshell: System V Edition, is also included. The CD-ROM contains UNIX in a Nutshell: System V Edition; UNIX Power Tools, 2nd Edition (with software); Learning the UNIX Operating System, 4th Edition; Learning the vi Editor, 5th Edition; sed & awk, 2nd Edition; and Learning the Korn Shell.

sed & awk, 2nd Edition

By Dale Dougherty & Arnold Robbins
2nd Edition March 1997
432 pages, ISBN 1-56592-225-5

sed & awk describes two text manipulation programs that are mainstays of the UNIX programmer's toolbox. This edition covers the sed and awk programs as they are mandated by the POSIX standard and includes discussion of the GNU versions of these programs.

lex & yacc, 2nd Edition

By John Levine, Tony Mason & Doug Brown
2nd Edition October 1992
366 pages, ISBN 1-56592-000-7

Shows programmers how to use two UNIX utilities, lex and yacc, in program development. You'll find tutorial sections for novice users, reference sections for advanced users, and a detailed index. Major MS-DOS and UNIX versions of lex and yacc are explored in depth. Also covers Bison and Flex.

Managing Projects with make, 2nd Edition

By Andrew Oram & Steve Talbott
2nd Edition October 1991
152 pages, ISBN 0-937175-90-0

make is one of UNIX's greatest contributions to software development, and this book is the clearest description of make ever written. It describes all the basic features and provides guidelines on meeting the needs of large, modern projects. Also contains a description of free products that contain major enhancements to make.

Writing GNU Emacs Extensions

By Bob Glickstein
1st Edition April 1997
236 pages, ISBN 1-56592-261-1

This book introduces Emacs Lisp and tells you how to make the editor do whatever you want, whether it's altering the way text scrolls or inventing a whole new "major mode." Topics progress from simple to complex, from lists, symbols, and keyboard commands to syntax tables, macro templates, and error recovery.

Tcl/Tk in a Nutshell

By Paul Raines & Jeff Tranter
1st Edition March 1999
456 pages, ISBN 1-56592-433-9

The Tcl language and Tk graphical toolkit are powerful building blocks for applications that feature a variety of commands with a wealth of options in each command. This quick reference briefly describes every command and option in the core Tcl/Tk distribution, as well as the most popular extensions. Keep it on your desk as you write scripts, and you'll be able to quickly find the particular option you need.

UNIX Tools

Exploring Expect

By Don Libes
1st Edition December 1994
602 pages, ISBN 1-56592-090-2

Written by the author of Expect, this is the first book to explain how this part of the UNIX toolbox can be used to automate Telnet, FTP, passwd, rlogin, and hundreds of other interactive applications. Based on Tcl (Tool Command Language), Expect lets you automate interactive applications that have previously been extremely difficult to handle with any scripting language.

Applying RCS and SCCS

By Don Bolinger & Tan Bronson
1st Edition September 1995
528 pages, ISBN 1-56592-117-8

Applying RCS and SCCS is a thorough introduction to these two systems, viewed as tools for project management. This book takes the reader from basic source control of a single file, through working with multiple releases of a software project, to coordinating multiple developers. It also presents TCCS, a representative "front-end" that addresses problems RCS and SCCS can't handle alone, such as managing groups of files, developing for multiple platforms, and linking public and private development areas.

Tcl/Tk Tools

By Mark Harrison
1st Edition September 1997
678 pages, Includes CD-ROM
ISBN 1-56592-218-2

One of the greatest strengths of Tcl/Tk is the range of extensions written for it. This book clearly documents the most popular and robust extensions—by the people who created them—and contains information on configuration, debugging, and other important tasks. The CD-ROM includes Tcl/Tk, the extensions, and other tools documented in the text both in source form and as binaries for Solaris and Linux.

Software Portability with imake, 2nd Edition

By Paul DuBois
2nd Edition September 1996
410 pages, ISBN 1-56592-226-3

This Nutshell Handbook®– the only book available on *imake* – is ideal for X and UNIX programmers who want their software to be portable. The second edition covers the current version of the X Window System (X11R6.1), using *imake* for non-UNIX systems such as Windows NT, and some of the quirks about using *imake* under OpenWindows/ Solaris.

How to stay in touch with O'Reilly

1. Visit Our Award-Winning Web Site

http://www.oreilly.com/

★ "Top 100 Sites on the Web" —*PC Magazine*
★ "Top 5% Web sites" —*Point Communications*
★ "3-Star site" —*The McKinley Group*

Our web site contains a library of comprehensive product information (including book excerpts and tables of contents), downloadable software, background articles, interviews with technology leaders, links to relevant sites, book cover art, and more. File us in your Bookmarks or Hotlist!

2. Join Our Email Mailing Lists

New Product Releases

To receive automatic email with brief descriptions of all new O'Reilly products as they are released, send email to:
listproc@online.oreilly.com
Put the following information in the first line of your message (*not* in the Subject field):
subscribe oreilly-news

O'Reilly Events

If you'd also like us to send information about trade show events, special promotions, and other O'Reilly events, send email to:
listproc@online.oreilly.com
Put the following information in the first line of your message (*not* in the Subject field):
subscribe oreilly-events

3. Get Examples from Our Books via FTP

There are two ways to access an archive of example files from our books:

Regular FTP

*   ftp to:
    ftp.oreilly.com
    (login: anonymous
    password: your email address)
*   Point your web browser to:
    ftp://ftp.oreilly.com/

FTPMAIL

*   Send an email message to:
    ftpmail@online.oreilly.com
    (Write "help" in the message body)

4. Contact Us via Email

order@oreilly.com
To place a book or software order online. Good for North American and international customers.

subscriptions@oreilly.com
To place an order for any of our newsletters or periodicals.

books@oreilly.com
General questions about any of our books.

software@oreilly.com
For general questions and product information about our software. Check out O'Reilly Software Online at **http://software.oreilly.com/** for software and technical support information. Registered O'Reilly software users send your questions to: **website-support@oreilly.com**

cs@oreilly.com
For answers to problems regarding your order or our products.

booktech@oreilly.com
For book content technical questions or corrections.

proposals@oreilly.com
To submit new book or software proposals to our editors and product managers.

international@oreilly.com
For information about our international distributors or translation queries. For a list of our distributors outside of North America check out:
http://www.oreilly.com/www/order/country.html

O'Reilly & Associates, Inc.
101 Morris Street, Sebastopol, CA 95472 USA
TEL   707-829-0515 or 800-998-9938
           (6am to 5pm PST)
FAX   707-829-0104

O'REILLY®

International Distributors

UK, EUROPE, MIDDLE EAST AND AFRICA (EXCEPT FRANCE, GERMANY, AUSTRIA, SWITZERLAND, LUXEMBOURG, LIECHTENSTEIN, AND EASTERN EUROPE)

INQUIRIES
O'Reilly UK Limited
4 Castle Street
Farnham
Surrey, GU9 7HS
United Kingdom
Telephone: 44-1252-711776
Fax: 44-1252-734211
Email: josette@oreilly.com

ORDERS
Wiley Distribution Services Ltd.
1 Oldlands Way
Bognor Regis
West Sussex PO22 9SA
United Kingdom
Telephone: 44-1243-779777
Fax: 44-1243-820250
Email: cs-books@wiley.co.uk

FRANCE

ORDERS
GEODIF
61, Bd Saint-Germain
75240 Paris Cedex 05, France
Tel: 33-1-44-41-46-16 (French books)
Tel: 33-1-44-41-11-87 (English books)
Fax: 33-1-44-41-11-44
Email: distribution@eyrolles.com

INQUIRIES
Éditions O'Reilly
18 rue Séguier
75006 Paris, France
Tel: 33-1-40-51-52-30
Fax: 33-1-40-51-52-31
Email: france@editions-oreilly.fr

GERMANY, SWITZERLAND, AUSTRIA, EASTERN EUROPE, LUXEMBOURG, AND LIECHTENSTEIN

INQUIRIES & ORDERS
O'Reilly Verlag
Balthasarstr. 81
D-50670 Köln
Germany
Telephone: 49-221-973160-91
Fax: 49-221-973160-8
Email: anfragen@oreilly.de (inquiries)
Email: order@oreilly.de (orders)

CANADA (FRENCH LANGUAGE BOOKS)

Les Éditions Flammarion ltée
375, Avenue Laurier Ouest
Montréal (Québec) H2V 2K3
Tel: 00-1-514-277-8807
Fax: 00-1-514-278-2085
Email: info@flammarion.qc.ca

HONG KONG

City Discount Subscription Service, Ltd.
Unit D, 3rd Floor, Yan's Tower
27 Wong Chuk Hang Road
Aberdeen, Hong Kong
Tel: 852-2580-3539
Fax: 852-2580-6463
Email: citydis@ppn.com.hk

KOREA

Hanbit Media, Inc.
Sonyoung Bldg. 202
Yeksam-dong 736-36
Kangnam-ku
Seoul, Korea
Tel: 822-554-9610
Fax: 822-556-0363
Email: hant93@chollian.dacom.co.kr

PHILIPPINES

Mutual Books, Inc.
429-D Shaw Boulevard
Mandaluyong City, Metro
Manila, Philippines
Tel: 632-725-7538
Fax: 632-721-3056
Email: mbikikog@mnl.sequel.net

TAIWAN

O'Reilly Taiwan
No. 3, Lane 131
Hang-Chow South Road
Section 1, Taipei, Taiwan
Tel: 886-2-23968990
Fax: 886-2-23968916
Email: benh@oreilly.com

CHINA

O'Reilly Beijing
Room 2410
160, FuXingMenNeiDaJie
XiCheng District
Beijing, China PR 100031
Tel: 86-10-86631006
Fax: 86-10-86631007
Email: frederic@oreilly.com

INDIA

Computer Bookshop (India) Pvt. Ltd.
190 Dr. D.N. Road, Fort
Bombay 400 001 India
Tel: 91-22-207-0989
Fax: 91-22-262-3551
Email: cbsbom@giasbm01.vsnl.net.in

JAPAN

O'Reilly Japan, Inc.
Kiyoshige Building 2F
12-Bancho, Sanei-cho
Shinjuku-ku
Tokyo 160-0008 Japan
Tel: 81-3-3356-5227
Fax: 81-3-3356-5261
Email: japan@oreilly.com

ALL OTHER ASIAN COUNTRIES

O'Reilly & Associates, Inc.
101 Morris Street
Sebastopol, CA 95472 USA
Tel: 707-829-0515
Fax: 707-829-0104
Email: order@oreilly.com

AUSTRALIA

WoodsLane Pty., Ltd.
7/5 Vuko Place
Warriewood NSW 2102
Australia
Tel: 61-2-9970-5111
Fax: 61-2-9970-5002
Email: info@woodslane.com.au

NEW ZEALAND

Woodslane New Zealand, Ltd.
21 Cooks Street (P.O. Box 575)
Waganui, New Zealand
Tel: 64-6-347-6543
Fax: 64-6-345-4840
Email: info@woodslane.com.au

LATIN AMERICA

McGraw-Hill Interamericana
Editores, S.A. de C.V.
Cedro No. 512
Col. Atlampa
06450, Mexico, D.F.
Tel: 52-5-547-6777
Fax: 52-5-547-3336
Email: mcgraw-hill@infosel.net.mx

O'REILLY®

O'REILLY™

O'Reilly & Associates, Inc.
101 Morris Street
Sebastopol, CA 95472-9902
1-800-998-9938

Visit us online at:
http://www.ora.com/
orders@ora.com

O'REILLY WOULD LIKE TO HEAR FROM YOU

Which book did this card come from?

_____

Where did you buy this book?
- ❑ Bookstore   ❑ Computer Store
- ❑ Direct from O'Reilly   ❑ Class/seminar
- ❑ Bundled with hardware/software
- ❑ Other _____

What operating system do you use?
- ❑ UNIX   ❑ Macintosh
- ❑ Windows NT   ❑ PC(Windows/DOS)
- ❑ Other _____

What is your job description?
- ❑ System Administrator   ❑ Programmer
- ❑ Network Administrator   ❑ Educator/Teacher
- ❑ Web Developer
- ❑ Other _____

❑ Please send me O'Reilly's catalog, containing
a complete listing of O'Reilly books and
software.

Name _____   Company/Organization _____

Address _____

City _____   State _____   Zip/Postal Code _____   Country _____

Telephone _____   Internet or other email address (specify network) _____

Nineteenth century wood engraving
of a bear from the O'Reilly &
Associates Nutshell Handbook®
Using & Managing UUCP.

POST CARD

||||

BUSINESS REPLY MAIL
FIRST CLASS MAIL PERMIT NO. 80 SEBASTOPOL, CA

Postage will be paid by addressee

O'Reilly & Associates, Inc.
101 Morris Street
Sebastopol, CA 95472-9902

||||||||||||||||||||||||||||||||||||||||||||||||